DAVID BUSCH'S
NIKON® D3500

GUIDE TO DIGITAL SLR PHOTOGRAPHY

David D. Busch

rockynook

David Busch's Nikon® D3500 Guide to Digital SLR Photography
David D. Busch

Project Manager: Jenny Davidson
Series Technical Editor: Michael D. Sullivan
Layout: Bill Hartman
Cover Design: Mike Tanamachi
Indexer: Valerie Haynes Perry
Proofreader: Mike Beady

ISBN: 978-1-68198-476-6
1st Edition (2nd printing, July 2022)

Rocky Nook, Inc.
1010 B Street, Suite 350
San Rafael, CA 94901
USA
www.rockynook.com

Distributed in the UK and Europe by Publishers Group UK
Distributed in the U.S. and all other territories by Ingram Publisher Services

Library of Congress Control Number: 2018957157

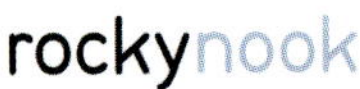

For Cathy

Acknowledgments

Thanks to everyone at Rocky Nook, including Scott Cowlin, managing director and publisher, for the freedom to let me explore the amazing capabilities of the Nikon D3500 in depth. I couldn't do it without my veteran production team, including project manager, Jenny Davidson, and series technical editor, Mike Sullivan. Also thanks to Bill Hartman, layout; Valerie Haynes Perry, indexing; Mike Beady, proofreading; Mike Tanamachi, cover design; and my agent, Carole Jelen, who has the amazing ability to keep both publishers and authors happy.

About the Author

With more than 2.5 million books in print, **David D. Busch** is the world's #1 selling digital camera guide author, and the originator of popular digital photography series like *David Busch's Pro Secrets* and *David Busch's Quick Snap Guides*. He has written more than four dozen hugely successful guidebooks and compact guides for Nikon digital SLR models, several dozen additional user guides for other camera models, as well as many popular books devoted to dSLRs, including *Mastering Digital SLR Photography, Fourth Edition* and *Digital SLR Pro Secrets*. As a roving photojournalist for more than 20 years, he illustrated his books, magazine articles, and newspaper reports with award-winning images. He's operated his own commercial studio, suffocated in formal dress while shooting weddings, and shot sports for a daily newspaper and an upstate New York college. His photos and articles have been published in magazines including *Popular Photography, Rangefinder, Professional Photographer*, and hundreds of other publications. He's also reviewed dozens of digital cameras for CNet Networks and other CBS publications. His advice has been featured on National Public Radio's *All Tech Considered*.

When About.com named its top five books on Beginning Digital Photography, debuting at the #1 and #2 slots were Busch's *Digital Photography All-In-One Desk Reference for Dummies* and *Mastering Digital Photography*. He's had as many as five of his books listed in the Top 20 of Amazon.com's Digital Photography Bestseller list—simultaneously! Busch's 200-plus other books published since 1983 include bestsellers like *Digital SLR Cameras and Photography for Dummies*.

Busch is a member of the Cleveland Photographic Society (www.clevelandphoto.org), which has operated continuously since 1887. Visit his website at http://www.nikonguides.com.

Contents

Chapter 3
Nikon D3500 Roadmap

33

Chapter 4
Playback and Shooting Menus

57

Chapter 5
Setup, Retouch, and Recent Settings Menus   91

Chapter 6
Nailing the Right Exposure
129

Chapter 7
Mastering the Mysteries of Autofocus
161

Chapter 8
Live View and Movie Making 179

Chapter 9
Advanced Shooting Tips for Your Nikon D3500 201

Chapter 10
Working with Lenses   217

Chapter 11
Making Light Work for You   247

Chapter 12
Troubleshooting and Prevention   281

Index   303

Preface

You don't want good pictures from your new Nikon D3500—you demand *outstanding photos*. After all, the Nikon D3500 is one of the most versatile entry-level cameras on the market. It boasts 24 megapixels of resolution with excellent low-light capabilities, fast autofocus, and high-definition video capabilities. But your gateway to pixel proficiency is dragged down by the minimalist pamphlet/user guide included in the box as a manual.

You know some of the basics are in there, somewhere, but you don't know where to start. In addition, the camera manual doesn't offer much information on photography or digital photography. Nor are you interested in spending hours or days studying a comprehensive book on digital SLR photography that doesn't necessarily apply directly to your D3500.

What you need is a guide that explains the purpose and function of the D3500's basic controls, how you should use them, and *why*. Ideally, there should be information about file formats, resolution, exposure, and special autofocus modes, but you'd prefer to read about those topics only after you've had the chance to go out and take a few hundred great pictures with your new camera. Why isn't there a book that summarizes the most important information in its first two or three chapters, with lots of illustrations showing what your results will look like when you use this setting or that? This is that book.

If you can't decide on what basic settings to use with your camera because you can't figure out how changing ISO or white balance or focus defaults will affect your pictures, you need this guide. I won't talk down to you, either; this book isn't padded with dozens of pages of checklists telling you how to take a travel picture, a sports photo, or how to take a snapshot of your kids in overly simplistic terms. There are no special sections devoted to "real world" recipes here. All of us do 100 percent of our shooting in the real world! So, I give you all the information you need to cook up great photos on your own!

Introduction

Despite its impressive feature list, the D3500 retains the ease of use that smooths the transition for those new to digital photography. For those just dipping their toes into the digital pond, the experience is warm and inviting. It has an all-new sensor (compared to the one found in its predecessor, the D3400) and a long list of features. The Nikon D3500 isn't a point-and-shoot camera (although you can activate its automatic features and use it like one). It's a tool for the most serious photography enthusiast.

Once you've confirmed that you made a wise purchase decision, the question comes up, *how do I use this thing?* All those cool features can be mind-numbing to learn, if all you have as a guide is the manual furnished with the camera. Help is on the way. I sincerely believe that this book is your best bet for learning how to use your new camera, and for learning how to use it well.

If you're a Nikon D3500 owner who's looking to learn more about how to use this great camera, you've probably already explored your options. There are DVDs and online YouTube tutorials—but who can learn how to use a camera by sitting in front of a television or computer screen? Do you want to watch a movie and click on HTML links, or do you want to go out and take photos with your camera? Videos are fun, but not the best answer.

There's always the manual furnished with the D3500. It's skimpy enough that Nikon also provides a downloadable PDF manual with more information. Either way, you're given very little guidance about *why* you should use particular settings or features. Its organization makes it difficult to find what you need. Multiple cross-references in the PDF send you searching back and forth between two or three sections of the book to find what you want to know. This electronic manual is also hobbled by black-and-white line drawings and tiny monochrome pictures that aren't very good examples of what you can do.

I've tried to make *David Busch's Nikon D3500 Guide to Digital SLR Photography* different from your other D3500 learn-up options. The roadmap sections use larger, color pictures to show you where all the buttons and dials are, and the explanations of what they do are longer and more comprehensive. I've tried to avoid overly general advice, including the two-page checklists on how to take a "sports picture" or a "portrait picture" or a "travel picture." You won't find half the content of this book taken up by generic chapters that tell you how to shoot landscapes, portraits, or product photographs. Instead, you'll find tips and techniques for using all the features of your Nikon D3500 to take *any kind of picture* you want. If you want to know where you should stand to take a picture of a quarterback dropping back to unleash a pass, there are plenty of books that will tell you that. This one concentrates on teaching you how to select the best autofocus mode, shutter speed, f/stop, or flash capability to take, say, a great sports picture under any conditions.

This book is not a lame rewriting of the manual that came with the camera. Some folks spend five minutes with a book like this one, spot some information that also appears in the original manual, and decide "Rehash!" without really understanding the differences. Yes, you'll find information here that is also in the owner's manual, such as the parameters you can enter when changing your D3500's operation in the various menus. Basic descriptions—before I dig in and start providing in-depth tips and information—may also be vaguely similar. There are only so many ways you can say, for example, "Hold the shutter release down halfway to lock in exposure." But not *everything* in the manual is included in this book. If you need advice on when and how to use the most important functions, you'll find the information here.

David Busch's Nikon D3500 Guide to Digital SLR Photography is aimed at Nikon and dSLR veterans as well as newcomers to digital photography and digital SLRs. Both groups can be overwhelmed by the options the D3500 offers, while underwhelmed by the explanations they receive in their user's manual. The manuals are great if you already know what you don't know, and you can find an answer somewhere in a booklet arranged by menu listings and written by a camera vendor employee who last threw together instructions on how to operate a camcorder.

Family Resemblance

If you've owned previous models in the Nikon digital camera line, and copies of my books for those cameras, you're bound to notice a certain family resemblance. Nikon has been very crafty in introducing upgraded cameras that share the best features of the models they replace, while adding new capabilities and options. You benefit in two ways. If you used a previous Nikon camera prior to switching to this latest D3500 model, you'll find that the parts that haven't changed have a certain familiarity for you, making it easy to make the transition to the newest model. There are lots of features and menu choices of the D3500 that are exactly the same as those in the most recent models. This family resemblance will help level the learning curve for you.

Similarly, when writing books for each new model, I try to retain the easy-to-understand explanations that worked for previous books dedicated to earlier camera models, and concentrate on expanded descriptions of things readers have told me they want to know more about, a solid helping of fresh sample photos, and lots of details about the latest and greatest new features. Rest assured, this book was written expressly for you, and tailored especially for the D3500.

Who Am I?

After spending many years as the world's most successful unknown author, I've become slightly less obscure in the past few years, thanks to a horde of camera guidebooks and other photographically oriented tomes. You may have seen my photography articles in the late, lamented *Popular Photography* magazine. I've also written about 2,000 articles for magazines like *Rangefinder, Professional Photographer*, and dozens of other photographic publications. But, first, and foremost, I'm a photo-journalist and made my living in the field until I began devoting most of my time to writing books. Although I love writing, I'm happiest when I'm out taking pictures, which is why I spend four to six weeks in the Florida Keys each winter as a base of operations for photographing the wildlife, wild natural settings, and wild people in the Sunshine State. In recent years, I've spent a lot of time overseas, too, photographing people and monuments. You'll find photos of some of these visual treasures within the pages of this book.

Like all my digital photography books, this one was written by a Nikon devotee with an incurable photography bug who has used Nikon cameras professionally for longer than I care to admit. Over the years, I've worked as a sports photographer for an Ohio newspaper and for an upstate New York college. I've operated my own commercial studio and photo lab, cranking out product shots on demand and then printing a few hundred glossy 8 × 10s on a tight deadline for a press kit. I've served as a photo-posing instructor for a modeling agency. People have actually paid me to shoot their weddings and immortalize them with portraits. I even prepared press kits and articles on photography as a PR consultant for a large Rochester, NY, company, which older readers may recall as an industry giant. My trials and travails with imaging and computer technology have made their way into print in book form an alarming number of times, including a few dozen on scanners and photography.

Like you, I love photography for its own merits, and I view technology as just another tool to help me get the images I see in my mind's eye. But, also like you, I had to master this technology before I could apply it to my work. This book is the result of what I've learned, and I hope it will help you master your Nikon D3500 digital SLR, too.

In closing, I'd like to ask a special favor: let me know what you think of this book. If you have any recommendations about how I can make it better, visit my website at www.nikonguides.com, click on the E-Mail Me tab, and send your comments, suggestions on topics that should be explained in more detail, or, especially, any typos. (The latter will be compiled on the Errata page you'll also find on my website.) I really value your ideas, and appreciate it when you take the time to tell me what you think! Some of the content of the book you hold in your hands came from suggestions I received from readers like you. If you found this book especially useful, tell others about it. Visit http://www.amazon.com/dp/1681984768 and leave a positive review. Your feedback is what spurs me to make each one of these books better than the last. Thanks!

1

Thinking Outside the Box

Although considered an "entry-level" model, the Nikon D3500, with its 24-megapixel resolution and long list of creativity-inspiring features, is considerably more versatile than any pocket-sized point-and-shoot camera and can certainly top even the most advanced smartphone cameras in features. Even with all that capability packed into a compact digital single-lens reflex (dSLR) body, you'll find "turn it on and shoot" ease of operation. With about 60 seconds' worth of instruction, you can go out and begin taking great pictures.

Try it. Insert a memory card and mount the lens (if you bought the D3500 at a store, they probably did that for you). Charge the battery and insert it into the camera. Remove the lens cap, turn the camera on (the button is concentric with the shutter release button), and then set the big ol' dial on top to the green AUTO icon. Point the D3500 at something interesting and press the shutter release. Presto! A pretty good picture will pop up on the color LCD on the back of the camera. Wasn't that easy?

But if you purchased this book, you're probably not going to be satisfied with pretty good photos. By buying a digital single-lens reflex camera with interchangeable optics, you've indicated an interest in capturing *incredible* images. The D3500 can do that, too. All you need is this book and some practice. The first step is to familiarize yourself with your camera. The first three chapters of this book will take care of that. Then, as you gain experience and skills, you'll want to learn more about how to improve your exposures, fine-tune the color, or use the essential tools of photography, such as electronic flash and available light. You'll want to learn how to choose and use lenses, too. All that information can be found in the other chapters of this book. The Nikon D3500 is not only easy to use, it's easy to *learn* to use.

As I've done with my guidebooks for previous Nikon cameras, I'm going to divide my introduction to the Nikon D3500 into several parts. The first part will cover what you absolutely *need* to know just to get started using the camera (you'll find that in this chapter). The second part is a Quick Start that offers a more comprehensive look at what you *should* know about the camera and its controls to use its features effectively (that'll be found in Chapter 2). Finally, you'll learn how to use the D3500's controls in Chapter 3, and then make key settings using the menu system, so you'll be able to fine-tune and tweak the D3500 to operate exactly the way you want in Chapters 4 and 5. While you probably should master everything in the first three chapters right away, you can take more time to learn about the settings described in Chapters 4 and 5, because you won't need to use all those options right away. However, I've included everything about menus and settings in those two chapters, so you'll find what you need, when you need it.

Perhaps you owned a previous Nikon camera, and wanted some of the added features the newer D3500 offers, such as full HD movie making and SnapBridge communication with smartphones and tablets. A few of you may even be someone like me, who often uses a more advanced Nikon dSLR as a preferred camera but finds the D3500 an alluring walk-about camera and backup because of its compact size and light weight.

If you fall into any of those categories, you may be able to skim through this chapter quickly and move on to the two that follow. The next few pages are designed to get your camera fired up and ready for shooting as quickly as possible. If you're new to digital SLRs, Nikon dSLRs, or even digital photography, you'll want to read through this introduction more carefully. After all, the Nikon D3500 is not a point-and-shoot camera, although, as I said, you can easily set it up in fully auto-mated Auto mode or use the semi-automated Program exposure mode and a basic autofocus setting for easy capture of grab shots. But, if you want a little more control over your shooting, you'll need to know more. So, I'm going to provide a basic pre-flight checklist that you need to complete before you really spread your wings and take off. You won't find a lot of detail in this chapter. Indeed, I'm going to tell you just what you absolutely *must* understand, accompanied by some interesting tidbits that will help you become acclimated to your D3500. I'll go into more depth and even repeat some of what I explain here in later chapters, so you don't have to memorize everything you see. Just relax, follow a few easy steps, and then go out and begin taking your best shots—ever.

In a Hurry?

Even a quick start like this one may be too much for those eager to begin using their cameras. Fortunately, Nikon has taken care of the most enthusiastic of the enthusiasts among you, with an expanded feature called the Guide mode, which can lead you through basic picture taking and reviewing steps, and simple camera setup procedures, with little help from me. If you want to try it out immediately, and then come back to read this chapter, you have three choices:

■ **Skim my two-minute introduction, then jump in.** The very last section of Chapter 2 has a short discussion explaining the Guide mode. Flip to it, glance through the intro, then grab your camera.

■ **Jump off the side of the boat now.** Rotate the mode dial (located on the top-right surface of the camera, southwest of the shutter release button) to the GUIDE position, and then figure out what to do from the menus and prompts on the screen. Take some photos, then come back to learn more about what you just did!

■ **Go Live!** If you're coming from a point-and-shoot camera and are used to composing and shooting your images using the LCD rather than a dSLR's cool through-the-lens optical viewfinder, you can jump into live view by reading the sidebar that's next.

LIVE VIEW CRASH COURSE

1. **Press the Live View lever.** It's located on the top-right panel of the camera next to the mode dial, and marked with an Lv label. (See Figure 1.1.) You can exit live view at any time by pressing the Lv lever again.

2. **Zoom in/out.** Check your view by pressing the Zoom In button (located on the right back panel of the D3500, as shown in Figure 1.2). A navigation box appears in the lower right of the LCD with a yellow box representing the portion of the image zoomed. Use the multi selector keys (that pad with the OK button in the center to the right of the LCD) to change the zoomed area within the full frame. Press the Zoom Out button (just below the Zoom In button) to zoom out again. Magnifying the live preview image has no effect on the area covered in the final image, of course.

3. **Shoot.** Press the shutter release all the way down to take a still picture or press the red-accented Movie button (on top of the camera, just to the southwest of the shutter release) to start motion picture filming. Stop filming by pressing the Movie button again.

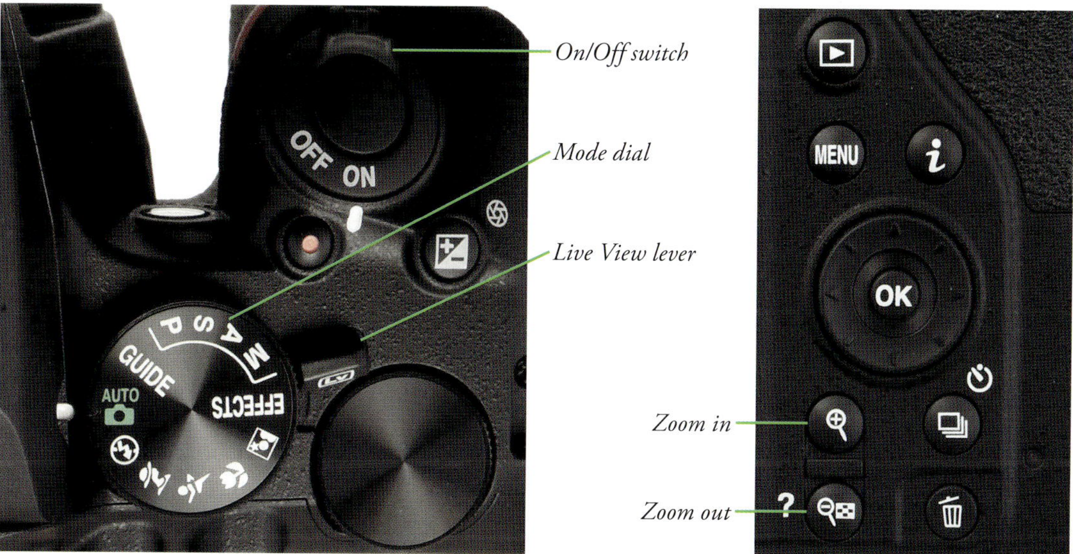

Figure 1.1 Location of the On/Off switch, mode dial, and Live View lever.

Figure 1.2 Zoom in/zoom out buttons.

First Things First

This section helps orient you with all the things that come in the box with your Nikon D3500, including what they do. I'll also describe some optional equipment you might want to have. If you want to get started immediately, skim through this section and jump ahead to "Initial Setup" later in the chapter.

The most important components in the impressive gold box your camera came in are the D3500 itself and lens. Unlike some other Nikon models, the D3500 is most often sold in a kit with a lens, such as the nifty, super-compact collapsible AF-P 18-55mm f/3.5-5.6 VR zoom. At introduction, it was also available in an expanded kit with an additional lens, the AF-P 70-300mm f/4.5-6.3G ED, for only $100 more. Also included is a battery, battery charger, and, if you're the nervous type, the neck strap. If you purchased your D3500 from a camera shop, as I did, the store personnel probably attached the neck strap for you, ran through some basic operational advice that you've already forgotten, tried to sell you a Secure Digital card (not included with the camera), and then, after they'd given you all the help you could absorb, sent you on your way with a handshake.

Perhaps you purchased your D3500 from one of those mass merchandisers that also sell washing machines and vacuum cleaners. In that case, you might have been sent on your way with only the handshake, or, maybe, not even that if you resisted the efforts to sell you an extended warranty. You save a few bucks at the big-box stores, but you don't get the personal service a professional photo retailer provides. It's your choice. There's a third alternative, of course. You might have purchased your camera from a mail order or Internet source, and your D3500 arrived in a big brown (or purple/red) truck. Your only interaction when you took possession of your camera was to scrawl your signature on an electronic clipboard.

In all three cases, the first thing to do is to carefully unpack the camera and double-check the contents listed below. While this level of setup detail may seem as superfluous as the instructions on a bottle of shampoo, checking the contents *first* is always a good idea. No matter who sells a camera, it's common to open boxes, use a particular camera for a demonstration, and then repack the box without replacing all the pieces and parts afterward. Someone might actually have helpfully checked out your camera on your behalf—and then mispacked the box. It's better to know *now* that something is missing so you can seek redress immediately. At a minimum, the box should hold the following:

- **Nikon D3500 digital camera.** It almost goes without saying that you should check out the camera immediately, making sure the color LCD on the back isn't scratched or cracked, the Secure Digital and battery doors open properly, and, when a charged battery is inserted and lens mounted, the camera powers up and reports for duty. Out-of-the-box defects like these are rare, but they can happen. It's probably more common that your dealer played with the camera or, perhaps, it was a customer return. That's why it's best to buy your D3500 from a retailer you trust to supply a factory-fresh camera.

- **Kit lens.** Nikon is predominantly offering this camera with one of two main kit lenses, the AF-P DX Nikkor 18-55mm f/3.5-5.6G VR and the same lens without the VR suffix (which represents Nikon's Vibration Reduction anti-shake technology). In addition, the company has created bundles that add a telephoto zoom, including: the AF-P DX Nikkor 70-300 f/4.5-6.3G ED in both VR and non-VR versions. A third kit lens that might have been furnished with your D3500 is the AF-S DX Nikkor 55mm-200mm f/4-5.6 ED VR II. I'll explain the meaning of all that alphabet soup, and how to choose the best lenses for your photography in Chapter 7.

- **BF-1B body cap/rear lens cap.** Nikon has been packaging D3500 kits with the kit lens(es) in separate compartments in the box, protected by a front lens cap and rear lens cap, and a protective body cap installed on the body. The latter keeps dust from infiltrating your camera when a lens is not mounted. Always carry a body cap (and rear lens cap) in your camera bag for those times when you need to have the camera bare of optics for more than a minute or two. (That usually happens when repacking a bag efficiently for transport, or when you are carrying an extra body or two for backup.) When not mounted on the lens, the body cap/lens cap nest together for compact storage.

- **Rechargeable Li-ion battery EN-EL14a.** You'll need to charge this 7.4V, 2030mAh (milliampere hour) battery before using it. I'll offer instructions later in this chapter.

- **Quick charger MH-24.** This charger is required to vitalize the EN-EL14a battery.

- **Neck strap.** Nikon provides you with a "steal me" neck strap emblazoned with the Nikon name, and while useful for showing off to your friends exactly which nifty new camera brand you bought, it's not very adjustable. I never attach the Nikon strap to my cameras, and instead opt for a more serviceable strap from UPstrap (www.upstrap-pro.com). If you carry your camera over one shoulder, as many do, I particularly recommend UPstrap (shown in Figure 1.3). It has a patented non-slip pad that offers reassuring traction and eliminates the contortions we sometimes go through to keep the camera from slipping off. I know several photographers who refuse to use anything else. If you do purchase an UPstrap, be sure to tell photographer-inventor Al Stegmeyer that I sent you hence.

Figure 1.3
Third-party neck straps like this UPstrap model, are often preferable to the Nikon-supplied strap.

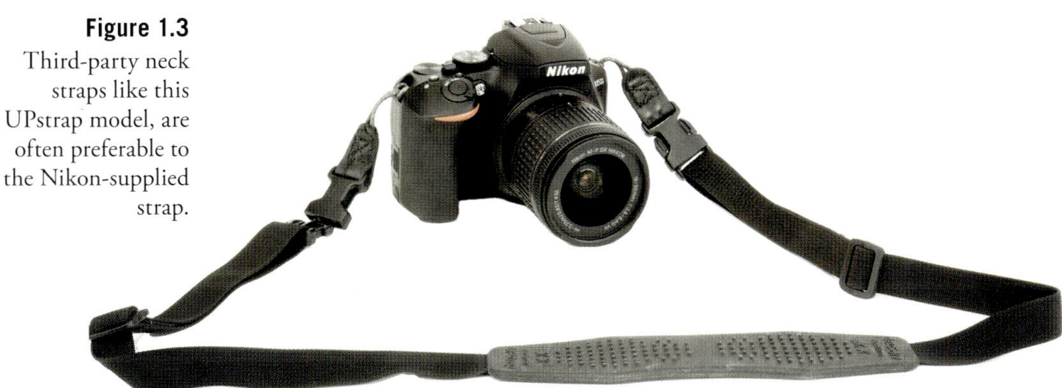

- **DK-17 eyepiece.** This is the square rubber eyecup that comes installed on the D3500. It slides on and off the viewfinder.

- **User manual/Quick Guide.** The only printed "user manual" you receive with the Nikon D3500 is a terse booklet that includes only the basic setup and usage information, and an even smaller quick-start guide pamphlet/poster. Many point-and-shoot cameras come with better printed materials. Both are decent for what they do, but they make a book like this one even more necessary.

- **Warranty and registration card.** Don't lose these! You can register your Nikon D3500 by mail or online (in the USA, the URL is www.nikonusa.com/register) and may need the information in this paperwork (plus the purchase receipt/invoice from your retailer) should you require Nikon service support.

Don't bother rooting around in the box for anything beyond what I've listed previously. There are a few things Nikon classifies as optional accessories, even though you (and I) might consider some of them essential. Here's a list of what you *don't* get in the box but might want to think about as an impending purchase. I'll list them roughly in the order of importance:

- **Secure Digital card.** First-time digital camera buyers are sometimes shocked that their new tool doesn't come with a memory card. Why should it? The manufacturer doesn't have the slightest idea of how much storage you require, or whether you want a slow/inexpensive card or one that's faster/more expensive, so why should they pack one in the box and charge you for it? Given the D3500's 24-megapixel resolution, you'll probably want an SD card with at least 16GB of capacity.

- **USB cable UC-E20.** You can use this optional cable to transfer photos from the camera to your computer (I don't recommend that because direct transfer uses a lot of battery power), or to upload and download settings between the camera and your computer (highly recommended). The Nikon UC-E6 cable works fine, but you can also use any generic USB 2.0 Micro-B cable, available at most retailers for a few bucks.

- **HDMI cable.** If you purchase an optional High-Definition Multimedia Interface (HDMI) cable, you can connect the D3500 to HD video devices, including TVs and monitors. Nikon's HC-E1 HDMI cable is a little pricey, so I recommend using any generic cable with a Type C connector.

- **Lens hoods.** In an effort to save themselves a few bucks, Nikon does not include a lens hood for either of the two kit lenses. I consider a lens hood an essential (not optional) accessory for all lenses, both for protection and for countering contrast-reducing flare when you're taking photos with a bright light source (such as the sun) located just outside the actual image area of the frame. The 18-55mm kit lens requires the HB-N106 bayonet hood, while the 70-300mm zoom uses the HB-77 bayonet hood. Don't leave home without them!

■ **Comprehensive manual.** Also not in the box is a comprehensive manual for the D3500. If you feel a need for something other than the abbreviated introductory printed pamphlet, you can visit the Nikon website for your country and download a more complete 354-page PDF Reference Manual you can view on your computer, laptop, phone, or tablet. Nikon also offers a Nikon Manual Viewer for your Android or iOS device that has direct links for downloading manuals and a convenient viewer for reading them. If you have this book, you probably don't need the Reference Manual, because I'm providing more complete descriptions of features and options.

■ **Extra EN-EL14a battery.** Even though you might get up to 1,550 shots from a single battery, it's easy to exceed that figure in a few hours of shooting sports at 5 fps or when using the built-in flash. Batteries can unexpectedly fail, too, or simply lose their charge from sitting around unused for a week or two. Buy an extra (I own four, in total), keep it charged, and free your mind from worry.

■ **Add-on Speedlight.** Your built-in flash can function as the main illumination for your photo, or it can be softened and used to fill in shadows. But, you'll have to own one or more external flash units if you want to trigger multiple add-on flash units. If you do much flash photography at all, consider an add-on Speedlight, such as the Nikon SB-500, as an important accessory.

■ **AC Adapter EH-5b/Power Connector EP-5a.** These two optional devices are used together to power the Nikon D3500 independently of the batteries. There are several typical situations where this capability can come in handy: when you're cleaning the sensor manually and want to totally eliminate the possibility that a lack of juice will cause the fragile shutter and mirror to spring to life during the process; when indoors shooting tabletop photos, portraits, class pictures, and so forth for hours on end; when using your D3500 for remote shooting as well as time-lapse photography; for extensive review of images on your television; or for file transfer to your computer. These all use prodigious amounts of power, which can be provided by this AC adapter. (Beware of power outages and blackouts when cleaning your sensor, however!)

■ **DR-6 right-angle viewer.** Used with the Nikon Eyepiece Adapter DK-22, it fastens in place of the standard square rubber eyecup and provides a 90-degree view for framing and composing your image at right angles to the original viewfinder. It's useful for low-level (or high-level) shooting. (Or, maybe, shooting around corners!)

■ **DG-2 magnifier/Eyepiece Adapter DK-22.** These replace the eyepiece to provide magnification of the center of the frame to ease focusing, particularly for close-up photography.

■ **SC-28 TTL flash cord.** Allows using Nikon Speedlights off-camera, while retaining all the automated features.

■ **SC-29 TTL flash cord.** Similar to the SC-28, this unit has its own AF-assist lamp, which can provide extra illumination for the D3500's autofocus system in dim light (which, not coincidentally, is when you'll probably be using an electronic flash).

- **Nikon Capture NX-i software.** Nikon's NEF (RAW) conversion and image-tweaking software is a free option that most D3500 owners won't need until they progress into extensive image editing.

- **BS-1 accessory shoe cover.** This is a sliding plastic piece that fits into the accessory shoe on top of the camera and protects its contents from damage. You can remove it (and probably lose it) when you attach an optional external electronic flash to the shoe. I always, without fail, tuck it into the same place each time (in my case, my right front pants pocket), and have yet to lose one. I've found a cheap source for these and will send you one for a few bucks—either a plain shoe cover or one with a built-in bubble level. Visit http://www.laserfairepress.com.

Initial Setup

This section familiarizes you with the controls most used to make adjustments: the multi selector and the command dial. You'll also find information on charging the battery, setting the clock, mounting a lens, and making diopter vision adjustments.

Once you've unpacked and inspected your camera, the initial setup of your Nikon D3500 is fast and easy. Basically, you just need to charge the battery, attach a lens, and insert a Secure Digital card. I'll address each of these steps separately, but if you already are confident you can manage these setup tasks without further instructions, feel free to skip this section entirely. I realize that some readers are ambitious, if inexperienced, and should, at the minimum, skim the contents of the next section, because I'm going to list a few options that you might not be aware of.

Mastering the Multi Selector

I'll be saving descriptions of most of the controls used with the Nikon D3500 until Chapter 3, which provides a complete "roadmap" of the camera's buttons and dials and switches. However, you may need to perform a few tasks during this initial setup process, and most of them will require the MENU button and the multi selector pad. The multi selector pad may remind you of the similar control found on many point-and-shoot cameras, and other digital SLRs. It consists of a thumbpad-sized button with raised arrows at the north, south, east, and west positions, raised indicators in between those locations, and a button in the center marked "OK." (See Figure 1.4.) The MENU button is easy to find: it's shown at upper left in the figure. It requires almost no explanation; when you want to access a menu, press it. To exit most menus, press it again.

With the D3500, the multi selector is used extensively for navigation; for example, to navigate among menus on the LCD or to choose one

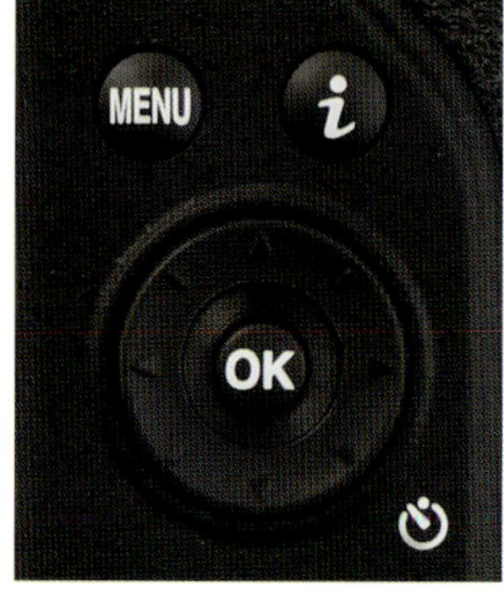

Figure 1.4 The multi selector pad has four directional buttons for navigating up/down/left/right, and an OK button to confirm your selection.

of the eleven focus points, to advance or reverse display of a series of images during picture review, or to change the kind of photo information displayed on the screen. The OK button is used to confirm your choices. So, from time to time in this chapter (and throughout this book), I'll be referring to the multi selector and its left/right/up/down buttons, and center OK button.

Setting the Clock

It's likely that your Nikon D3500's internal clock hasn't been set to your local time, so you may need to do that first. (The in-camera clock might have been set for you by someone checking out your camera prior to delivery.) If you do need to set the clock, the flashing CLOCK indicator on the LCD will be the giveaway. You'll find complete instructions for setting the four options for the date/time (time zone, actual date and time, the date format, and whether you want the D3500 to conform to Daylight Savings Time) in Chapter 5. However, if you think you can handle this step without instruction, press the MENU button, and then use the multi selector to scroll down to the Setup menu (it's marked with a wrench icon), press the multi selector button to the right, and then press the down button to scroll down to the Time Zone and Date entry, and press the right button again. The options will appear on the screen that appears next. Keep in mind that you'll need to reset your camera's internal clock from time to time, as it is not 100 percent accurate. (If you use SnapBridge to link the camera to your smart device, you can tell the D3500 to use that device's satellite information to correct its internal clock.) Of course, your camera will not explode if the internal clock is inaccurate, but your images will have the wrong time stamped on them. You may also need to reset your camera's internal clock if you travel and you want the time stamp on your pictures to reflect the time where the images were shot, and not the time back home.

Battery Included

Your Nikon D3500 is a sophisticated hunk of machinery and electronics, but it needs a charged battery to function, so rejuvenating the EN-EL14a lithium-ion battery pack furnished with the camera should be your first step. A fully charged power source should be good for a minimum of 1,550 shots, based on standard tests defined by the Camera & Imaging Products Association (CIPA) document DC-002. Nikon touts this figure as an improvement over the previous model, which was capable of just 1200 shots using CIPA standards. Of course, in the real world, the life of the battery will depend on several factors, including how often you review the shots you've taken on the LCD screen, whether you are shooting in live view or capturing video, as well as how many pictures you take with the built-in flash. In practice, you'll want to keep track of how many pictures *you* are able to take in your own typical circumstances, and use that figure as a guideline, instead.

All rechargeable batteries undergo some degree of self-discharge just sitting idle in the camera or in the original packaging. Lithium-ion power packs of this type typically lose a small amount of their charge every day, even when the camera isn't turned on. Li-ion cells lose their power through a chemical reaction that continues when the camera is switched off. It's very likely that the battery purchased with your camera is at least partially pooped out, so you'll want to revive it before going out for some serious shooting.

A BATTERY AND A SPARE

I always recommend purchasing Nikon-brand batteries (for about $60) over less-expensive third-party packs, even though the $30 substitute batteries may offer more capacity at a lower price (some top the 1,230 mAh offered by the Nikon battery). My reasoning is that it doesn't make sense to save $10 on a component for a sophisticated camera, especially since batteries have been known to fail in potentially harmful ways. You need only look as far as Nikon's own 2012 recall of its EN-EL15, and the free replacement of the same battery in 2016 because it wasn't fully compatible with all the latest Nikon models. Nikon shipped out thousands of free replacement cells. You're unlikely to get the same support from a third-party battery supplier that sells under a half-dozen or more different brand names and may not even have an easy way to get the word out that a recall has been issued.

If your pictures are important to you, always have at least one spare battery available, and make sure it is an authentic Nikon product.

Charging the Battery

When the battery is inserted into the MH-24 charger properly (it's impossible to insert it incorrectly), as you can see at upper right in Figure 1.5, the contacts on the battery line up and mate with matching contacts inside the charger. When properly connected, an orange charge light begins flashing, and remains flashing until the status lamp glows steadily, indicating that charging is finished. Nikon says that roughly one hour and 50 minutes are required to fully charge the battery. When the battery is charged, slide the latch on the bottom of the camera and ease the battery in, as shown at lower left in Figure 1.5.

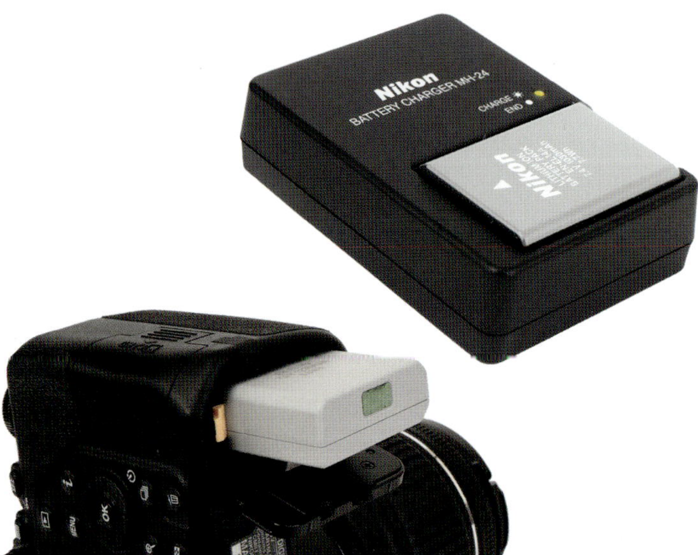

Figure 1.5
When the charger is plugged in, a flashing status light will illuminate while the battery is being charged (upper right). Insert the battery in the camera; it only fits one way (lower left).

Final Steps

Your Nikon D3500 is almost ready to fire up and shoot. You'll need to select and mount a lens, adjust the viewfinder for your vision, and insert a Secure Digital card. Each of these steps is easy, and if you've used any Nikon before, you already know exactly what to do. I'm going to provide a little extra detail for those of you who are new to the Nikon or SLR worlds.

Mounting the Lens

As you'll see, my recommended lens mounting procedure emphasizes protecting your equipment from accidental damage and minimizing the intrusion of dust. If your D3500 has no lens attached, select the lens you want to use and loosen (but do not remove) the rear lens cap. I generally place the lens I am planning to mount vertically in a slot in my camera bag, where it's protected from mishaps, but ready to pick up quickly. By loosening the rear lens cap, you'll be able to lift it off the back of the lens at the last instant, so the rear element of the lens is covered until then.

After that, remove the body cap by rotating the cap away from the release button. You should always mount the body cap when there is no lens on the camera, because it helps keep dust out of the interior of the camera, as the D3500 does not have an automatic sensor cleaning system like that found on more upscale Nikon dSLRs. The body cap also protects the camera's innards from damage caused by intruding objects (including your fingers, if you're not cautious).

Once the body cap has been removed, remove the rear lens cap from the lens, set it aside, and then mount the lens on the camera by matching the alignment indicator on the lens barrel with the white dot on the camera's lens mount. (See Figure 1.6.) Rotate the lens toward the shutter release until it seats securely. Some lenses are trickier to mount than others, especially telephoto lenses with special collars for attaching the lens itself to a tripod.

Figure 1.6
Match the indicator on the lens with the white dot on the camera mount to properly align the lens with the bayonet mount.

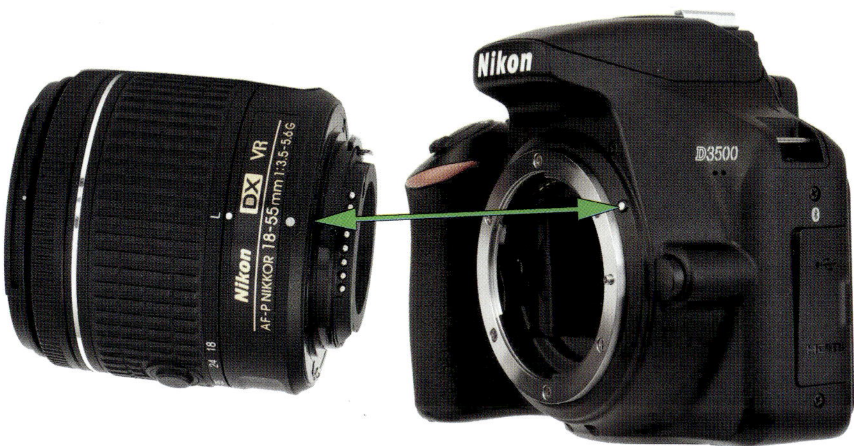

If you own a Nikon retractable lens (currently only the two AF-P 18-55mm kit lenses and an older AF-S version of the same lens), if you power up the camera with the lens retracted, you'll see a message "Before taking photos, rotate the zoom ring to extend the lens." Press the lens barrel button and rotate the zoom ring toward the shutter release to extract the lens to its shooting length.

Then, if your lens has a focus mode switch, set it to AF or M/A (Autofocus). If the optional lens hood is bayoneted on the lens in the reversed position (which makes the lens/hood combination more compact for transport), twist it off and remount with the "petals" (if present) facing outward. (See Figure 1.7.) A lens hood protects the front of the lens from accidental bumps, and reduces flare caused by extraneous light arriving at the front of the lens from outside the picture area.

Adjusting Diopter Correction

Those of us with less than perfect eyesight can often benefit from a little optical correction in the viewfinder. Your contact lenses or glasses may provide all the correction you need, but if you are a glasses wearer and want to use the D3500 without your glasses, you can take advantage of the camera's built-in diopter adjustment, which can be varied from –1.7 to +0.5 correction. Press the shutter release halfway to illuminate the indicators in the viewfinder, then rotate the diopter adjustment control next to the viewfinder (see Figure 1.8) while looking through the viewfinder until the indicators appear sharp. Should the available correction be insufficient, Nikon offers nine different DK-20C Diopter-Adjustment Viewfinder Correction lenses for the viewfinder window, ranging from –5 to +3, at a cost of about $16.

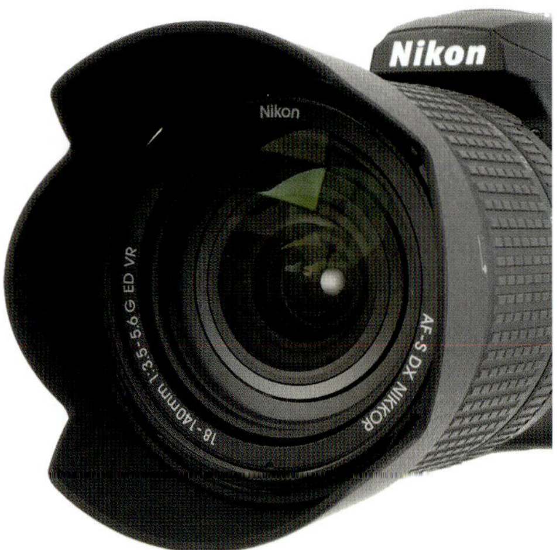

Figure 1.7 A lens hood protects the lens from extraneous light and accidental bumps.

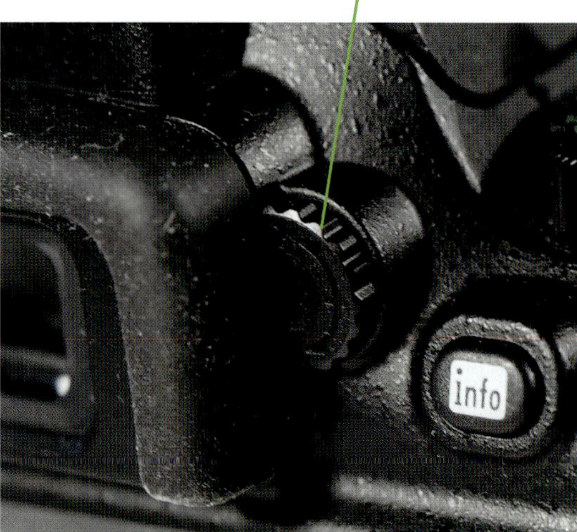

Figure 1.8 Viewfinder diopter correction from –1.7 to +0.5 can be dialed in.

Inserting a Secure Digital Card

You've probably set up your D3500 so you can't take photos without a Secure Digital card inserted. (There is a Slot Empty Release Lock entry in the Setup menu that enables/disables shutter release functions when a memory card is absent—you'll learn about that in Chapter 5.) So, your final step will be to insert a Secure Digital card. Slide the cover on the right side of the camera toward the back, and then open it. (You should only remove the memory card when the camera is switched off, or, at the very least, the yellow-green card access light [just to the northeast of the "trash can" icon on the back of the camera] that indicates the D3500 is writing to the card is not illuminated.)

Insert the memory card with the label facing the back of the camera oriented so the edge with the gold edge connectors goes into the slot first. (See Figure 1.9.) Close the door, and, if this is your first use of the card, format it (described next). When you want to remove the memory card later, press the card inward, and it will pop right out.

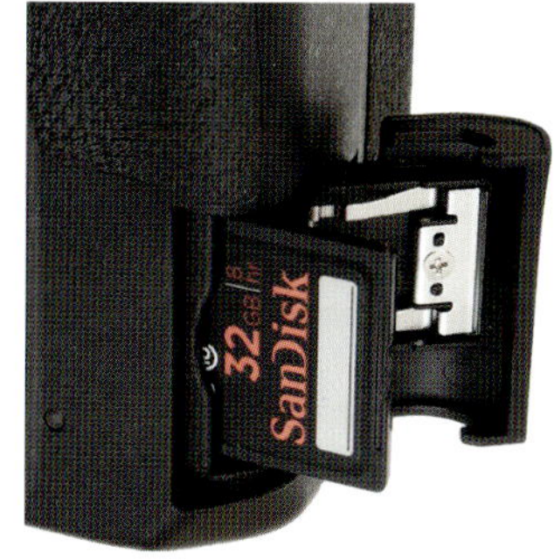

Figure 1.9 The Secure Digital card is inserted with the label facing the back of the camera.

Formatting a Memory Card

There are three ways to create a blank Secure Digital card for your D3500, and two of them are at least partially wrong. Here are your options, both correct and incorrect:

- **Transfer (move) files to your computer.** When you transfer (rather than copy) all the image files to your computer from the Secure Digital card (either using a direct cable transfer or with a card reader), the old image files are erased from the card, leaving the card blank. Theoretically. Unfortunately, this method does *not* remove files that you've labeled as Protected (by pressing the Protect button to the right of the viewfinder window [it's marked with a key icon] while viewing the image on the LCD), nor does it identify and lock out parts of your SD card that have become corrupted or unusable since the last time you formatted the card. Therefore, I recommend always formatting the card, rather than simply moving the image files, each time you want to make a blank card. The only exception is when you *want* to leave the protected/ unerased images on the card for a while longer, say, to share with friends, family, and colleagues.

- **(Don't) Format in your computer.** With the SD card inserted in a card reader or card slot in your computer, you can use Windows or Mac OS to reformat the memory card. Don't! The operating system won't necessarily arrange the structure of the card the way the D3500 likes to see it (in computer terms, an incorrect *file system* may be installed). The only way to ensure that the card has been properly formatted for your camera is to perform the format in the camera itself. The only exception to this rule is when you have a seriously corrupted memory card that your camera refuses to format. Sometimes it is possible to revive such a corrupted card by allowing the operating system to reformat it first, then trying again in the camera. However, this works only with SD and SDHC cards; all SDXC cards (those with capacities of 64GB and up) use a special file system called exFAT and should only be formatted in a camera like the D3500.

- **Setup menu format.** To use the recommended method to format a memory card, press the MENU button, use the up/down buttons of the multi selector (that thumb-pad-sized control to the right of the LCD) to choose the Setup menu (which is represented by that wrench icon), navigate to the Format Memory Card entry with the right button of the multi selector, and select Yes from the screen that appears. Press OK (in the center of the multi selector pad) to begin the format process.

HOW MANY SHOTS?

The D3500 provides a fairly accurate estimate of the number of shots remaining on the LCD, as well as at the lower-right edge of the viewfinder display when the display is active. (Tap the shutter release button to activate it.)

It is only an estimate, because the actual number will vary, depending on the capacity of your memory card, the file format(s) you've selected (more on those later), and the content of the image itself. (Some photos may contain large areas that can be more efficiently squeezed down to a smaller size.)

For example, an 8GB card can hold about 524 shots in the format known as JPEG Fine at the D3500's maximum resolution (Large) format; 1,100 shots using the Normal JPEG setting; or 2,000 shots with Basic JPEG setting. When numbers exceed 1,000, the D3500 displays a figure and decimal point, followed by a K superscript, so that 1,900 shots (or thereabouts) is represented by [1.9]^K on the LCD and viewfinder.

Table 1.1 shows the typical number of shots you can expect using a 16GB SD memory card (which I expect will be a popular size card among D3500 users as prices continue to plummet during the life of this book). All figures are by actual count with my own 16GB SD card. Take those numbers and cut them in half if you're using an 8GB SD card or double them if you have a 32GB card. (You can use the Shooting menu's Image Quality option to change the file/formats in column 1, and to change the image sizes in columns 2, 3, and, 4, or change either value using the information edit display, described in Chapters 2 and 3.)

Table 1.1 Typical Shots with a 16GB Memory Card

	Large	Medium	Small
JPEG Fine	1,048	1,756	3,400
JPEG Normal	2,200	3,000	6,600
JPEG Basic	4,000	6,600	13,000
RAW	534	N/A	N/A
RAW+JPEG Fine	352	N/A	N/A

2

Nikon D3500 Quick Start

Now it's time to fire up your Nikon D3500 and take some photos. The easy part is turning on the power—the On/Off switch is on the right side, concentric with the shutter release button. Turn on the camera, and, if you mounted a lens and inserted a fresh battery and memory card—as I prompted you in the last chapter—you're ready to begin. You'll need to select a release mode, exposure mode, metering mode, focus mode, and, if need be, elevate the D3500's built-in flash.

But first, you need to learn how to use the screen that allows you to make most of the key adjustments and settings available with the D3500: the information edit display. Some of these choices can also be made using the menu system, as you'll learn in Chapters 4 and 5, but the information edit display is almost always faster.

Using the Information Edit Display

You can use the information edit display to change many of the D3500's basic settings. You shouldn't skip this section, because it provides basic information on how to change settings, including choosing exposure, metering, and autofocus modes.

There are *two* "information" buttons on the D3500, which can lead to confusion among new owners of this camera. The pair is shown in Figure 2.1. At top left you can see the Info button; its sole function is to turn the rear-panel LCD display on (if it's not visible) or off (if it is). Turning off the LCD information display when you're using the viewfinder saves power and can avoid a distraction that can be annoying when shooting in dark surroundings, such as a concert.

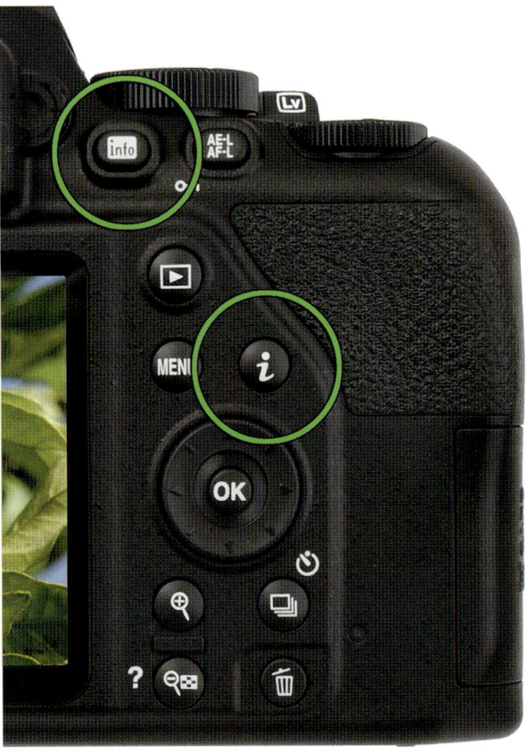

Figure 2.1
Info button (top left); Information edit button (center right).

The information edit or *i* button is pressed once to produce the shooting information display (see Figure 2.2) if it is not visible. Then press the *i* button a second time to activate the information edit display (see Figure 2.3), which is the screen you can use to make many adjustments, including those I will describe in this chapter.

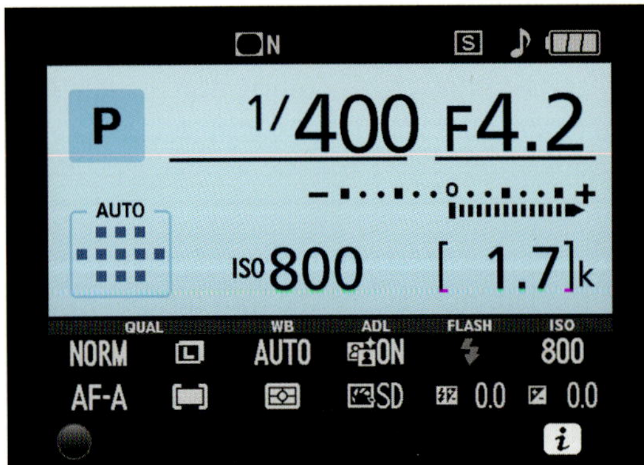

Figure 2.2 Press the Info button to turn the information screen on or off.

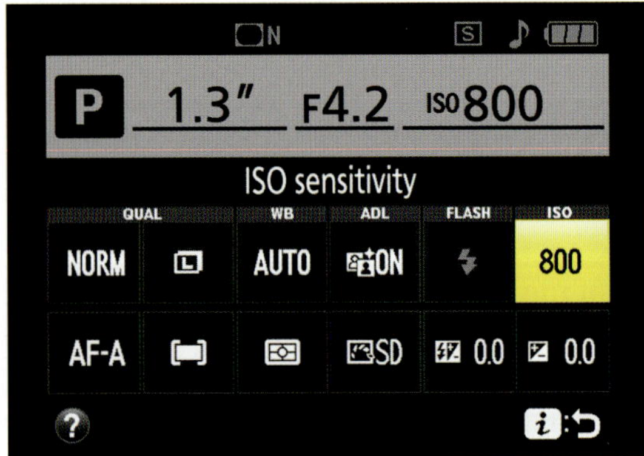

Figure 2.3 Pressing the *i* button gives you access to the information edit screen to modify your options.

The difference between the two is simple: the Info button just turns the shooting information screen on or off; the information edit (*i*) button allows you to make changes to the settings shown. Throughout most of this book I will just refer to the information edit button as the *i* button. Here's a breakdown of how they work:

- **Info button.** Press to toggle the shooting information screen on or off. That's all it does.
- **Information edit (*i*) button.** If the LCD monitor is blank, press once to go directly to the information edit display. If a screen is already displayed, the *i* button toggles between the shooting information screen and the information edit screen.

SCREEN OPTIONS

Your screen may not look exactly like the illustrations, as the D3500 allows you to choose several different color schemes, and opt for either a "Graphic" display or the "Classic" version shown in the figures. You can find out how to switch among these display modes in Chapter 5, using the Info Display Format entry in the Setup menu.

To change any settings, follow these steps:

1. **Overkill reminder.** If the LCD screen is blank, press the *i* button to access the information edit screen. Each time you press the *i* button, the screen toggles between the *shooting information* screen and the *information edit* screens.
2. **Highlight the setting to be changed.** Use the multi selector pad's left/right/up/down buttons to navigate to the settings at the bottom of the screen to the option you want to change.
3. **Access settings screen.** Press the OK button in the center of the multi selector pad to produce a screen where you can change options, as seen in Figure 2.4. The available settings screens include image size, image quality, ISO, focus modes, and other settings.

Figure 2.4
Choose your settings.

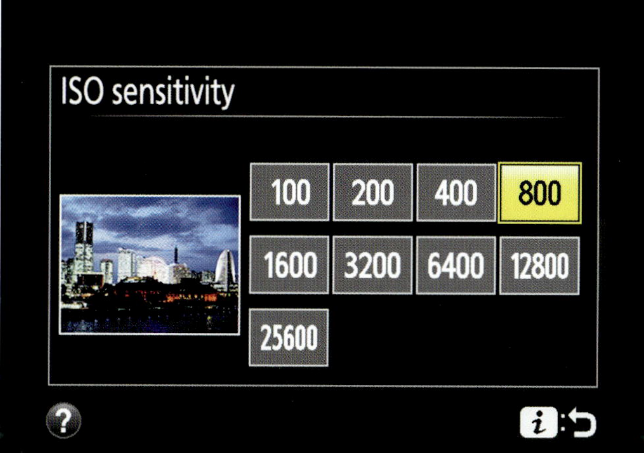

4. **Select option.** Use the up/down buttons to move the yellow highlighting to the desired option within the settings screen.

5. **Confirm.** Press the OK button to confirm your choice.

6. **Exit.** Press the *i* button to exit the screen.

Choosing a Release Mode

This section shows you how to choose from single-frame, continuous mode, quiet shutter release, self-timer mode, and remote control modes.

This shooting mode determines when (and how often) the D3500 makes an exposure. If you're coming to the dSLR world from a point-and-shoot camera, you might have used a model that labels these options as drive modes, dating back to the film era when cameras could be set for single-shot or "motor drive" (continuous) shooting modes. Your D3500 has four release (shooting/drive) modes: Single frame, Continuous (Burst), Quiet Shutter Release, and Self-timer.

Your camera has a dedicated button available to help you select one of these release modes quickly. It's located on the back-right panel of the D3500. You can see its location, just above the icon of the trash can, in Figure 2.1, above. Press the button, and then select the mode you want using the left/right directional buttons. A thumbnail appears at left when you press the button to provide a hint about what that release mode is used for. Press the *i* button to back out of the screen, or the OK button to confirm your highlighted choice and exit.

- **Single frame.** In this mode, a picture is taken each time the shutter release is pressed down all the way. The thumbnail shows a woman posing in a flower garden.

- **Continuous.** The camera records images at roughly a 5-frames-per-second rate as long as the shutter button is held down, or until an area of memory in the camera called a *buffer* fills, and the D3500 stops shooting until enough pictures are written to the memory card to allow more to be captured. Continuous shooting is useful for grabbing action shots of sports, or for capturing fleeting expressions (especially of children). The screen's thumbnail shows a motocross rider making a leap.

- **Quiet Shutter Release.** Think of this as a "quieter" shooting mode rather than a true "quiet" mode. In this mode, the camera takes a single picture when the shutter button is pressed all the way down, just as in Single frame mode. However, the camera's internal beeper won't chirp when autofocus is achieved, and after the shutter trips, capturing the image, the camera's viewing mirror doesn't flip back down until you release the shutter button. So, taking a picture in Quiet Shutter Release mode results in a single "clunk" sound as the mirror flips up and the shutter opens/closes, eventually followed by a second "clunk" when you release pressure on the shutter button. Theoretically, that's quieter than the "beep-clunk-clunk" heard in Single frame mode. The icon shows a concert hall, a typical venue where you'd want the quietest possible operation.

■ **Self-timer.** In this mode, press the shutter release down all the way, and, by default, the camera takes a single picture 10 seconds later. However, you can also specify 2-, 5-, and 20-second delays in the Setup menu's Self-timer entry, as well as tell the camera to fire off from 1 to 9 shots when the timer has elapsed. (Chapter 5 will show you how to do this.) Multiple shots are a good way to thwart those accidental (or intentional) blinkers or yawners who might otherwise spoil a family portrait.

The self-timer is a good way to get into the picture yourself, or to allow the vibration induced in a tripod-mounted camera to settle down after you've "punched" the shutter release. A white lamp on the front of the camera will blink while the timer counts down, then remain on continuously for about two seconds just before the picture is taken. Any time you use the camera on a tripod (with the self-timer or otherwise) make sure there is no bright light shining on the viewfinder window; if so, cover it or replace the rubber eyecup with the DK-5 eyepiece cap and block the window.

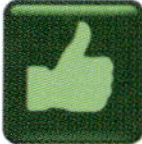

Tip

If you plan to dash in front of the camera to join the scene, consider using manual focus so the D3500 won't refocus on your fleeing form and produce unintended results. (Nikon really needs to offer an option to autofocus at the *end* of the self-timer cycle.)

Selecting a Shooting Mode

This section shows you how to choose an exposure mode. If you'd rather have the D3500 make all of the decisions for you, just rotate the mode dial to the green Auto setting and jump to the section titled "Reviewing the Images You've Taken." If you'd rather choose one of the Scene modes, tailored to specific types of shooting situations, or try out the camera's semi-automatic modes, continue reading this section.

The Nikon D3500 has three types of shooting modes: advanced modes/exposure modes; a second set, which Nikon labels Scene modes; and a third type of mode called Special Effects (represented by the EFFECTS position on the mode dial). The advanced modes include Programmed auto (or Program mode), Aperture-priority auto, Shutter-priority auto, and Manual exposure mode. These are the modes you'll use most often after you've learned all your D3500's features, because they allow you to specify how the camera chooses its settings when making an exposure, for greater creative control.

The Scene modes take full control of the camera, make all the decisions for you, and don't allow you to override the D3500's settings. They are most useful while you're learning to use the camera, because you can select an appropriate mode (Auto, Auto/No Flash, Portrait, Sports, Close-up, or Night Portrait) and fire away. You'll end up with decent photos using appropriate settings, but your opportunities to use a little creativity (say, to overexpose an image to create a silhouette, or to delib-erately use a slow shutter speed to add a little blur to an action shot) are minimal. The D3500 also has a Guide mode, with four simplified menus, Shoot, View/Delete, Retouch, and Setup, that provides fast access only to the most frequently used settings. I'll explain Guide mode later in this chapter, after you've had an introduction to the three types of options that are available in its menus. I'll cover EFFECTS in Chapter 4.

Choosing a Scene Mode

The six Auto/Scene modes can be selected by rotating the mode dial on the top right of the Nikon D3500 to the appropriate icon (shown in Figure 2.5):

- **Auto.** In this mode, the D3500 makes all the exposure decisions for you, and will pop up the internal flash if necessary under low-light conditions. The camera automatically focuses on the subject closest to the camera (unless you've set the lens to manual focus), and the autofocus assist illuminator lamp on the front of the camera will light up to help the camera focus in low-light conditions.
- **Auto (Flash Off).** Identical to Auto mode, except that the flash will not pop up under any circumstances. You'd want to use this in a museum, during religious ceremonies, concerts, or any environment where flash is forbidden or distracting.
- **Portrait.** Use this mode when you're taking a portrait of a subject standing relatively close to the camera and want to de-emphasize the background, maximize sharpness, and produce flat-tering skin tones. The built-in flash will pop up if needed.

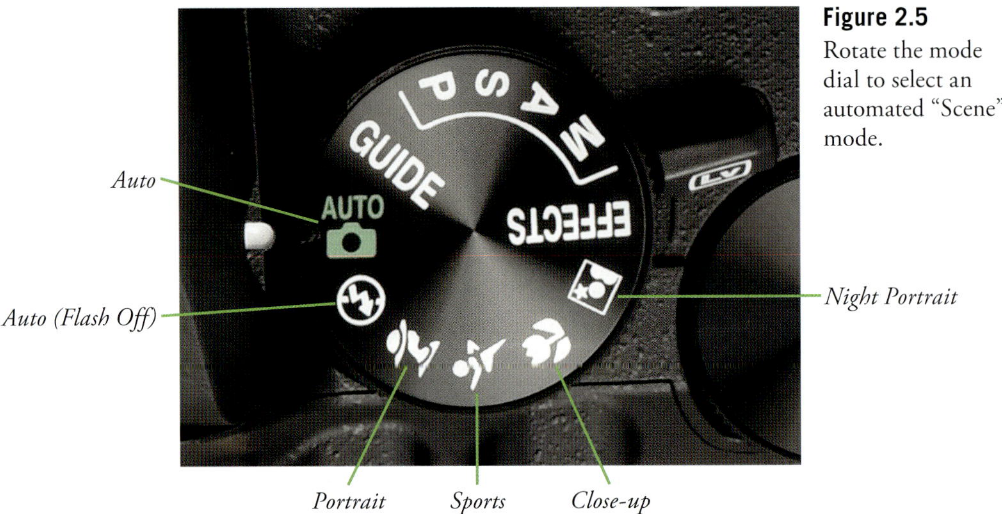

Figure 2.5
Rotate the mode dial to select an automated "Scene" mode.

■ **Sports.** Use this mode to freeze fast-moving subjects. The D3500 selects a fast shutter speed to stop action, and focuses continuously on the center focus point while you have the shutter release button pressed halfway. However, you can select one of the other two focus points to the left or right of the center by pressing the multi selector left/right buttons. The built-in electronic flash and focus assist illuminator lamp are disabled.

■ **Close-up.** This mode is helpful when you are shooting close-up pictures of a subject from about one foot away or less, such as flowers, bugs, and small items. The D3500 focuses on the closest subject in the center of the frame, but you can use the multi selector right and left buttons to focus on a different point. Use a tripod in this mode, as exposures may be long enough to cause blurring from camera movement. The built-in flash will pop up if needed.

■ **Night Portrait.** Choose this mode when you want to illuminate a subject in the foreground with flash (it will pop up automatically, if needed), but still allow the background to be exposed properly by the available light. The camera focuses on the closest main subject. Be prepared to use a tripod or a vibration-resistant lens like the 18-55 VR kit lens to reduce the effects of camera shake. (You'll find more about VR and camera shake in Chapter 10.)

Choosing an Advanced Mode

If you're very new to digital photography, you might want to set the camera to P (Program mode) and start snapping away. That mode will make all the appropriate settings for you for many shooting situations. If you have more photographic experience, you might want to opt for one of the semi-automatic modes, or even Manual mode. These advanced modes all let you apply a little more creativity to your camera's settings. Figure 2.6 shows the position of the modes described next.

■ **P (Program).** This mode allows the D3500 to select the basic exposure settings, but you can still override the camera's choices to fine-tune your image, while maintaining metered exposure, as I'll describe in Chapter 6.

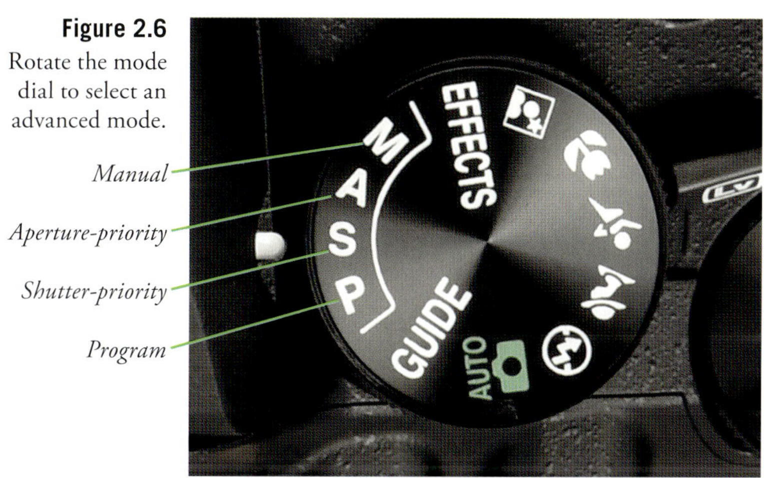

Figure 2.6
Rotate the mode dial to select an advanced mode.

Manual

Aperture-priority

Shutter-priority

Program

- **S (Shutter-priority).** This mode is useful when you want to use a particular shutter speed to stop action or produce creative blur effects. Choose your preferred shutter speed, and the D3500 will select the appropriate f/stop for you.

- **A (Aperture-priority).** Choose when you want to use a particular lens opening, especially to control sharpness or how much of your image is in focus. Specify the f/stop you want, and the D3500 will select the appropriate shutter speed for you.

- **M (Manual).** Select when you want full control over the shutter speed and lens opening, either for creative effects or because you are using a studio flash or other flash unit not compatible with the D3500's automatic flash metering.

Choosing a Metering Mode

This section shows you how to choose the area the D3500 will use to measure exposure: giving emphasis to the center of the frame, evaluating many different areas of the frame, or measuring light from a small spot in the center of the frame.

The metering mode you select determines how the D3500 calculates exposure. You might want to select a particular metering mode for your first shots, although the default Matrix metering is probably the best choice as you get to know your camera. (It is used automatically in any of the D3500's Scene modes.) I'll explain when and how to use each of the three metering modes later. To change metering modes, use the information edit screen. (You can also specify metering mode using the Shooting menu, as I'll describe in Chapter 6.)

1. **Access information edit screen.** Press the *i* button and navigate to the metering selection using the multi selector buttons.

2. **View options.** Press OK to select the option.

3. **Select metering mode.** Use the multi selector up/down buttons to choose Matrix, Center-weighted, or Spot metering (described below and represented by the icons shown in Figure 2.7).

4. **Confirm setting.** Press OK to confirm your choice.

5. **Exit.** Press the *i* button to exit, or just tap the shutter release button.

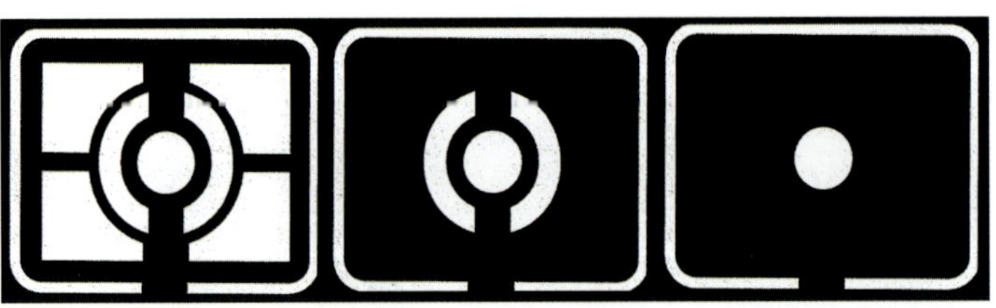

Figure 2.7
Metering mode icons are (left to right): Matrix, Center-weighted, Spot.

- **Matrix metering.** The standard metering mode; the D3500 attempts to intelligently classify your image and choose the best exposure based on readings from a 420-segment color CCD sensor that interprets light reaching the viewfinder using a database of hundreds of thousands of patterns.

- **Center-weighted metering.** The D3500 meters the entire scene but gives the most emphasis to the central area of the frame, measuring about 8mm.

- **Spot metering.** Exposure is calculated from a smaller 3.5 mm central spot, about 2.5 percent of the image area.

You'll find a detailed description of each of these modes in Chapter 6.

Choosing Focus Modes

This section shows you how to select *when* the D3500 calculates focus: all the time (continuously), only once when you press a control like the shutter release button (single autofocus), or manually when you rotate a focus ring on the lens.

The Nikon D3500 can focus your pictures for you or allow you to manually focus the image using the focus ring on the lens (I'll help you locate this ring in Chapter 3). Switching between automatic and manual focus is easy. You can move the AF/MF (autofocus/manual focus) or M/A-M (manual fine-tune autofocus/manual) switch found on most lenses (but not on some kit lenses) mounted on your camera. If you want to use manual focus and your lens does not have either type of switch, you can use the Shooting menu entry, described in Chapter 4, instead.

When using autofocus, you have additional choices. The D3500 has eleven autofocus zones that can be used to zero in on a particular subject area in your image. (See Figure 2.8.) In addition, you can select *when* the D3500 applies its focusing information to your image prior to exposure. I'll describe both in the next two sections.

Figure 2.8
The D3500 can select which of eleven focus zones to use, or allow you to make the choice, depending on the autofocus area mode you specify.

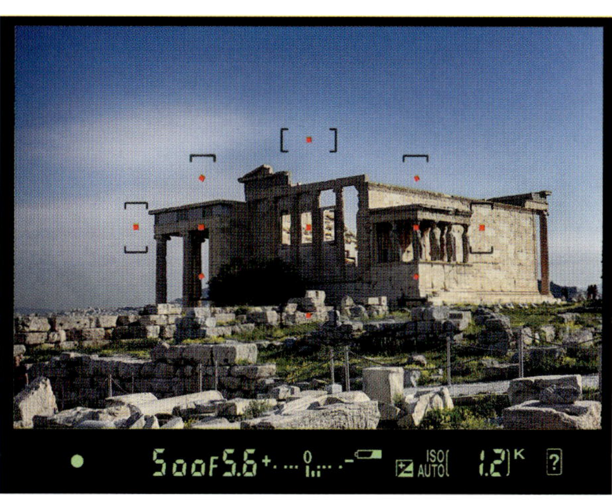

Choosing Autofocus-Area Mode

You can set the AF-area mode using the information edit screen.

1. Press the *i* button and navigate to the AF-area mode selection (it's second from the left in the bottom row) using the multi selector buttons.

2. Press OK to select the option.

3. Use the multi selector up/down buttons to choose Single-point AF, Dynamic-area AF, 3D-tracking (11 points), or Auto-area AF (described below).

4. Press OK to confirm your choice.

5. Press the *i* button to exit, or just tap the shutter release button.

The four modes, described in more detail in Chapter 7, are as follows:

- **Single-point.** You always choose which of the eleven points are used, and the Nikon D3500 sticks with that focus bracket, no matter what. This mode is best for non-moving subjects.

- **Dynamic-area.** You can choose which of the eleven focus zones to use, but the D3500 will switch to another focus mode when using AF-C or AF-A mode (described next) and the subject moves. This mode is great for sports or active children.

- **3D-tracking (11 points).** You can select the focus zone, but when not using AF-S mode, the camera refocuses on the subject if you reframe the image.

- **Auto-area.** This default mode chooses the focus point for you and can use distance information when working with a lens that has a G or D suffix in its name. (See Chapter 10 for more on the difference between G/D lenses and other kinds of lenses.)

Choosing Focus Mode

When you are using Program, Aperture-priority, Shutter-priority, or Manual exposure mode, you can select the autofocus mode *when* the D3500 measures and locks in focus prior to pressing the shutter release down all the way and taking the picture. The focus mode is chosen using the information edit screen.

1. Press the *i* button and navigate to the focus mode selection (it's at left in the bottom row) using the multi selector buttons.

2. Press OK to select the option.

3. Use the multi selector up/down buttons to choose AF-A, AF-S, AF-C, or M (described next).

4. Press OK to confirm your choice.

5. Press the *i* button to exit, or just tap the shutter release button.

The four focus modes when not using live view are as follows (there are additional autofocus modes, including Face Priority, available when shooting in live view):

- **Auto-servo AF (AF-A).** This default setting switches between AF-C and AF-S, as described below.

- **Single-servo AF (AF-S).** This mode, sometimes called *single autofocus*, locks in a focus point when the shutter button is pressed down halfway, and the focus confirmation light glows at bottom left in the viewfinder. The focus will remain locked until you release the button or take the picture. This mode is best when your subject is relatively motionless.

- **Continuous-servo AF (AF-C).** This mode, sometimes called *continuous autofocus*, sets focus when you partially depress the shutter button (or other autofocus activation button), but continues to monitor the frame and refocuses if the camera or subject is moved. This is a useful mode for photographing sports and moving subjects.

- **Manual focus (M).** When focus is set to manual, you always focus manually using the focus ring on the lens. The focus confirmation indicator in the viewfinder provides an indicator when correct focus is achieved.

Adjusting White Balance and ISO

This section describes some optional features you can select if you feel you need to choose the white balance or change the camera's sensitivity setting.

There are a few other settings you can make if you're feeling ambitious, but don't feel ashamed if you postpone using these features until you've racked up a little more experience with your D3500.

If you like, you can custom-tailor your white balance (color balance) and ISO (sensitivity) settings. I'll explain more about what these settings are, and why you might want to change them, in Chapter 4. To start out, it's best to set white balance (WB) to Auto, and ISO to ISO 200 for daylight photos, and ISO 400 for pictures in dimmer light. (Don't be afraid of ISO 1600, however; the D3500 does a *much* better job of producing low-noise photos at higher ISOs than many other cameras.) You'll find complete recommendations for both these settings in Chapter 4. You can adjust either one now using the information edit screen, as described multiple times in this chapter. I won't repeat the instructions again. The WB (for white balance) and ISO settings are third and fifth from the left in the top row in the information edit screen (respectively).

Reviewing the Images You've Taken

Here you'll discover how to review the images you've taken in a basic way. I'll provide more detailed options for image review in Chapter 4.

The Nikon D3500 has a broad range of playback and image review options, and I'll cover them in more detail in Chapter 4. For now, you'll want to learn just the basics. Here is all you really need to know at this time, as shown in Figure 2.9:

- **Display an image.** Press the Playback button (marked with a white right-pointing triangle) at the upper-left corner of the back of the camera to display the most recent image on the LCD.
- **Scroll among images.** Spin the command dial left or right to review additional images. You can also use the multi selector left/right buttons. Press right to advance to the next image or left to go back to a previous image.

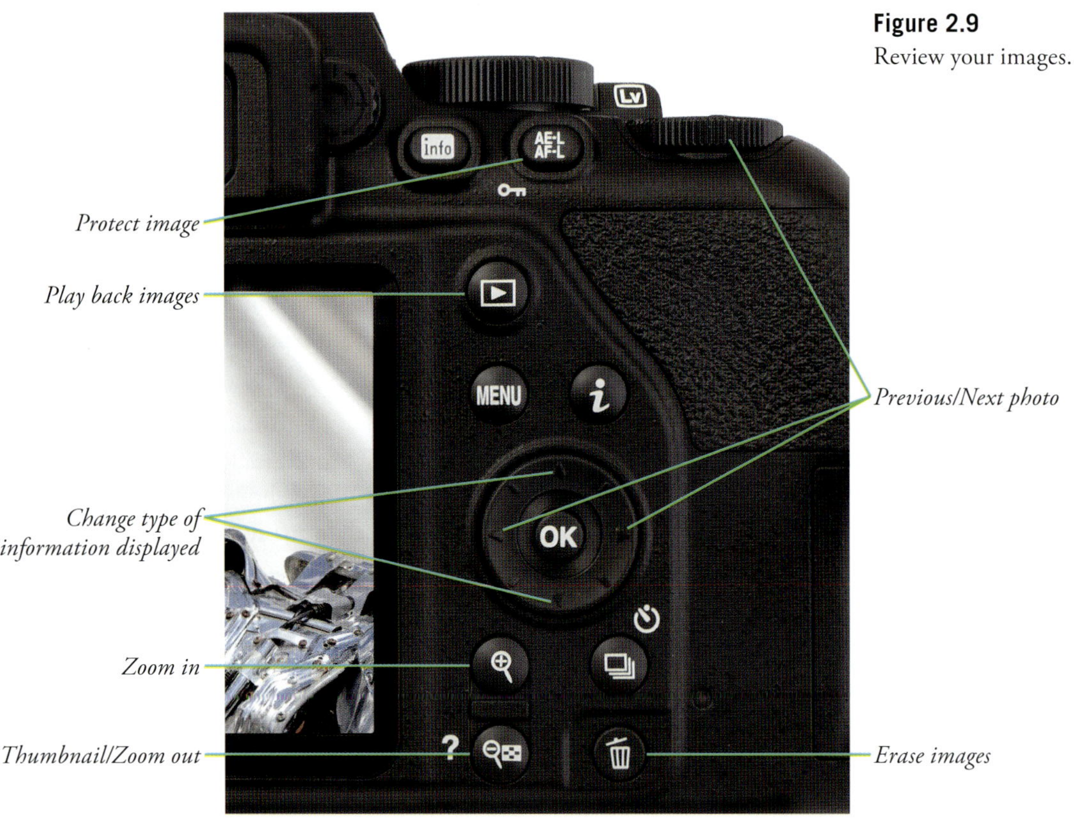

Figure 2.9
Review your images.

- **Change image information display.** Press the multi selector button up or down to change among overlays of basic image information or detailed shooting information. I'll show you how to specify the types of information shown in Chapter 4.

- **Magnify/reduce image on screen.** Press the Zoom In button repeatedly to zoom in on the image displayed; the Zoom Out button reduces the image. A thumbnail representation of the whole image appears in the lower-right corner with a yellow rectangle showing the relative level of zoom. At intermediate zoom positions, the yellow rectangle can be moved around within the frame using the multi selector.

- **Protect images.** Press the Protect button to mark an image and shield it from accidental erasure (but not from reformatting of the memory card).

- **Delete current image.** Press the Trash button twice to remove the photo currently being displayed.

- **Exit playback.** Press the Playback button again, or just tap the shutter release button to exit playback view.

You'll find information on viewing thumbnail indexes of images, automated playback, and other options in Chapter 4.

Using the Built-in Flash

> This section provides a quick introduction to your camera's built-in flash. You'll find more information on flash photography in Chapter 11.

Working with the D3500's built-in flash (as well as external flash units like the Nikon SB-500) deserves a chapter of its own, and I'm providing one (see Chapter 11). But the built-in flash is easy enough to work with that you can begin using it right away, either to provide the main lighting of a scene or as supplementary illumination to fill in the shadows.

The built-in flash will pop up automatically as required in Auto, Portrait, Close-up, and Night Portrait Scene modes. To use the built-in flash in Manual, Aperture-priority, Shutter-priority, or Program modes, just press the flash pop-up button (shown in Figure 2.10). When the flash is fully charged, a lightning bolt symbol will appear at the right side of the viewfinder display. When using P (Program) and A (Aperture-priority) exposure modes, the D3500 will select a shutter speed for you automatically from the range of 1/200th to 1/60th seconds. In S (Shutter-priority) and M (Manual) modes, you select the shutter speed from 1/200th to 30 seconds.

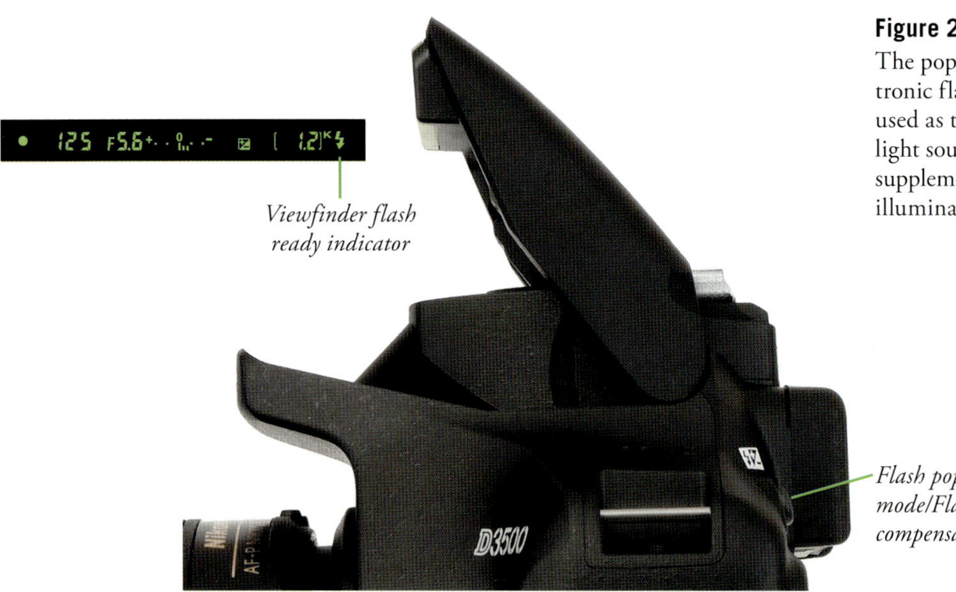

*Viewfinder flash
ready indicator*

*Flash pop-up/Flash
mode/Flash
compensation button*

Figure 2.10
The pop-up elec-
tronic flash can be
used as the main
light source or for
supplemental
illumination.

Transferring Photos to Your Computer

When you're ready to transfer your photos to your computer, you'll find everything you need to know in this section.

The final step in your picture-taking session will be to transfer the photos you've taken to your computer for printing, further review, or image editing. Your D3500 allows you to print directly to PictBridge-compatible printers and to create print orders right in the camera, plus you can select which images to transfer to your computer. I'll outline those options in Chapter 4.

I always recommend using a card reader attached to your computer to transfer files, because that process is generally a lot faster and doesn't drain the D3500's battery. However, you can also use a cable for direct transfer (an extra-cost option because Nikon no longer includes a USB cable in the box), which may be your only option when you have the cable and a computer, but no card reader (perhaps you're using the computer of a friend or colleague, or at an Internet café).

To transfer images from the camera to a Mac or PC computer using the USB cable:

1. Turn off the camera.
2. Pry back the cover that protects the D3500's USB port, and plug the USB cable furnished with the camera into the USB port. (See Figure 2.11.)

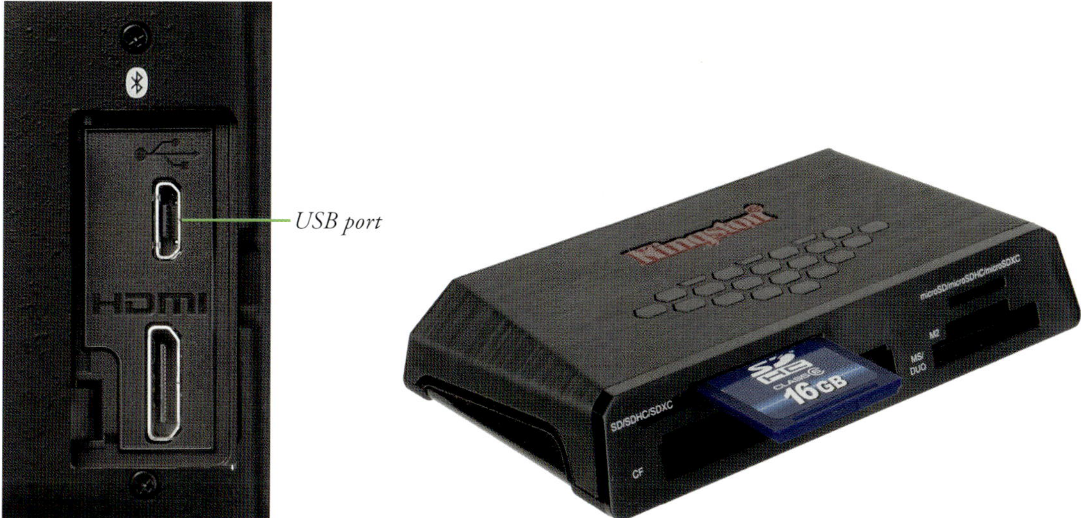

Figure 2.11 Images can be transferred to your computer using a USB cable.

Figure 2.12 A card reader is the fastest way to transfer photos.

3. Connect the other end of the USB cable to a USB port on your computer.

4. Turn on the camera. The operating system itself, or installed software such as Nikon ViewNX-i usually detects the camera and offers to copy or move the pictures. Or, the camera appears on your desktop as a mass storage device, enabling you to drag and drop the files to your computer.

To transfer images from a Secure Digital card to the computer using a card reader, as shown in Figure 2.12, do the following:

1. Turn off the camera.

2. Slide open the memory card door and remove the SD card.

3. Insert the Secure Digital card into your memory card reader. Your installed software detects the files on the card and offers to transfer them. The card can also appear as a mass storage device on your desktop, which you can open and then drag and drop the files to your computer.

Using the Guide Mode

The Nikon D3500 is one of the few Nikon digital SLRs to have a clever "mode" installed right on the mode dial in the form of the Guide mode, shown in Figure 2.13. This mode gives you fast access to some of the most-used commands, through an easy to navigate series of screens that lead you right through accessing the functions you need to shoot, view, or delete your photos, or set up the D3500 camera.

The Guide mode doesn't really need much in the way of instructions—once you rotate the mode dial to the GUIDE position you can easily figure out what you want to do by following through the menus and prompts. But that's the whole idea—the Guide mode is designed for absolute newbies to the Nikon D3500, who want to do simple tasks without the need to read even the abbreviated instructions provided in the manual. Of course, I'm going to provide instructions for using this menu anyway, because the mere thought of going out and taking pictures with nothing but training wheels for support is frightening for some who've purchased the D3500 camera as their first digital camera or digital SLR.

Rotate the mode dial to GUIDE and the LCD lights up with the screen, as shown in Figure 2.13. If it is not visible, press the MENU button located to the left of the LCD to make it appear. You can choose guides for shooting, viewing/deleting images, retouching photos, and setting up your camera. Use the left/right buttons on the multi selector pad to highlight Shoot, View/Delete, Retouch, or Set up, and then press the OK button in the center of the pad.

Shoot Options

If you choose Shoot, you'll see a simple menu like the one shown in Figure 2.14. There are only two options, Easy Operation and Advanced Operation. You can use the up/down buttons to highlight one, then press the multi selector right button to view that menu.

Easy Operation

This mode lists functions like Auto, No Flash, Distant Subjects, Close-ups, Moving Subjects, Portraits, Night Portraits, and Photograph Night Landscapes. (If you haven't jumped directly to this section from the beginning of the chapter, you might recognize that some of these options correspond to the Scene modes that are also built into the mode dial.)

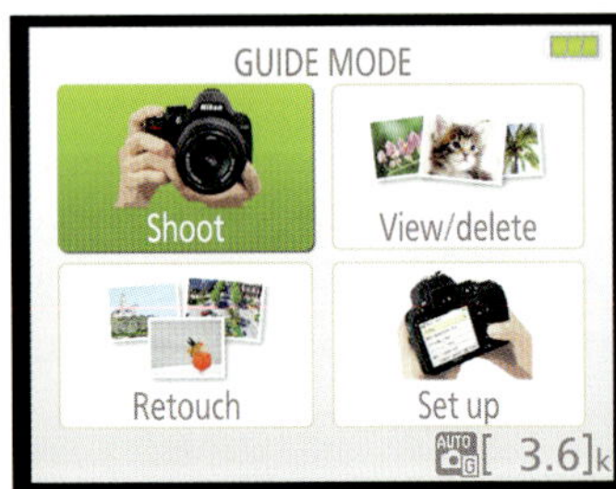

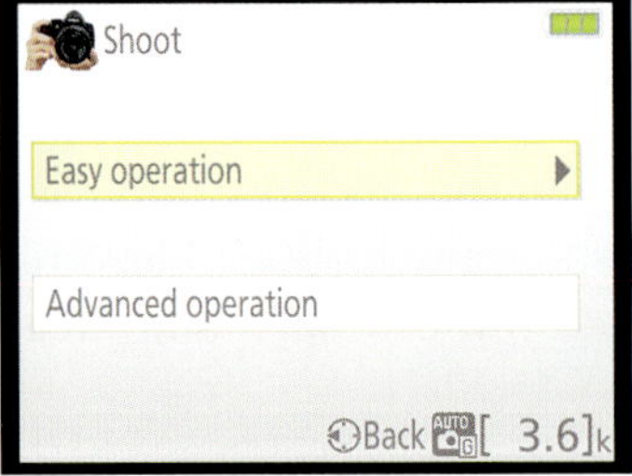

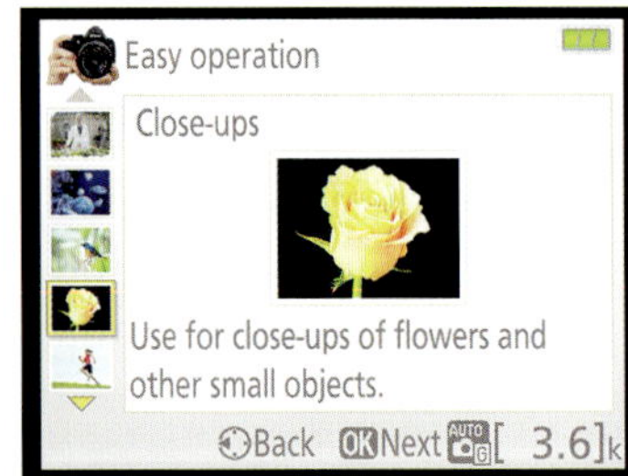

Figure 2.13 Rotate the mode dial to GUIDE to use the ultra-easy Guide mode.

Figure 2.14 Easy Operation corresponds to the Scene modes located on the mode dial.

Figure 2.15 Choose any of these available easy operations and you'll be shown a screen with instructions on how to take the picture.

Just follow these steps:

1. **Select mode.** The first page of the Easy Operation choices is shown in Figure 2.15. You can scroll with the multi selector's up/down buttons to view them all. Select one by highlighting it and pressing the right multi selector button.

2. **Instruction screen appears.** You'll be shown a screen explaining the mode you've selected and its functions. For example, if you've selected Sleeping Faces, the screen says "The camera is now in 'Portrait' mode with the release mode set to single frame." This screen usually (but not always) lingers for a few seconds to give you time to read it, then proceeds to the next step. You can jump to that step immediately by pressing the right button.

3. **Select Shooting Mode or More Settings.** The next screen, seen at left in Figure 2.16, allows you to choose whether to frame your shot using the optical viewfinder, use live view to take still photos while viewing the actual sensor image on the LCD monitor on the back of the camera, or shoot movies. You can also scroll down to More Settings to set things like Flash Mode, Release Mode, or ISO sensitivity (Figure 2.16, right). Press the right button or OK to switch to your selected shooting mode, or to use More Settings.

4. **Take Photos.** When the D3500 exits the Guides, you can shoot photos using the chosen mode until you rotate the mode dial from the Guide position to another setting or turn the camera off.

Advanced Operation

This choice is as easy to use as Easy Operation, but it may ask you to manually make some settings on the camera to get the effect you're asking for. It includes eight options: Soften Backgrounds, Bring More into Focus, Freeze Motion (People), Freeze Motion (Vehicles), Show Water Flowing, Capture Reds in Sunsets, Take Bright Photos, and Take Dark (low key) Photos. (See Figure 2.17, left.)

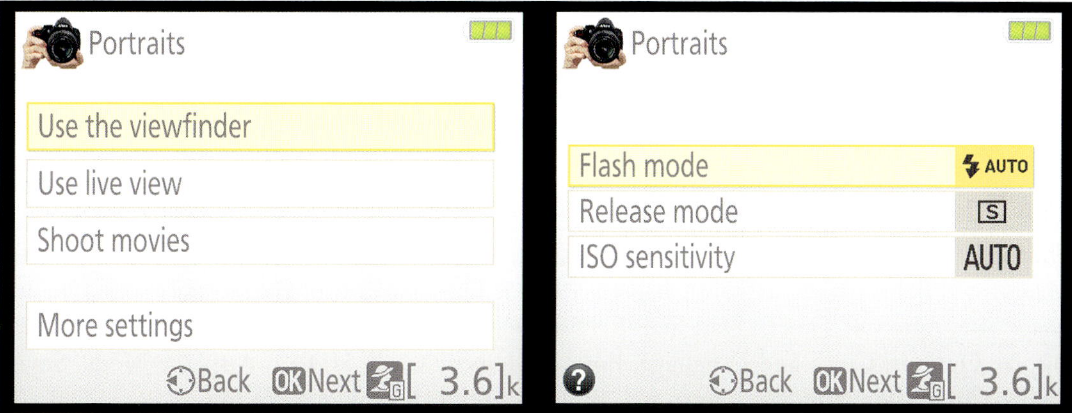

Figure 2.16 Select a shooting mode or more settings (left); additional settings are available, too (right).

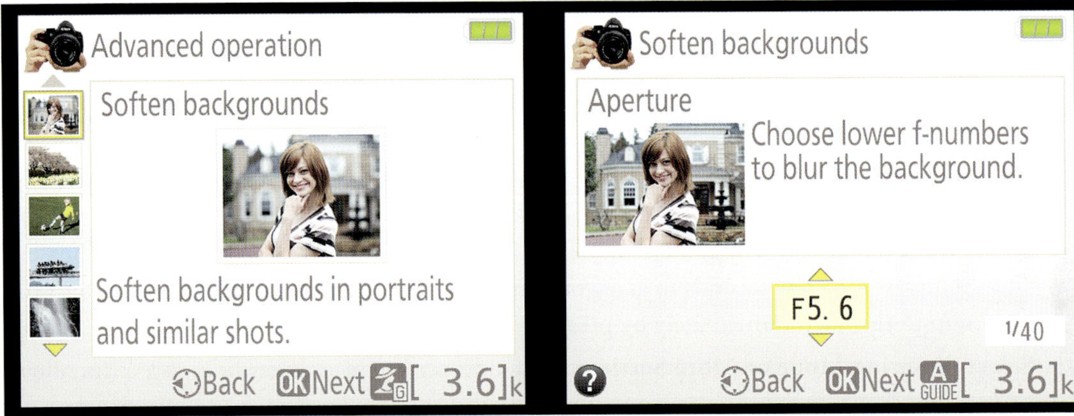

Figure 2.17 Choose an advanced option (left) and the D3500 will show you how to use it (right).

Selecting any of them sets up the camera for that type of picture and provides you with a screen of information explaining how to take the picture. For example, with Soften Backgrounds, the D3500 will ask you to choose a lower f/stop so the background will blur (Figure 2.17, right). Nikon's choice of words isn't always the best: by "lower f-number" they mean a *larger* f/stop, which happens to have a *smaller* absolute number. For example, f/6.3 is a "lower" number than f/8, which means it is a larger f/stop and provides less *depth-of-field* that results in a slightly blurrier background. Don't worry: I'll explain all about f/stops and exposure (Chapter 4) and depth-of-field (Chapter 5).

View/Delete Options

This screen has five options you can select to activate functions (when not in Guide mode). These include View Single Photos, View Multiple Photos, Choose a Date (select images to view from a calendar of dates), View a Slide Show, and Delete Photos.

Retouch Options

This screen has six options for retouching functions: Trim, Filter Effects (cross screen), Filter Effects (soft), Photo Illustration, Miniature Effect, and Selective Color.

Set Up Options

This screen has 13 options that correspond to the choices available in the Shooting and Setup menus that I'll describe in detail in Chapters 4 and 5. The choices available include Image Quality, Image Size, Auto Off Timers, Date Stamp, Display and Sound Settings, Movie Settings, Playback Display Options, Clock and Language, Format Memory Card, HDMI, Airplane Mode, Smart Device Connection, and Slot Empty Release Lock. You can explore them in Guide mode if you like, or read how and why you might want to change these options in Chapters 4 and 5.

3

Nikon D3500 Roadmap

With the D3500, Nikon has continued its emphasis on creating a super-compact, entry-level digital SLR that retains the convenience and easy access to essential controls. Most of the Nikon D3500's key functions and settings that are changed frequently can be accessed directly using either the information edit (*i*) button or the modest array of dials, buttons, and knobs that populate the camera's surface. With so many quick-access controls available, you'll find that the bulk of your shooting won't be slowed down by a visit to the vast thicket of text options called Menuland.

However, if you want to operate your D3500 efficiently, you'll need to learn the location, function, and application of all these controls. You may have seen advice from well-meaning digital SLR veterans who tell you that a guide like this one isn't necessary because, "everything is in the user's manual." Sure it is! And a Road Atlas has every town, hamlet, and metropolitan area of the whole country. But planning the best route to your destination doesn't require a suffocating amount of information: what you need is expert advice (or a GPS!).

While the *basics* on each control is in the skimpy pamphlet supplied with the camera, Nikon grudgingly supplies you with more useful information only within the virtual pages of a downloadable PDF manual, which you'll have to consult using your computer or smart device. If you check out the "Getting to Know the Camera" pages in Nikon's manual, you'll find compressed views of the front, back, top, and bottom of the D3500 within tiny black-and-white line drawings and a couple insets. There the drawings with more than four dozen callouts point to various buttons and dials crammed into the illustrations. If you can find the control you want within this cramped layout, you'll still need to flip back and forth among multiple pages (individual buttons can have several different cross-references!) to locate the information.

I originated the up-close-and-personal, full-color, street-level roadmap (rather than a satellite view) that I use in this book and my previous camera guidebooks. I provide you with an entire chapter filled with many different views, and lots of explanation accompanying each zone of the camera.

By the time you finish this chapter, you'll have a basic understanding of every control and what it does. I'm not going to delve into menu functions here—you'll find a discussion of your Setup, Shooting, and Playback menu options in Chapters 4 and 5. Everything here is devoted to the button pusher and dial twirler in you.

You'll also find this "roadmap" chapter a good guide to the rest of the book, as well. I'll try to provide as much detail here about the use of the main controls as I can, but some topics (such as autofocus and exposure) are too complex to address in depth right away. So, I'll point you to the relevant chapters that discuss things like setup options, exposure, use of electronic flash, and working with lenses with the occasional cross-reference.

I wish it were possible to explain all there is to know about every feature the first time a feature is introduced. I get emails from readers wanting to know why I didn't just explain how to use the flash when I pointed out the location of the Flash button in the roadmap chapter. However, I know you'd rather not slog through an impenetrable 200-page chapter and won't mind jumping to the menu and flash chapters for a full explanation. Compared to some other books, one or two cross-references is a small price to pay for more efficient organization. Instead, in this chapter I'm going to provide you with just enough information about each control to get you started, and go into more detail after you've had a chance to absorb the basics.

Nikon D3500: Front View

This is the side of the D3500 seen by your subjects as you snap away. For the photographer, though, the front is the surface your fingers curl around as you hold the camera, and there are really only a few buttons to press, all within easy reach of the fingers of your left and right hands. There are additional controls on the lens itself. You'll need to look at several different views to see everything.

Figure 3.1 shows the front of the camera with the lens removed, so you can take a peek at some of your D3500's innards. The most important components you can see from this angle include:

- **AF-assist illuminator/Self-timer lamp/Red-eye reduction lamp.** This LED provides a blip of light shortly before a flash exposure to cause the subjects' pupils to close down, reducing the effect of red-eye reflections off their retinas. When using the self-timer, this lamp also flashes to mark the countdown until the photo is taken and serves to provide some extra illumination in dark environments to assist the autofocus system.

- **Aperture lever.** This lever pivots to physically move the diaphragm inside the lens to the f/stop that will be used to take the picture. The actual size of the aperture is determined by the setting calculated by the D3500's exposure system, or specified by you in manual exposure mode, and conveyed to the camera through the electrical contacts located at the top edge of the lens mount.

Figure 3.1

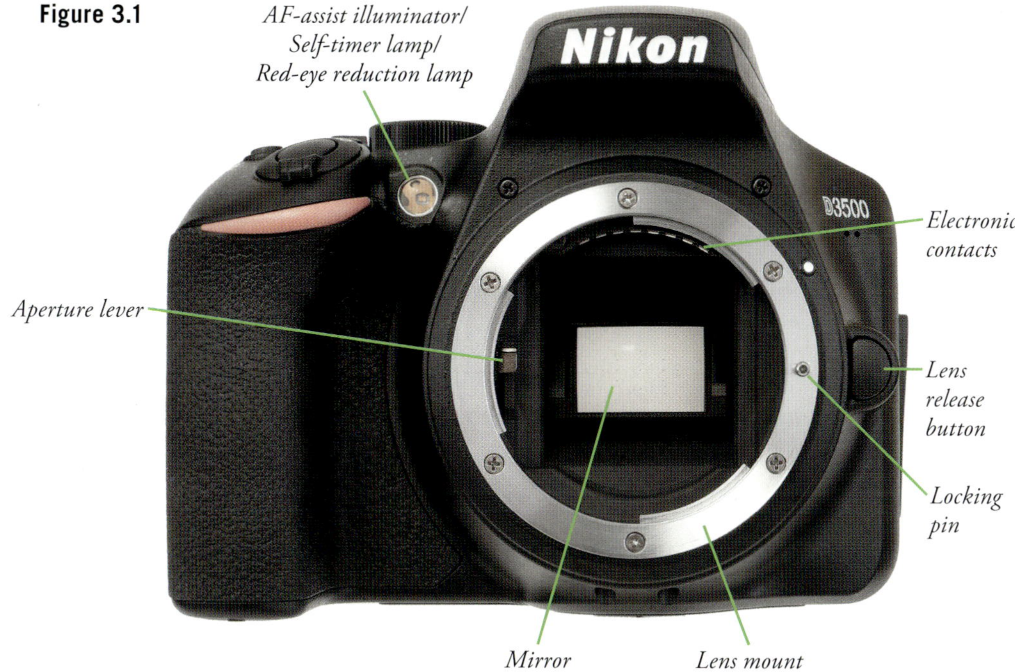

- **Electronic contacts.** These eight contact points mate with matching points on the bayonet mount of the lens itself, and allow two-way communication between the camera and lens for functions like aperture size and autofocus information.

- **Mirror.** This flip-up mirror directs the image seen by the lens upward to the viewing screen and exposure metering system, and thence onward to the eyepiece of the optical viewfinder. Eleven semi-silvered locations on the mirror allow some illumination to be directed downward to the autofocus mechanism located on the floor of the compartment.

- **Lens mount.** This precision bayonet mount mates with the matching mount on the back of each compatible lens. The mount configuration is basically unchanged since the original Nikon F was introduced in 1959, with only a few changes. The D3500 version, for example, lacks something called a *lens indexing ring* that communicates the maximum aperture of older lenses (non-autofocus) to the camera, as well as an *autofocus motor/pin* that controls the focus of lenses with the AF (not AF-S or AF-P) designation. As a result of these changes, the D3500 provides full functionality only with lenses marked AF-S/AF-P (or the equivalent with non-Nikkor optics). You'll find more information about lens compatibility in Chapter 10.

- **Lens release button.** Press this button to retract the locking pin on the lens mount so a lens can be rotated to remove it from the camera.

- **Locking pin.** This pin slides inside a matching hole in the lens to keep it from rotating until the lens release button is pressed.

Figure 3.2 shows a front view of the Nikon D3500 from a 45-degree angle. The main components you need to know about are as follows:

- **Shutter release button.** Angled on top of the hand grip is the shutter release button, which has multiple functions. Press this button down halfway to lock exposure and focus. Press it down all the way to actually take a photo or sequence of photos if you're using the Continuous shooting mode. Tapping the shutter button when the D3500's exposure meters have turned themselves off reactivates them, and a tap can be used to remove the display of a menu or image from the rear color monitor.

- **On/Off switch.** Turns the D3500 on or off.

- **Hand grip.** This provides a comfortable hand-hold, and also contains the D3500's battery.

- **Memory card door.** Slide this door toward the back of the camera to provide access to the SD memory card slot.

- **DC power port.** Connect the optional EP-5a power cable from the EH-5b AC adapter through this port.

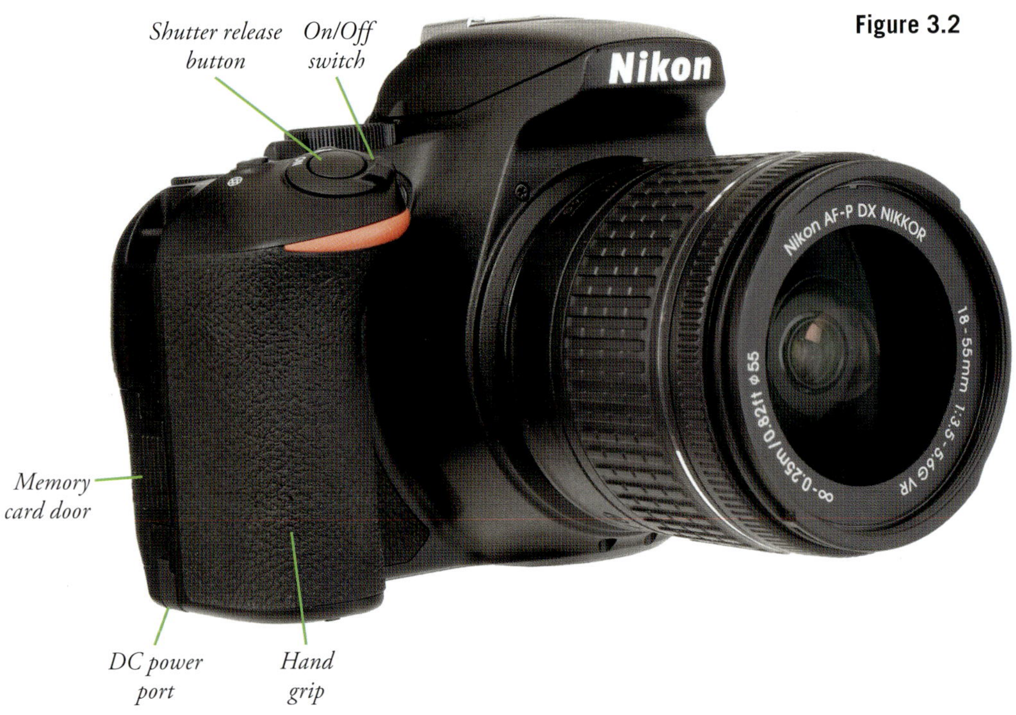

Figure 3.2

You'll find more controls on the other side of the D3500, shown in Figure 3.3. The main points of interest shown include:

- **Pop-up flash.** The flash elevates from the top of the camera, theoretically reducing the chances of red-eye reflections, because the higher light source is less likely to reflect back from your subjects' eyes into the camera lens. In practice, the red-eye effect is still possible (and likely) and can be further minimized with the D3500's red-eye reduction lamp (which flashes before the exposure, causing the subjects' pupils to contract), and the after-shot red-eye elimination offered in the Retouch menu. (Your image editor may also have anti-red-eye tools.) Of course, the best strategy is to use an external Speedlight that mounts on the accessory shoe on top of the camera (and thus is even higher) or a flash that is off-camera entirely.
- **Microphone.** This monaural microphone records sound when shooting movies.
- **Lens mount index mark.** Align the dot on the base of the lens with this index to mount the lens, then rotate toward the shutter release.
- **Lens autofocus/manual switch (not shown).** Found on many lenses, this switch can be used to change from manual (M) to autofocus (A or A/M—the latter designation meaning that the lens can be manually adjusted even when using autofocus mode). Most lenses have this switch, but not all do.
- **Port cover.** This panel protects the D3500's input/output connectors.
- **Camera strap eyelet.** Attach a camera strap here.

Figure 3.3

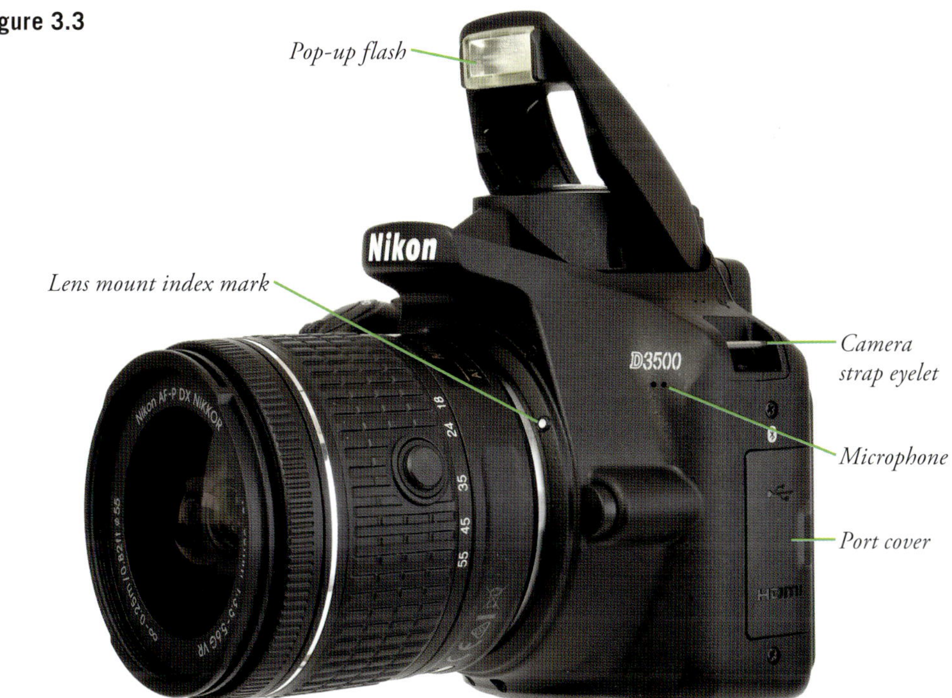

The main features on the side of the Nikon D3500 (under the cover that protects the connectors from dust and moisture) are the ports themselves. In Figure 3.4 you can see:

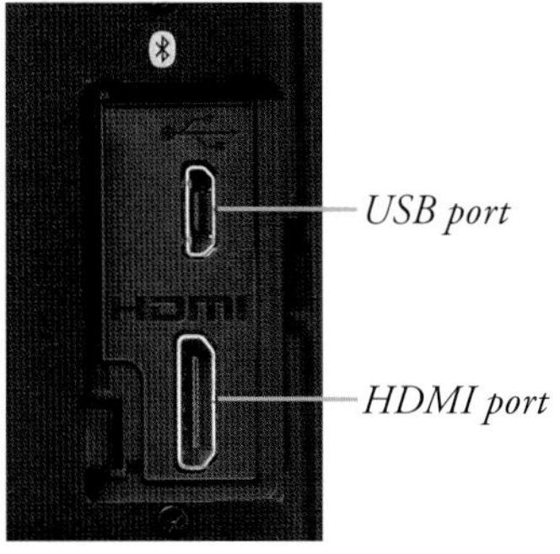

Figure 3.4

- **USB port.** The optional USB cable UC-E6 (or a generic USB 2.0 Micro-B cable) can be connected to a USB port in your computer to transfer photos.

- **HDMI port.** Connect your camera to an HDTV television or monitor using this port. You'll have to buy a mini-C HDMI cable for this option, as one is not furnished with the camera.

The Nikon D3500's Business End

The back panel of the Nikon D3500 bristles with almost a dozen different controls, buttons, and knobs. That might seem like a lot of controls to learn, but you'll find that it's a lot easier to press a dedicated button and spin a dial than to jump to a menu every time you want to access one of these features.

The key buttons and components shown in Figure 3.5 and their functions are as follows:

- **Flash button.** (Flash pop-up/Flash mode button.) This button releases the built-in flash so it can flip up and start the charging process. If you decide you do not want to use the flash, you can turn it off by pressing the flash head back down. Hold down this button while spinning the command dial to choose a flash mode. Hold down this button while also pressing the exposure compensation button on the top panel of the D3500 to add/subtract flash exposure compensation. I'll explain how to use the various flash modes (red-eye reduction, front/rear curtain sync, and slow sync) in Chapter 11, along with some tips for adjusting flash exposure.

- **Viewfinder window/eyecup.** You can frame your composition by peering into the viewfinder. It's surrounded by a soft rubber eyecup that seals out extraneous light when pressing your eye tightly up to the viewfinder, and it also protects your eyeglass lenses (if worn) from scratching. It can be removed and replaced by the DK-5 eyepiece cap when you use the camera on a tripod, to ensure that light coming from the back of the camera doesn't venture inside and possibly affect the exposure reading. Shielding the viewfinder with your hand may be more convenient (unless you're using the self-timer to get in the photo yourself).

- **Diopter wheel.** Rotate to adjust the viewfinder for your eyesight.

- **AE-L/AF-L/Protect button.** This triple-duty button can be used to protect an image from accidental erasure. When reviewing a picture on the LCD, press once to protect the image, a second time to unprotect it. A key symbol appears when the image is displayed to show that it is protected. (This feature safeguards an image from erasure when deleting or transferring pictures only; when you format a card, protected images are removed along with all the others.) When shooting pictures, the button locks the exposure or focus that the camera sets when you

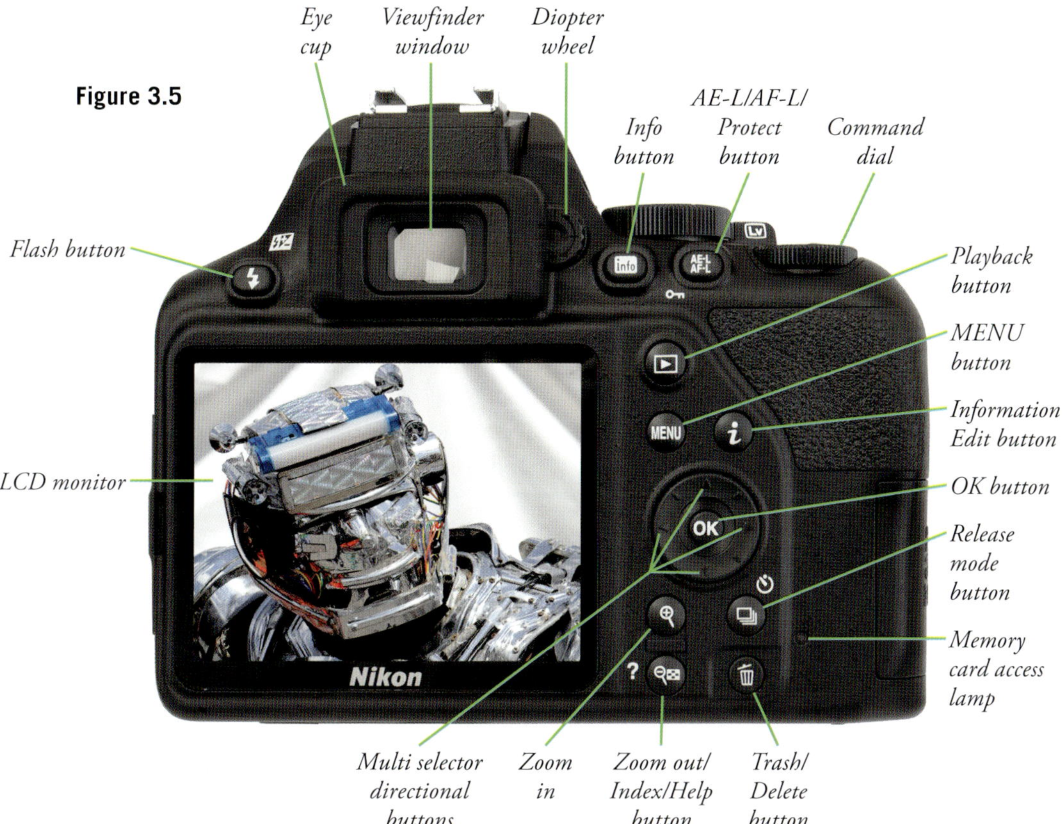

Figure 3.5

partially depress the shutter button. The exposure lock indication (AE-L icon) appears in the viewfinder. If you want to recalculate exposure or autofocus with the shutter button still partially depressed, press the button again. The exposure/autofocus will be unlocked when you release the shutter button or take the picture. To retain the exposure/autofocus lock for subsequent photos even if you move the camera, keep the button pressed while shooting.

■ **Command dial.** The command dial is used to set or adjust many functions, such as shutter speed, either alone or when another button is depressed simultaneously.

■ **LCD monitor.** This 3-inch display shows live view previews, images, and thumbnails for review, menus, and informational screens.

■ **Playback button.** Press this button to review images you've taken, using the controls and options I'll explain in the next section. To remove the displayed image from view, press the Playback button again, or simply tap the shutter release button.

■ **MENU button.** Summons/exits the menu displayed on the rear LCD monitor of the D3500. When you're working with submenus, this button also serves to exit a submenu and return to the main menu.

■ **Zoom In.** In Playback mode, press to zoom in on an image.

- **Zoom Out/Index/Help button.** In Playback mode, use this button to change from full-screen view to 4, 9, or 72 thumbnails or calendar view, and to zoom out from a magnified image. I'll explain zooming and other playback options in the next section. When viewing most menu items on the LCD monitor, pressing this button produces a concise Help screen with tips on how to make the relevant setting.

- **Info button.** Turns the LCD monitor display on or off.

- **Information Edit button.** When shooting pictures, press this button to restore the shooting information display; press a second time to produce the information edit screen used to make many camera settings, such as metering mode, white balance, or ISO. Press this button to activate the shooting information display. Press again to remove the information display (or simply tap the shutter release button). The display will also clear after the period you've set for LCD monitor display (the default value is 20 seconds). The information display can be set to alternate between modes that are best viewed under bright daylight, as well as in dimmer illumination.

- **Multi selector directional buttons.** This joypad-like button can be shifted up/down and side to side to provide several functions, including AF point selection, scrolling around a magnified image, or trimming a photo. Within menus, pressing the up/down buttons moves the on-screen cursor up or down; pressing toward the right selects the highlighted item and displays its options; pressing left cancels and returns to the previous menu.

- **OK button.** Use this button to confirm a selection. When working with menus, press the MENU button instead to back out without making a selection.

- **Memory card access lamp.** When lit or blinking, this lamp indicates that the memory card is being accessed.

- **Trash/Delete button.** Press to erase the image shown on the LCD monitor. A display will pop up on the screen asking you to select Yes to delete the photo or press the Playback button to cancel.

- **Release mode button.** Press to pop up the Release mode setting screen.

Playing Back Images

Reviewing images is a joy on the Nikon D3500's big 3-inch LCD. Here are the basics involved in reviewing images on the LCD monitor screen (or on a television screen you have connected with a cable). You'll find more details about some of these functions later in this chapter, or, for more complex capabilities, in the chapters that I point you to. This section just lists the must-know information.

- **Start review.** To begin review, press the Playback button at the upper-left corner of the back of the D3500. The most-recently viewed image or movie will appear on the LCD monitor. (Movies are marked with an icon that has film sprocket holes in thumbnail mode, or a movie camera symbol in other review modes.)

- **Playback folder.** Image review generally shows you the images in the currently selected folder on your memory card. A given card can contain several folders (a new one is created anytime you exceed 9999 images in the current folder). You can use the Playback folder menu option in the Playback menu (as I'll explain in Chapter 4) to select a specific folder or direct the D3500 to display images from all the folders on the memory card.

- **View thumbnail images.** To change the view from a single image to four, nine, or 72 thumbnails, or calendar view, follow the instructions in the "Viewing Thumbnails" section that follows.

- **Zoom in and out.** To zoom in or out, press the Zoom In and Zoom Out buttons, following the instructions in the "Zooming the Nikon D3500 Playback Display" in the next section. (It also shows you how to move the zoomed area around using the multi selector pad.)

- **Move back and forth.** To advance to the next image, rotate the command dial to the right or press the right edge of the multi selector pad; to go back to a previous shot, rotate the command dial to the left or press the left edge of the multi selector. When you reach the beginning/end of the photos in your folder, the display "wraps around" to the end/beginning of the available shots.

- **See different types of data.** To change the type of information about the displayed image that is shown, press the up and down portions of the multi selector pad. To learn what data is available, read the "Working with Photo Information" section later in this chapter.

- **Retouch image.** Press the *i* button while a single image is displayed on the screen to jump to a screen that allows you to select whether to apply a rating, retouch an image, or send the photo to your smart device. (I'll explain ratings in Chapter 4, and the workings of the Retouch and SnapBridge in Chapter 5.)

- **Remove images.** To delete an image that's currently on the screen, press the Trash/Delete button once, and then select Yes to confirm the deletion. To select and delete a group of images, use the Delete option in the Playback menu to specify particular photos to remove, as described in more detail in Chapter 4.

- **Cancel playback.** To cancel image review, press the Playback button again, or simply tap the shutter release button.

Zooming the Nikon D3500 Playback Display

Here's how to zoom in and out on your images during picture review:

1. **Zoom in.** When an image is displayed (use the Playback button to start), press the Zoom In button to fill the screen with a slightly magnified version of the image. You can keep pressing the Zoom In button to magnify a portion of the image up to 38X if you used the Large resolution setting when shooting the photo. An image at Medium resolution can be magnified up to 28X, while Small images can be zoomed in up to 19X. (See Figure 3.6.)

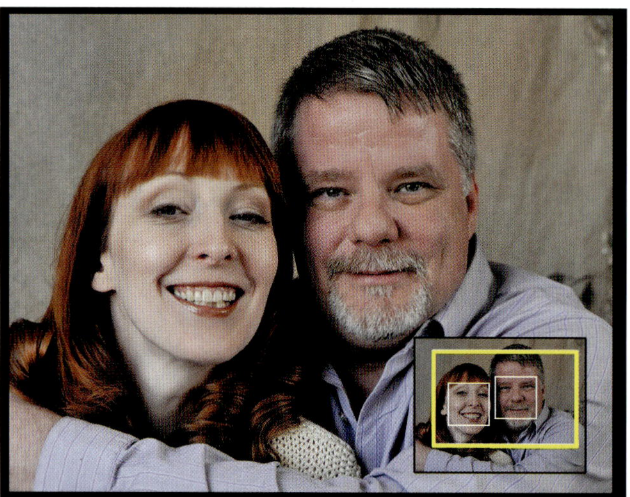

Figure 3.6
The D3500 incorporates a small thumbnail image with a yellow box showing the current zoom area, and one or more white boxes to mark any faces detected in the scene.

2. **Inset shows zoomed area highlighted in yellow.** A navigation window appears in the lower-right corner of the LCD monitor showing the entire image. Keep pressing to continue zooming in. The yellow box in the navigation window shows the zoomed area within the full image. The entire navigation window vanishes from the screen after a few seconds, leaving you with a full-screen view of the zoomed portion of the image.

3. **Faces marked in navigation window.** If a face is detected in the scene, a white box appears around it within the navigation box (as seen in Figure 3.6). If multiple faces are found (up to 35 different faces may be detected) use the multi selector directional buttons to move to a different face. You can press the *i* button, highlight Face Zoom in the box that pops up, and press OK to zoom in on the selected face.

4. **Move zoomed view around within full image.** Use the multi selector buttons to move the zoomed area around within the image. The navigation window will reappear for reference when zooming or scrolling around within the display. Use the command dial to move to the same zoomed area of the next/previous image.

5. **Zoom Out.** Use the Zoom Out/Thumbnail button to zoom back out of the image. If you continue pressing the Zoom Out button from the full-screen view, you'll be shown four, nine, and 72 thumbnails, plus a calendar view. These are all described in the next section.

6. **Exit Zoom.** To exit Zoom In/Zoom Out display, keep pressing the Zoom Out button until the full-screen/full-image/information display appears again.

Viewing Thumbnails

The Nikon D3500 provides other options for reviewing images in addition to zooming in and out. You can switch between single image view and four, nine, or 72 reduced-size thumbnail images on a single LCD monitor screen.

Pages of thumbnail images offer a quick way to scroll through a large number of pictures quickly to find the one you want to examine in more detail. The D3500 lets you switch quickly from single- to four- to nine- to 72-image views, with a scroll bar displayed at the right side of the screen to show you the relative position of the displayed thumbnails within the full collection of images in the active folder on your memory card. Figure 3.7 offers a comparison between three levels of thumbnail views. The Zoom In and Zoom Out/Thumbnail buttons are used.

- **Add thumbnails.** To increase the number of thumbnails on the screen, press the Zoom Out button. The D3500 will switch from single image to four thumbnails to nine thumbnails to 72 thumbnails, and then to calendar view (discussed next). Additional presses in calendar view toggle back and forth between highlighting calendar dates, or showing pictures taken on that date (see "Working with Calendar View," next). (The display doesn't cycle back to single image again.)

- **Reduce number of thumbnails.** To decrease the number of thumbnails on the screen, press the Zoom In button to change from calendar view to 72 to nine thumbnails to four thumbnails, or from four to single-image display. Continuing to press the Zoom In button once you've returned to single-image display starts the zoom process described in the previous section.

- **Change highlighted thumbnail area.** Use the multi selector to move the yellow highlight box around among the thumbnails.

- **Protect and delete images.** When viewing thumbnails or a single-page image, press the Protect button (on the upper right of the back of the D3500, marked with a key icon and AE-L/AF-L label) to preserve the image against accidental deletion (a key icon is overlaid over the full-page or thumbnail image) or the Protect button again to remove the key icon.

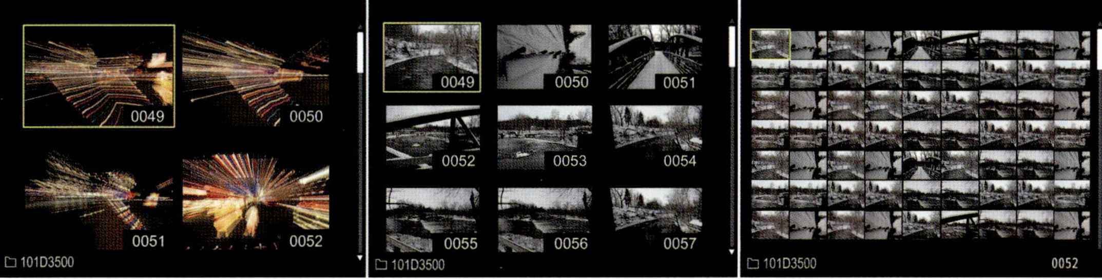

Figure 3.7 Switch between four thumbnails (left), nine thumbnails (center), or 72 thumbnails (right), by pressing the Zoom Out and Zoom In buttons.

- **Exit image review.** Tap the shutter release button or press the Playback button to exit image review. You don't have to worry about missing a shot because you were reviewing images; a half-press of the shutter release automatically brings back the D3500's exposure meters, the autofocus system, and cancels image review.

Working with Calendar View

Once in calendar view, you can sort through images arranged by the date they were taken. This feature is especially useful when you're traveling and want to see only the pictures you took in, say, a particular city on a certain day.

- **Change dates.** Use the multi selector or main dial to move through the date list. If your memory card has pictures taken on a highlighted date, they will be arrayed in a scrolling list at the right side of the screen (see Figure 3.8).

- **View a date's images.** Press the Zoom Out button to toggle between the date list to the scrolling thumbnail list of images taken on that date. When viewing the thumbnail list, you can use the multi selector up/down keys to scroll through the available images.

- **Preview an image.** In the thumbnail list, when you've highlighted an image you want to look at, press the Zoom In button to see an enlarged view of that image without leaving the calendar view mode. The zoomed image replaces the date list.

- **Delete images.** Press the Trash button and select Yes to delete a highlighted image in the thumbnail list. In the date list view, pressing the Trash button and selecting Yes removes all the images taken on that date (use with caution!). In either case, you can press the Playback button when the confirmation screen appears to cancel the deletion process.

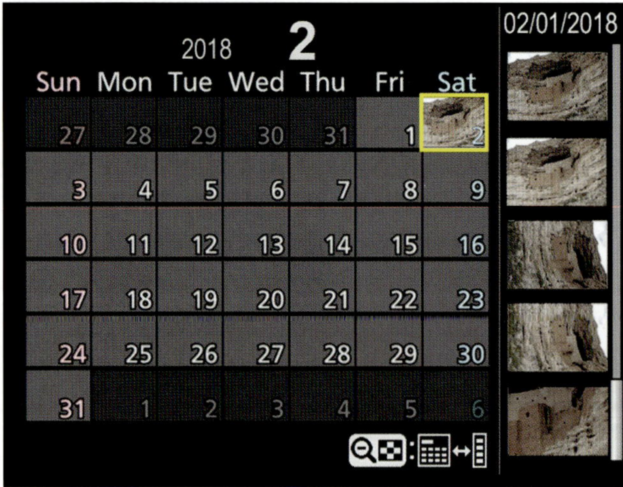

Figure 3.8
Calendar view allows you to browse through all images on your memory card taken on a certain date.

■ **Exit calendar view.** In thumbnail view, if you highlight an image and press the OK button, you'll exit calendar view and the highlighted image will be shown on the LCD monitor in the display mode you've chosen. (See "Working with Photo Information" to learn about the various display modes.) In date list view, pressing the Zoom In button exits calendar view and returns to 72 thumbnails view. You can also exit calendar view by tapping the shutter release (to turn off the LCD to ready the camera for shooting) or by pressing the MENU button.

Working with Photo Information

When reviewing an image on the screen, your D3500 can supplement the image itself with a variety of shooting data, ranging from basic information presented at the bottom of the LCD monitor display, to optional text overlays that detail virtually every shooting option you've selected. (You must first activate any or all of the optional displays. I'll provide step-by-step instructions on how to activate them in Chapter 4.) This section will show you the type of information available after each has been enabled. Most of the data is self-explanatory, so the labels in the accompanying figures should tell you most of what you need to know. To change to any of these views while an image is on the screen in playback mode, press the multi selector up/down buttons.

■ **File information screen.** The basic full-image review display is officially called the file information screen and looks like Figure 3.9.

■ **No information.** This screen displays your image only, with no data shown.

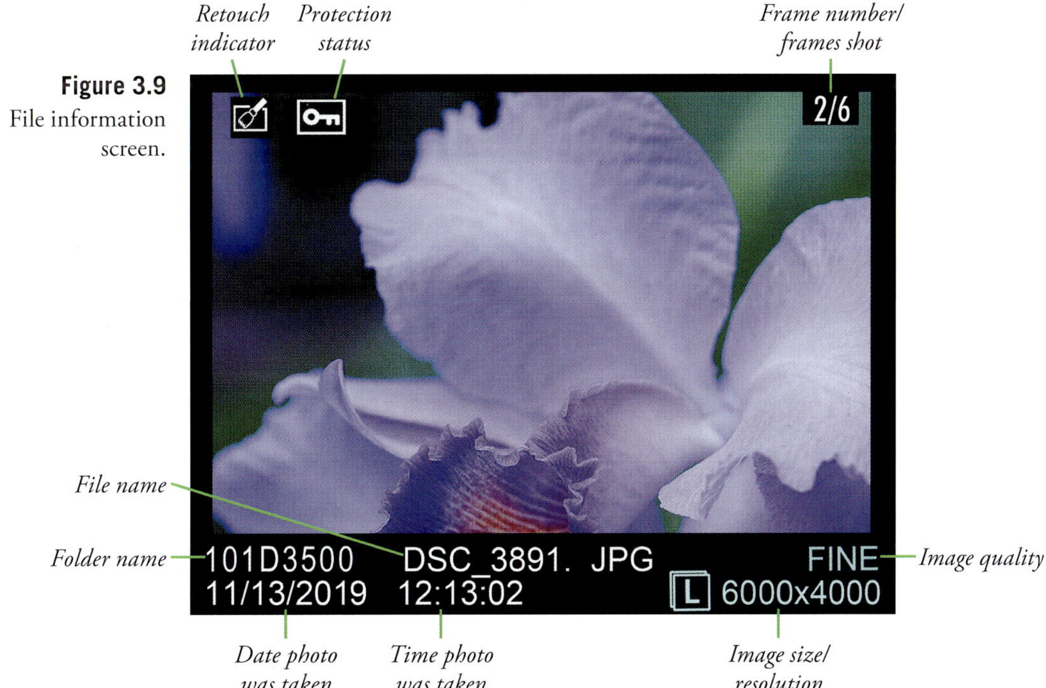

Figure 3.9 File information screen.

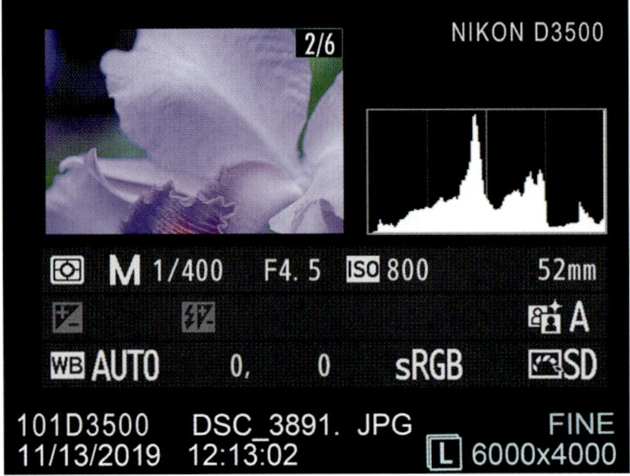

Figure 3.10 Overview data.

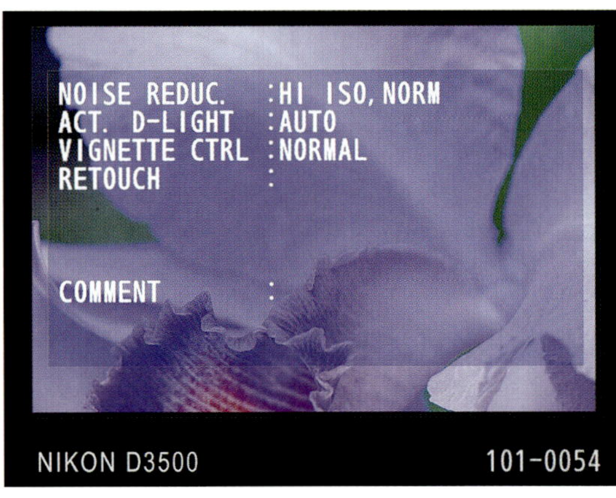

Figure 3.11 Shooting Data screen 1.

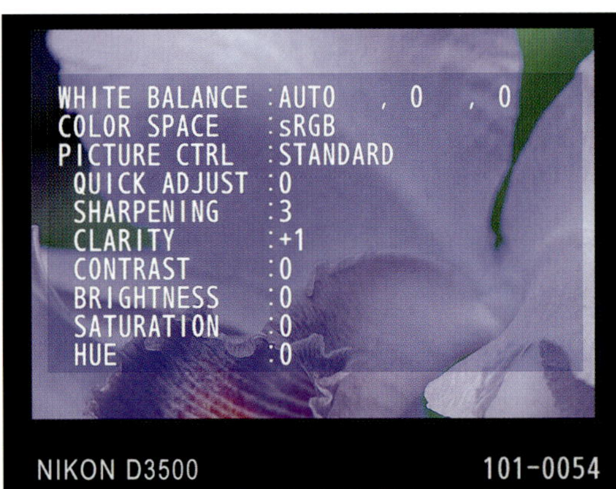

Figure 3.12 Shooting Data screen 2.

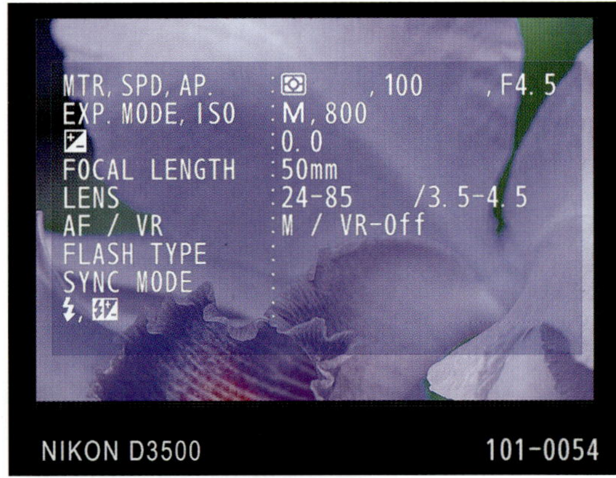

Figure 3.13 Shooting Data screen 3.

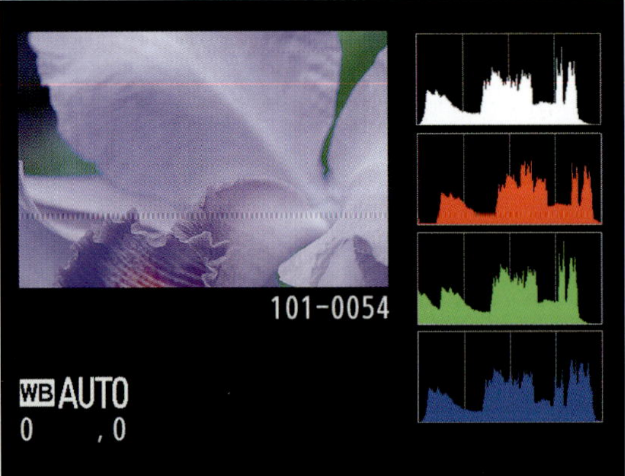

Figure 3.14 RGB histogram.

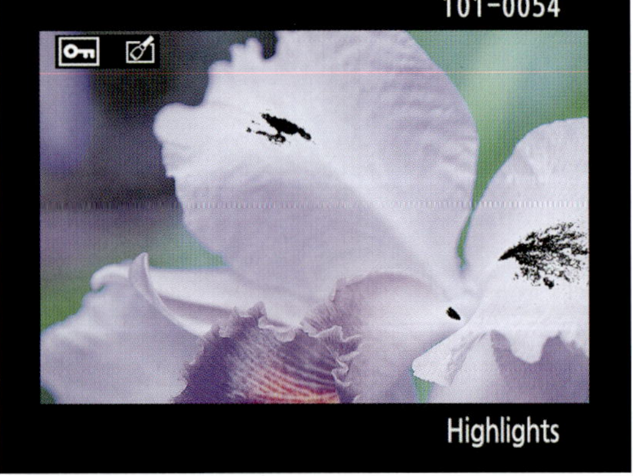

Figure 3.15 Highlights display.

- **Overview data.** This screen adds more data, including metering mode, shutter speed, f/stop, and ISO setting, and looks like Figure 3.10

- **Shooting Data 1.** This screen shows noise reduction information, Active D-Lighting, retouching effects that have been applied, and your user comments, as shown in Figure 3.11.

- **Shooting Data 2.** This screen shows white balance data and adjustments, sharpness and saturation settings, and other parameters (see Figure 3.12).

- **Shooting Data 3.** This screen tells you everything else you might want to know about a picture you've taken, including metering mode, exposure mode, exposure compensation, lens information, and all the details of any built-in or external dedicated flash units you might have used. See Figure 3.13.

- **RGB histogram.** This shows the image accompanied by a brightness histogram, as well as red, green, and blue histograms, which you can see in Figure 3.14. The histogram is a kind of chart that represents an image's exposure, and how the darkest areas, brightest areas, and middle tones have been captured. Histograms are easy to work with, and I'll show you how in Chapter 6.

- **Highlights.** When the Highlights display is active (see Figure 3.15), any overexposed areas will be indicated by a flashing black border. As I am unable to make the printed page flash, you'll have to check out this effect for yourself.

Shooting Information Display/Information Edit Screen

As first described in Chapter 2, the back-panel color LCD monitor can be used to provide a wealth of information (the shooting information display) and access to a number of settings (the information edit screen). The information edit screen can help you avoid some trips to Menuland, by making some basic adjustments available using the color LCD's speedy settings view.

To activate/deactivate the shooting information display, press the Info button on top of the camera. When the screen is visible, you'll see settings like those shown in Figure 3.16. Two versions are available: the "Classic" version, which has a clean, text-based format, and the "Graphic" version, which includes a smattering of graphics—particularly in Scene modes, when a representation of the mode dial appears briefly as you change modes. (See Figure 3.17.) Use Info Display from the Setup menu to specify which of these two versions to use. You can choose the display type for Auto/Scene modes and advanced P, S, A, and M modes separately, while choosing a blue, black, or orange color scheme. Light-on-dark is usually easier to read in dim lighting conditions, while the reverse scheme is better under bright lighting.

When the shooting information display is shown, press the *i* button to activate the information edit menu. Use the multi selector left/right buttons to highlight one of the adjustments, then press the OK button to produce a screen of options for that setting.

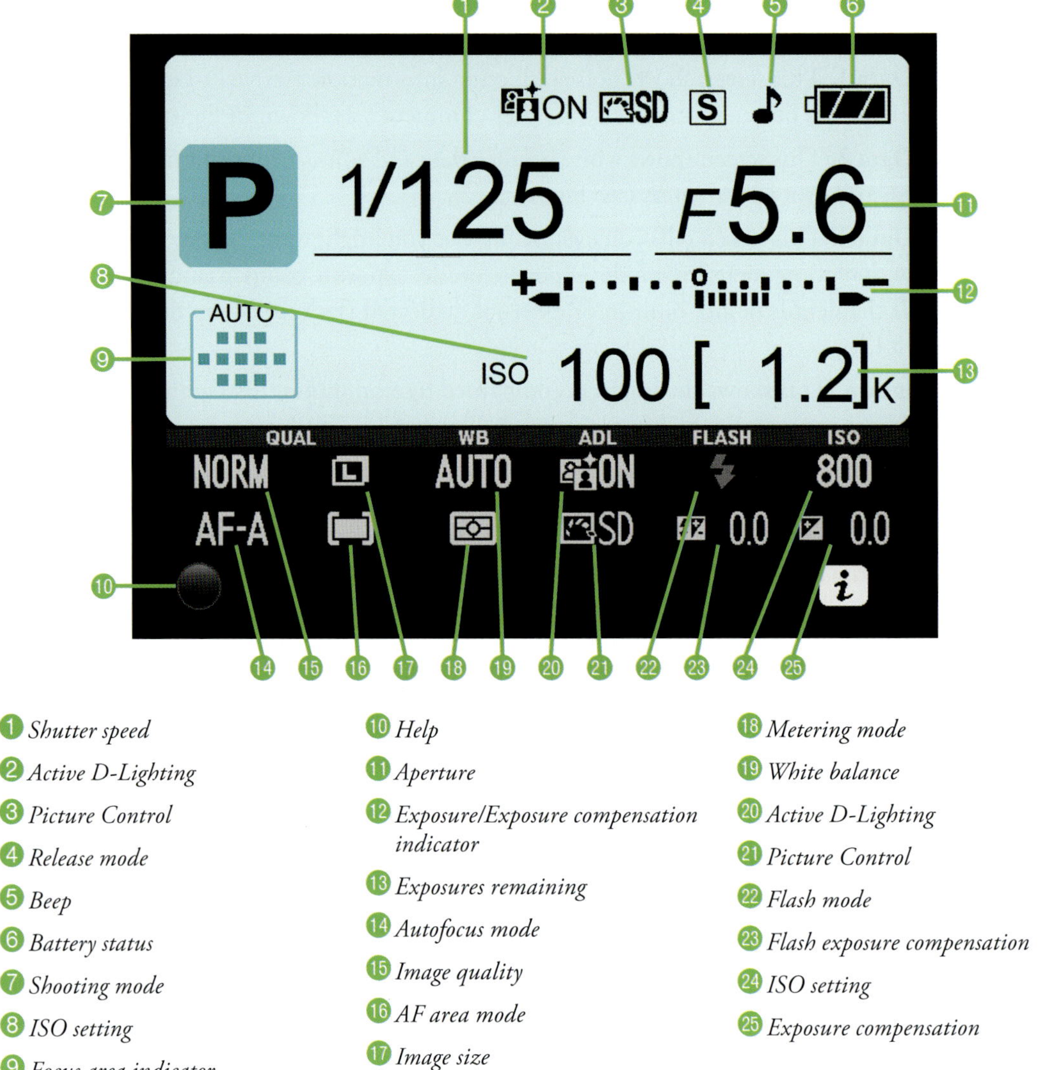

1 *Shutter speed*

2 *Active D-Lighting*

3 *Picture Control*

4 *Release mode*

5 *Beep*

6 *Battery status*

7 *Shooting mode*

8 *ISO setting*

9 *Focus area indicator*

10 *Help*

11 *Aperture*

12 *Exposure/Exposure compensation indicator*

13 *Exposures remaining*

14 *Autofocus mode*

15 *Image quality*

16 *AF area mode*

17 *Image size*

18 *Metering mode*

19 *White balance*

20 *Active D-Lighting*

21 *Picture Control*

22 *Flash mode*

23 *Flash exposure compensation*

24 *ISO setting*

25 *Exposure compensation*

Figure 3.16 The shooting information display shows basic information on the color LCD monitor. Information edit can be accessed pressing the information edit (i) button.

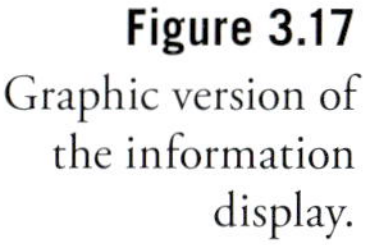

Figure 3.17
Graphic version of the information display.

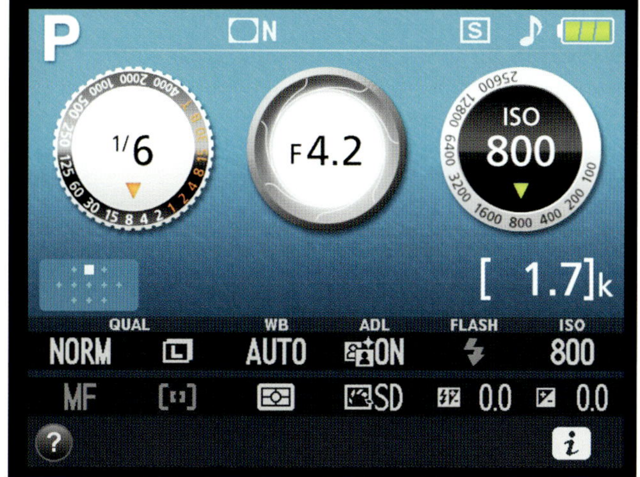

The shooting information displayed on the LCD monitor displays status information about most of the shooting settings. Some of the items also appear in the viewfinder, such as the shutter speed and aperture and the exposure level. This display remains active for about eight seconds, then shuts off if no operations are performed with the camera. The display also turns off when you press the shutter release halfway. You can re-activate the display by pressing the Zoom In, Info, Zoom Out, or Fn buttons (except when the behavior of the latter button has been set to white balance compensation). The display also appears when the exposure compensation/aperture button is pressed in P, S, or A exposure modes, or when the Flash button is pressed in any exposure mode other than Auto (Flash Off). In other words, the shooting information display appears whenever you're likely to need it and can be summoned at other times by pressing the Info button on the back of the camera next to the viewfinder. Many of the settings shown in Figure 3.16 are described below.

- **Exposure mode.** This indicator tells you whether the D3500 is set for one of the Scene modes, or for Program, Aperture-priority, Shutter-priority, or Manual exposure modes. An asterisk appears next to the P when you have used Flexible Program mode, which allows you to depart from the camera's programmed exposure setting to set a different combination of shutter speed/aperture that produces the same exposure. You'll find more about this feature in Chapter 4.

- **Image size.** Shows whether the D3500 is shooting Large, Medium, or Small sizes.

- **Image quality.** Shows current image quality, including JPEG, RAW, and RAW+JPEG Fine.

- **White balance.** One of the white balance settings will appear here, depending on the selection you've made.

- **Release mode.** Indicates whether the D3500 is set for Single frame, Continuous, or one of the Self-timer/Remote modes.

- **Focus mode.** Shows AF-C, AF-S, AF-A, and manual focus modes.

- **Autofocus-area indicator.** Displays the autofocus area status, from among Single-point, Dynamic-area, Auto-area, and 3D-tracking (11 points), all discussed earlier.

- **Metering mode.** Indicates whether Matrix, Center-weighted, or Spot metering has been selected.

- **ISO/ISOAuto indicators.** Displayed to show the currently set ISO value or that the D3500 is set to adjust ISO for you automatically.

- **Electronic analog display.** This is a continuous scale that shows that correct exposure is achieved when the indicator is in the center, and how many stops off exposure is when the indicator veers to the right (underexposure) or left (overexposure). This scale is also used to display other information, such as exposure compensation.

- **Exposure compensation.** Appears when you've dialed in exposure compensation. Monitor this indicator, as it's easy to forget that you've told the Nikon D3500 to use more or less exposure than what its (reasonably intelligent) metering system would otherwise select.

- **Flash compensation.** Reminds you that you've tweaked the D3500's electronic flash exposure system with more or less exposure.

- **Number of exposures/additional functions.** This indicator shows the number of exposures remaining on your memory card, as well as other functions, such as the number of shots remaining until your memory buffer fills.

- **Battery status.** Three segments show the approximate battery power remaining.

- **Flash mode.** The current mode for the D3500's built-in electronic flash unit is shown here.

- **Active D-Lighting status.** Shows whether this feature is active or turned off.

- **Beep indicator.** Indicates that a helpful beep will sound during the countdown in Self-timer mode. The beep also chirps when the D3500 successfully focuses when using Sports scene mode, as well as in AF-S or AF-A Autofocus modes. No beep sounds in AF-C mode, or when the subject is moving while in AF-A mode (because the D3500 effectively switches to AF-C mode at that point).

- **Aperture/additional functions.** The selected f/stop appears here.

- **Shutter speed/additional functions.** Here you'll find the shutter speed, ISO setting, color temperature, and other useful data.

- **Help indicator.** Press the Help/Zoom Out button to receive more information about a setting.

- **Eye-Fi Status (not shown).** Appears when you have an Eye-Fi card installed in the D3500.

Going Topside

The top surface of the Nikon D3500 (see Figure 3.18) has its own set of frequently accessed controls.

- **Accessory shoe.** Slide an electronic flash into this mount when you need a more powerful Speedlight. A dedicated flash unit, like the Nikon SB-400, SB-600, SB-700, or SB-900/910, can use the multiple contact points shown to communicate exposure, zoom setting, white balance information, and other data between the flash and the camera. There's more on using electronic flash in Chapter 11.

- **Power switch.** Rotate this switch clockwise to turn on the Nikon D3500 (and virtually all other Nikon dSLRs).

- **Shutter release button.** Partially depress this button to lock in exposure and focus. Press all the way to take the picture. Tapping the shutter release when the camera has turned off the autoexposure and autofocus mechanisms reactivates both. When a review image is displayed on the back-panel color LCD monitor, tapping this button removes the image from the display and reactivates the autoexposure and autofocus mechanisms.

Figure 3.18

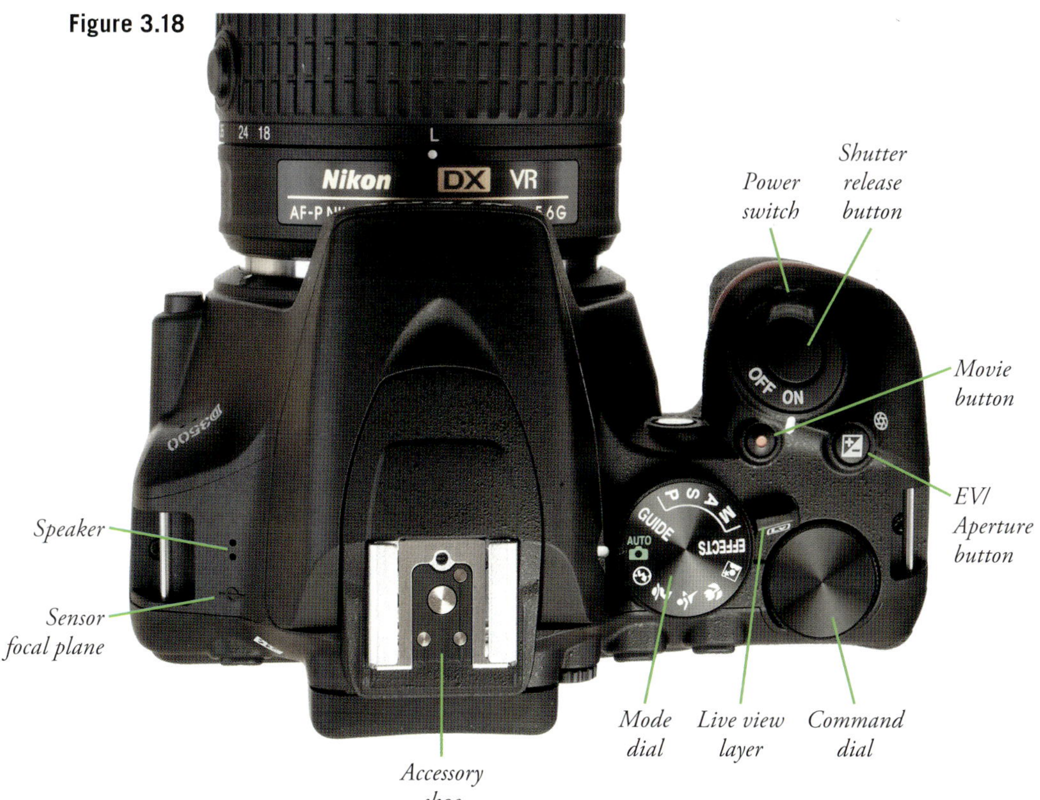

- **EV/Aperture button.** Press this button while spinning the command dial to change the aperture in Manual exposure mode (there is no need to press the button to change the aperture in Aperture-priority mode). Hold down this button and spin the command dial to add or subtract exposure when using Program, Aperture-priority, or Shutter-priority modes. This facility allows you to "override" the settings the camera has made and create a picture that is lighter or darker. This is called *exposure compensation.* You can "apply" exposure compensation in Manual mode, too, but in that case the exposure isn't really changed. The D3500 simply tells you how much extra or reduced exposure you are requesting, using a display in the viewfinder and LCD monitor which I'll describe later in this chapter. Finally, the button can be used in conjunction with the flash button on the front of the camera to set flash exposure compensation. Hold down both buttons and spin the command dial to adjust the amount of flash exposure. (I'll explain this process in Chapter 11.)

- **Live view lever.** Rotate to activate/deactivate live view.

- **Sensor focal plane.** This indicator shows the *plane* of the sensor, for use in applications where exact measurement of the distance from the focal plane to the subject are necessary. (These are mostly scientific/close-up applications.)

- **Mode dial.** Rotate the mode dial to choose between Program, Aperture-priority, Shutter-priority, and Manual exposure modes, as well as Auto, Auto (No Flash), Portrait, Sports, Close-up, and Night Portrait scene modes. You can also select Effects modes and Guide mode. Your choice will be displayed on the LCD monitor and in the viewfinder, both described in the next sections.

- **Movie button.** Press this button to start shooting video; press a second time to stop capture.

- **Speaker.** Sounds emitted by your D3500, including audio during video playback, are emitted from this speaker.

Lens Components

Figure 3.19 displays the components of a typical lens. I'm showing the older AF-S version of Nikon's collapsible kit lens rather than the AF-P version. It includes several additional components that you'll encounter on other lenses in the Nikon line-up, such as an A/M autofocus mode switch and VR on/off control. The lens is shown in collapsed and extended modes. Components found on typical lenses include:

- **Filter thread.** Most lenses have a thread on the front for attaching filters and other add-ons. Some also use this thread for attaching a lens hood (you screw on the filter first, and then attach the hood to the screw thread on the front of the filter). Some lenses, such as the AF-S Nikkor 14-24mm f/2.8G ED lens, have no front filter thread, either because their front elements are too curved to allow mounting a filter and/or because the front element is so large that huge filters would be prohibitively expensive. Some of these front-filter-hostile lenses allow using smaller filters that drop into a slot at the back of the lens.

Figure 3.19

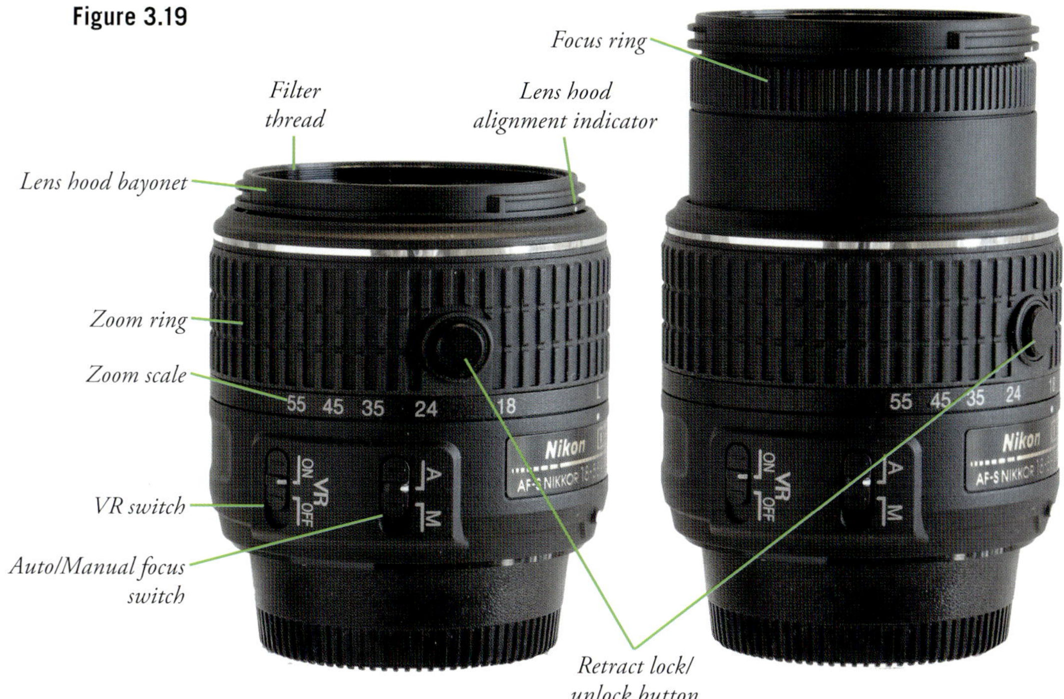

- **Lens hood bayonet.** This lens uses the bayonet to mount the lens hood. Such lenses generally will have a lens hood alignment indicator on the edge showing how to align the lens hood with the bayonet mount.

- **Focus ring.** This is the ring you turn when you manually focus the lens or fine-tune autofocus adjustment. It's a narrow ring at the very front of the lens (on the 18-55mm kit lens), or a wider ring located somewhere else.

- **Focus scale (not shown).** This is a readout found on many lenses that rotates in unison with the lens's focus mechanism to show the distance at which the lens has been focused. It's a useful indicator for double-checking autofocus, roughly evaluating depth-of-field, and for setting manual focus guesstimates. Chapter 10 deals with the mysteries of lenses and their controls in more detail.

- **Zoom scale.** These markings on the lens show the current focal length selected.

- **Zoom ring.** Turn this ring to change the zoom setting.

- **Autofocus/Manual focus switch.** Allows you to change from automatic focus to manual focus.

- **Aperture ring (not shown).** Some lenses have a ring that allows you to set a specific f/stop manually, rather than use the camera's internal electronic aperture control. An aperture ring is useful when a lens is mounted on a non-automatic extension ring, bellows, or other accessory that doesn't couple electronically with the camera. Aperture rings also allow using a lens on an older camera that lacks electronic control. In recent years, Nikon has been replacing lenses that have aperture rings with versions that only allow setting the aperture with camera controls.

- **Vibration reduction switch.** Lenses with Nikon's Vibration Reduction (VR) feature include a switch for turning the stabilization feature on and off, and, in some cases, for changing from normal vibration reduction to a more aggressive "active" VR mode useful for, say, shooting from moving vehicles. More on VR and other lens topics in Chapter 10.

Underneath Your Nikon D3500

- There's not a lot going on with the bottom panel of your Nikon D3500. You'll find the battery compartment access door and a tripod socket, which secures the camera to a tripod. The socket accepts other accessories, such as flash brackets and quick release plates that allow rapid attaching and detaching of the D3500 from a matching platform affixed to your tripod.

- Figure 3.20 shows the underside view of the camera.

Figure 3.20

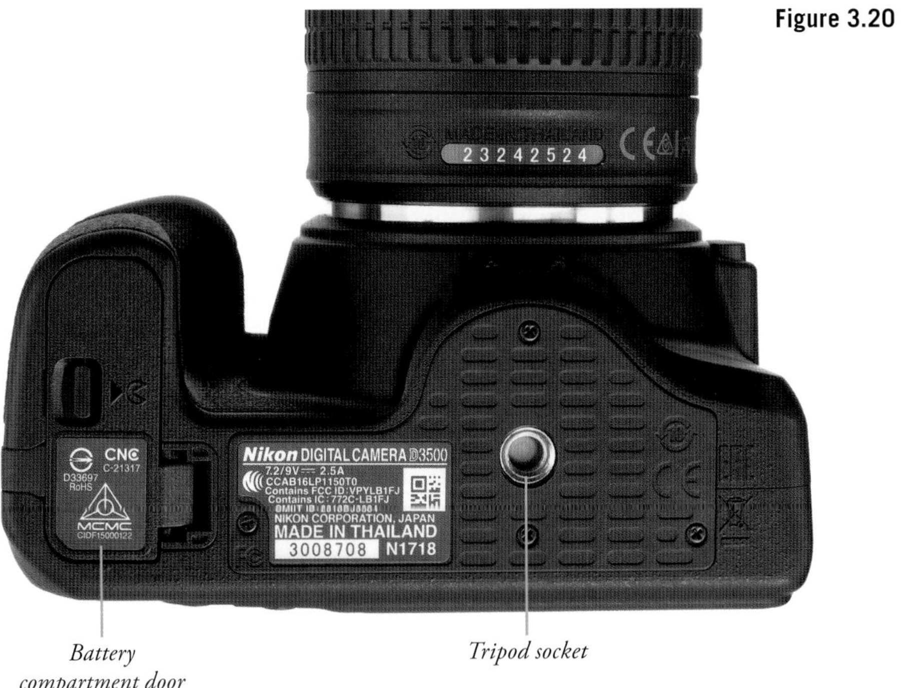

*Battery
compartment door*

Tripod socket

Looking Inside the Viewfinder

Much of the important shooting status information is shown inside the viewfinder of the Nikon D3500. Not all of this information will be shown at any one time. Figure 3.21 shows what you can expect to see. These readouts include:

- **Focus points.** Can display the 11 areas used by the D3500 to focus. The camera can select the appropriate focus zone for you, or you can manually select one or all of the zones, as described in Chapters 1 and 7. The currently selected active focus point can be highlighted with red illumination, depending on focus mode.

- **Battery indicator.** Appears when the D3500's battery becomes depleted. (The current battery condition appears on the LCD monitor, so you're not totally surprised.)

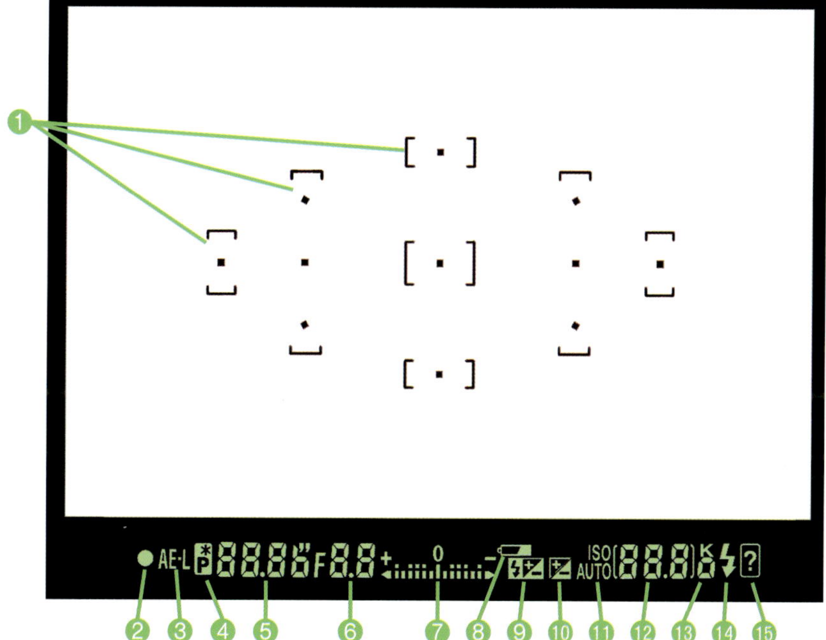

1 *Focus points*

2 *Focus confirmation indicator*

3 *Autoexposure lock indicator*

4 *Flexible program indicator*

5 *Shutter speed*

6 *Aperture*

7 *Electronic analog exposure display*

8 *Battery indicator*

9 *Flash compensation indicator*

10 *Exposure compensation indicator*

11 *Automatic ISO indicator*

12 *Number of exposures remaining/ Number of shots remaining before buffer fills/White balance recording indicator/Exposure compensation value/Flash compensation value/ISO sensitivity.*

13 *Thousands of exposures*

14 *Flash ready indicator*

15 *Warning indicator*

Figure 3.21

- **Focus confirmation indicator.** This green dot stops blinking (and a beep will sound if you haven't deactivated the beep feature) when the subject covered by the active autofocus zone is in sharp focus, whether focus was achieved by the AF system or by you using manual focusing.

- **Autoexposure lock indicator.** Shows that exposure has been locked.

- **Shutter speed.** Displays the current shutter speed selected by the camera or by you in Manual exposure mode.

- **Aperture.** Shows the current aperture chosen by the D3500's autoexposure system or specified by you when using Manual exposure mode.

- **Automatic ISO indicator.** Shown as a reminder that the D3500 has been set to adjust ISO sensitivity automatically. It flashes when the exposure meters are active as a warning to you that the camera may be adjusting the ISO setting.

- **Electronic analog exposure display.** This scale shows the current exposure level, with the bottom indicator centered when the exposure is correct as metered. The indicator may also move to the left or right to indicate over- or underexposure (respectively). The scale is also used to show the amount of exposure compensation dialed in.

- **Flash compensation indicator.** Appears when flash EV changes have been made.

- **Exposure compensation indicator.** This is shown when exposure compensation (EV) changes have been made. It's easy to forget you've dialed in a little more or less exposure, and then shoot a whole series of pictures of a different scene that doesn't require such compensation. Beware!

- **Flash ready indicator.** This icon appears when the flash is fully charged.

- **Number of exposures remaining/Number of shots remaining before buffer fills/White balance recording indicator/Exposure compensation value/Flash compensation value/ISO sensitivity.** Normally displays the number of exposures remaining on your memory card, but while shooting it changes to show a number that indicates the number of frames that can be taken in Continuous shooting mode using the current settings. This indicator also shows other information, such as exposure/flash compensation values, and whether the D3500 is connected to a PC through a USB cable. A question mark indicates an error condition of some sort, such as a full memory card or flash error.

4

Playback and Shooting Menus

For an entry-level camera, the Nikon D3500 has a remarkable number of options and settings you can use to customize the way your camera operates. Not only can you change shooting settings used at the time the picture is taken, but you can adjust the way your camera behaves. Indeed, if your D3500 doesn't operate in exactly the way you'd like, chances are you can make a small change in the Playback, Shooting, and Setup menus that will tailor the D3500 to your needs.

This chapter will help you sort out the settings for two of the D3500's menus. These are the Playback and Shooting menus, which determine how the D3500 displays images on review, and how it uses many of its shooting features to take a photo. I'll cover the Setup and Retouch menus in Chapter 5.

As I've mentioned before, this book isn't intended to replace the manual you received with your D3500, nor have I any interest in rehashing its contents. You'll still find the original manual useful as a standby reference that lists every possible option in exhaustive (if mind numbing) detail—without really telling you how to use those options to take better pictures. There is, however, some unavoidable duplication between the Nikon manual and this chapter, because I'm going to explain all the key menu choices and the options you may have in using them. You should find, though, that I will give you the information you need in a much more helpful format, with plenty of detail on why you should make some settings that are particularly cryptic.

I'm not going to waste a lot of space on some of the more obvious menu choices in these chapters. For example, you can probably figure out, even without my help, that the Beep option in the Setup menu with the solid-state beeper in your camera sounds off during various activities (such as the self-timer countdown). In this chapter, I'll devote no more than a sentence or two to the blatantly obvious settings and concentrate on the more confusing aspects of D3500 setup, such as autofocus. I'll start with an overview of using the D3500's menus themselves.

Anatomy of the Nikon D3500's Menus

For this entry-level camera, Nikon has tried to simplify the menu system, reducing five separate menu listings found in more upscale cameras in the Nikon line (Playback, Photo Shooting, Movie Shooting, Custom Settings, and Setup) to three. (The Custom Settings menu has been banished, and its options distributed among the three remaining menus.) There are also two "bonus" menus: the Retouch menu, which contains functions you can apply to your images rather than operational options; and the Recent Settings menu, which simply displays the 20 most recent menu items you've accessed. If you've never used a Nikon digital SLR before, this chapter will help you learn how to access and apply all these choices and, most importantly, *why* you might want to use a particular option or feature. The Nikon D3500's menu lineup is quite sound, and easy to learn.

If you're switching from a previous Nikon dSLR, you *really* need this chapter. As always, in making its menu improvements, Nikon continues to confound long-time users by changing the names of many menu items, shuffling their order, and hiding old favorite options in places you might never think to look. (Entries for redefining the AE-L/AF-L control and AE lock are now tucked away under a heading called "Buttons," for example.) Nikon must certainly love menu layouts, because it uses so many different versions of them in its various digital SLR cameras, with little consistency beyond family resemblance among them.

If you're lucky enough to be able to work with more than one Nikon camera, you also gain the opportunity to learn several different menu systems in the bargain. It's fortunate that so many menu options are duplicated in the information edit screen, because you can change many settings there and avoid the Lewis Carroll–like trip through Menuland entirely.

The MENU button and basic operation of the D3500's menus are simple. Press the MENU button, located on the right side of the LCD monitor. The menus consist of a series of five separate screens with rows of entries, as shown in Figure 4.1. (Note that when the D3500 is set to the green Auto icon on the mode dial, or Scene modes, some menu choices are not available.)

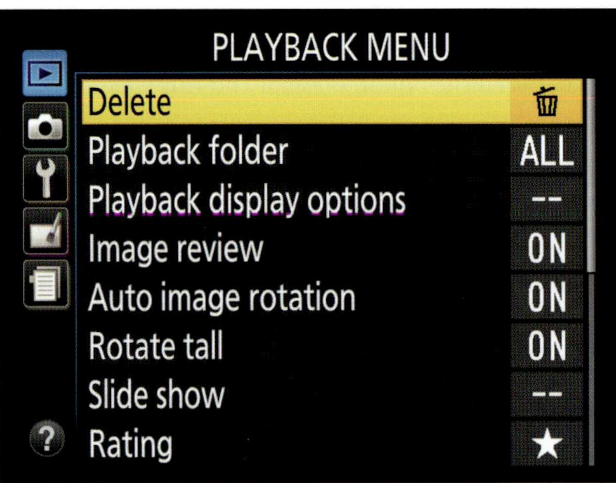

Figure 4.1
The most recently accessed menu appears when you press the MENU button.

There are three columns of information in each menu screen.

- The left-hand column includes an icon representing each of the top-level menu screens. From the top in Figure 4.1, they are Playback (right-pointing triangle icon), Shooting (camera icon), Setup (wrench), Retouch (a paintbrush), and Recent Settings (a tabbed page), with Help access represented by a question mark at the bottom of the column.

- The center column includes the name representing the function of each choice in the currently selected menu. For example, Image Review represents the menu entry for turning automatic playback of each image shot on or off.

- The right-hand column has an icon or text that shows either the current setting for that menu item or text or an icon that represents the function of that menu entry. In Figure 4.1, a trash can icon shows that you can use the Delete entry for removing images, while the text ON appears next to the Rotate Tall entry, indicating that the D3500 has been set to rotate vertical images on the LCD monitor.

Navigating among the various menus is easy and follows a consistent set of rules.

- **Press MENU to start.** Press the MENU button to display the main menu screens.

- **Navigate with the multi selector pad.** The multi selector pad, located to the right of the LCD monitor, has indents at the up/down/left/right positions. Press these "buttons" to navigate among the menu selections. Press the left button to move highlighting to the left column; then press the up/down buttons to scroll up or down among the five top-level menus.

- **Highlighting indicates active choice.** As each top-level menu is highlighted, its icon will first change from black-and-white to yellow/amber, white, and black. As you use the multi selector's right button to move into the column containing that menu's choices, you can then use the up/down buttons to scroll among the individual entries. If more than one screen full of choices is available, a scroll bar appears at the far right of the screen, with a position slider showing the relative position of the currently highlighted entry.

- **Select a menu item.** To work with a highlighted menu entry, press the OK button in the center of the multi selector on the back of the D3500 or just press the right button on the multi selector. Any additional screens of choices will appear, like the one you can see in Figure 4.2. You can move among them using the same multi selector movements.

- **Choose your menu option.** You can confirm a selection by pressing the OK button or, frequently, by pressing the right button on the multi selector once again. Some functions require scrolling to a Done menu choice or include an instruction to set a choice using some other button.

- **Leaving the menu system.** Pressing the multi selector left button usually backs you out of the current screen and pressing the MENU button again usually does the same thing. You can exit the menu system at any time by tapping the shutter release button. If you haven't confirmed your choice for a particular option, no changes will be made.

- **Quick return.** The Nikon D3500 "remembers" the top-level menu and specific menu entry you were using (but not any submenus) the last time the menu system was accessed (even if you have subsequently turned the camera off), so pressing the MENU button brings you back to where you left off.

The top-level menus are color coded, and a bar in that color is displayed in a partial bracket at the top and left edges of the menu entries when one of those menus is highlighted. The colors are Playback menu (blue); Shooting menu (green); Setup menu (orange); Retouch menu (purple); and Recent Settings (gray). Note that the descriptions for each menu entry in Chapters 4 and 5 include a list of options, usually with a default value noted. If no default value is listed, there is none for that menu command.

Playback Menu Options

The blue-coded Playback menu entries are used to select options related to the display, review, and printing of the photos you've taken. The choices you'll find include:

- Delete
- Playback Folder
- Playback Display Options
- Image Review
- Auto Image Rotation
- Rotate Tall
- Slide Show
- Rating
- Select to Send to Smart Device

Delete

Options: Selected (default), Select Date, All

Choose this menu entry and you'll be given three choices: Selected, Select Date, and All. If you choose Selected, you'll see an image selection screen like the one shown in Figure 4.2. Then, follow these instructions:

1. **Review thumbnails.** Use the multi selector up/down/left/right buttons to scroll among the available images.

2. **Examine image.** When you highlight an image you think you might want to delete, press the Zoom In button to temporarily enlarge that image so you can evaluate it further. When you release the button, the selection screen returns.

3. **Mark/unmark images.** To mark an image for deletion, press the Zoom Out/Thumbnail button (*not* the Trash button). A trash can icon will appear overlaid on that image's thumbnail. To unmark an image, press the Zoom Out/Thumbnail button again.

4. **Remove images.** When you've finished marking images to delete, press OK. A final screen will appear asking you to confirm the removal of the image(s). Choose Yes to delete the image(s) or No to cancel deletion, and then press OK. If you selected Yes, then you'll return to the Playback menu; if you chose No, you'll be taken back to the selection screen to mark/unmark images.

5. **Exit.** To back out of the selection screen, press the MENU button.

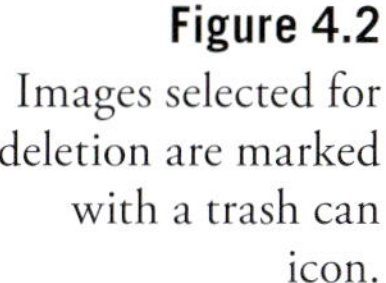

Figure 4.2

Images selected for deletion are marked with a trash can icon.

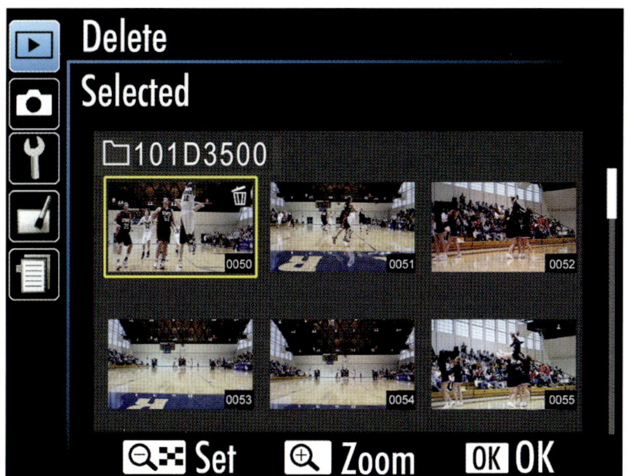

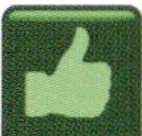

Tip

Using the Delete menu option to remove images will have no effect on images that have been marked as protected with the Protect key.

Keep in mind that deleting images though the Delete process is slower than just wiping out the whole card with the Format command, so using Format is generally much faster than choosing Delete: All, and also is a safer way of returning your memory card to a fresh, blank state.

Playback Folder

Options: D3500, All (default), Current

Images created by your Nikon D3500 are deposited into folders on your memory card. These folders have names like 100D3500 or 101D3500, but you can change those default names to something else using the Folders option in the Setup menu, described later in Chapter 5.

With a freshly formatted memory card (formatting is covered under the Setup menu), the D3500 starts with a default name: 100D3500. When that folder fills with the maximum of 999 images, the camera automatically creates a new folder numbered one higher, such as 101D3500. If you use the same memory card in another camera, that camera will also create its own folder (say, 102NCD40 for a Nikon D40). Thus, you can end up with several folders on the same memory card, at least one for each camera the card is used in, until you eventually reformat the card and folder creation starts anew. In Chapter 5, in the section on the Setup menu, I'll show you how to create folders with names you select yourself using the Storage Folder option.

This menu item allows you to choose which folders are accessed when displaying images using the D3500's Playback facility.

Your choices are as follows:

- **D3500.** The camera displays the images in the folder with the indicated name.

- **All.** All folders containing images that the D3500 can read will be accessed, regardless of which camera created them. You might want to use this setting if you swap memory cards among several cameras and want to be able to review all the photos. You will be able to view images even if they were created by a non-Nikon camera if those images conform to a specification called the Design Rule for Camera File systems (DCF).

- **Current.** The D3500 will display only images in the current Active Folder, as specified in the Setup menu. For example, if you have been shooting heavily at an event and have already accumulated more than 999 shots and the D3500 has created a new folder for the overflow, you'd use this setting to view only the most recent photos, which reside in that new current folder. You can change the current folder to any other specific folder on your memory card using the Active Folder option in the Setup menu, described in Chapter 5.

Playback Display Options

Options: None (Image Only), Highlights, RGB Histogram, Shooting Data, Overview

You'll recall from Chapter 2 that a great deal of information, available on multiple screens, can be displayed when reviewing images. This menu item helps you reduce/increase the clutter by specifying which information and screens will be available.

This menu option presents you with a screen of possible display screens, which I showed you in the previous chapter. You can scroll among the options and select from None (image only), Highlights, RGB Histogram, Shooting Data (three different screens), and Overview. (See Figure 4.3.)

To activate or deactivate an info option, scroll to that option and press the right multi selector button to add a check mark to the box next to that item. Press the right button to unmark an item that has previously been checked.

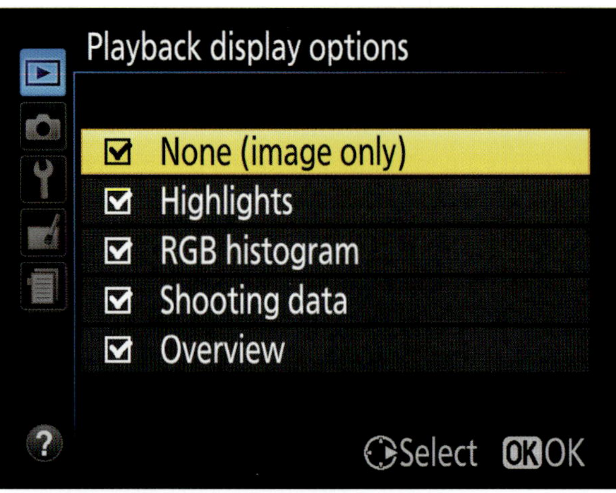

Figure 4.3
Choose Playback Display options.

Image Review

Options: On (default), Off

There are certain shooting situations in which it's useful to have the picture you've just shot pop up on the LCD monitor automatically for review. Perhaps you're fine-tuning exposure or autofocus and want to be able to see whether your most recent image is acceptable. Or, maybe you're the nervous type and just want confirmation that you actually took a picture. Instant review has saved my bacon a few times; for example, when I was shooting with studio flash in Manual mode and didn't notice that the shutter speed had been set to (a non-syncing) 1/320th second by mistake.

A lot of the time, however, it's a better idea to *not* automatically review your shots in order to conserve battery power (the LCD monitor is one of the major juice drains in the camera) or to speed up or simplify operations. For example, if you've just fired off a burst of eight shots at 5 fps during a football game do you *really* need to have each and every frame display as the D3500 clears its buffer and stores the photos on your memory card? Or, when you're shooting at an acoustic concert, wouldn't it be smart to disable image review so the folks behind you aren't hit with a blast of light from that luminous 3-inch LCD every time you take a picture? This menu operation allows you to choose which mode to use:

- **On.** At this default setting, image review is automatic after every shot is taken.
- **Off.** Images are displayed only when you press the Playback button.

Auto Image Rotation

Options: On (default), Off

This command tells the D3500 to embed information indicating how the camera was rotated when the picture was taken, enabling the camera and compatible software to read this data and rotate the image during review or editing.

Rotate Tall

Options: On (default), Off

When you rotate the D3500 to photograph vertical subjects in portrait (tall), rather than landscape (wide) orientation, you probably don't want to view them tilted onto their sides later on, either on the camera LCD monitor or within your image viewing/editing application on your computer. The D3500 is way ahead of you. It has a directional sensor built in that can detect whether the camera was rotated when the photo was taken and hide this information in the image file itself.

The orientation data is applied in two different ways. It can be used by the D3500 to automatically rotate images when they are displayed on the camera's LCD monitor, or you can ignore the data and let the images display in non-rotated fashion (so you have to rotate the camera to view them in their proper orientation). Your image-editing application, such as Adobe Photoshop Elements, can also use the embedded file data to automatically rotate images on your computer screen.

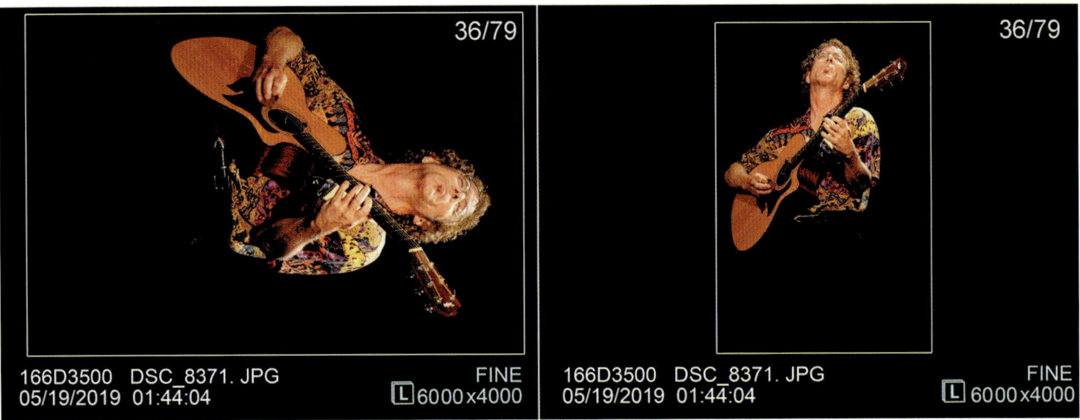

Figure 4.4 With Rotate Tall turned off (left), vertical images appear large on the LCD monitor, but you must turn the camera to view them upright. With Rotate Tall turned on (right), vertical images are shown in a smaller size, but oriented for viewing without turning the camera.

But either feature works only if you've told the D3500 to place orientation information in the image file, so it can be retrieved when the image is displayed. You must set Auto Image Rotation to On. Once you've done that, the D3500 will embed information about orientation in the image file, and both your D3500 and your image editor can rotate the images for you as the files are displayed.

This menu choice deals only with whether the image should be rotated when displayed on the *camera LCD monitor*. (If you de-activate this option, your image-editing software can still read the embedded rotation data and properly display your images.) When Rotate Tall is turned off, the Nikon D3500 does not rotate pictures taken in vertical orientation, displaying them as shown in Figure 4.4, left. The image is large on your LCD screen, but you must rotate the camera to view it upright.

When Rotate Tall is turned on, the D3500 rotates pictures taken in vertical orientation on the LCD monitor screen so you don't have to turn the camera to view them comfortably. However, this orientation also means that the longest dimension of the image is shown using the shortest dimension of the LCD, so the picture is reduced in size, as you can see in Figure 4.4, right.

So, turn this feature On (as well as Auto Image Rotation in the Playback menu), if you'd rather not turn your camera to view vertical shots in their natural orientation, and don't mind the smaller image. Turn the feature Off if, as I do, you'd rather see a larger image and are willing to rotate the camera to do so.

Slide Show

Options: Start, Image Type, Frame Interval

The D3500's Slide Show feature is a convenient way to review images in the current playback folder one after another, without the need to manually switch between them. To activate, just choose Start from this entry in the Playback menu. If you like, you can choose Frame Interval before commencing the show in order to select an interval of 2, 3, 5, or 10 seconds between "slides."

During playback, you can press the OK button to pause the slide show (in case you want to examine an image more closely). When the show is paused, a menu pops up, as shown in Figure 4.5, with choices to restart the show (by pressing the OK button again); change the interval between frames; or to exit the show entirely.

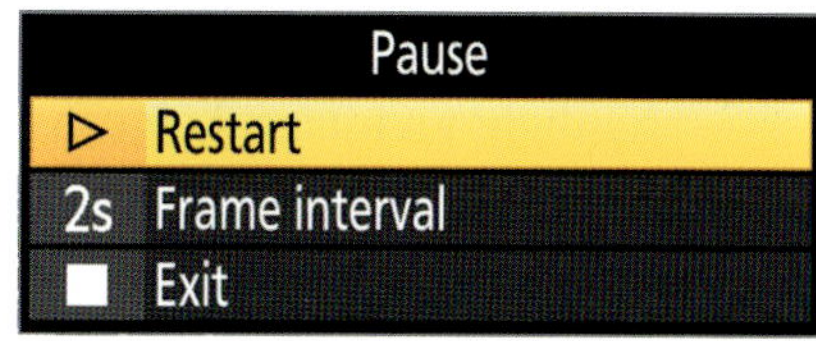

Figure 4.5 Press the OK button to pause the slide show, change the interval between slides, or to exit the presentation.

As the images are displayed, press the up/down multi selector buttons to change the amount of information presented on the screen with each image. For example, you might want to review a set of images and the settings used to shoot them. At any time during the show, press the up/down buttons until the informational screen you want is overlaid on the images.

As the slide show progresses, you can press the left/right multi selector buttons to move back to a previous frame or jump ahead to the next one. The slide show will then proceed as before. Press the MENU button to exit the slide show and return to the menu, or the Playback button to exit the menu system totally. As always, while reviewing images, you can tap the MENU button to exit the show and return to the menus or tap the shutter release button if you want to remove everything from the screen and return to shooting mode.

At the end of the slide show, as when you've paused it, you'll be offered the choice of restarting the sequence, changing the frame interval, or exiting the slide show feature completely.

Rating

Options: Apply one to five stars

Rating allows you to mark pictures according to quality using a 1- to 5-star system or mark them using any other criterion you want to use (if you make up your own categories corresponding to the number of stars). If you want to apply a quality rating to images or movies you've shot (or use the rating system to represent some other criteria), you can use this entry to give particular images one, two, three, four, or five stars, or turn the rating off.

Suppose you were photographing a track meet with multiple events. You could apply a one-star rating to jumping events, two stars to relays, three stars to throwing events, four stars to hurdles, and five stars to dashes. Then, using the Image Jump feature, you could review only images of one particular type.

With a little imagination you can apply the rating system to all sorts of categories. At a wedding, you could classify pictures of the bride, the groom, guests, attendants, and parents of the couple. If you were shooting school portraits, one rating could apply to first grade, another to second grade, and so on. Given a little thought, this feature has many more applications than you might think. There are two ways to add ratings, using this menu entry to rate one or multiple images, or directly from playback view to mark images one at a time. To use this menu entry:

1. Select Rating from the Playback menu and press the right multi selector button.
2. A screen appears allowing you to browse through the image.
3. Highlight an image. You can press the Zoom In button to view it full frame.
4. With the Zoom Out button held in, use the up/down multi selector buttons to choose a rating from one to five stars. You can also press the Trash button to mark the picture for later deletion.
5. Press OK to confirm and finish.
6. When done rating, choose MENU to exit.

You can also rate images without using the menu:

1. In Playback mode, display an image in full-frame or zoom views, or use thumbnail view to highlight it.
2. Press the *i* button to show playback display options Rating and Retouch.
3. Select Rating and press OK.
4. Press the left/right multi controller buttons to choose from one to five stars. You can also press the Trash button to mark the picture for later deletion.
5. Press OK to confirm and exit.

Select to Send to Smart Device

Options: Select Image(s), Deselect All

You'll need to scroll down to access this last entry in the Playback menu. Use it to mark images you want to upload to a smart device using the D3500's SnapBridge capabilities, described in Chapter 9.

Shooting Menu Options

The Shooting menu options (see Figure 4.6) are likely to be the most frequently accessed settings, with changes made to one or more of them during a particular session fairly common. You might make such adjustments as you begin a shooting session, or when you move from one type of subject to another. Nikon makes accessing many changes easiest through the information edit screen via the *i* button, and I recommend that method for making changes to the

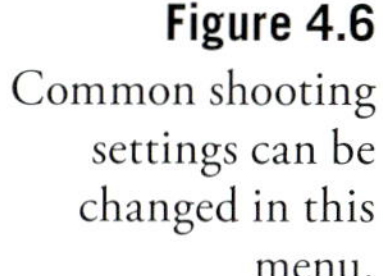

Figure 4.6
Common shooting settings can be changed in this menu.

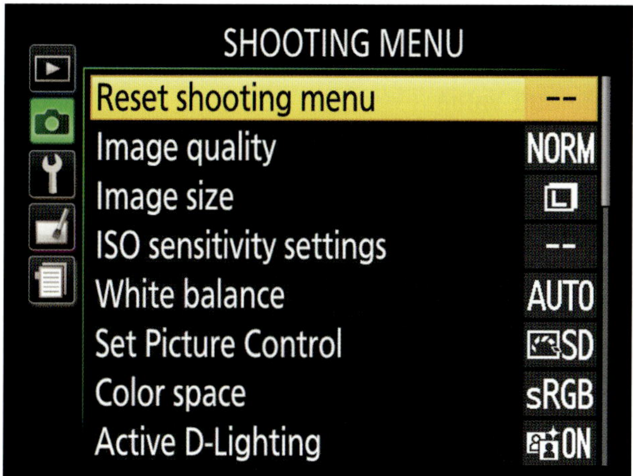

entries duplicated there. You can readily see the current settings for any of these—and the other settings visible on the shooting information screen—and then press the *i* button, use the multi selector directional buttons to navigate to the entry you want to use, press OK, and make your change in a few seconds. Using the equivalent Shooting menu entries usually takes a little longer.

This section explains the options of the Shooting menu and how to use them. The options you'll find in these green-coded menus include:

- Reset Shooting Menu
- Image Quality
- Image Size
- ISO Sensitivity Settings
- White Balance
- Set Picture Control
- Color Space
- Active D-Lighting
- Noise Reduction

- Vignette Control
- Auto Distortion Control
- Focus Mode
- AF-Area Mode
- Built-in AF-Assist Illuminator
- Metering
- Flash Cntrl for Built-In Flash/ Optional Flash
- Movie Settings

Reset Shooting Menu

Options: Yes

If you select Yes, the Shooting menu settings shown in Table 4.1 will be set to their default values. It has no effect on the settings in other menus, or any of the other camera settings.

You'd want to use this Reset option when you've made a bunch of changes (say, while playing around with them as you read this chapter), and now want to put them back to the factory defaults.

Table 4.1 Values Reset

Setting	Default Value
Release Mode	All modes except Sports: Single Frame Sports mode: Continuous
Focus Point	Center
Flexible Program	Off
AE-L/AF-L Hold	Off
Flash Modes	Auto, Portrait, Child, Close-up, Vivid, POP, Toy modes: Automatic Night Portrait: Auto-Slow Sync Photo Illustration: Flash Off Program, Aperture-priority, Shutter-priority, Manual modes: Fill Flash
Exposure Compensation	Off
Flash Compensation	Off

Image Quality

Options: NEF (RAW)+JPEG Fine, NEF (RAW), JPEG Fine, JPEG Normal (default), JPEG Basic

You can choose the image quality settings used by the D3500 to store its files. The quickest way to do that is with the information edit screen. You can also use this menu option, if you prefer. There is no real advantage to using this menu instead of the information edit screen. (See Figure 4.7.)

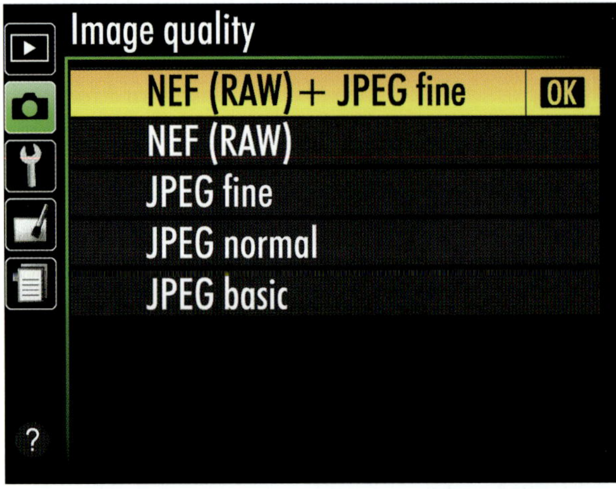

Figure 4.7
Choose Image Quality options here.

You have two choices to make:

- **Level of JPEG compression (Fine, Normal, Basic).** To reduce the size of your image files and allow more photos to be stored on a given memory card, the D3500 uses JPEG compression to squeeze the images down to a smaller size. This compacting reduces the image quality a little, so you're offered your choice of Fine (a 1:4 reduction), Normal (1:8 reduction), and Basic (1:16) compression. You can see examples of the results of compression in Figure 4.8. I'll explain more about JPEG compression later in this section.

- **JPEG, RAW, or both.** You can elect to store only JPEG versions of the images you shoot, or you can save your photos as RAW images, which Nikon calls NEF, for Nikon Electronic Format files. RAW images consume more than twice as much space on your memory card. Or, you can store both RAW and JPEG Basic files at once as you shoot. Many photographers elect to save *both* JPEG and RAW, so they'll have a JPEG Basic version that might be usable as-is, as well as the original "digital negative" RAW file in case they want to do some processing of the image later. You'll end up with two different versions of the same file: one with a .jpg extension, and one with the .nef extension that signifies a Nikon RAW file.

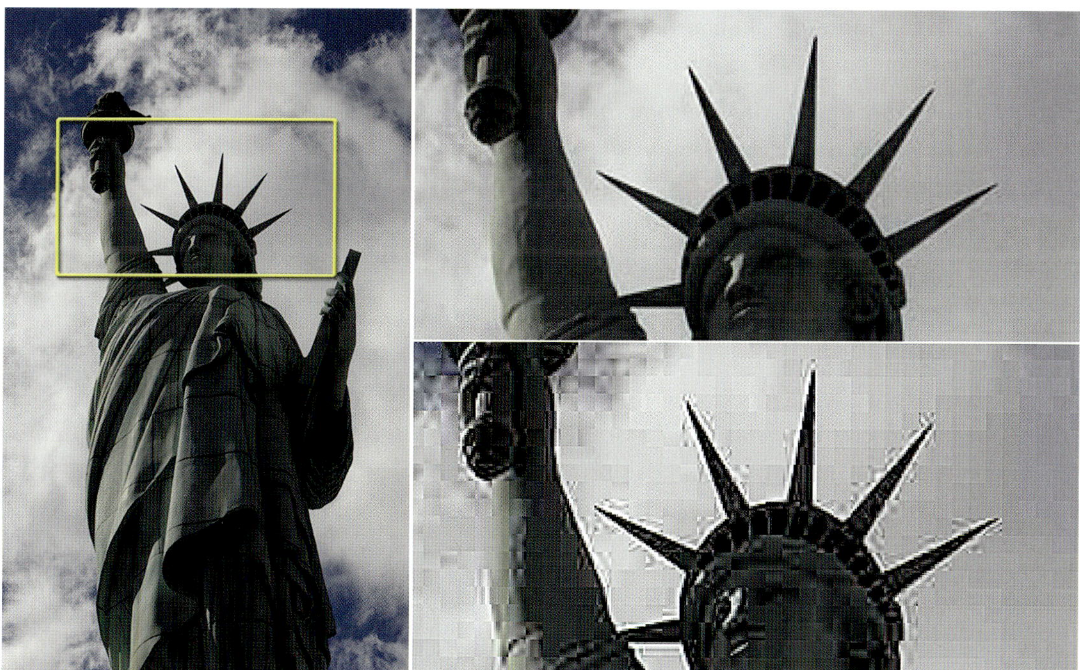

Figure 4.8 JPEG compression yields little image quality loss (top); extreme compression produces visible loss of detail (bottom).

To choose the combination you want, access the Shooting menu, scroll to Image Quality, and select it by pressing OK or the multi selector right button. Scroll to highlight the setting you want, and either press OK or push the multi selector right button to confirm your selection.

In practice, you'll probably use the JPEG Fine or NEF (RAW)+JPEG Fine selections most often, although beginners concerned about squeezing many images onto a card, or who display them only online may prefer a more compact JPEG setting. Why so many choices, then? There are some advantages to using the JPEG Normal and JPEG Basic settings. Settings that are less than max allow stretching the capacity of your memory card so you can shoehorn quite a few more pictures onto a single memory card. That can come in useful when on vacation and you're running out of storage, or when you're shooting non-critical work that doesn't require 24 megapixels of resolution (such as photos taken for real estate listings, web page display, photo ID cards, or similar applications). Some photographers like to record RAW+JPEG Fine so they'll have a moderate-quality JPEG file for review only and no intention of using for editing purposes, while retaining access to the original RAW file for serious editing.

For most work, using lower resolution and extra compression is false economy. You never know when you might actually need that extra bit of picture detail. Your best bet is to have enough memory cards to handle all the shooting you want to do until you have the chance to transfer your photos to your computer or a personal storage device.

However, reduced image quality can sometimes be beneficial if you're shooting sequences of photos rapidly, as the D3500 is able to hold more of them in its internal memory buffer before transferring to the memory card. Still, for most sports and other applications, you'd probably rather have better, sharper pictures than longer periods of continuous shooting. Do you really need 10 shots of a pass reception in a football game, or six slightly different versions of your local basketball star driving in for a layup?

JPEG vs. RAW

You'll sometimes be told that Nikon's NEF or RAW files are the "unprocessed" image information your camera produces, before it's been modified. That's nonsense. RAW files are no more unprocessed than camera film is after it's been through the chemicals to produce a negative or transparency. Your digital image undergoes a significant amount of processing before it is saved as a RAW file.

A RAW file is more similar to a film camera's processed negative. It contains all the information captured by the sensor, but with no sharpening and no application of any special filters or other settings you might have specified when you took the picture. Those settings are *stored* with the RAW file, so they can be applied when the image is converted to a form compatible with your favorite image editor. However, using RAW conversion software such as Adobe Camera Raw or Nikon Capture NX, you can override those settings and apply settings of your own. You can select essentially the same changes there that you might have specified in your camera's picture-taking options.

RAW exists because sometimes we want to have access to all the information captured by the camera, before the camera's internal logic has processed it and converted the image to a standard file format. RAW doesn't save as much space as JPEG. What it does do is preserve all the information captured by your camera after it's been converted from analog to digital form.

So, why don't we always use RAW? Some photographers avoid using Nikon's RAW NEF files on the misguided conviction that they don't want to spend time in an image editor. But, if your basic settings are okay, such work is *optional*, and needs to be applied only when a particular image needs to be fine-tuned.

Although some photographers do save *only* in RAW format, it's common to use RAW+JPEG Fine, or, if you're confident about your settings, just shoot JPEG and eschew RAW altogether. In some situations, working with a RAW file can slow you down a little. RAW images take longer to store on the memory card and must be converted from RAW to a format your image editor can handle, whether you elect to go with the default settings in force when the picture was taken or make minor adjustments to the settings you specified in the camera.

As a result, those who depend on speedy access to images or who shoot large numbers of photos at once may prefer JPEG over RAW. These photographers include wedding and sports shooters, who may take hundreds to more than a thousand pictures within a few hours.

JPEG was invented as a more compact file format that can store most of the information in a digital image, but in a much smaller size. JPEG predates most digital SLRs and was initially used to squeeze down files for transmission over slow dial-up connections. JPEG provides smaller files by compressing the information in a way that loses some image data. JPEG remains a viable alternative because it offers several different quality levels. At the highest-quality Fine level, you might not be able to tell the difference between the original RAW file and the JPEG version. If you don't mind losing some quality, you can use more aggressive Normal compression with JPEG to cut the size again.

Image Size

Options: Large (default), Medium, Small

The next menu command in the Shooting menu lets you select the resolution, or number of pixels captured as you shoot with your Nikon D3500. Your choices range from Large (L—6,000 × 4,000, 24 megapixels), Medium (M—4,496 × 3,000, 13.5 megapixels), and Small (S—2,992 × 2,000, 6 megapixels). There are no additional options available from the Image Size menu screen. Keep in mind that if you choose NEF (RAW) or NEF (RAW)+JPEG Fine, only the Large image size can be selected. The other size options are grayed out and unavailable.

ISO Sensitivity Settings

Options: ISO Sensitivity (default, ISO 100 in PSAM modes; Auto for other modes); Auto ISO Sensitivity Control (default, On); Maximum Sensitivity (default, 25600); Minimum Shutter Speed (default, Auto)

ISO governs how sensitive your Nikon D3500 is to light. Low ISO settings, such as ISO 100 or ISO 200 mean that you may have to use wider lens openings or slower shutter speeds. Faster ISO settings, on the other hand, let you take pictures in lower light levels, with faster shutter speeds (say, to freeze action) or with smaller lens openings (to produce a larger range in which objects are in sharp focus). I'll explain all these factors in more detail in Chapter 6.

This menu entry allows you to set an ISO sensitivity value, from ISO 100 (at the low end) through ISO 25600. You can also choose Auto, which allows the Nikon D3500 to change the ISO setting as you shoot if the setting you have made isn't high enough to produce the best combination of shutter speed and lens opening for a sharp picture. The Auto feature can be used when you're working in Auto, Scene, Program, Shutter-priority, Aperture-priority, or Manual exposure modes. This feature can be used both with available-light shots, and those using electronic flash.

Auto ISO is available with P, S, A, and M exposure modes when you're using a type-E or type-G lens (lens types are explained in Chapter 10). When Auto ISO is active, if the ISO rating that you've chosen doesn't provide enough sensitivity to take an optimal picture (that is one that is well-exposed, but also has a shutter speed that's fast enough to stop action, and an aperture that produces an acceptable range of sharpness), the camera can increase the ISO automatically.

This capability can be a convenience (and, at times, a life-saver), but is also fraught with pitfalls. For example, it is possible that the D3500 could, if not given some guidance, choose an ISO setting far higher than what you intended, producing pictures that might be unacceptably graining for a given purpose. In such cases, you might have preferred to keep your original ISO setting and optimize exposure through some other means, such as supplementary flash or using a tripod with a longer shutter speed.

Fortunately, the D3500 does not easily lead you astray. Automatic ISO shifts are possible only if you've activated that feature in this menu, and, when implemented by the camera, you're given fair warning by an ISO-Auto indicator on the shooting information screen and in the viewfinder. Better yet, you can lay down some rules that the D3500 will use before it meddles with the ISO setting you originally specified.

The lower half of the ISO sensitivity settings screen has three choices. One of them, On/Off, is self-explanatory; you can enable or disable the ISO Auto feature by choosing the appropriate option. The other two, available only when Auto is turned on, are Max. Sensitivity and Min. Shutter Speed. These lead you to separate screens you can use to lay down the ground rules.

Here's a quick explanation of how your options operate:

- **Off.** Set ISO Sensitivity Auto Control to Off, and the ISO setting will not budge from whatever value you have specified. Use this setting when you don't want any ISO surprises, or when ISO increases are not needed to counter slow shutter speeds. For example, if the D3500 is mounted on a tripod, you can safely use slower shutter speeds at a relatively low ISO setting, so there is no need for a speed bump.

- **On.** At other times, you may want to activate the feature. For example, if you're hand-holding the camera and the D3500, set for Program (P) or Aperture-priority (A) mode, wants to use a shutter speed slower than, say, 1/30th second, it's probably a good idea to increase the ISO to avoid the effects of camera shake. If you're using a telephoto lens (which magnifies camera shake), a shutter speed of 1/125th second or higher might be the point where an ISO bump would be a good idea. In that case, you can turn on the ISO Sensitivity Auto Control, or remember to boost the ISO setting yourself.

- **Maximum sensitivity.** If the idea of unwanted noise bothers you, you can avoid using an ISO setting that's higher than you're comfortable with. This parameter sets the highest ISO setting the D3500 will use in ISO-Auto mode. You can choose from ISO 200, 400, 800, 1600, 3200, or 6400, as the max ISO setting the camera will use. Use a low number if you'd rather not take any photos at a high ISO without manually setting that value yourself. Dial in a higher ISO number if getting the photo at any sensitivity setting is more important than worrying about noise.

- **Minimum shutter speed.** You can decide the shutter speed that's your personal "danger threshold" in terms of camera shake blurring. That is, if you feel you can't hand-hold the camera at a shutter speed slower than 1/30th second, you can tell the D3500 that when the metered exposure will end up with a speed slower than that, ISO-Auto should kick in and do its stuff. When the shutter speed is *faster* (shorter) than the speed you specify, ISO-Auto will not take effect and the ISO setting you've made yourself remains in force. The default value is 1/30th second, because in most situations, any shutter speed longer/slower than 1/30th is to be avoided, unless you're using a tripod, monopod, or looking for a special effect. If you're working with a telephoto lens and find even a relatively brief shutter speed "dangerous," you can set a minimum shutter speed threshold of 1/250th second. Of course, lenses with vibration reduction (VR) built in can raise your minimum shutter speed threshold preference.

White Balance

Options: Auto (default), Incandescent, Fluorescent (seven types), Direct Sunlight, Flash, Cloudy, Shade, Preset Manual

The Shooting menu's White Balance settings are considerably more flexible than those available from the information edit screen, so you may want to use this menu entry instead. The information edit screen lets you choose one of six predefined settings, plus Auto and PRE (which is a user-definable white balance you can base on the lighting in a scene of your choice). The White Balance menu, on the other hand, has more choices of presets, and gives you the additional option of fine-tuning the white balance precisely.

Different light sources have difference "colors," at least as perceived by your D3500's sensor. Indoor illumination tends to be somewhat reddish, while daylight has, in comparison, a more bluish tinge. If the color balance the camera is using doesn't match the light source, you can end up with a color rendition that is off-kilter, as you can see in Figure 4.9.

This menu entry allows you to choose one of the white balance values from among Auto, incandescent, seven varieties of fluorescent illumination (the information edit screen only lets you switch to whichever fluorescent setting you define here), direct sunlight, flash, cloudy, shade, or a preset value taken from an existing photograph or a measurement you make.

When you select the White Balance entry on the Shooting menu, you'll see an array of choices like those shown in Figure 4.10. (One additional choice, PRE Preset Manual, is not visible until you scroll down to it.) Choose the predefined value you want by pressing the multi selector right button, or press OK.

If you choose Fluorescent, you'll be taken to another screen that presents seven different types of lamps, from sodium-vapor through warm-white fluorescent down to high-temperature mercury-vapor. If you know the exact type of non-incandescent lighting being used, you can select it, or settle on a likely compromise. Press the multi selector right button again or press OK to select the fluorescent lamp variation you want to use.

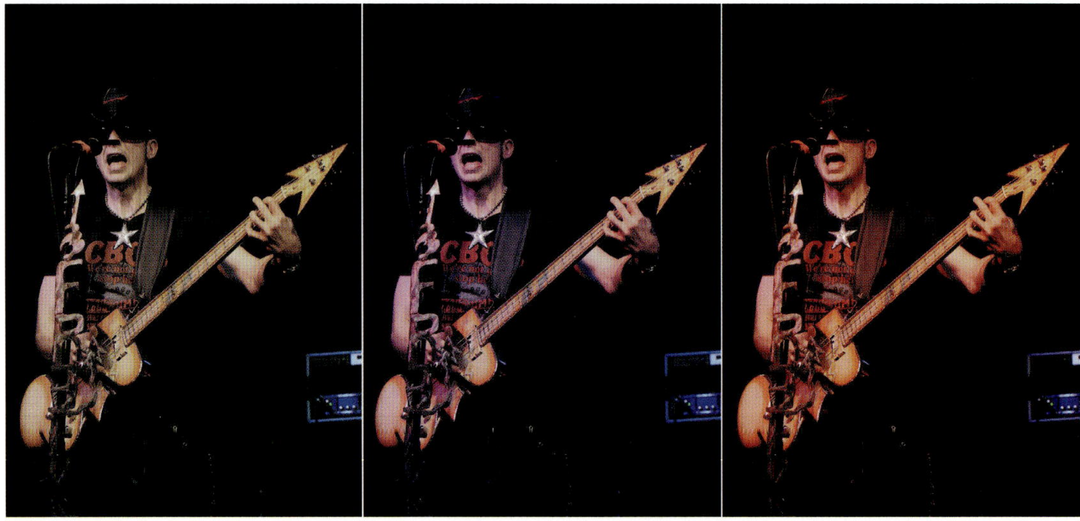

Figure 4.9 Adjusting color temperature can provide different results of the same subject at settings of 3,400K (left), 5,000K (middle), and 2,800K (right).

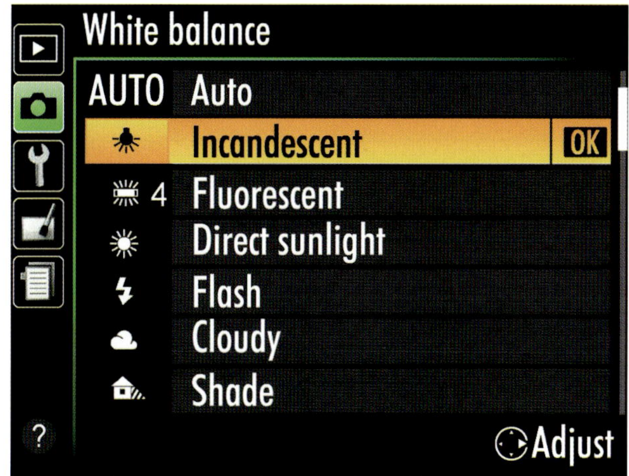

Figure 4.10
The White Balance menu has predefined values, plus the option of setting a preset you measure yourself.

When you've finished choosing a fluorescent light source *and for all other predefined values* (Auto, Incandescent, Direct Sunlight, Flash, Cloudy, or Shade), you'll next be taken to the fine-tuning screen shown in Figure 4.11 (and which uses the incandescent setting as an example). The screen shows a grid with two axes, an amber/blue axis extending left/right, and a green/magenta axis extending up and down the grid. By default, the grid's cursor is positioned in the middle, and a readout to the right of the grid shows the cursor's coordinates on the A-B axis (yes, I know the display has the end points reversed) and G-M axis at 0,0.

You can use the multi selector's up/down and right/left buttons to move the cursor to any coordinate in the grid, thereby biasing the white balance in the direction(s) you choose. The amber/blue axis makes the image warmer or colder (but not actually yellow or blue). Similarly, the green/magenta axis preserves all the colors in the original image, but gives them a tinge biased toward green or

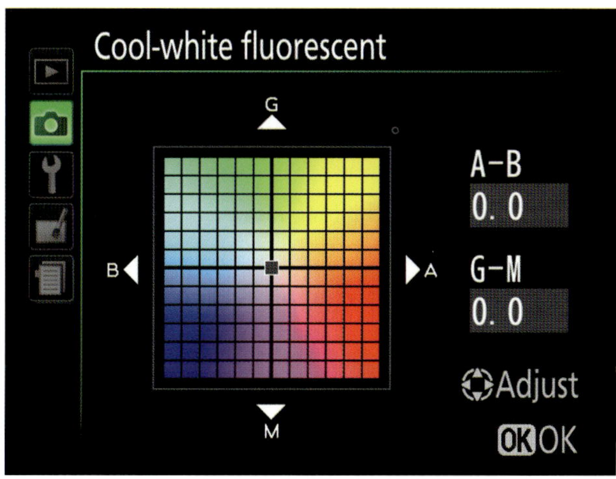

Figure 4.11
Specific white balance settings can be fine-tuned by changing their bias in the amber/blue, green/magenta directions—or along both axes simultaneously.

magenta. Each increment equals about five mired units, but you should know that mired values aren't linear; five mireds at 2,500K produces a much stronger effect than five mireds at 6,000K. If you really want to fine-tune your color balance, you're better off experimenting and evaluating the results of a particular change.

When you've fine-tuned white balance, an asterisk appears next to the white balance icon in both the Shooting menu and shooting information screen shown on the LCD monitor, as a tip-off that this tweaking has taken place.

Using Preset Manual White Balance

If automatic white balance or one of the predefined settings available aren't suitable, you can set a custom white balance using the Preset Manual menu option. You can apply the white balance from a scene, either by shooting a new picture on the spot and using the resulting white balance (Measure) or using an image you have already shot (Use Photo). To perform direct measurement from your current scene using a reference object (preferably a neutral gray or white object), follow these steps:

1. Place the neutral reference under the lighting you want to measure.
2. Choose Preset Manual from the White Balance screen in the Shooting menu (you may need to scroll down to see it).
3. Select Measure from the screen that appears by scrolling to it and pressing the multi selector right button or pressing OK.
4. A warning message appears, Overwrite existing preset data? Choose Yes.
5. An instructional message appears for a few seconds telling you to take a photo of a white or gray object that fills the viewfinder under the lighting that will be used for shooting. Do that!
6. After you've taken the photo, if the D3500 was able to capture the white balance data, a message Data Acquired appears on the shooting information screen, and the PRE white balance setting is shown. If the D3500 was not able to capture white balance data, a pop-up message appears, and you should try again.

The preset value you've captured will remain in the D3500's memory until you replace that white balance with a new captured value. You can also use the white balance information from a picture you've already taken, using the Use Photo option, as described next:

1. Choose Preset Manual from the White Balance menu.
2. Select Use Photo.
3. The most recently shot picture will appear, with a menu offering to use This Image or Select Image.
4. Press OK to use the displayed image or choose Select Image to specify another picture on your memory card.

A WHITE BALANCE LIBRARY

Consider dedicating a low-capacity memory card to stow a selection of images taken under a variety of lighting conditions. If you want to "recycle" one of the color temperatures you've stored, insert the card and select it with the Use Photo option.

5. If you want to select a different image, you can choose which folder on your memory card, then navigate through the selected images, using the standard D3500 image selection screen shown several times previously in this chapter.

6. When the photo you'd like to use is highlighted, press OK to select it.

7. You'll be returned to the Shooting menu, where you can press the MENU button to exit, or just tap the shutter release.

Set Picture Control

Options: Various; Default: Standard

The pictures you take with your D3500 can be individually fine-tuned in an image editor, of course, but you can also choose certain kinds of adjustments that are made to every picture, as you shoot, using the camera's Picture Controls options. While there are only seven predefined styles offered: (Standard, Neutral, Vivid, Monochrome, Portrait, Landscape, and Flat), you can *edit* the settings of any of those styles (but not rename them) so they better suit your taste.

In Set Picture Controls, available only in P, S, A, and M modes, choose from one of the predefined styles and follow these steps:

1. Choose Set Picture Control from the Shooting menu. The screen shown in Figure 4.12 appears. Note that Picture Controls that have been modified from their standard settings have an asterisk next to their name.

2. Scroll down to the Picture Control you'd like to use.

3. Press OK to activate the highlighted style. (Although you can usually select a menu item by pressing the multi selector right button; in this case, that button activates editing instead.)

4. Press the MENU button or tap the shutter release to exit the menu system.

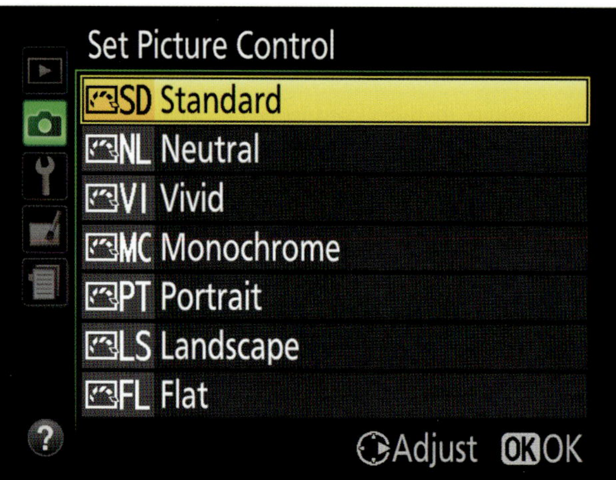

Figure 4.12
You can choose from seven predefined Picture Controls.

Editing a Picture Control Style

You can change the parameters of any of Nikon's predefined Picture Controls. You are given the choice of using the quick-adjust/fine-tune facility to modify a Picture Control with a few sliders, or to view the relationship of your Picture Controls on a grid. To make quick adjustments for Portrait, Landscape, Standard, or Vivid styles, follow these steps:

1. Choose Set Picture Control from the Photo Shooting menu.

2. Scroll down to the Picture Control you'd like to edit.

3. Press the multi selector right button to produce the adjustment screen shown in Figure 4.13.

4. Use the Quick Adjust slider to exaggerate the attributes of the Portrait, Landscape, Standard, or Vivid styles (quick adjustments are not available with other styles, including Neutral, Monochrome, or Flat).

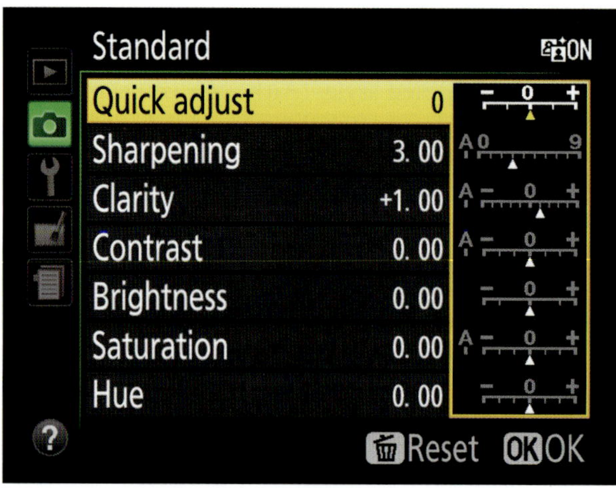

Figure 4.13
Sliders can be used to make quick adjustments to your Picture Control styles.

5. Scroll down to the Sharpening, Clarity, Contrast, Brightness, Saturation, and Hue sliders with the multi selector up/down buttons, then use the left/right buttons to decrease or increase the effects. A line will appear under the original setting in the slider whenever you've made a change from the defaults. Note: You can't adjust contrast and brightness when Active D-Lighting (discussed later in this chapter) is active. A helpful icon at upper right in the dialog box will alert you when ADL is enabled. Turn it off to make those Picture Control adjustments.

6. Instead of making changes with the slider's scale, you can move the cursor to the far left and choose A (for auto) when working with the Sharpening, Clarity, Contrast, and Saturation sliders. The D3500 will adjust these parameters automatically, depending on the type of scene it detects.

7. Press the Trash button to reset the values to their defaults.

8. Press OK when you're finished making adjustments.

CLARIFYING CLARITY

The Sharpening, Contrast, Brightness, Saturation, and Hue parameters are virtually self-explanatory, because you've probably worked with them many times in Photoshop or another image editor. The use for Clarity, however, may be unclear to you. Think of Clarity as a type of sharpening/enhancing effect applied to the mid tones of an image. High values produce contrasty and vivid images with darkened colors and improved detail in the midtones. Low values reduce midtone detail and flatten colors. The D3500 applies +1 Clarity by default to Standard, Vivid, Landscape, and Monochrome Picture Controls.

Editing the Monochrome style is similar, except that the parameters differ slightly. Sharpening and Contrast are available, but instead of Saturation and Hue, you can choose a filter effect (Yellow, Orange, Red, Green, or none) and choose a toning effect (black-and-white, plus seven levels of Sepia, Cyanotype, Red, Yellow, Green, Blue Green, Blue, Purple Blue, and Red Purple). (Keep in mind that once you've taken a JPEG photo using a Monochrome style, you can't convert the image back to full color. Shoot using RAW+JPEG, and you'll get a monochrome JPEG, plus the RAW file that retains all the color information.)

When you press the Zoom In button, the adjustment toggles between manual setting and automatic. Each of these provides varying amounts of five different attributes: sharpness, contrast, color mode, saturation, and hue. The individual parameters affect your images in various ways.

- **Sharpening.** This affects the contrast of the edges or outlines of your image, making a photo look more or less sharp.

- **Clarity.** Sharpening and enhancing of the midtones, as mentioned earlier.

FILTERS VS. TONING

Although some of the color choices seem to overlap, you'll get very different looks when choosing between Filter Effects and Toning. Filter Effects add no color to the monochrome image. Instead, they reproduce the look of black-and-white film that has been shot through a color filter. That is, Yellow will make the sky darker and the clouds will stand out more, while Orange makes the sky even darker and sunsets more full of detail. The Red filter produces the darkest sky of all and darkens green objects, such as leaves. Human skin may appear lighter than normal. The Green filter has the opposite effect on leaves, making them appear lighter in tone. Figure 4.14 shows the same scene shot with no filter, then Yellow, Green, and Red filters.

The Sepia, Blue, Green, and other toning effects, on the other hand, all add a color cast to your monochrome image. Use these when you want an old-time look or a special effect, without bothering to recolor your shots in an image editor. You can see toning effects in Figure 4.15.

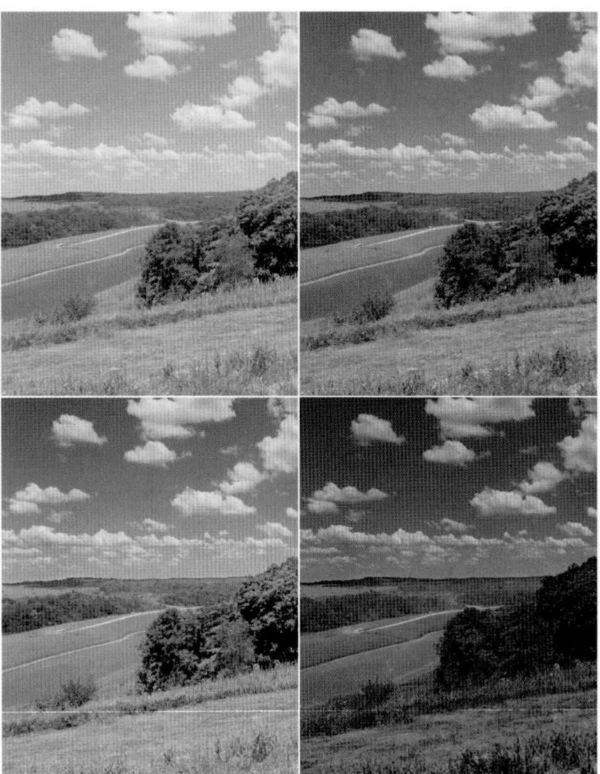

Figure 4.14 No filter (upper left); Yellow filter (upper right); Green filter (lower left); and Red filter (lower right).

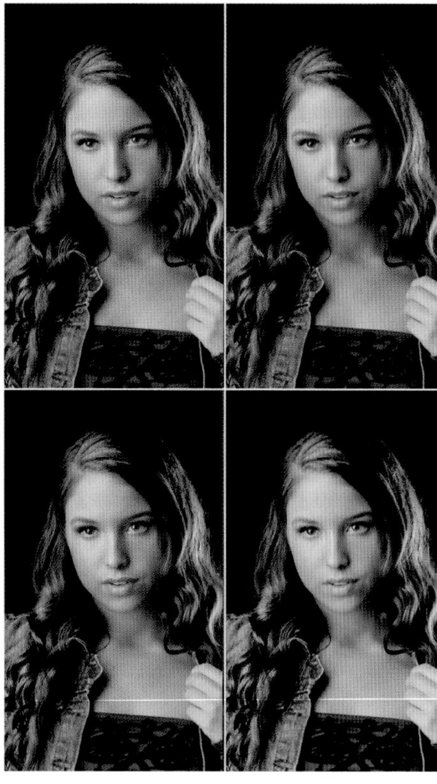

Figure 4.15 Sepia (upper left); Blue (upper right); Purple (lower left); and Green (lower right).

■ **Contrast.** This factor affects an attribute called *tone compensation*, which controls whether detail is visible or lost in the brightest areas and darkest areas of your image. An image with high contrast shows less detail in the highlights and shadows but produces a more dramatic appearance. A lower-contrast image has more detail in those areas, but, if contrast is too low, the image may appear to be flat and dull.

■ **Saturation.** The richness of the colors is determined by the saturation setting. For example, a deep red rose is fully saturated, while one that appears more pinkish is still, technically, red, but the color is less saturated and more muted.

■ **Hue.** Think of hue as rotating all the colors in an image around a color wheel. Positive hue adjustments bias reds toward the orange end of the spectrum, greens more toward the blue, and blues become purplish. Going the other way around the wheel, reds become more purple, blues more green, and greens become more yellow.

Color Space

Options: sRGB (default), Adobe RGB

The Nikon D3500's Color Space option gives you the choice of two different color spaces (also called *color gamuts*), named Adobe RGB (because it was developed by Adobe Systems in 1998), and sRGB (supposedly because it is the *standard* RGB color space). These two color gamuts define a specific set of colors that can be applied to the images your D3500 captures.

You're probably surprised that the Nikon D3500 doesn't automatically capture *all* the colors we see. Unfortunately, that's impossible because of the limitations of the sensor and the filters used to capture the fundamental red, green, and blue colors, as well as that of the phosphors used to display those colors on your camera and computer monitors. Nor is it possible to *print* every color our eyes detect, because the inks or pigments used don't absorb and reflect colors perfectly.

Instead, the colors that can be reproduced by a given device are represented as a color space that exists within the full range of colors we can see. That full range is represented by the odd-shaped splotch of color shown in Figure 4.16, as defined by scientists at an international organization back in 1931. The colors possible with Adobe RGB are represented by the larger, black triangle in the figure, while the sRGB gamut is represented by the smaller white triangle.

Regardless of which triangle—or color space—is used by the D3500, you end up with 16.8 million different colors that can be used in your photograph. (No one image will contain all 16.8 million!) But, as you can see from the figure, the colors available will be *different.*

Adobe RGB is what is often called an *expanded* color space, because it can reproduce a range of colors that is spread over a wider range of the visual spectrum. Adobe RGB is useful for commercial and professional printing. You don't need this range of colors if your images will be displayed primarily on your computer screen or output by your personal printer.

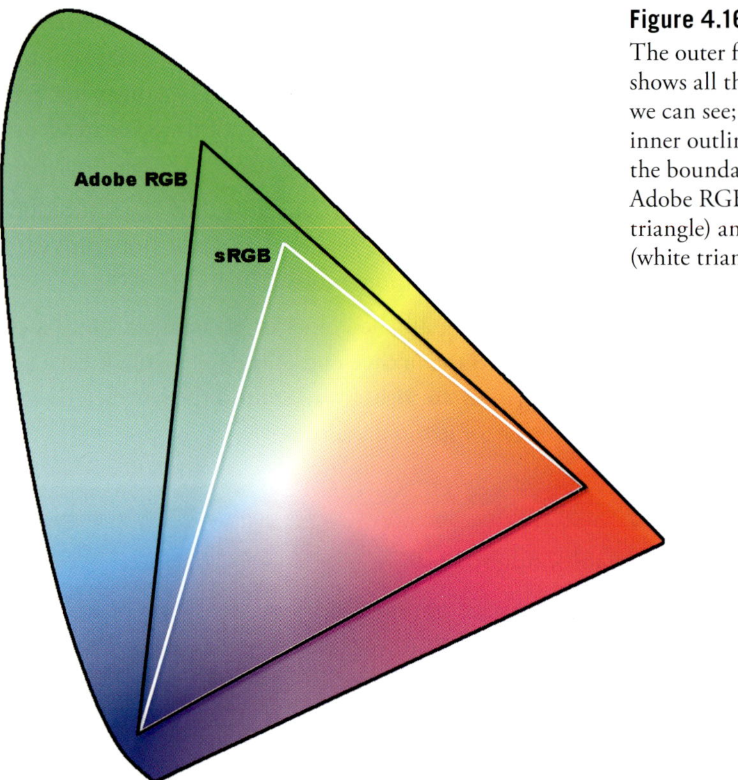

Figure 4.16
The outer figure shows all the colors we can see; the two inner outlines show the boundaries of Adobe RGB (black triangle) and sRGB (white triangle).

The other color space, sRGB, is recommended for images that will be output locally on the user's own printer, as this color space matches that of the typical inkjet printer fairly closely. While both Adobe RGB and sRGB can reproduce the exact same 16.8 million absolute colors, Adobe RGB spreads those colors over a larger portion of the visible spectrum, as you can see in the figure. Think of a box of crayons (the jumbo 16.8 million crayon variety). Some of the basic crayons from the original sRGB set have been removed and replaced with new hues not contained in the original box. Your "new" box contains colors that can't be reproduced by your computer monitor, but which work just fine with a commercial printing press.

Active D-Lighting

Options: On (default), Off

D-Lighting is a feature that improves the rendition of detail in highlights and shadows when you're photographing high-contrast scenes (those which have dramatic differences between the brightest areas and the darkest areas that hold detail). It's been available as an internal retouching option that could be used *after* the picture has been taken and has been found in Nikon's lower-end cameras (by that I mean the Coolpix point-and-shoot line) for some time, and has gradually worked its way up through the company's dSLR products. You'll find this post-shot feature in the Retouch menu.

A new wrinkle, however, is the *Active D-Lighting* capability introduced with Nikon's recent cameras, which, unlike the Retouch menu post-processing feature, applies its improvements *while you are actually taking the photo.* That's good news and bad news. It means that, if you're taking photos in a contrasty environment, Active D-Lighting can automatically improve the apparent dynamic range of your image as you shoot, without additional effort on your part. However, you'll need to disable the feature once you leave the high-contrast lighting behind, and the process does take some time to apply as you shoot. You wouldn't want to use Active D-Lighting for continuous shooting of sports subjects, for example. There are many situations in which the selective application of D-Lighting using the Retouch menu is a better choice.

For best results, use your D3500's Matrix metering mode, so the Active D-Lighting feature can work with a full range of exposure information from multiple points in the image. Active D-Lighting works its magic by subtly *underexposing* your image so that details in the highlights (which would normally be overexposed and become featureless white pixels) are not lost. At the same time, it adjusts the values of pixels located in midtone and shadow areas so they don't become too dark because of the underexposure. Highlight tones will be preserved, while shadows will eventually be allowed to go dark more readily. Bright beach or snow scenes, especially those with few shadows (think high noon, when the shadows are smaller) can benefit from using Active D-Lighting. Figure 4.17 shows a typical example.

You have just two choices: Off and On. You'll want to experiment to see which types of situations can benefit your shooting the most.

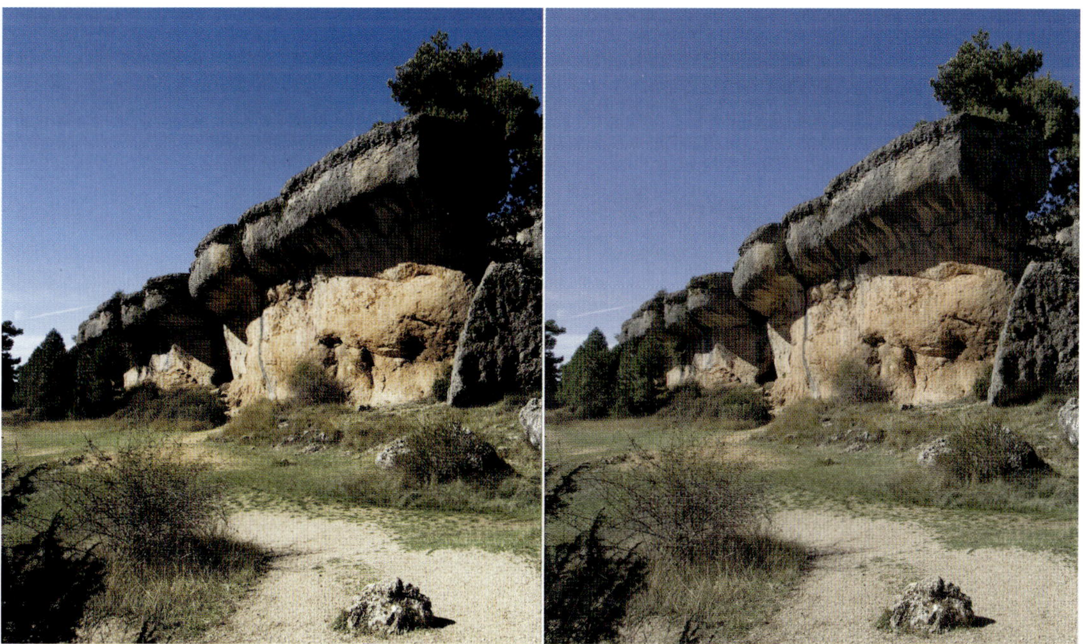

Figure 4.17 No D-Lighting (left); Active D-Lighting (right).

Noise Reduction

Options: On (default), Off

Visual noise is that awful graininess caused by long exposures and high ISO settings, and which shows up as multicolored specks in images. This setting, the first on the second page of the Shooting menu (see Figure 4.18), helps reduce noise, which is rarely desirable in a digital photograph. There are easier ways to add texture to your photos.

High ISO noise commonly appears when you raise your camera's sensitivity setting above ISO 800. This type of visual noise appears as a result of the amplification needed to increase the sensitivity of the sensor. While higher ISOs do pull details out of dark areas, they also amplify non-signal information randomly, creating noise.

A similar noisy phenomenon occurs during long time exposures, which allow more photons to reach the sensor, increasing your ability to capture a picture under low-light conditions. However, the longer exposures also increase the likelihood that some pixels will register random phantom photons, often because the longer an imager is "hot" the warmer it gets, and that heat can be mistaken for photons.

While high ISO settings are the usual culprit, some noise is created when you're using shutter speeds longer than eight seconds. Extended exposure times allow more photons to reach the sensor but increase the likelihood that some photosites will react randomly even though not struck by a particle of light. Moreover, as the sensor remains switched on for the longer exposure, it heats, and this heat can be mistakenly recorded as if it were a barrage of photons.

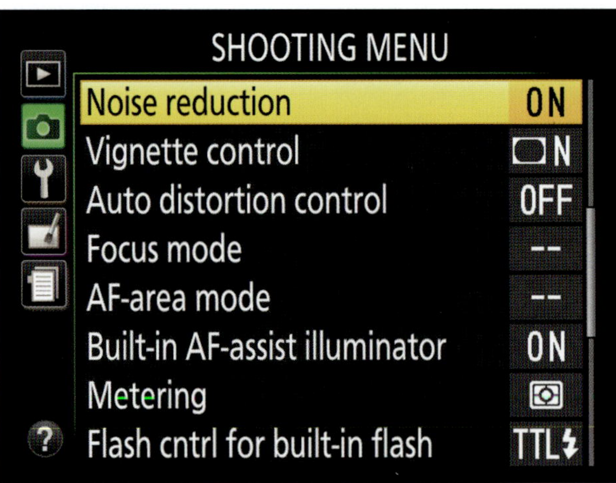

Figure 4.18
The second page of the Shooting menu.

While noise reduction does minimize the grainy effect, it can do so at the cost of some sharpness. This menu setting can be used to activate or deactivate the D3500's noise-canceling operation.

- **Off.** This setting disables the default level of noise reduction (the D3500 applies *some* noise reduction at all times, even when you select Off). Use it when you want the maximum amount of detail present in your photograph, even though higher noise levels will result. This setting also eliminates the delay caused by the more aggressive noise reduction process that occurs after the picture is taken (this delay is roughly the same amount of time that was required for the exposure). If you plan to use only lower ISO settings (thereby reducing the noise caused by high ISO values), the noise levels produced by longer exposures may be acceptable. For example, you might be shooting a waterfall at ISO 100 with the camera mounted on a tripod, using a neutral-density filter and a long exposure to cause the water to blur. (Try exposures of 2 to 16 seconds, depending on the intensity of the light and how much blur you want.) (See Figure 4.19.) To maximize detail in the non-moving portions of your photos for the exposures that are eight seconds or longer, you can switch off long exposure noise reduction.

- **On.** When exposures are eight seconds or longer, by default the Nikon D3500 takes a second, blank exposure to compare that to the first image. (While the second image is taken, the warning **Job nr** appears in the viewfinder.) Noise (pixels that are bright in a frame that *should* be completely black) in the "dark frame" image is subtracted from your original picture, and only the noise-corrected image is saved to your memory card. Because the noise-reduction process effectively doubles the time required to take a picture, you won't want to use this setting when you're rushed. Some noise can be removed later on, using tools in your image editor.

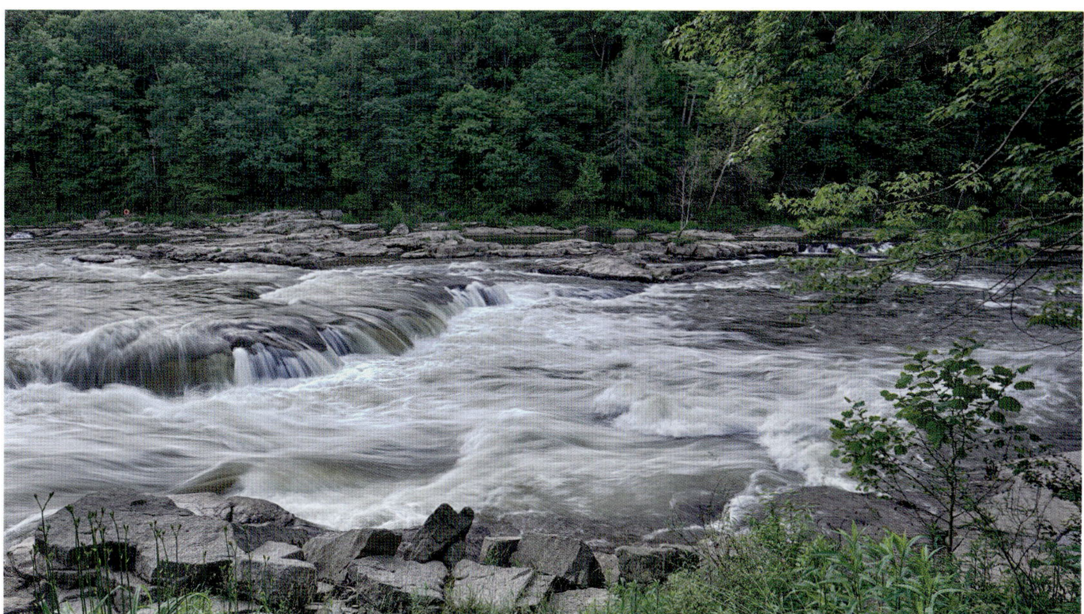

Figure 4.19 A long exposure with the camera mounted on a tripod produces this traditional waterfall photo.

Vignette Control

Options: High, Normal (default), Low, Off

Some lenses may not be up to the challenge of covering the frame evenly, producing darkening in the corners of your images at certain focal lengths. (See Figure 4.20.) You generally won't have this problem with full-frame (FX) lenses, which were designed to cover an area much larger than the D3500's DX format. Indeed, the otherwise superb original version of the Nikon 70-200 f/2.8 VR zoom exhibited vignetting on full-frame cameras but performed like a champ on DX models.

If you consistently encounter vignetting, this option may help. It reduces darkening at the periphery of images when using non-DX/non-perspective control lenses of the G and D type. (I will explain the nomenclature of Nikon's lens alphabet soup in Chapter 10.) You can choose from High, Normal, Low, and Off. It's difficult to quantify exactly how much corner-brightening each setting provides. Your best bet is to shoot some blank walls of a single color with lenses that seem to have this problem and try a few at each of the settings. Then select the value that best seems to counter vignetting with your particular lenses.

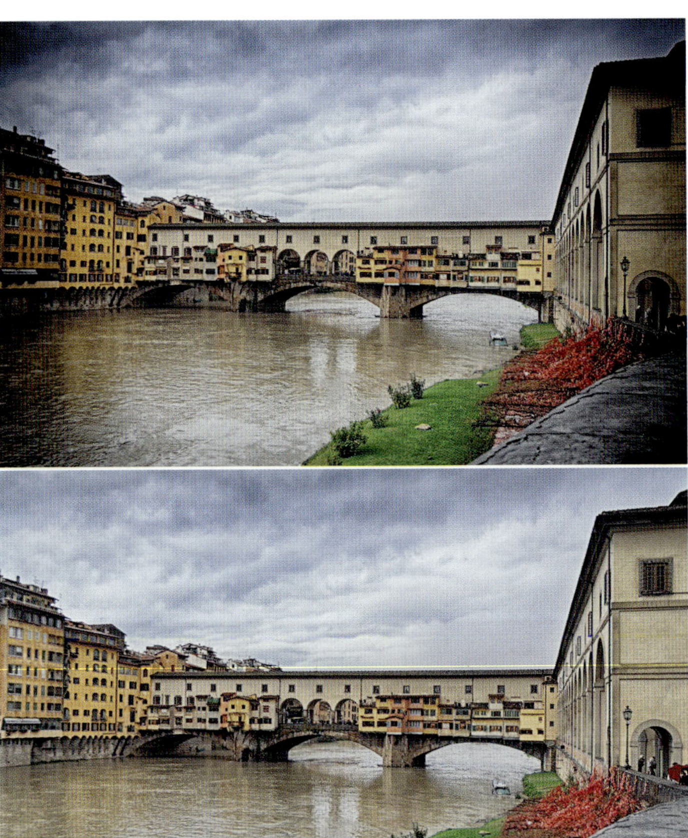

Figure 4.20
Darkened corners caused by vignetting (top); corrected (bottom).

Auto Distortion Control

Options: Off (default), On

Wide-angle lenses can produce a bowing-in effect, called *barrel distortion*, that's most noticeable at the edges of images. Telephoto lenses can produce the opposite effect, an inward-bending effect called *pincushion distortion.* If you notice this problem in your pictures, you can partially nullify the effects by using Auto Distortion Control. If you have no distortion problems, leave it off, because the less manipulation of your images in the camera, the better. I'll explain these distortions in more detail in Chapter 10.

Focus Mode

Options: Viewfinder, Live View/Movies

You can select a focus mode for the D3500 to use when working with P, S, A, or M exposure modes. You can choose modes separately for use when shooting using the optical viewfinder and when shooting stills or movies in live view. I'll explain how to choose a focus mode in Chapter 7.

- **Viewfinder.** Select from AF-A (Auto-servo AF), AF-S (Single-servo AF), AF-C (Continuous-servo AF), and Manual focus.
- **Live View/Movies.** Choose from AF-S (Single-servo AF), AF-C (Continuous-servo AF), and Manual focus.

AF-Area Mode

Options: Single-point AF, Dynamic-area AF, 3D-tracking (11 points), Auto-area (default)

This entry is a duplication of the autofocus area mode options in the information edit menu, as described in Chapter 1, but with the addition of options for choosing an autofocus zone when using live view, too. You'll find more about autofocus and focus modes in Chapter 7. When you select this entry, you'll be given a choice of Viewfinder and Live View/Movie modes.

To recap, the four choices when using the viewfinder to compose your images are as follows:

- **Single-point AF.** You always choose which of the eleven points are used, and the Nikon D3500 sticks with that focus bracket, no matter what. This mode is best for non-moving subjects.
- **Dynamic-area AF.** You can choose which of the eleven focus zones to use, but the D3500 will switch to another focus mode when using AF-C or AF-A mode and the subject moves. This mode is great for sports or active children.
- **3D-tracking (11 points).** You can select the focus zone, but when not using AF-S mode, the camera refocuses on the subject if you reframe the image.
- **Auto-area.** This default mode chooses the focus point for you and can use distance information when working with a lens that has a G or D suffix in its name. (See Chapter 10 for more on the difference between G/D lenses and other kinds of lenses.)

If you're using live view to shoot stills or are shooting movies, you can specify four different AF-area selection modes:

- **Face-priority AF.** The D3500 detects faces and automatically chooses those faces to focus on.
- **Wide-area AF.** When shooting non-portrait subjects, such as landscapes, you can select the focus zone using the multi selector.
- **Normal-area AF.** Most useful when the camera is mounted on a tripod, you can select any area on the live view frame to focus on.
- **Subject-tracking AF.** Autofocus will lock onto a subject and keep focus on that subject even if it moves throughout the frame.

I'll explain the mysteries of autofocus in detail in Chapter 7.

Built-In AF-Assist Illuminator

Options: On (default), Off

Use this setting to control the AF-assist lamp built into the Nikon D3500 when using the optical viewfinder.

- **On.** This default value will cause the AF-assist illuminator lamp to fire when lighting is poor, but only if Single-servo autofocus (AF-S) or Automatic autofocus (AF-A) are active, or you have selected the center focus point manually and either Single-point or Dynamic-area autofocus (rather than Auto-area autofocus) has been chosen. It does not operate in Manual focus modes, in AF-C mode, or when AF-A has switched to its AF-C behavior, nor when Landscape or Sports scene modes are used.

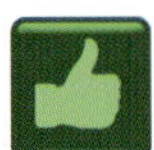

Tip

With some lenses, the lens hood can block the AF-assist lamp's illumination; you may have to remove the hood in low-light situations. Your hand may also block the lamp.

- **Off.** Use this to disable the AF-assist illuminator. You'd find that useful when the lamp might be distracting or discourteous (say, at a religious ceremony or acoustic music concert), or your subject is located closer than one foot, eight inches or farther than about 10 feet. One downside of turning AF-assist off is that the D3500 may be unable to focus accurately in situations where it really, really needs the extra light from the supplementary lamp. You may have to focus manually in such situations.

Metering

Options: Matrix metering (default), Center-weighted metering, Spot metering

This is a duplicate of the settings you can make from the information edit screen. I'll explain each of the Nikon D3500's three metering modes in more detail in Chapter 6. As I explained in Chapter 1, the three modes are as follows:

- **Matrix metering.** The standard metering mode; the D3500 attempts to intelligently classify your image and choose the best exposure based on readings from a 420-segment color CCD sensor that interprets light reaching the viewfinder using a database of hundreds of thousands of patterns.

- **Center-weighted metering.** The D3500 meters the entire scene but gives the most emphasis to the central area of the frame, measuring about 8mm in diameter.

- **Spot metering.** Exposure is calculated from a smaller 3.5 mm central spot, about 2.5 percent of the image area.

Flash Cntrl for Built-In Flash/Optional Flash

Options: TTL (default), Manual

This setting is used to adjust the features of the Nikon D3500's built-in pop-up electronic flash, or optional Nikon SB-300, SB-400, or SB-500 add-on flash units, or other Nikon-compatible flash, which fit in the accessory shoe on top of the camera. (The label of this setting changes to Optional Flash when a compatible external unit is mounted.) Its settings are in force when you are using Program, Shutter-priority, Aperture-priority, or Manual exposure modes (but not when using any of the Scene modes). You can read more about using the D3500's flash capabilities in Chapter 11.

You have two options with this setting:

- **TTL.** When selected, the built-in flash or external flash operate in iTTL (intelligent through the lens) exposure mode to automatically choose an exposure based on measuring the light from a "pre-flash" (fired an instant before the picture is taken) as it reflects back to the camera. Use this setting under most circumstances. As you'll learn in Chapter 11, the D3500 can even balance the flash output with the daylight or other illumination to allow the flash to fill in dark shadows or provide supplementary light.

- **Manual.** In this mode, the flash always fires using a preselected output level, which ranges from full power to 1/32 power. Use this mode when you want a certain exposure for every shot, say, to deliberately under- or overexpose an image for a special effect.

Optical VR

Options: On (default)/Off

This entry appears *only* if you have a Nikon lens with the AF-P designation mounted on your D3500. It allows you to switch the vibration reduction on or off. All Nikon non-AF-P lenses with VR have a built-in switch for adjusting the VR feature; AF-P lenses dispense with that control.

Movie Settings

Options: Frame Size/Frame Rate, Movie Quality, Microphone, Wind Noise Reduction

The Movie Settings entries are explained in more detail in Chapter 8. You have the following choices:

- **Frame Size/Frame Rate.** Choose your resolution. Use the Movie Settings entry in the Shooting menu. Or, when live view is activated, and before you start shooting your video clip, you can select the resolution/frame rate of your movie. All use *progressive scan,* in which all the lines are captured one after another in order. Your options are as follows:
  - 1,920 × 1,080 at 60/50 fps, progressive scan (60p/50p) (default)
  - 1,920 × 1,080 at 30/25 fps, progressive scan (30p/25p)
  - 1,920 × 1,080 at 24 fps, progressive scan (24p)
  - 1,280 × 720 at 60/50 fps, progressive scan (60p/50p)
- **Movie Quality.** Choose High quality (to capture up to 10 minutes of action at 60p, or 20 minutes at 30p and 24p) or the default Normal quality (for up to 20 minutes at 60p or 29 minutes, 59 seconds of video per clip at 30p and 24p).
- **Microphone.** Here, you can set audio sensitivity for the built-in microphone. Choose from Auto Sensitivity (the default), Manual Sensitivity, or Microphone Off. With the Manual Sensitivity setting, a set of volume unit (VU) meter bars appears on the menu screen showing the current sound levels. Press the right directional button to access a screen where you can select a manual sensitivity level from 1 to 20.
- **Wind Noise Reduction.** Gusts of wind can interfere with clear recording of your desired audio, so this options allows you to turn a built-in wind noise reduction feature on or off. In quiet surroundings you'll want to keep the default Off setting for overall better sound quality.
- **Manual Movie Settings.** Switch from Off (the default value) to On if you want to make manual adjustments to the shutter speed or ISO sensitivity when you are working in Manual exposure mode. You can then select shutter speeds as high as 1/4,000th second, and as slow as 1/30th second (for 24p, 25p, and 30p frame rates) or 1/50th/1/60th for 50p/60p frame rates. While you can adjust ISO in Manual exposure movie mode, Auto ISO cannot be used.

5

Setup, Retouch, and Recent Settings Menus

In this chapter, I'm going to introduce you to the final three tabs in the Nikon D3500 menu system: the Setup, Retouch, and Recent Settings menus. In the section on the Setup menu, you'll discover how to format a memory card, set the date/time and LCD monitor brightness, and do other maintenance and configuration tasks. You'll learn how to use the Retouch menu to remove red-eye and fix photos right in your camera. The Recent Settings menu displays a list of the last 20 menu items used—a sort of "favorites" display for quick access.

Setup Menu Options

The orange-coded Setup menu (see Figure 5.1 for its first page) has a long list of entries. In this menu you can make additional adjustments on how your camera *behaves* before or during your shooting session, as differentiated from the Shooting menu, which adjusts how the pictures are actually taken.

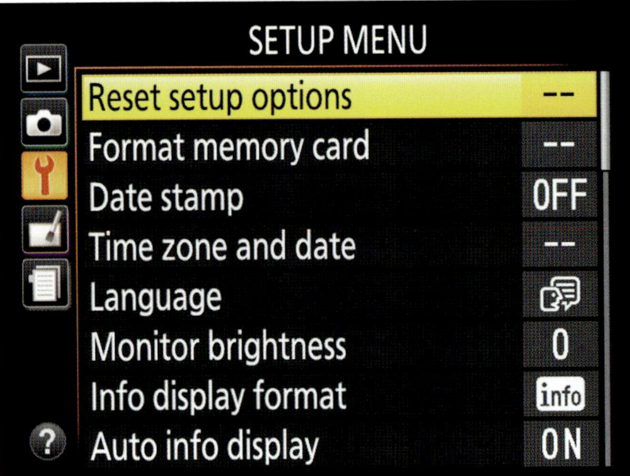

Figure 5.1
The first page of the Setup menu.

Your choices include:

- Reset Setup Options
- Format Memory Card
- Date Stamp
- Time Zone and Date
- Language
- Monitor Brightness
- Info Display Format
- Auto Info Display
- Auto Off Timers
- Self-Timer
- Lock Mirror Up for Cleaning

- Image Dust Off Ref Photo
- Image Comment
- Copyright Information
- Beep
- Flicker Reduction
- Buttons
- Rangefinder
- Manual Focus Ring in AF Mode
- File Number Sequence
- Storage Folder
- File Naming

- HDMI
- Location Data
- Airplane Mode
- Connect to Smart Device
- Send to Smart Device (Auto)
- Bluetooth
- Eye-Fi Upload
- Conformity Marking
- Slot Empty Release Lock
- Reset All Settings
- Firmware Version

Reset Setup Options

If you select Yes, the Setup menu settings shown in Table 5.1 will be set to their default values. It has no effect on the settings in other menus, or any of the other camera settings. Note that there is also a Reset option in the Shooting menu to return your shooting settings to their defaults.

You'd want to use this Reset option when you've made a bunch of changes (say, while playing around with them as you read this chapter), and now want to put them back to the factory defaults. Your choices are Yes and No. *Only settings that are changed with this menu option are listed in the table below.* Some don't have settings you can change, such as Format Memory Card, Conformity Marking, and Firmware Version. Others retain the settings you make and ignore this reset, including Time Zone and Date, Language, and Storage Folder.

Table 5.1 Values Reset

Setting	Default Value
Date Stamp	Off
Time Zone and Date	
Sync with Smart Device	Off
Daylight Savings Time	Off
Monitor Brightness	0
Info Display Format	Graphic; White background
Auto/Scene/Effects Modes	Graphic; White background
P/S/A/M Modes	Graphic; Black background
Auto Info Display	On
Auto Off Timers	Normal
Self-Timer	
Self-Timer Delay	10 sec.
Number of Shots	1 shot
Remote On Duration	1 min.
Beep	Low
Flicker Reduction	Auto
Buttons	
Assign Fn button	ISO sensitivity
Assign AE-L/AF-L button	AE/AF lock
Shutter-release button AE-L	Off
AF activation	Enable
Manual Focus Ring in AF Mode	Enable
File Number Sequence	Off
File Naming	DSC
HDMI	
Output resolution	Auto
Device control	On
Location data	
Download from smart device	No
Airplane Mode	Disable
Send to Smart Device (Auto)	Off
Bluetooth	
Network Connection	Disable
Send While Off	On
Eye-Fi Upload	Enable
Slot Empty Release Lock	Release locked

If you really want to change (almost) *all* Setup settings to their defaults, use Reset All Settings, described later in this chapter. It preserves only the Language, Time Zone and Date, and GUIDE mode options, and wipes out your Copyright Information, Image Comments, and other entries.

Format Memory Card

Options: Format card

I recommend using this menu entry to reformat your memory card after each shoot. While you can move files from the memory card to your computer, leaving behind a blank card, or delete files using the Playback menu's Delete feature, both of those options can leave behind stray files (such as those that have been marked as Protected). Format removes those files completely and beyond retrieval (unless you use a special utility program) and establishes a spanking-new fresh file system on the card, with all the file allocation table (FAT or exFAT) pointers (which tell the camera and your computer's operating system where all the images reside) efficiently pointing where they are supposed to on a blank card.

To format a memory card, choose this entry from the Setup menu, highlight Yes on the screen that appears, and press OK.

Date Stamp

Options: Off (default), Date, Date and Time, Date Counter

You can superimpose the date, time, or both on your photographs, or imprint a date counter that shows the number of days (or years and days, or months, years, and days) between when the picture was taken and a date (in the past or future) that you select. The good news is that this feature can be useful for certain types of photographs used for documentation. While the D3500's time/date stamp may not be admissible in a court of law, it makes a convincing (or convenient) in-picture indication of when the shot was made. This feature works only with JPEG images; you cannot use Date Imprint with pictures taken using the RAW or RAW+Fine settings.

The bad news, especially if you use the feature accidentally, is that the imprint is a permanent part of the photograph. You'll have to polish up your Photoshop skills if you want to remove it, or, at the very least, crop it out of the picture area. Date and time are set using the format you specify in the World Time setting of the Setup menu, described in the next section. Your options are as follows:

- **Off.** Deactivates the date/time imprint feature.
- **Date.** The date is overlaid on your image in the bottom-right corner of the frame, and appears in the shooting information display. If you've turned on Auto Image Rotation the date is overlaid at the bottom-right corner of vertically oriented frames.
- **Date and Time.** Both date and time are imprinted in the same positions.
- **Date Counter.** This option imprints the current date on the image, but also adds the number of days that have elapsed since a particular date in the past that you specify, *or* the days remaining until an upcoming date in the future.

Using the Date Counter

If you're willing to have information indelibly embedded in your images, the Date Counter can be a versatile feature. You can specify several parameters in advance (or at the time you apply the Date Counter) and activate the overprinting *only* when you want it.

- **Off.** Select this from the main Date Imprint screen. Choosing Off disables the imprinting of date, date/time, *and* the Date Counter. When disabled, no date or counter information is shown, regardless of how you have set the other parameters.

- **Choose date.** When you enter the Date Counter screen, one option lets you enter up to three different dates for your countdown/countup. When you activate the Date Counter, you can choose from the three dates (or a new date you enter to replace one of the three) and use that for your date counting imprint.

- **Display options.** Also in the Date Counter screen, you can select Display Options, which allows you to specify Number of Days, Years and Days, or Years, Months, and Days for the Date Counter readout imprinted on your images.

- **Done.** When you've finished entering date and display options, choose Done to return to the Setup menu. (You *must* do this. If you press the MENU button or tap the shutter release button at this point, your changes will not be confirmed.)

Here are some applications for the Date Counter:

- **Tracking a newborn.** Enter the child's birthday as one of your three dates. Select Number of Days as your display option for a newborn. Then, as often as you like, activate the Date Counter and take a picture or two. The number of days since the baby's birth will be displayed right on the picture. (Remember to turn the feature off when shooting other pictures of the child, or of other subjects!)

- **Document construction projects.** Enter the start date of the project, activate the Date Counter, and take pictures of the construction progress. Each photo will show exactly how many days have elapsed since ground was broken (or the cornerstone laid, or that non-bearing wall demolished to begin remodeling).

- **Long-term documentation.** Perhaps you'd like to record the appearance of your favorite nature spot at different times of the year. Choose the first day of spring as your start date, then shoot pictures at intervals for an entire year, activating the Date Counter as needed. The results will be interesting—and maybe a revelation. With the Years, Months, and Days selected as a display option, you can continue your documentation for years!

- **Countdown.** Something big scheduled for a particular day? Choose that date in the future as your counter, and any photo you take with imprinting activated will show the days remaining until the big day.

Time Zone and Date

Options: Time Zone, Date and Time, Sync with Smart Device, Date Format, Daylight Saving Time

Use this menu entry to adjust the D3500's internal clock. Your options include:

- **Time zone.** A small map will pop up on the setting screen and you can choose your local time zone. I sometimes forget to change the time zone when I travel (especially when going to Europe), so my pictures are all time-stamped incorrectly. I like to use the time stamp to recall exactly when a photo was taken, so keeping this setting correct is important.

- **Date and Time.** Use this setting to enter the exact year, month, day, hour, minute, and second, using a 24-hour clock.

- **Sync with Smart Device.** Allows the camera clock to be updated using information from your smart device when it is linked to the D3500.

- **Date format.** Choose from Year/month/day (Y/M/D), Month/day/year (M/D/Y), or Day/month/year (D/M/Y) formats.

- **Daylight saving time.** Use this to turn daylight saving time On or Off. Because the date on which DST takes effect has been changed from time to time, if you turn this feature on you may need to monitor your camera to make sure DST has been implemented correctly.

Language

Options: List of languages

Choose the language for menu display. Note that Nikon has pared down the list of languages available, depending on where the D3500 is sold. Here in the USA, the *only* choices are English, Spanish, French, and Portuguese. I suspect these might be the default offerings in *all* of North and South America. If you live elsewhere, Nikon has previously supplied language choices that include Arabic, Traditional Chinese, Simplified Chinese, Czech, Danish, Dutch, English, Finnish, French, German, Greek, Hindi, Hungarian, Indonesian, Italian, Japanese, Korean, Norwegian, Polish, Portuguese, Romanian, Russian, Spanish, Swedish, Thai, Turkish, and Ukrainian.

Monitor Brightness

Options: 0 (default); Values from +5 to −5

Choose this menu option to adjust the intensity of the display using the LCD Brightness option. A grayscale strip appears on the LCD monitor, as shown in Figure 5.2. Use the multi selector up/down keys to adjust the brightness to a comfortable viewing level over a range of +5 to −5. Under the lighting conditions that exist when you make this adjustment, you should be able to see all 10 swatches from black to white. If the two end swatches blend together, the brightness has been set too low. If the two whitest swatches on the right end of the strip blend together, the brightness is too high. Brighter settings use more battery power, but can allow you to view an image on the LCD

Figure 5.2
Adjust the LCD brightness so that all the grayscale strips are visible.

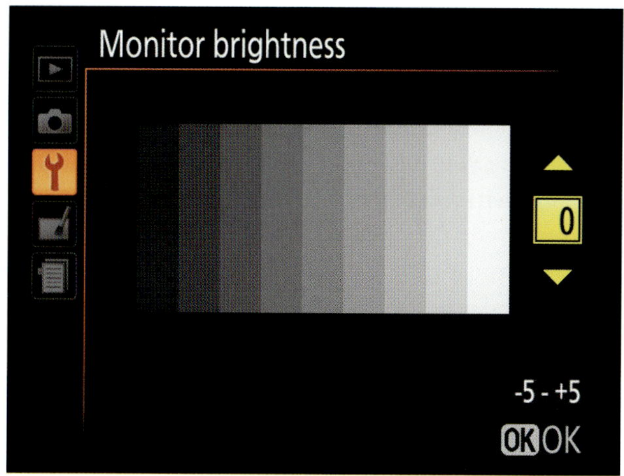

outdoors in bright sunlight. When you have the brightness you want, press OK to lock it in and return to the menu.

Info Display Format

Options: Classic, Graphic (default); Separate display formats for Auto/Scene/Effects modes and P/S/A/M modes

You can choose the format the Nikon D3500 uses for its shooting information screen. Two formats are available. You can choose one format for Auto, Scene, and Effects modes, and a different one for P/S/A/M modes, or have both the same.

- **Classic.** This is a mostly text-based format with a few icons. You'll find this format the fastest to use once you've grown accustomed to the D3500 and its features, as all the information is clustered in a no-nonsense way that is easy to read.

- **Graphic.** This format mixes text and graphics, and includes a facsimile of the mode dial that appears briefly on the left side of the screen as you change from one exposure mode to the other. It's prettier to look at and adds a little flair to the display, because you can choose black, white, or orange backgrounds, but I find it distracting.

You can change the shooting information display to the format of your choice using three easy-to-understand screens:

1. Choose Info Display format from the Setup menu.

2. Choose either Auto/Scene/Effects or P/S/A/M and press the multi selector right button.

3. Navigate to the Classic or Graphic combination of your choice, in Black, White, or Blue background colors. Then press OK.

4. You'll be returned to the first screen you saw, where you can again choose Auto/Scene/Effects or P/S/A/M or press the MENU button (or tap the shutter release) to exit.

Auto Info Display

Options: On (default), Off

This setting controls when the shooting information display is shown on the LCD monitor. The display is a handy tool for checking your settings as you shoot. It does use up battery power, so you might want to turn off the automatic display if you don't need to review your settings frequently, or if you especially want to conserve battery power. The shooting information display can be viewed any time by pressing the Info button at the lower-left side of the back of the D3500. You can choose whether to display Auto/Scene modes or P, S, A, and M modes individually. Here's how this option works for both types of modes:

- **On.** The D3500 will display the shooting information screen if the shutter release button is pressed halfway and released. As always, the information display goes away when you press the shutter release halfway and hold it. If you've set Image Review to Off in the Playback menu, the shooting information screen also appears as soon as the photograph is taken. If Image Review is set to On, the shooting information screen appears only when the shutter release is pressed halfway and released, or if the Info button is pressed, but not immediately after the picture is taken. (Instead, the picture you just took is shown.)
- **Off.** The shooting information screen is not displayed when you press the shutter release button halfway and release it. You can activate the display by pressing the Info button.

Auto Off Timers

Options: Short, Normal (default), Long, Custom

This is the first entry on the second page of the Setup menu. (See Figure 5.3.) Use this setting to determine how long the D3500's LCD monitor and viewfinder displays are shown, and how long exposure meters continue to function after the last operation, such as autofocusing, focus point selection, and so forth, was performed. You can choose a short timer to save power, or a longer value

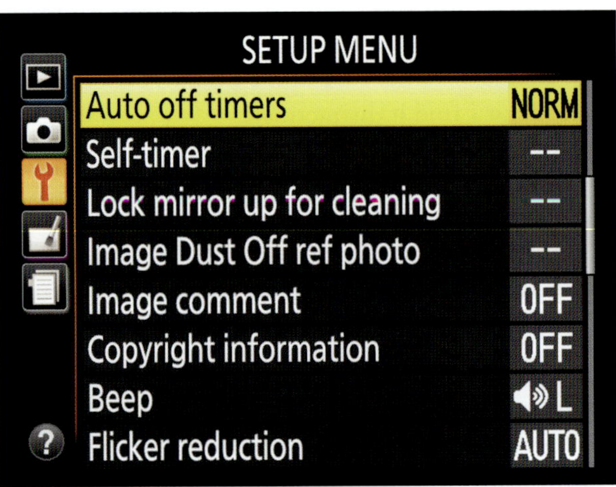

Figure 5.3

The second page of the Setup menu.

to keep the camera "alive" for a longer period of time. When the Nikon EH5a/EH-5b AC adapter is connected to the D3500, the exposure meters will remain on indefinitely, and when the D3500 is connected to a computer or PictBridge-compatible printer, the LCD and viewfinder displays do not turn off automatically.

Sports shooters and some others prefer longer delays, because they are able to keep their camera always "at the ready" with no delay to interfere with taking an action shot that unexpectedly presents itself. Extra battery consumption is just part of the price paid. For example, when I am shooting football, a meter-off delay of 16 seconds is plenty, because the players lining up for the snap is my signal to get ready to shoot. But for basketball or soccer, I typically set a longer limit, because action is virtually continuous.

Of course, if the meters have shut off, and if the power switch remains in the On position, you can bring the camera back to life by tapping the shutter button. You can select generic times such as Short, Norm, and Long as the auto-off delay, or specify custom times for playback/menus, image review, and exposure meters.

SAVING POWER WITH THE NIKON D3500

There are several settings techniques you can use to stretch the longevity of your D3500's battery. To get the most from each charge, consider these steps:

- **Image Review.** Turn off automatic image review after each shot. You can still review your images by pressing the Playback button. Or, leave image review on, but set the display for the minimum 4 seconds with this Auto Off Timers custom command.

- **Auto meter-off-delay.** Set to 4 seconds using Auto Off Timers if you can tolerate such a brief active time.

- **Reduce LCD brightness.** In the Setup menu's LCD Brightness option, select the lowest of the seven brightness settings that work for you under most conditions. If you're willing to shade the LCD with your hand, you can often get away with lower brightness settings outdoors, which will further increase the useful life of your battery.

- **Turn off the shooting information display.** You can always turn it on manually by pressing the Info button.

- **Reduce internal flash use.** No flash at all or fill flash use less power than a full blast.

- **Cancel VR.** Turn off vibration reduction if your lens (such as the 18-55mm VR kit lens) has that feature and you feel you don't need it. Remember that you must use the menu entry to disable VR on AF-P lenses that have it; other VR lenses include an On/Off switch.

- **Use a card reader.** When transferring pictures from your D3500 to your computer, use a card reader instead of the USB cable. Linking your camera to your computer and transferring images using the cable takes longer and uses a lot more power.

Your delay options are as follows:

- **Short.** LCD Monitor Playback/Menus: 20 seconds; LCD Review: 4 seconds; Live View: 5 minutes; Standby Timer: 4 seconds.
- **Norm.** LCD Monitor Playback/Menus: 1 minute; LCD Review: 4 seconds; Live View: 10 minutes; Standby Timer: 8 seconds.
- **Long.** LCD Monitor Playback/Menus: 5 minutes; LCD Review: 20 seconds; Live View: 20 minutes; Standby Timer: 60 seconds.
- **Custom: Playback/Menus.** Choose 8, 12, 20, 60 seconds, or 10 minutes.
- **Custom: Image Review.** Choose 4, 8, 20, 60 seconds, or 10 minutes.
- **Custom: Live View.** Choose 30 seconds, 1, 3, or 5 minutes.
- **Custom: Standby timer.** Choose 4, 8, 20, 60 seconds, or 30 minutes.

Self-Timer

Options: Self-timer delay (default: 10 seconds), Number of shots (default: 1)

This setting lets you choose the length of the self-timer shutter release delay. The default value is 10 seconds. You can also choose 2, 5, and 20 seconds, as well as multiple shots (2 to 9) at the end of the elapsed time. If I have the camera mounted on a tripod or other support, I can set a two-second delay that is sufficient to let the camera stop vibrating after I've pressed the shutter release. Remember that you can't adjust the delay or number of shots using the Release Mode button; you must make those adjustments here.

Lock Mirror Up for Cleaning

Options: None

Because the D3500 does not have automatic sensor cleaning, from time to time you'll need to clean the sensor manually. Use this menu entry to raise the mirror and open the shutter so you'll have access to the sensor for cleaning with a blower, brush, or swab. You don't want power to fail while you're poking around inside the camera, so this option is available only when sufficient battery power (at least 60 percent) is available. Using a fully charged battery or connecting the D3500 to an EP-5a/EH5b AC adapter is an even better idea.

Image Dust Off Ref Photo

Options: Start; Clean Sensor, Then Start

This menu choice lets you "take a picture" of any dust or other particles that may be adhering to your sensor. The D3500 will then append information about the location of this dust to your photos, so that the Image Dust Off option in Capture NX can be used to mask the dust in the NEF image.

To use this feature, select Dust Off Ref Photo, choose either Start or Clean Sensor, Then Start, and then press OK. If directed to do so, the camera will first perform a self-cleaning operation by applying ultrasonic vibration to the low-pass filter that resides on top of the sensor. Then, a screen will appear asking you to take a photo of a bright featureless white object 10 cm (about four inches) from the lens. Nikon recommends using a lens with a focal length of at least 50mm. Point the D3500 at a solid white card and press the shutter release. An image with the extension .ndf will be created, and can be used by Nikon Capture NX-i as a reference photo if the "dust off" picture is placed in the same folder as an image to be processed for dust removal. This setting is not available if battery power is low.

Image Comment

Options: Attach Comment, Input Comment

The Image Comment is your opportunity to add personal information about yourself (including contact info), or even a description of where the image was taken (e.g., Seville Photos 2012), although text entry with the Nikon D3500 is a bit too clumsy for doing a lot of individual annotation of your photos. (But you still might want to change the comment each time, say, you change cities during your travels.) The embedded comments can be read by many software programs, including Nikon ViewNX-i or Capture NX-D.

You can enter text using the same procedure described next for entering copyright information.

Copyright Information

Options: Attach Copyright Information, Artist, Copyright

This is an expansion of the Image Comment capability, allowing you to specify the name of the "artist" (photographer), and enter copyright information. Use the standard Nikon text entry screen described next. Highlight the Attach Copyright Information option and press the right multi selector button to mark/unmark it to control whether your copyright data is embedded in each photo as taken.

The standard text entry screen can be used to enter your comment, with up to 36 characters available. For the copyright symbol, most just embed a lowercase "c" within opening and closing parentheses: (c). (Technically, you must use Copr. instead, as I did for Figure 5.4.) You can enter text by choosing Input Comment, turning attachment of the comment On or Off using the Attach Comment entry, and selecting Done when you're finished working with comments. If you find typing with a cursor too tedious, you can enter your comment in Nikon Capture NX-D and upload it to the camera though a USB cable.

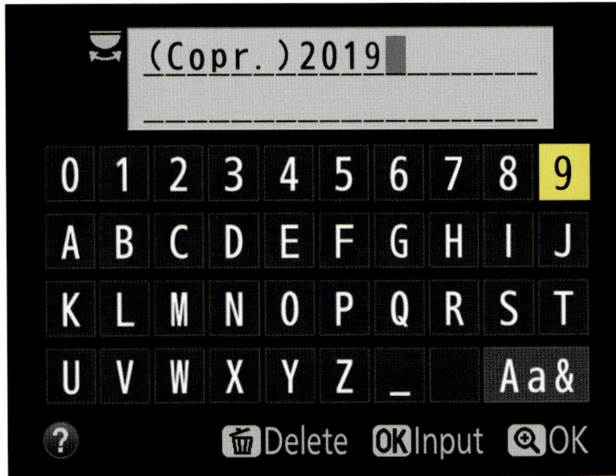

Figure 5.4

Enter a comment on this screen.

Now is a good time to review text entry, because you can use it to enter comments, rename folders, and perform other functions.

1. Press MENU and select the Setup menu.

2. Scroll to Image Comment with the multi selector up/down buttons and press the multi selector right button.

3. Scroll down to Input Comment and press the multi selector right button to confirm your choice.

4. Use the multi selector navigational buttons to scroll around within the array of alphanumerics, as shown in Figure 5.4. There is a full array of uppercase, lowercase, and symbol characters. They can't be viewed all at once, so you may need to scroll up or down to locate the one you want. Then, enter your text:

   - Press the OK button to insert the highlighted character. The cursor will move one place to the right to accept the next character.

   - Rotate the command dial button to move the cursor within the line of characters that have been input.

   - To remove a character you've already input, move the cursor with the command dial to highlight that character, and then press the Trash button.

   - When you're finished entering text, press the Zoom In button to confirm your entry and return to the Image Comment screen.

5. In the Image Comment screen, scroll down to Attach Comment and press the multi selector right button to activate the comment, or to disable it.

6. When finished, press OK to confirm and exit.

Beep

Options: High, Low (default), Off

The Nikon D3500's internal beeper provides a (usually) superfluous chirp to signify various functions, such as the countdown of your camera's self-timer or autofocus confirmation in AF-S mode or AF-A mode with a static subject. You can (and probably should) switch it off if you want to avoid the beep because it's annoying, impolite, or distracting (at a concert or museum), or undesired for any other reason. It's one of the few ways to make the D3500 a bit quieter. (I've actually had new dSLR owners ask me how to turn off the "shutter sound" the camera makes; such an option was available in the point-and-shoot camera they'd used previously.) Your choices are High, Low, and Off. When the beeper is active, a musical note icon is shown in the shooting information display.

Flicker Reduction

Options: Auto (default), 50Hz, 60Hz

This option reduces flicker and banding, which can occur when shooting in Live View mode and Movie mode under fluorescent and mercury vapor illumination, because the cycling of these light sources interacts with the frame rate of the camera's video system. In the United States, you'd choose the 60Hz frequency; in locations where 50Hz current is the norm, select that option instead.

Buttons

Options: Assign AE-L/AF-L Button, Shutter Release Button AE-L, AF Activation

This is the first entry on the third page of the Setup menu (See Figure 5.5). Here, you can define the action that the AE-L/AF-L, and shutter release button perform when pressed alone, and whether AF activation occurs when the shutter release button is pressed halfway. Each of the buttons has its own set of actions that you can define for use in P/S/A/M modes.

Figure 5.5
The third page of
the Setup menu.

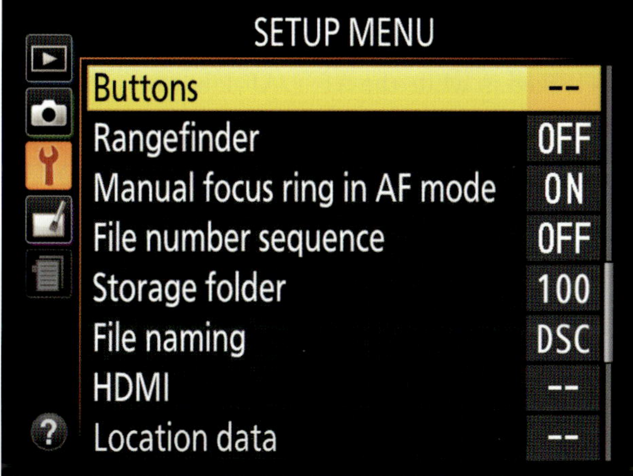

AE-L/AF-L Button

When the Nikon D3500 is set to its default values, a half-press of the shutter release locks in the current autofocus setting in AF-S mode, or in AF-A mode if your subject is not moving. (The camera will refocus if the subject moves and the D3500 is set for AF-C or AF-A mode.) That half-press also activates the exposure meter, but, ordinarily, the exposure changes as the lighting conditions in the frame change.

However, sometimes you want to lock in focus and/or exposure, and then reframe your photo. For that, and for other focus/exposure locking options, Nikon gives you the AE-L/AF-L button (located on the back of the camera to the right of the viewfinder window), and a variety of behavior combinations for it. This setting allows you to define whether the Nikon D3500 locks exposure, focus, or both when the button is pressed, so the AE-L/AF-L button can be used for these functions in addition to, or instead of, a half-press of the shutter release. It can also be set so that autofocus starts *only* when the button is pressed; in that case, a half-press of the shutter release initiates autoexposure, but the AE-L/AF-L button *must* be pressed to start the autofocusing process. These options can be a little confusing, so I'll offer some clarification:

- **AE/AF lock.** Lock both focus and exposure while the AE-L/AF-L button is pressed and held down, even if the shutter release button has not been pressed. This is the default value, and is useful when you want to activate and lock in exposure and focus independently of the shutter release button. Perhaps your main subject is off-center; place that subject in the middle of the frame, lock in exposure and focus, and then reframe the picture while holding the AE-L/AF-L button.

- **AE lock only.** Lock only the exposure while the AE-L/AF-L button is pressed. The exposure is fixed when you press and hold the button, but autofocus continues to operate (say, when you press the shutter release halfway) using the AF-A, AF-S, or AF-C mode you've chosen.

- **AE lock (Hold).** Exposure is locked when the AE-L/AF-L button is pressed, and remains locked until the button is pressed again, or the exposure meter-off delay expires. Use this option when you want to lock exposure at some point, but don't want to keep your thumb on the AE-L/AF-L button.

- **AF lock only.** Focus is locked in while the AE-L/AF-L button is held down, but exposure will continue to vary as you compose the photo and press the shutter release button.

- **AF-ON.** The AE-L/AF-L button is used to initiate autofocus. This setting is useful when you want to frame your photo, press the shutter release halfway to lock in exposure, but don't want the D3500 to autofocus until you tell it to. I use this for sports photography when I am waiting for some action to move into the frame before starting autofocus. For example, I might press the AE-L/AF-L button just before a racehorse crosses the finish line. This technique is called *back button focus,* and is described in Chapter 7.

Shutter Release Button AE-L

When you choose On, exposure will lock when the shutter release is pressed halfway. Select Off, and you must lock exposure using the AE-L/AF-L button (when it is defined to lock exposure, as described above).

AF Activation

Select Enable (On) and the D3500 will focus when the shutter release is pressed halfway. Choose Disable (Off) instead, and the shutter release button doesn't activate autofocus. The Off option is required for the back button focus procedure mentioned above. While the technique is not excessively complex, it needs the full step-by-step description provided in Chapter 7.

Rangefinder

Options: Off (default), On

The rangefinder is a clever feature that supplements the green focus confirmation indicator at the left edge of the viewfinder by transforming the analog exposure indicator as an "in-focus/out-of-focus" scale to show that correct focus has been achieved when focusing manually.

Some lenses don't offer autofocus features with the Nikon D3500, because they lack the internal autofocus motor the D3500 requires. (They are able to autofocus on other Nikon cameras, except for the D3xxx-series, D5xxx-series, D60, and D40/D40x, because those other cameras include an autofocus motor in the body.) Many manual focus lenses that never had autofocus features can also be used with the D3500 in manual focus mode. You'll find more information about this limitation in Chapter 10, but all you need to know is that Nikon lenses with the AF-S or AF-P designation in the lens name *will* autofocus on the D3500, while those with the AF, AI, or AI-S designation will not. Specifications for lenses from other vendors will indicate whether the lens includes an autofocus motor or not.

When a non-autofocus lens is mounted on the Nikon D3500, and the camera has been set for any exposure mode except for Manual (M)—that is, any of the Scene or Effects modes, plus Program, Aperture-priority, or Shutter-priority—manual focus mode is automatically activated. You can manually focus by turning the focus ring on the lens (set the lens to manual focus if it is an AF-type lens) and watching the sharpness of the image on the focusing screen. The focus confirmation indicator at the lower-left corner of the viewfinder will illuminate when correct focus is achieved, if your lens has a maximum aperture of f/5.6 or larger (that is, a larger number, such as f/4.5, f/4, and so forth).

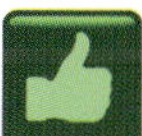

> **Tip**
>
> Note that this feature is not available when shooting in Manual *exposure* mode, nor when using live view. The D3500 shows whether exposure is under, over, or correct, instead. Use the focus confirmation lamp to monitor manual focus in this mode.

The readout in the viewfinder is not analog (that is, continuous). Only the six indicators shown in Figure 5.6 are displayed. Two centered rectangles indicate that correct focus has been achieved; when all 12 are shown, it means that correct focus cannot be indicated. Three and six rectangles show that slight or major focus corrections are needed, respectively.

Turn the Rangefinder On with this setting option if you want an additional manual focusing aid. With a manual focus lens and the Rangefinder operating, the analog exposure display at bottom right in the viewfinder will be replaced by a rangefinder focusing scale. Indicators on the scale like those in Figure 5.6 show when the image is in sharp focus, as well as when you have focused somewhat in front of, or behind the subject.

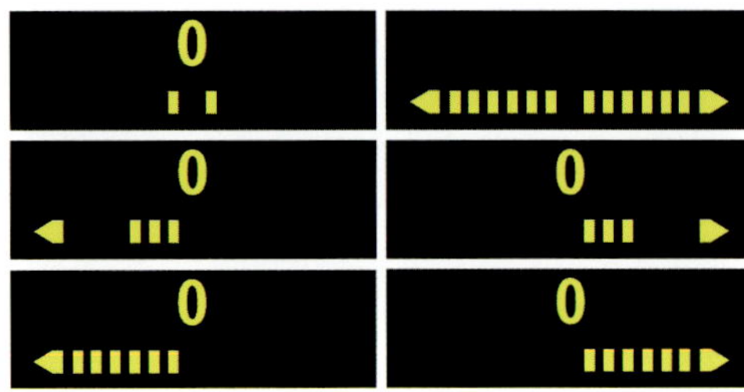

Figure 5.6 Upper left: Correct focus; upper right: focus is grossly incorrect; center left: focus slightly in front of the subject; center right: focus slightly behind the subject; bottom left: focus significantly in front of the subject; bottom right: focus significantly behind the subject.

Follow these steps to use the Rangefinder:

1. Press the multi selector buttons to choose a focus point that coincides with the subject you'd like to be in focus.

2. Rotate the focusing ring, watching the rangefinder scale at the bottom of the viewfinder. If the current sharp focus plane is *in front* of the point of desired focus, the rangefinder scale will point toward the left side of the viewfinder. The greater the difference, the more bars (either three or six bars) shown in the rangefinder.

3. When the current focus plane is *behind* the desired point of focus, the rangefinder indicator will point to the right.

4. When the subject you've selected with the focus zone bracket is in sharp focus, only two bars will appear, centered under the 0, and the focus confirmation indicator will stop blinking.

Manual Focus Ring in AF Mode

Options: Enable, Disable (default)

This entry is not illustrated in the figure. It is displayed *only* when you have mounted a lens on the D3500 that supports the feature. It allows you to fine-tune focus with compatible lenses when the D3500 is set to autofocus mode. With many lenses, the focus ring cannot be rotated when in an AF mode; you must switch to manual focus to gain control over focus. If you try to turn the focus ring without taking this step, you can damage the gearing. There are four different lens configurations available from Nikon that allow you to use manual focus to fine-tune while AF is active:

- **Lenses with an A-M switch.** With these lenses, you must exit autofocus and set the lens switch to the M position to safely tine-tune your lenses.

- **Lenses with an A/M-M switch.** These lenses will automatically disengage the AF motor while you're rotating the focus ring, so you can safely fine-tune. There may be a small time lag before the motor disengages.

- **Lenses with an M/A-M switch.** These lenses smoothly disengage the motor as soon as you begin rotating the focus ring. This feature is more commonly found on professional lenses that benefit from increased responsiveness.

- **Lenses without an AF/MF switch of any kind.** Nikon does not provide a definitive list of these lenses, so I am making an assumption here, because the only lenses in my collection that allow using the Manual Focus Ring in AF Mode entry are AF-P optics that lack the switch. All three of the kit lenses (18-55mm and both 70-300mm lenses) do activate the entry. When enabled, the focus ring does move freely in AF mode.

When this choice is enabled, you can autofocus by pressing the shutter release button halfway, and then, with the button still depressed, fine-tune the focus with the lens's focus ring. Release the shutter button and press it down halfway to refocus/fine-tune again.

File Number Sequence

Options: On, Reset, Off (default)

The Nikon D3500 will automatically apply a file number to each picture you take, using consecutive numbering for all your photos over a long period of time, spanning many different memory cards, starting over from scratch when you insert a new card, or when you manually reset the numbers. Numbers are applied from 0001 to 9999, at which time the D3500 "rolls over" to 0001 again.

The camera keeps track of the last number used in its internal memory and, if File Number Sequence is turned On, will apply a number that's one higher, or a number that's one higher than the largest number in the current folder on the memory card inserted in the camera. You can also start over each time a new folder has been created on the memory card, or reset the current counter back to 0001 at any time. Here's how it works:

- **On.** When you insert a new memory card in the camera, format an existing card, or create a new folder yourself, the D3500 saves the next photo you take, and applies a number one higher than the last picture taken, or one number higher than the highest file number in the current folder (whichever is larger). Numbering proceeds up to 9999, at which point a new folder is created and numbering starts over at 0001.

- **Off.** At this default setting, if you're using a blank/reformatted memory card, or a new folder is created, the next photo taken will be numbered 0001. File number sequences will be reset every time you use or format a card, or a new folder is created. A reset will occur automatically and a new folder created when an existing folder on your memory card contains 999 shots.

■ **Reset.** If the current folder is empty, file numbering starts over at 0001. If the folder does contain images, the next photo you save will be numbered one higher than the highest file number in the current folder. I generally use the On setting, but this Reset option can come in handy if you shoot a *lot* of images. Your D3500 can actually lock up if you happen to have a folder numbered 999 that contains 999 photos *or* one numbered 9999. To resolve the dilemma, select this menu entry, choose Reset, and then replace the current memory card with a fresh one.

This event is not as rare as you might think. Your camera allows you to create a folder numbered 999 (you don't have to wait for that number to turn up on its own), and then all you have to do is store 999 pictures in that folder to trigger the lockup. With larger memory cards and continuous shooting, photo number 999 can be captured in a single shooting session.

HOW MANY SHOTS, REALLY?

The file numbers produced by the D3500 don't provide information about the actual number of times the camera's shutter has been tripped—called actuations. For that data, you'll need a third-party software solution, such as the free Opanda iExif (www.opanda.com) for Windows or the non-free ($39.95) GraphicConverter for Macintosh (www.lemkesoft.com). These utilities can be used to extract the true number of actuations from the Exif information embedded in a JPEG file.

Storage Folder

Options: Select Folder by Number, Select From List

This entry is useful if you want to store images in a folder other than the one created and selected by the Nikon D3500; you can switch among available folders on your memory card, or create your own folder. Remember that any folders you create will be deleted when you reformat your memory card.

The Nikon D3500 automatically creates a folder on a newly formatted memory card with a name like 100D3500, and when it fills with 999 images, it will automatically create a new folder with a number incremented by one (such as 101D3500). The "D3500" portion of the folder name is always created by the camera; you can override the camera-assigned folder number and specify your own number for the last three characters, from 100 to 999. When traveling, I often use "dates" such as 902 for September 2, and so forth for folder. From October to December, I just cycle back to 1, 2, and 3—the goal is to separate each day's shots; the folder numbers are deleted on the memory card when I reformat after the images have been copied to my computer. Be sure to be aware of the Folder 999 numbering quandary I described above. To change the currently active folder:

1. Choose Storage Folder in the Setup menu.

2. Scroll down to Select Folder From List and press the multi selector right button.

3. From among the available folders shown, scroll to the one that you want to become active for image storage and playback. (Handy when displaying slide shows.)

4. Press the OK button to confirm your choice, or press the multi selector right button to return to the Setup menu.

Or you can create your own folders. Perhaps you're traveling and have a high-capacity memory card and want to store the images for each day (or for each city that you visit) in a separate folder. Maybe you'd like to separate those wedding photos you snapped at the ceremony from those taken at the reception. To create your own folder, or to rename an existing folder:

1. Choose Storage Folder in the Setup menu.

2. Scroll down to Select Folder by Number and press the multi selector right button.

3. Use the left/right buttons to choose which of the three digits to change, and the up/down buttons to increment/decrement the numbers.

4. Press OK when finished to confirm your choice and exit.

File Naming

Option: Choose three-letter prefix. Default: DSC

The D3500, like other cameras in the Nikon product line, automatically applies a name like _DSC0001.jpg or DSC_0001.nef to your image files as they are created. You can use this menu option to change the names applied to your photos, but only within certain strict limitations. In practice, you can change only three of the eight characters, the *DSC* portion of the file name. The other five are mandated either by the Design Rule for Camera File System (DCF) specification that all digital camera makers adhere to or to industry conventions.

DCF limits file names created by conforming digital cameras to a maximum of eight characters, plus a three-character extension (such as .jpg, .nef, or .wav in the case of audio files) that represents the format of the file. The eight-plus-three (usually called 8.3) length limitation dates back to an evil and frustrating computer operating system that we older photographers would like to forget (its initials are D.O.S.), but which, unhappily, lives on as the wraith of a file naming convention.

Of the eight available characters, four are used to represent, in a general sense, the type of camera used to create the image. By convention, one of those characters is an underline, placed in the first position (as in _DSCxxxx.xxx) when the image uses the Adobe RGB color space and in the fourth position (as in DSC_xxxx.xxx) for sRGB and RAW (NEF) files. That leaves just three characters for the manufacturer (and you) to use. Nikon, Sony, and some other vendors use DSC (which may or may not stand for Digital Still Camera, depending on who you ask), while Canon prefers IMG. The remaining four characters are used for numbers from 0000 to 9999, which is why your D3500 "rolls over" to DSC_0000 again when the 9999 number limitation is reached.

When you select File Naming, you'll be shown the current settings for both sRGB (and RAW) and Adobe RGB. Press the right multi selector button, and you'll be taken to the (mostly) standard Nikon text entry screen and allowed to change the DSC value to something else. In this version of the text entry screen, however, only the numbers from 0 to 9 and characters A to Z are available; the file name cannot contain other characters. As always, press the OK button to confirm your new setting.

Because the default DSC characters don't tell you much, don't hesitate to change them to something else. I use 350 for my D3500 and ND5 for my Nikon D5. If you don't need to differentiate between different camera models, you can change the three characters to anything else that suits your purposes, including your initials (DDB_ or JFK_, for example), or even customize for particular shooting sessions (EUR_, GER_, FRA_, and IND_ when taking vacation trips). You can also use the file name flexibility to partially overcome the 9999 numbering limitation. You could, for example, use the template 501_ to represent the first 10,000 pictures you take with your D3500, and then 502_ for the next 10,000, and 503_ for the 10,000 after that.

That's assuming that you don't rename your image files in your computer. In a way, file naming verges on a moot consideration, because they apply *only* to the images as they exist in your camera. After (or during) transfer to your computer, you can change the names to anything you want, completely disregarding the 8.3 limitations (although it's a good idea to retain the default extensions). If you shot an image file named DSC_4832.jpg in your camera, you could change it to Paris_EiffelTower_32.jpg later on. Indeed, virtually all photo transfer programs allow you to specify a template and rename your photos as they are moved or copied to your computer from your camera or memory card.

I usually don't go to that bother (I generally don't use transfer software; I just drag and drop images from my memory card to folders I have set up), but renaming can be useful for those willing to take the time to do it.

HDMI

Options: Output Resolution; Device Control, On, Off

This setting is used to control the HDMI format used to play back camera images and movies on a High-Definition Television (HDTV) using a special cable not supplied by Nikon. Note that this setting controls *only* the output from your D3500 to the device. It has no effect on the resolution of your images or your movie clips. Your choices:

- **Output resolution.** You can choose Auto, in which case the camera selects the right format, or, to suit your particular HDTV, one of four progressive scan options: 480p—640 × 480 pixels; 576p—720 × 576 pixels; 720p—1280 × 720 pixels, and 1080p—1920 × 1080 pixels; plus one interlaced scan option, 1080i—1920 × 1080 pixels.

■ **Device control.** You can select On or Off. This option applies when the D3500 is connected to a television that supports HDMI-CEC remote control operations. When you select On, if both the camera and HDTV are powered up, you will see a Play/Slideshow menu on the TV screen, and you can use the TV remote control as if it were the multi selector directional buttons and OK button during picture review and slide shows. An indicator reading CEC will appear in the camera viewfinder in place of the exposures remaining indicator. Select Off, and the television remote control is disabled.

Location Data

Options: Download From Smart Device, Position

This menu entry has options for using the Nikon D3500 when linked to a smart device that has GPS capabilities, and is available only when that device has not been set up for the camera.

■ **Download From Smart Device.** Enables/disables embedding GPS information obtained from your device in the D3500's image files. See Chapter 9 for information about using this option.

■ **Position.** This is an information display, rather than a selectable option. You can view the location information added to your images from the smart device's GPS data. Data in movie files is reported at the start of the recording.

Airplane Mode

Options: Enable, Disable (default)

Like the Airplane mode on your smartphone or tablet, this option turns off the D3500's Wi-Fi and Bluetooth capabilities. I enable the feature any time I am not planning to use Eye-Fi cards or SnapBridge, because it saves a lot of power. This is the first entry in the fourth page of the Setup menu. (See Figure 5.7.)

Figure 5.7
The fourth page of the Setup menu.

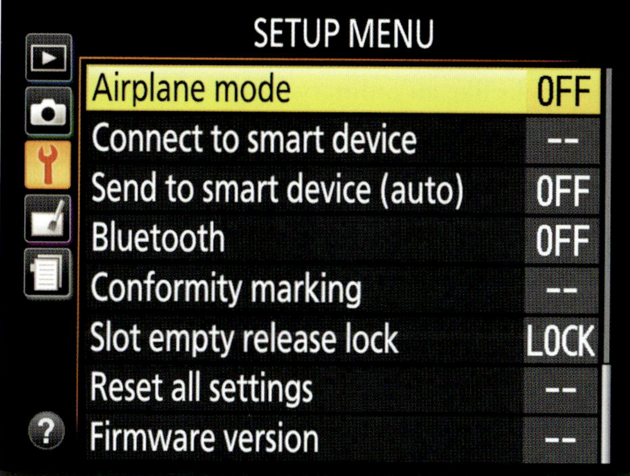

Connect to Smart Device

Options: Adjust the settings for connecting to smart devices

The D3500 has built-in Wi-Fi communications without the need of an add-on device. Use this entry to set up your SnapBridge connection to your smartphone or tablet. Your D3500's other connectivity options will be covered in detail in Chapter 9, and the instructions for setting up your smart device won't be repeated here.

Send to Smart Device (Auto)

Options: On, Off (default)

You can instruct your D3500 to automatically upload new still photos (but not movies) to your smart device when the camera and device are linked. If they are not connected, the D3500 will mark a maximum of 1,000 photos and upload them the next time a wireless connection is made. See Chapter 9 for detailed information on using this feature.

Bluetooth

Options: Network Connection: Enable/Disable; Paired Devices: View Paired Devices; Send While Off: On, Off

Use this entry to enable or disable Bluetooth connections with your smart device, or to see what devices you have paired. The option you'll use most frequently, however, is Send While Off. When turned on, wireless communication will continue even if the camera is powered down or the standby timer expires. As you might guess, that can consume a lot of power, especially if you have a lot of images queued up for transmission. It's safer to leave the automatic upload disabled.

Eye-Fi Upload

Options: Enable, Disable

This option is displayed in the menu *only* when a compatible Eye-Fi memory card is being used in the D3500. The Eye-Fi card looks like an ordinary SDHC memory card, but has built-in Wi-Fi capabilities, so it can be used to transmit your photos as they are taken directly to a computer over a Wi-Fi network, or, unlike the D3500's built-in Wi-Fi feature, upload directly to Facebook and other online sites. When an Eye-Fi card is inserted, and you've enabled the card by choosing Enable in this menu entry, one of four informational icons representing current connection and upload status will appear in its shooting information screen. If you are using an Eye-Fi card, you must set both Airplane Mode and Bluetooth > Network Connection to Disable. Because Eye-Fi has recently discontinued support for its older (but still commonly used) cards, and the D3500 has its own Wi-Fi capabilities, I no longer recommend using these cards. Set this menu option to Disable, and you can continue to use your Eye-Fi cards as ordinary memory cards, but without drawing unnecessary power.

Conformity Marking

Options: Display only—no selections

This entry does nothing but display the various international standards with which the D3500 complies. It's included here because Nikon can easily update the listing during a firmware upgrade. The alternative might be to print new labels (like the one on the base of the D3500) each time a change is made.

Slot Empty Release Lock

Options: Release Locked (default), Enable Release

This entry gives you the ability to snap off "pictures" without a memory card installed—or, alternatively, to lock the camera shutter release if no card is present. It is sometimes informally called Play mode, because you can experiment with your camera's features or even hand your D3500 to a friend to let them fool around, without any danger of pictures actually being taken.

Back in our film days, we'd sometimes finish a roll, rewind the film back into its cassette surreptitiously, and then hand the camera to a child to take a few pictures—without actually wasting any film. It's hard to waste digital film, but "shoot without card" mode is still appreciated by some, especially camera vendors who want to be able to demo a camera at a store or trade show, but don't want to have to equip each and every demonstrator model with a memory card. Choose Enable Release to activate "play" mode or Release Locked to disable it. The pictures you actually "take" are displayed on the LCD with the legend "Demo" superimposed on the screen, and they are, of course, not saved.

Reset All Settings

Options: Reset, Do Not Reset

Resets all settings, including Copyright Information, and other user-generated settings, except Language and Time Zone and Date.

Firmware Version

Options: Reset, Do Not Reset (default)

You can see the current firmware release in use in this menu listing. You can learn how to update firmware in Chapter 12.

Retouch Menu Options

The Retouch menu has eight entries on its first screen (see Figure 5.8). This menu allows you to create a new copy of an existing image with trimmed or retouched characteristics. You can apply D-Lighting, remove red-eye, create a monochrome image, apply filter effects, rebalance color, overlay one image on another, and compare two images side-by-side. Just select a picture during playback mode, as described below, or you can also go directly to this Retouch menu, select a retouching feature, and then choose a picture from the standard D3500 picture selection screen shown earlier.

The Retouch menu is most useful when you want to create a modified copy of an image on the spot, for immediate printing or e-mailing without first importing into your computer for more extensive editing. You can also use it to create a JPEG version of an image in the camera when you are shooting RAW-only photos.

While you can retouch images that have already been processed by the Retouch menu, you can apply up to 10 different effects, in total, but only once per effect (except for Image Overlay). You may notice some quality loss with repeated applications. For the Retouch menu entries, I'm going to list the options in the description only.

To create a retouched copy of an image:

1. While browsing among images in playback mode, press the *i* button when an image you want to retouch is displayed on the screen. A menu will pop up allowing you to choose from Rating, Retouch, or Select to Send to Smart Device. Choose Retouch.

2. From the Retouch menu, select the option you want and press the multi selector right button. The Nikon D3500's standard image selection screen appears. Scroll among the images as usual with the left/right multi selector buttons, press the Zoom In button to examine a highlighted image more closely, and press OK to choose that image.

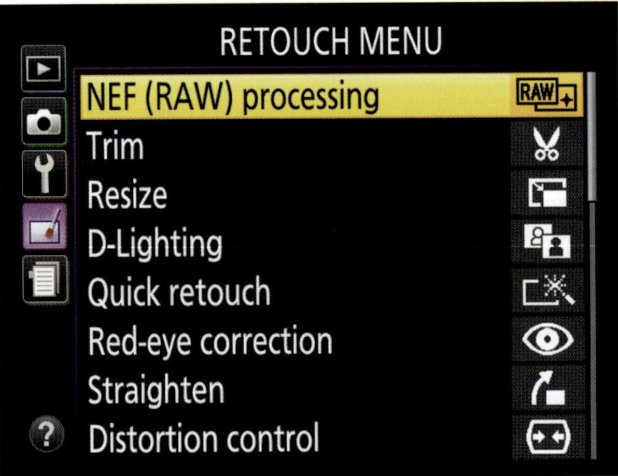

Figure 5.8
The Retouch menu allows simple in-camera editing.

3. Work with the options available from that particular Retouch menu feature and press OK to create the modified copy, or Playback to cancel your changes.

4. The retouched image will bear a file name that reveals its origin. For example, if you make a Small Picture version of an image named DSC_0112.jpg, the reduced-size copy will be named SSC_0113.jpg. Copies incorporating other retouching features would be named CSC_0113.jpg instead.

Here are the Retouch menu options:

- NEF (RAW) Processing
- Trim
- Resize
- D-Lighting
- Quick Retouch
- Red-Eye Correction
- Straighten
- Distortion Control
- Perspective Control
- Fisheye
- Filter Effects
- Monochrome
- Image Overlay
- Color Outline
- Photo Illustration
- Color Sketch
- Miniature Effect
- Selective Color
- Painting
- Edit Movie
- Side-by-Side Comparison

NEF (RAW) Processing

Use this tool to create a JPEG version of any image saved in either straight RAW (with no JPEG version) or RAW+Fine (with a Fine JPEG version). You can select from among several parameters to "process" your new JPEG copy right in the camera.

1. Choose a RAW image. Select NEF (RAW) Processing from the Retouch menu. You'll be shown the standard Nikon D3500 image selection screen. Use the left/right buttons to navigate among the RAW images displayed. Press OK to select the highlighted image.

2. In the NEF (RAW) processing screen, shown in Figure 5.9, you can use the multi selector up/down keys to select from five different attributes of the RAW image information to apply to your JPEG copy. Choose Image Quality (Fine, Normal, or Basic), Image Size (Large, Medium, or Small), White Balance, Exposure Compensation, Set Picture Control, High ISO Noise Reduction, Color Space, Vignette Control, and D-Lighting parameters.

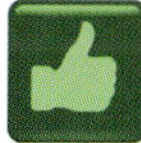

Tip

The White Balance and Vignette parameters cannot be selected for images created with the Image Overlay tool. Exposure compensation cannot be adjusted for images taken using Active D-Lighting, and both white balance and optimize image settings cannot be applied to pictures taken using any of the Scene modes.

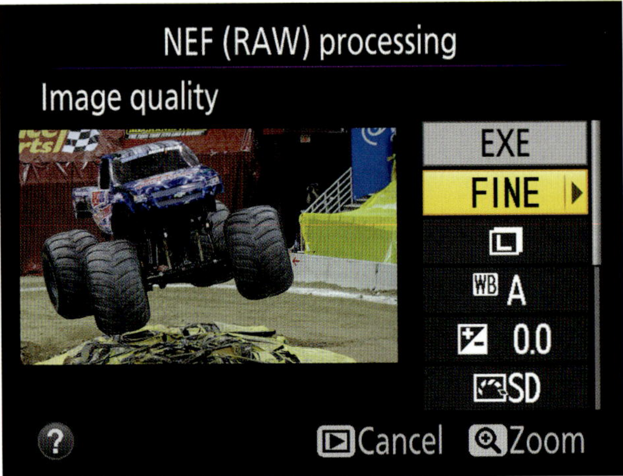

Figure 5.9
Adjust parameters and then save your JPEG copy from a RAW original file.

3. Press the Zoom In button to magnify the image temporarily while the button is held down.

4. Press the Playback button if you change your mind, to exit from the processing screen.

5. When all parameters are set, highlight EXE (for Execute) and press OK. The D3500 will create a JPEG file with the settings you've specified, and show an Image Saved message on the LCD when finished.

Trim

This option creates copies in specific sizes based on the final size you select, chosen from among 3:2, 4:3, and 5:4 aspect ratios (proportions). You can use this feature to create smaller versions of a picture for e-mailing without the need to first transfer the image to your own computer. If you're traveling, create your smaller copy here, insert the memory card in a card reader at an Internet café, your library's public computers, or some other computer, and e-mail the reduced-size version. Just follow these steps:

1. **Select your photo.** Choose Trim from the Retouch menu. You'll be shown the standard Nikon D3500 image selection screen. Scroll among the photos using the multi selector left/right buttons, and press OK when the image you want to trim is highlighted. While selecting, you can temporarily enlarge the highlighted image by pressing the Zoom In button.

2. **Choose your aspect ratio.** Rotate the command dial to change from 3:2, 4:3, 5:4, 1:1, and 16:9 aspect ratios. These proportions happen to correspond to the proportions of common print sizes, plus HDTV, including the two most popular sizes: 4 × 6 inches (3:2) and 8 × 10 inches (5:4). (See Table 5.2.)

3. **Crop in on your photo.** Press the Zoom In button to crop your picture. The pixel dimensions of the cropped image at the selected proportions will be displayed in the upper-left corner (see Figure 5.10) as you zoom. The current framed size is outlined in yellow within an inset image in the lower-right corner.

4. **Move cropped area within the image.** Use the multi selector left/right and up/down buttons to relocate the yellow cropping border within the frame.

5. **Save the cropped image.** Press OK to save a copy of the image using the current crop and size, or press the Playback button to exit without creating a copy. Copies created from JPEG Fine, Normal, or Standard have the same Image Quality setting as the original; copies made from RAW files or any RAW+JPEG setting will use JPEG Fine compression.

Table 5.2 Trim Sizes

Aspect Ratio	Sizes Available
3:2	5760 × 3840; 5120 × 3416; 4480 × 2984; 3840 × 2560; 3200 × 2128; 2560 × 1704; 1920 × 1280; 1280 × 856; 960 × 640; 640 × 424
4:3	5328 × 4000; 5120 × 3840; 4480 × 3360; 3840 × 2880; 3200 × 2400; 2560 × 1920; 1920 × 1440; 1280 × 960; 960 × 720; 640 × 480
5:4	5008 × 4000; 4800 × 3840; 4208 × 3360; 3600 × 2880; 2992 × 2400; 2400 × 1920; 1808 × 1440; 1200 × 960; 896 × 720; 608 × 480
1:1	3840 × 3840; 3360 × 3360; 2880 × 2880; 2400 × 2400; 1920 × 1920; 1440 × 1440; 960 × 960; 720 × 720; 480 × 480
16:9	6016 × 3384; 5760 × 3240; 5120 × 2880; 4480 × 2520; 3840 × 2160; 3200 × 1800; 2560 × 1440; 1920 × 1080; 1280 × 720; 960 × 536; 640 × 360

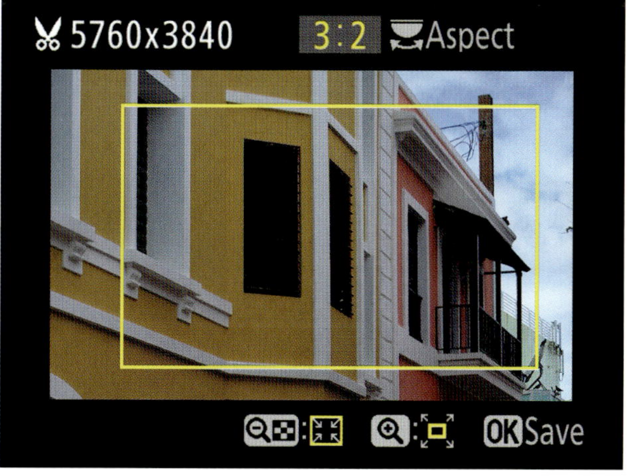

Figure 5.10
The Trim feature of the Retouch menu allows in-camera cropping.

Resize

This option creates smaller copies of the selected images. It can be applied while viewing a single image in full-frame mode (just press the *i* button as described above), or accessed from the Retouch menu (especially useful if you'd like to select and resize multiple images).

1. **Select images.** If accessing from the Retouch menu, you can choose to select multiple images, or jump directly to the following two steps.
2. **Choose Size.** Next, select the size for the finished copy, from 2.5M (1920 × 1280 pixels), 1.1M (1280 × 856 pixels), 0.6M (960 × 640 pixels), 0.3M (640 × 424 pixels), or 0.1M (320 × 216 pixels).
3. **Confirm.** Press OK to create your copy.

D-Lighting

This option brightens the shadows of pictures that have already been taken, similarly to the Active D-Lighting feature described in Chapter 4. It is a useful tool for backlit photographs or any image with deep shadows with important detail. Once you've selected your photo for modification, you'll be shown side-by-side images with the unaltered version on the left, and your adjusted version on the right. Press the multi selector's up/down buttons to choose from High, Normal, or Low corrections. Press the Zoom In button to magnify the image. When you're happy with the corrected image on the right, compared to the original on the left, press OK to save the copy to your memory card.

Quick Retouch

This option brightens the shadows of pictures that have already been taken. Once you've selected your photo for processing, use the multi selector up/down keys in the screen that pops up (see Figure 5.11). The amount of correction that you select (High, Normal, or Low) will be applied to

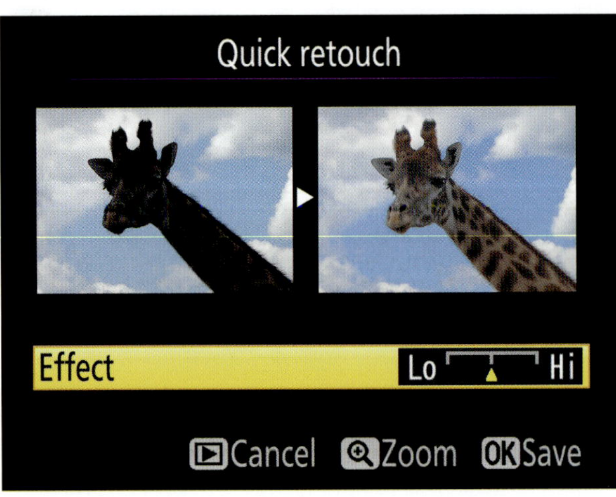

Figure 5.11
Quick Retouch applies D-Lighting, enhanced contrast, and added saturation to an image.

the version of the image shown at right. The left-hand version of the image shows the uncorrected version. While working on your image, you can press the Zoom In button to temporarily magnify the original photo.

Quick Retouch brightens shadows, enhances contrast, and adds color richness (saturation) to the image. Press OK to create a copy on your memory card with the retouching applied.

Red-Eye Correction

This Retouch menu tool can be used to remove the residual red-eye look that remains after applying the Nikon D3500's other remedies, such as the red-eye reduction lamp. (You can use the red-eye tools found in most image editors, as well.)

Your Nikon D3500 has a moderately useful red-eye reduction flash mode. Unfortunately, your camera is unable, on its own, to totally *eliminate* the red-eye effects that occur when an electronic flash (or, rarely, illumination from other sources) bounces off the retinas of the eye and into the camera lens. Animals seem to suffer from yellow or green glowing pupils, instead; the effect is equally undesirable. The effect is worst under low-light conditions (exactly when you might be using a flash) as the pupils expand to allow more light to reach the retinas. The best you can hope for is to *reduce* or minimize the red-eye effect.

The best way to truly eliminate red-eye is to raise the flash up off the camera so its illumination approaches the eye from an angle that won't reflect directly back to the retina and into the lens. The extra height of the built-in flash may not be sufficient, however. That alone is a good reason for using an external flash. If you're working with your D3500's built-in flash, your only recourse may be to switch on the red-eye reduction flash mode. That causes a lamp on the front of the camera to illuminate with a half-press of the shutter release button, which may result in your subjects' pupils contracting, decreasing the amount of the red-eye effect. (You may have to ask your subject to look at the lamp to gain maximum effect.)

If your image still displays red-eye effects, you can use the Retouch menu to make a copy with red-eye reduced further. First, select a picture that was taken with flash (non-flash pictures won't be available for selection). After you've selected the picture to process, press OK. The image will be displayed on the LCD monitor. You can magnify the image with the Zoom In button, scroll around the zoomed image with the multi selector buttons, and zoom out with the Zoom Out button. While zoomed, you can cancel the zoom by pressing the OK button. When you are finished examining the image, press OK again. The D3500 will look for red-eye, and, if detected, create a copy that has been processed to reduce the effect. If no red-eye is found, a copy is not created.

Straighten

Use this to create a corrected copy of a crooked image, rotated by up to five degrees, in increments of one-quarter of a degree. Use the right directional button to rotate clockwise, and the left directional button to rotate counterclockwise. Press OK to make a corrected copy, or the Playback button to exit without saving a copy.

Distortion Control

This option produces a copy with reduced barrel distortion (a bowing out effect) or pincushion distortion (an inward-bending effect), both most noticeable at the edges of a photo. You can select Auto to let the D3500 make this correction, or use Manual to make the fix yourself visually. Use the right directional button to reduce barrel distortion and the left directional button to reduce pincushion distortion. In both cases, some of the edges of the photo will be cropped out of your image. Press OK to make a corrected copy, or the Playback button to exit without saving a copy. Note that Auto cannot be used with images exposed using the Auto Distortion Control feature described earlier in this chapter. Auto works only with type G and type D lenses (see Chapter 10 for a description of what these lenses are), and does not work well with certain lenses, such as fisheye lenses and perspective control lenses.

Perspective Control

This option is the first on the second page of the Retouch menu (see Figure 5.12). It lets you adjust the perspective of an image, reducing the falling back effect produced when the camera is tilted to take in the top of a tall subject, such as a building. Use the multi selector buttons to "tilt" the image in various directions and visually correct the distortion. (See Figure 5.13.)

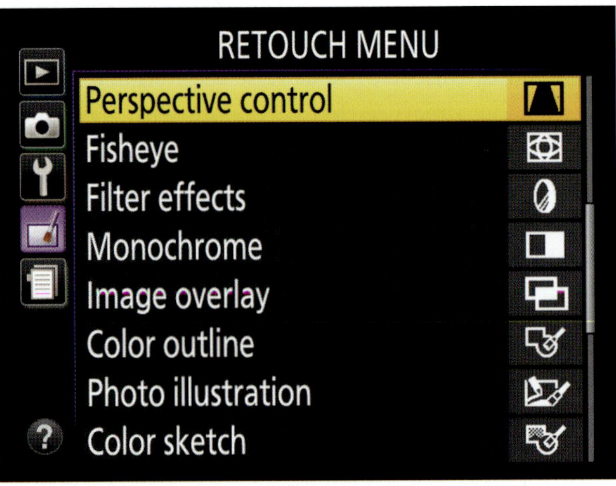

Figure 5.12
Perspective Control is the first entry on the second page of the Retouch menu.

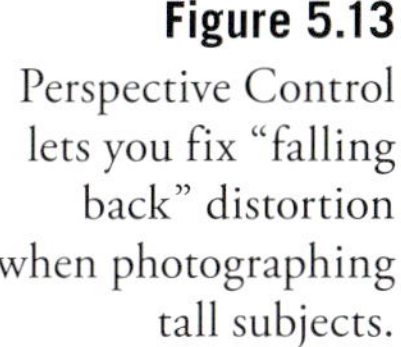

Figure 5.13
Perspective Control lets you fix "falling back" distortion when photographing tall subjects.

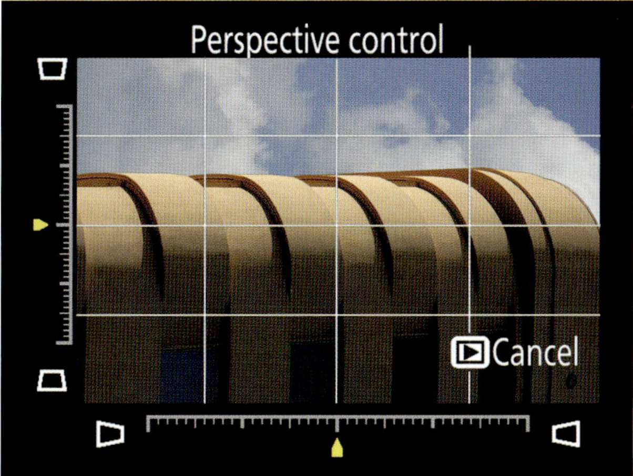

Fisheye

This feature emulates the extreme curving effect of a fisheye lens. Use the right directional button to increase the effect, and the left directional button to decrease it. Press OK to make a corrected copy, or the Playback button to exit without saving a copy. Figure 5.14 shows an example image.

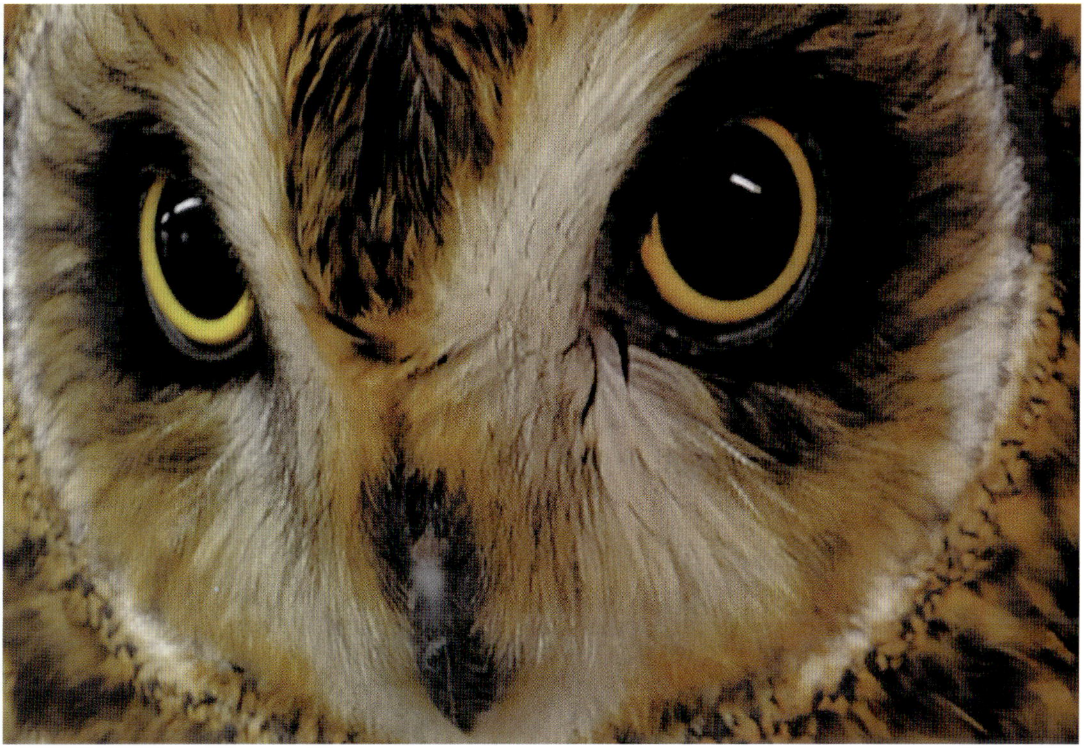

Figure 5.14 You can apply a fisheye effect to an image.

Filter Effects

Add effects somewhat similar to photographic filters with this tool. Your choices are as follows:

- **Skylight.** This option makes the image slightly less blue.

- **Warm.** Use this filter to add a rich warm cast to the duplicate.

- **Cross screen.** This option adds radiating star points to bright objects—such as the reflection of light sources on shiny surfaces. You can choose four different attributes of your stars:

  - **Number of points.** You can select from four, six, or eight points for each star added to your image.

  - **Filter amount.** Select from three different intensities, represented by two, three, and four stars in the menu (this doesn't reflect the actual number of stars in your image, which is determined by the number of bright areas in the photo).

  - **Filter angle.** Select from three different angles: steep, approximately 45 degrees, and a shallower angle.

  - **Length of points.** Three different lengths for the points can be chosen: short, medium, and long.

- **Soft.** Creates a dreamy, soft-focus version of your image. You can compare the "before" and "after" versions using a screen much like the one used for D-Lighting.

Monochrome

This Retouch choice allows you to produce a copy of the selected photo as a black-and-white image, sepia-toned image, or cyanotype (blue-and-white) image. You can fine-tune the color saturation of the previewed Sepia or Cyanotype version by pressing the multi selector up button to increase color richness, and the down button to decrease saturation. When satisfied, press OK to create the monochrome duplicate. (See Figure 5.15.)

Image Overlay

Option: Combine two RAW photos

This feature allows you to combine two RAW photos (only NEF files can be used) in a composite image that Nikon claims is better than a "double exposure" created in an image-editing application, because the overlays are made using RAW data. To produce this composite image, follow these steps:

1. Choose Image Overlay. A screen will be displayed, with the Image 1 box highlighted.

2. Press OK and the Nikon D3500's image selection screen appears. Choose the first image for the overlay and press OK.

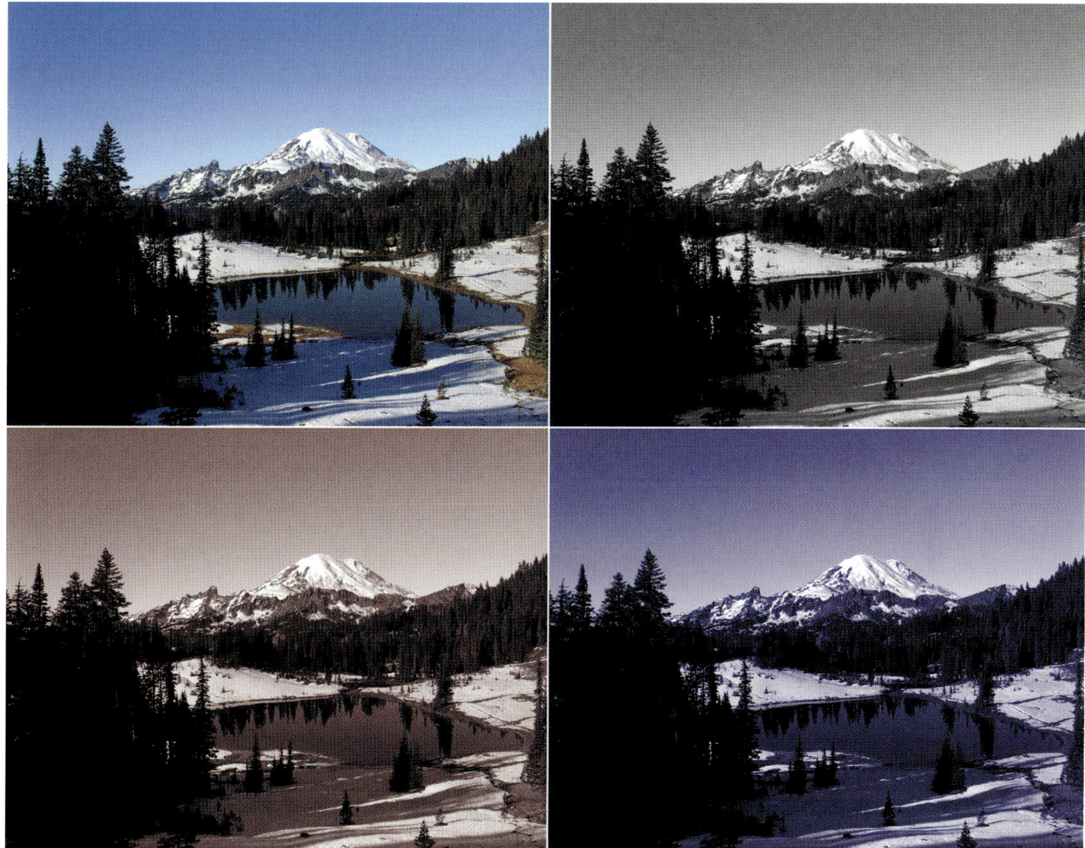

Figure 5.15 Create a black-and-white, sepia, or cyanotype version of a full-color image.

3. Press the right multi selector button to highlight the Image 2 box, and press OK to produce the image selection screen. Choose the second image for the overlay.

4. By highlighting either the Image 1 or Image 2 boxes and pressing the multi selector up/down buttons, you can adjust the "gain," or how much of the final image will be "exposed" from the selected picture. You can choose from X0.5 (half-exposure) to X2.0 (twice the exposure) for each image. The default value is 1.0 for each, so that each image will contribute equally to the final exposure.

5. Use the multi selector right button to highlight the Preview box and view the combined picture. Press the Zoom In button to enlarge the view.

6. When you're ready to store your composite copy, press the multi selector down button when the Preview box is highlighted to select Save, and press OK. The combined image is stored on the memory card.

Color Outline

This option creates a copy of your image in outline form (see Figure 5.16), which Nikon says you can use for "painting." You might like the effect on its own. It's a little like the Find Edges command in Photoshop and Photoshop Elements, but you can perform this magic in your camera! A slider appears that allows you to adjust the size of the outlines.

Photo Illustration

Applies the same look to an image that the Photo Illustration EFFECTS mode does, as explained in Chapter 6. It also includes an adjustment for tweaking the outlines.

Color Sketch

This option creates a copy of your image in outline form, too, but retains some of the colors of the original image. You can specify Vividness (color saturation) and adjust the outlines.

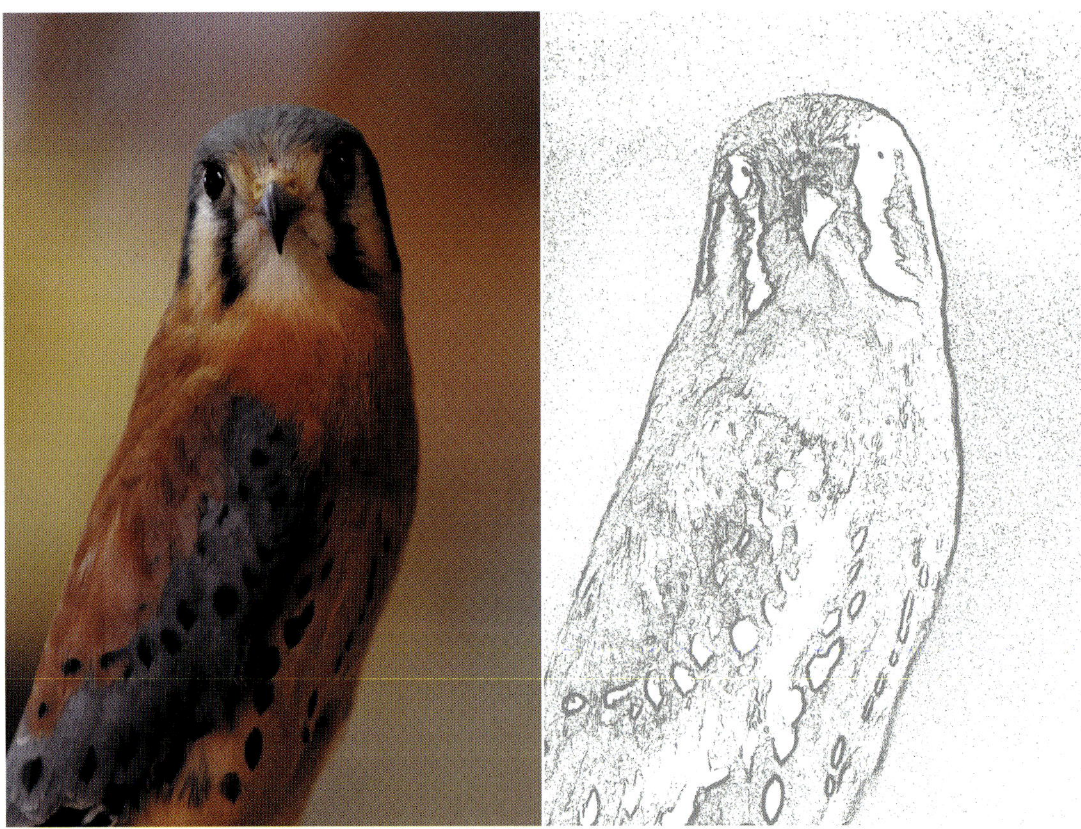

Figure 5.16 The Color Outline retouching feature creates an outline image (right), but it's not in color (like the original, left).

Miniature Effect

This is a clever effect, and it's hampered by a misleading name and the fact that its properties are hard to visualize (which is not a great attribute for a visual effect). This tool doesn't create a "miniature" picture, as you might expect. What it does is mimic tilt/shift lens effects that angle the lens off the axis of the sensor plane to drastically change the plane of focus, producing the sort of look you get when viewing some photographs of a diorama, or miniature scene. Confused yet? It's the first entry on the last screen of the Retouch menu. (See Figure 5.17.)

Perhaps the best way to understand this capability is to actually modify a picture using it. Just follow these steps:

1. **Take your best shot.** Capture an image of a distant landscape or other scene, preferably from a slightly elevated viewpoint.

2. **Access Miniature Effect.** When viewing the image during playback, press the multi selector center button to access the Retouch menu, and select Miniature Effect. A screen like the one shown at left in Figure 5.18 appears.

3. **Adjust selected area.** A wide yellow box (or a tall yellow box if the image is rotated to vertical perspective on playback) highlights a small section of the image. (No, we're not going to create a panorama from that slice; this Nikon super-tricky feature has fooled you yet again.) Use the up/down buttons (or left/right buttons if the image is displayed vertically) to move the yellow box, which represents the area of your image that will be rendered in (fairly) sharp focus. The rest of the image will be blurred.

Figure 5.17

The last screen in the Retouch menu.

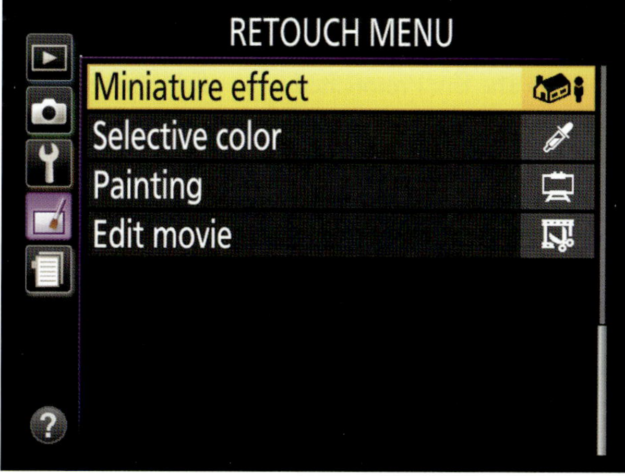

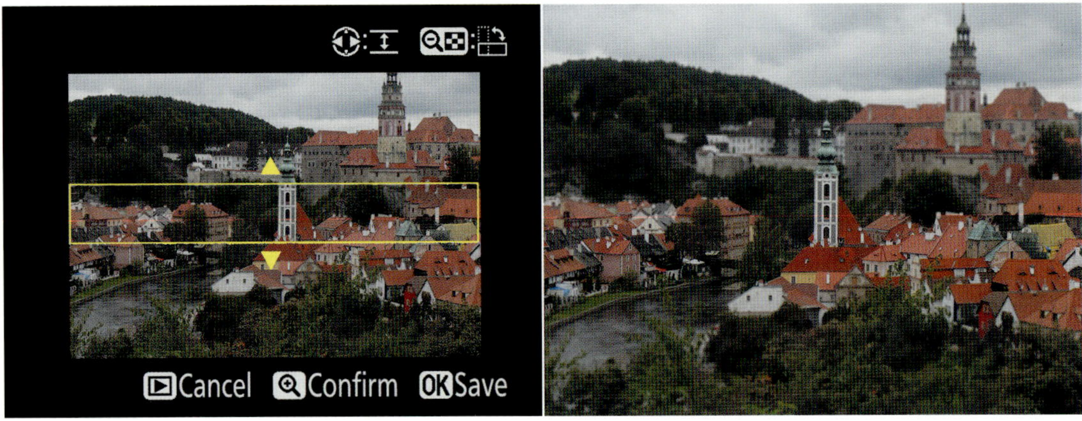

Figure 5.18 Left: Choose the area for sharp focus by moving the yellow box within the frame. Right: The photo with the diorama/miniature effect applied.

4. **Preview area to be in sharp focus.** Press the Zoom In button to preview the area that will be rendered in sharp focus. Nikon labels this control Confirm, but that's just to mislead you. It's actually just a preview that lets you "confirm" that this is the area you want to emphasize.

5. **Apply the effect.** Press the OK button to apply the effect (or the Playback button to cancel). Your finished image will be rendered in a weird altered-focus way, as shown at right in Figure 5.18.

Selective Color

Use the multi selector to move the cursor over an object and press the AE-L/AF-L button to select that color, which will remain in the final retouched copy of the image, while the other colors are converted to black-and-white. You can press the Zoom In/Zoom Out buttons to choose a specific color more precisely. Rotate the command dial to expand/contract the color range of hues to match the selected color. (See Figure 5.19.)

Painting

Creates a copy with a weird, almost HDR effect, which, fortunately, the D3500 will preview for you before you decide to discard it. Or, maybe you'll like it.

Edit Movie

You can trim your movies to exclude extraneous "footage." You'll find instructions for using this feature in Chapter 8.

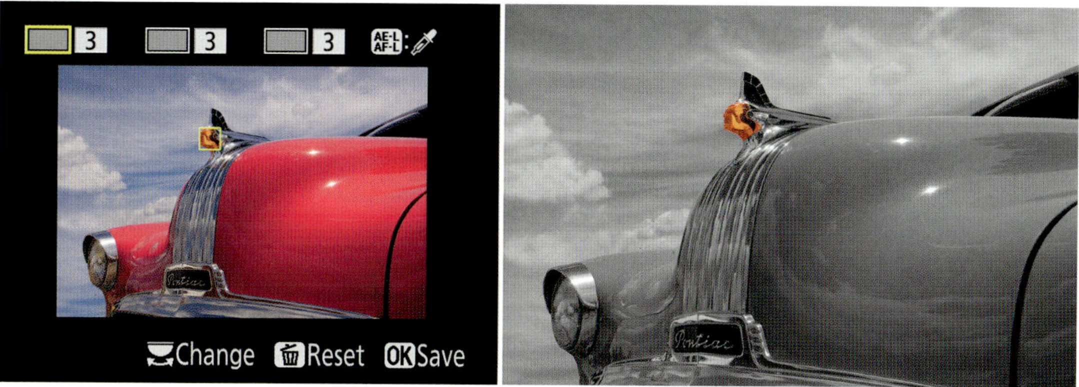

Figure 5.19 Left: Choose a color to preserve. Right: All non-selected colors will be rendered in black-and-white.

Side-by-Side Comparison

Use this option to compare a retouched photo side-by-side with the original from which it was derived. This option is shown on the pop-up menu that appears when you are viewing an image (or copy) full screen and press the *i* button.

1. Press the Playback button and review images in full-frame mode until you encounter a source image or retouched copy you want to compare. The retouched copy will have the retouching icon displayed in the upper-left corner. Press OK.

2. The Retouch menu appears, with Side-by-Side Comparison added at the bottom. Scroll down to that entry and press OK.

3. The original and retouched image will appear next to each other, with the retouching options you've used shown as a label above the images.

4. Highlight the original or the copy with the multi selector left/right buttons, and press the Zoom In button to magnify the image to examine it more closely.

5. If you have created more than one copy of an original image, select the retouched version shown, and press the multi selector up/down buttons to view the other retouched copies. The up/down buttons will also let you view the other image used to create an Image Overlay copy.

6. When done comparing, press the Playback button to exit.

Using Recent Settings

The last menu in the D3500's main menu screen is Recent Settings (see Figure 5.20), which simply shows an ever-changing roster of the 20 menu items you used most recently. Press the up/down buttons to highlight an entry, and the right button to select it. To remove an entry from the Recent Settings listing, highlight it and press the Trash button.

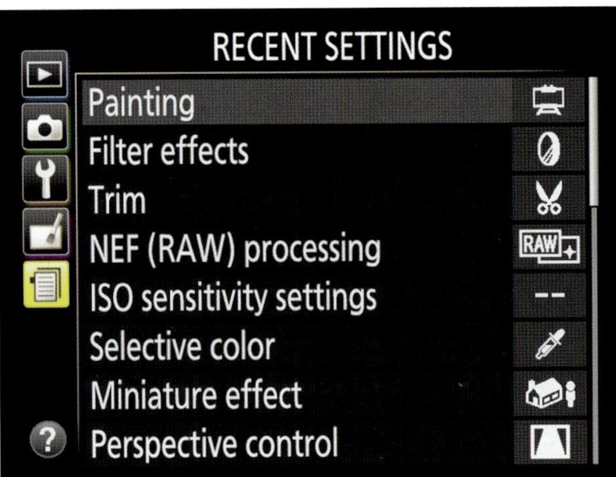

Figure 5.20

The most recent menu items you've accessed appear in the Recent Settings menu.

6

Nailing the Right Exposure

When you bought your Nikon D3500, you probably thought your days of worrying about getting the correct exposure were over. To paraphrase an old tagline dating back to the 19th Century—the goal is, "you press the button, and the camera does the rest." For the most part, that's a realistic objective. The D3500 is one of the smartest cameras available when it comes to calculating the right exposure for most situations. You can generally choose Auto, one of the Scene modes, or spin the mode dial to switch to Program (P), Aperture-priority (A), or Shutter-priority (S) and shoot away.

For example, when you shoot with the main light source behind the subject, you end up with *back-lighting*, which can result in an overexposed background and/or an underexposed subject. The Nikon D3500 recognizes backlit situations nicely, and can properly base exposure on the main subject, producing a decent photo. Features like Active D-Lighting (discussed in Chapter 4) can fine-tune exposure as you take photos, to preserve detail in the highlights and shadows.

But what if you *want* to underexpose the subject, to produce a silhouette effect? Or, perhaps, you might want to flip up the D3500's built-in flash unit to fill in the shadows on your subject. The more you know about how to use your D3500, the more you'll run into situations where you want to creatively tweak the exposure to provide a different look than you'd get with a straight shot.

This chapter shows you the fundamentals of exposure, so you'll be better equipped to override the Nikon D3500's default settings when you want to, or need to. After all, correct exposure is one of the foundations of good photography, along with accurate focus and sharpness, appropriate color balance, freedom from unwanted noise and excessive contrast, as well as pleasing composition.

The Nikon D3500 gives you a great deal of control over all of these, although composition is entirely up to you. You must still frame the photograph to create an interesting arrangement of subject matter, but all the other parameters are basic functions of the camera. You can let your D3500 set them for you automatically, you can fine-tune how the camera applies its automatic settings, or you can make them yourself, manually. The amount of control you have over exposure, sensitivity (ISO settings), color balance, focus, and image parameters like sharpness and contrast make the D3500 a versatile tool for creating images.

In the next few pages, I'm going to give you a grounding in one of those foundations, and explain the basics of exposure, either as an introduction or as a refresher course, depending on your current level of expertise. When you finish this chapter, you'll understand most of what you need to know to take well-exposed photographs creatively in a broad range of situations.

Getting a Handle on Exposure

In the most basic sense, exposure is all about light. Exposure can make or break your photo. Correct exposure brings out the detail in the areas you want to picture, providing the range of tones and colors you need to create the desired image. Poor exposure can cloak important details in shadow, or wash them out in glare-filled featureless expanses of white. However, getting the perfect exposure requires some intelligence—either that built into the camera or the smarts in your head—because digital sensors can't capture all the tones we are able to see. If the range of tones in an image is extensive, embracing both inky black shadows and bright highlights, we often must settle for an exposure that renders most of those tones—but not all—in a way that best suits the photo we want to produce. One solution is to use High Dynamic Range (HDR) photography—taking two (or more) exposures and combining them to create a single image with a full range of tones.

You may have heard about the traditional "exposure triangle" of aperture (quantity of light, light passed by the lens), shutter speed (the amount of time the shutter is open), and the ISO sensitivity of the sensor—all working proportionately and reciprocally to produce an exposure. The trio is itself affected by the amount of illumination that is available to work with. So, if you double the amount of light, increase the aperture by one stop, make the shutter speed twice as long, or boost the ISO setting 2X, you'll get twice as much exposure. Similarly, you can increase any of these factors while decreasing one of the others by a similar amount to keep the same exposure.

Working with any of the three controls involves trade-offs. Larger f/stops provide less depth-of-field, while smaller f/stops increase depth-of-field (and potentially at the same time can *decrease* sharpness through a phenomenon called *diffraction*). Shorter shutter speeds do a better job of reducing the effects of camera/subject motion, while longer shutter speeds make that motion blur more likely. Higher ISO settings increase the amount of visual noise and artifacts in your image, while lower ISO settings reduce the effects of noise. (See Figure 6.1.)

Exposure determines the look, feel, and tone of an image, in more ways than one. Incorrect exposure can impair even the best-composed image by cloaking important tones in darkness, or by washing them out so they become featureless to the eye. On the other hand, correct exposure brings out the detail in the areas you want to picture, and provides the range of tones and colors you need to create the desired image. However, getting the perfect exposure can be tricky, because digital sensors can't capture all the tones we are able to see. If the range of tones in an image is extensive, embracing both inky black shadows and bright highlights, the sensor may not be able to capture

Figure 6.1

The traditional exposure triangle includes aperture, shutter speed, and ISO sensitivity.

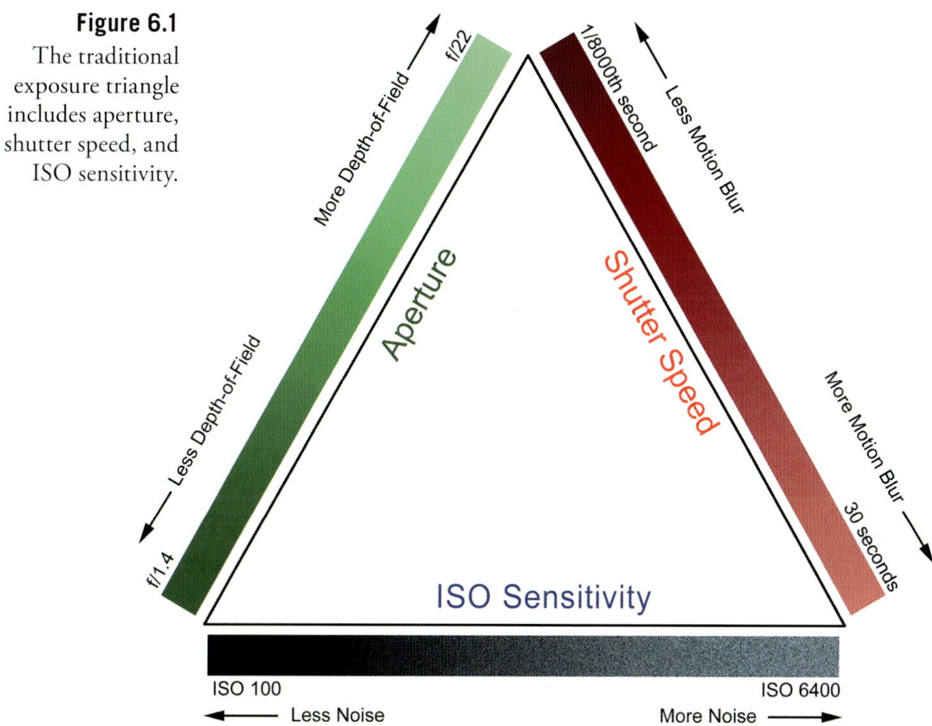

them all. Sometimes, we must settle for an exposure that renders most of those tones—but not all—in a way that best suits the photo we want to produce. You'll often need to make choices about which details are important, and which are not, so that you can grab the tones that truly matter in your image.

Look at two bracketed exposures presented in Figure 6.2. For the image at top left, the highlights are well exposed, but everything else in the shot is seriously underexposed. The version at the top right, taken an instant later with the tripod-mounted camera, shows detail in the shadow areas, but the highlights are completely washed out. The camera's sensor simply can't capture detail in both dark areas and bright areas in a single shot. With digital camera sensors, it's tricky to capture detail in both highlights and shadows in a single image, because the number of tones, the *dynamic range* of the sensor, is limited.

With digital camera sensors, it's tricky to capture detail in both highlights and shadows in a single image, because the number of tones, the *dynamic range* of the sensor, is limited. The solution, in this particular case, was to resort to a technique called high dynamic range (HDR) photography, in which the two exposures from Figure 6.2, top, were combined in an image editor such as Photoshop, or a specialized HDR tool like Photomatix. The resulting shot is shown at the bottom of the figure. I'll explain more about HDR photography later in this chapter. For now, though, I'm going to concentrate on showing you how to get the best exposures possible without resorting to such tools, using only the features of your D3500.

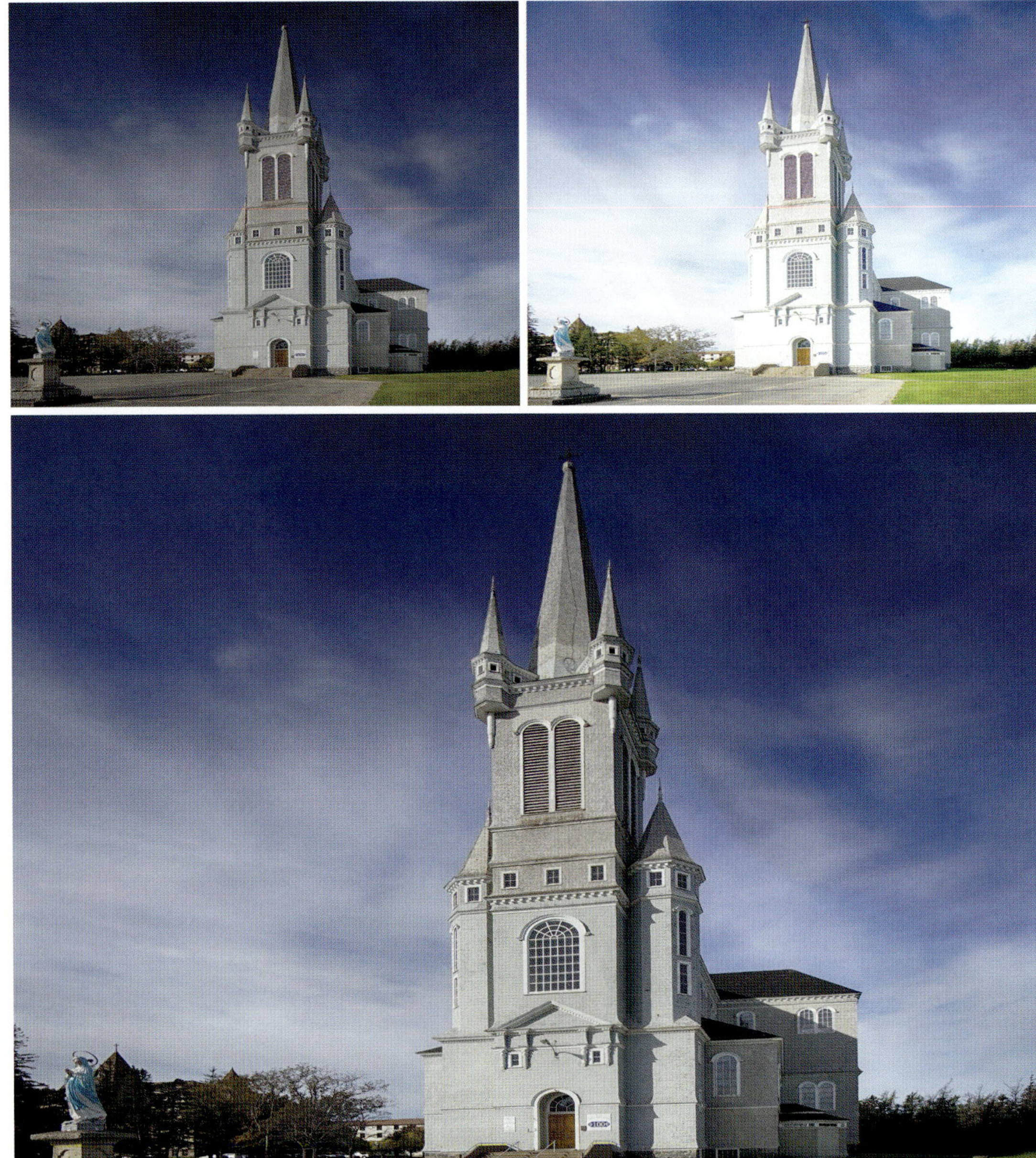

Figure 6.2 At top, the image is exposed for the highlights (left) and shadows (right). At bottom, combining the two exposures produces the best compromise image.

To understand exposure, you need to understand the six aspects of light that combine to produce an image. Start with a light source—the sun, an interior lamp, or the glow from a campfire—and trace its path to your camera, through the lens, and finally to the sensor that captures the illumination. Here's a brief review of the things within our control that affect exposure, listed in "chronological" order (that is, as the light moves from the subject to the sensor):

- **Light at its source.** Our eyes and our cameras—film or digital—are most sensitive to that portion of the electromagnetic spectrum we call *visible light*. That light has several important aspects that are relevant to photography, such as color and harshness (which is determined primarily by the apparent size of the light source as it illuminates a subject). But, in terms of exposure, the important attribute of a light source is its *intensity*. We may have direct control over intensity, which might be the case with an interior light that can be brightened or dimmed. Or, we might have only indirect control over intensity, as with sunlight, which can be made to appear dimmer by introducing translucent light-absorbing or reflective materials in its path.

- **Light's duration.** We tend to think of most light sources as continuous. But, as you'll learn in Chapter 11, the duration of light can change quickly enough to modify the exposure, as when the main illumination in a photograph comes from an intermittent source, such as an electronic flash.

- **Light reflected, transmitted, or emitted.** Once light is produced by its source, either continuously or in a brief burst, we are able to see and photograph objects by the light that is reflected from our subjects toward the camera lens; transmitted (say, from translucent objects that are lit from behind); or emitted (by a candle or television screen). When more or less light reaches the lens from the subject, we need to adjust the exposure. This part of the equation is under our control to the extent we can increase the amount of light falling on or passing through the subject (by adding extra light sources or using reflectors), or by pumping up the light that's emitted (by increasing the brightness of the glowing object).

- **Light passed by the lens.** Not all the illumination that reaches the front of the lens makes it all the way through. Filters can remove some of the light before it enters the lens. Inside the lens barrel is a variable-sized diaphragm that produces an opening called an *aperture* that dilates and contracts to control the amount of light that enters the lens. You, or the D3500's autoexposure system, can control exposure by varying the size of the aperture. The relative size of the aperture is called the *f/stop*. (See Figure 6.3.)

- **Light passing through the shutter.** Once light passes through the lens, the amount of time the sensor receives it is determined by the D3500's shutter, which can remain open for as long as 30 seconds (or even longer if you use the Bulb setting) or as briefly as 1/4,000th second.

- **Light captured by the sensor.** Not all the light falling onto the sensor is captured. If the number of photons reaching a particular photosite doesn't pass a set threshold, no information is recorded. Similarly, if too much light illuminates a pixel in the sensor, then the excess isn't recorded or, worse, spills over to contaminate adjacent pixels. We can modify the minimum and maximum number of pixels that contribute to image detail by adjusting the ISO setting. At higher ISOs, the incoming light is amplified to boost the effective sensitivity of the sensor.

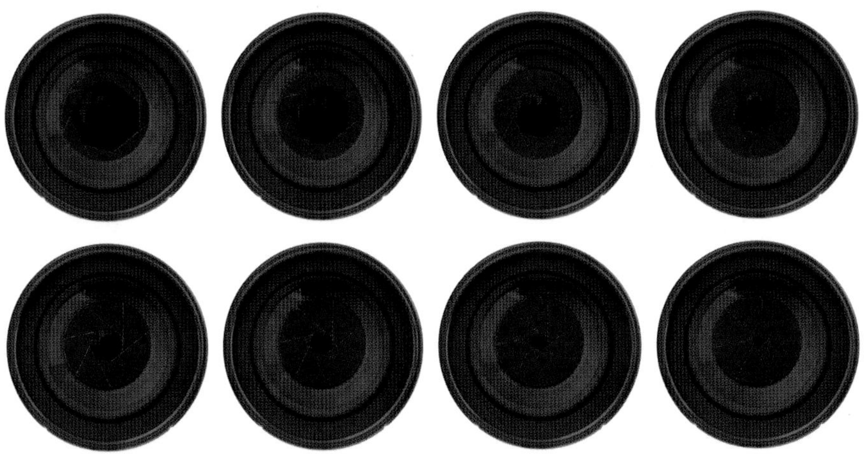

Figure 6.3
Top row (left to right): f/2, f/2.8, f/4, f/5.6; bottom row: f/8, f/11, f/16, f/22.

F/STOPS AND SHUTTER SPEEDS

If you're *really* new to more advanced cameras (and I realize that many ambitious amateurs do purchase the D3500 as their first digital SLR), you might need to know that the lens aperture, or f/stop, is a ratio, much like a fraction, which is why f/2 is larger than f/4, just as 1/2 is larger than 1/4. However, f/2 is actually *four times* as large as f/4. (If you remember your high school geometry, you'll know that to double the area of a circle, you multiply its diameter by the square root of two: 1.4.)

Lenses are usually marked with intermediate f/stops that represent a size that's twice as much/half as much as the previous aperture. So, a lens might be marked: f/2, f/2.8, f/4, f/5.6, f/8, f/11, f/16, f/22, with each larger number representing an aperture that admits half as much light as the one before, as shown in Figure 6.3.

Shutter speeds are actual fractions (of a second), but the numerator is omitted, so that 60, 125, 250, 500, 1000, and so forth represent 1/60th, 1/125th, 1/250th, 1/500th, and 1/1,000th second. To avoid confusion, Nikon uses quotation marks to signify longer exposures: 2", 2"5, 4", and so forth representing 2.0-, 2.5-, and 4.0-second exposures, respectively.

As I mentioned, quantity of light, light passed by the lens, the amount of time the shutter is open, and the sensitivity of the sensor, all work proportionately and reciprocally to produce an exposure. That is, if you double the amount of light, increase the aperture by one stop, make the shutter speed twice as long, or boost the ISO setting 2X, you'll get twice as much exposure. Similarly, you can increase any of these factors while decreasing one of the others by a similar amount to keep the same exposure.

Most commonly, exposure settings are made using the aperture and shutter speed, followed by adjusting the ISO sensitivity, if it's not possible to get the preferred exposure (that is, the one that uses the "best" f/stop or shutter speed for the depth-of-field or action stopping we want). Table 6.1 shows equivalent exposure settings using various shutter speeds and f/stops.

Table 6.1 Equivalent Exposures

Shutter speed	f/stop	Shutter speed	f/stop
1/30th second	f/22	1/500th second	f/5.6
1/60th second	f/16	1/1,000th second	f/4
1/125th second	f/11	1/2,000th second	f/2.8
1/250th second	f/8	1/4,000th second	f/2

When the D3500 is set for P mode, the metering system selects the correct exposure for you automatically, but you can change quickly to an equivalent exposure by spinning the command dial until the desired equivalent exposure combination is displayed. An asterisk next to the P on the display indicates that you've adjusted the exposure combination. You can use this Flexible Program feature more easily if you remember that you need to rotate the command dial toward the left when you want to increase the amount of depth-of-field or use a slower shutter speed; rotate to the right when you want to reduce the depth-of-field or use a faster shutter speed. The need for more/less DOF and slower/faster shutter speed are the primary reasons you'd want to use Flexible Program. This program shift mode does not work when you're using flash.

In Aperture-priority (A) and Shutter-priority (S) modes you can change to an equivalent exposure, but only by either adjusting the aperture (the camera chooses the shutter speed) or shutter speed (the camera selects the aperture). I'll cover all these exposure modes later in the chapter.

F/STOPS VERSUS STOPS

In photography parlance, *f/stop* always means the aperture or lens opening. However, for lack of a current commonly used word for one exposure increment, the term *stop* is often used. (In the past, EV served this purpose, but Exposure Value and its abbreviation have since been inextricably intertwined with its use in describing Exposure Compensation.) In this book, when I say "stop" by itself (no *f/*), I mean one whole unit of exposure, and am not necessarily referring to an actual f/stop or lens aperture. So, adjusting the exposure by "one stop" can mean both changing to the next shutter speed increment (say, from 1/125th second to 1/250th second) or the next aperture (such as f/4 to f/5.6). Similarly, 1/3-stop or 1/2-stop increments can mean either shutter speed or aperture changes, depending on the context. Be forewarned.

How the D3500 Calculates Exposure

Your D3500 calculates exposure by measuring the light that passes through the lens and is bounced up by the mirror to sensors located near the focusing surface, using a pattern you can select (more on that later) and based on the assumption that each area being measured reflects about the same amount of light as a neutral gray card that reflects a "middle" gray of about 12 to 18 percent reflectance. (The photographic "gray cards" you buy at a camera store have an 18 percent gray tone; your camera is calibrated to interpret a somewhat darker 12 percent gray; I'll explain more about this later.) That "average" 12 to 18 percent gray assumption is necessary, because different subjects reflect different amounts of light. In a photo containing, say, a white cat and a dark gray cat, the white cat might reflect five times as much light as the gray cat. An exposure based on the white cat will cause the gray cat to appear to be black, while an exposure based only on the gray cat will make the white cat washed out.

This is more easily understood if you look at some photos of subjects that are dark (they reflect little light), those that have predominantly middle tones, and subjects that are highly reflective. The next figure shows some images of actual cats (actually, the *same* cat rendered in black, gray, and white varieties through the magic of Photoshop), with each of the three strips exposed using a different cat for reference.

Correctly Exposed

The three pictures shown at top in Figure 6.4 represent how the black, gray, and white cats would appear if the exposure were calculated by measuring the light reflecting from the middle, gray cat, which, for the sake of illustration, we'll assume reflects approximately 12 to 18 percent of the light that strikes it. The exposure meter sees an object that it thinks is a middle gray, calculates an exposure based on that, and the feline in the center of the strip is rendered at its proper tonal value. Best of all, because the resulting exposure is correct, the black cat at left and white cat at right are rendered properly as well.

When you're shooting pictures with your D3500, and the meter happens to base its exposure on a subject that averages that "ideal" middle gray, then you'll end up with similar (accurate) results. The camera's exposure algorithms are concocted to ensure this kind of result as often as possible, barring any unusual subjects (that is, those that are backlit, or have uneven illumination). The D3500 has three different metering modes (described on the next few pages), each of which is equipped to handle certain types of unusual subjects, as I'll outline.

Overexposed

The strip of three images in the middle of Figure 6.4 shows what would happen if the exposure were calculated based on metering the leftmost, black cat. The light meter sees less light reflecting from the black cat than it would see from a gray middle-tone subject, and so figures, "Aha! I need to add exposure to brighten this subject up to a middle gray!" That lightens the black cat, so it now appears to be gray.

But now, the cat in the middle that was *originally* middle gray is overexposed and becomes light gray. And the white cat at right is now seriously overexposed, and loses detail in the highlights, which have become a featureless white.

Underexposed

The third possibility in this simplified scenario is that the light meter might measure the illumination bouncing off the white cat, and try to render that feline as a middle gray. A lot of light is reflected by the white kitty, so the exposure is *reduced*, bringing that cat closer to a middle gray tone. The cats that were originally gray and black are now rendered too dark. Clearly, measuring the gray cat—or a substitute that reflects about the same amount of light, is the only way to ensure that the exposure is precisely correct. (See the bottom strip of images in Figure 6.4.)

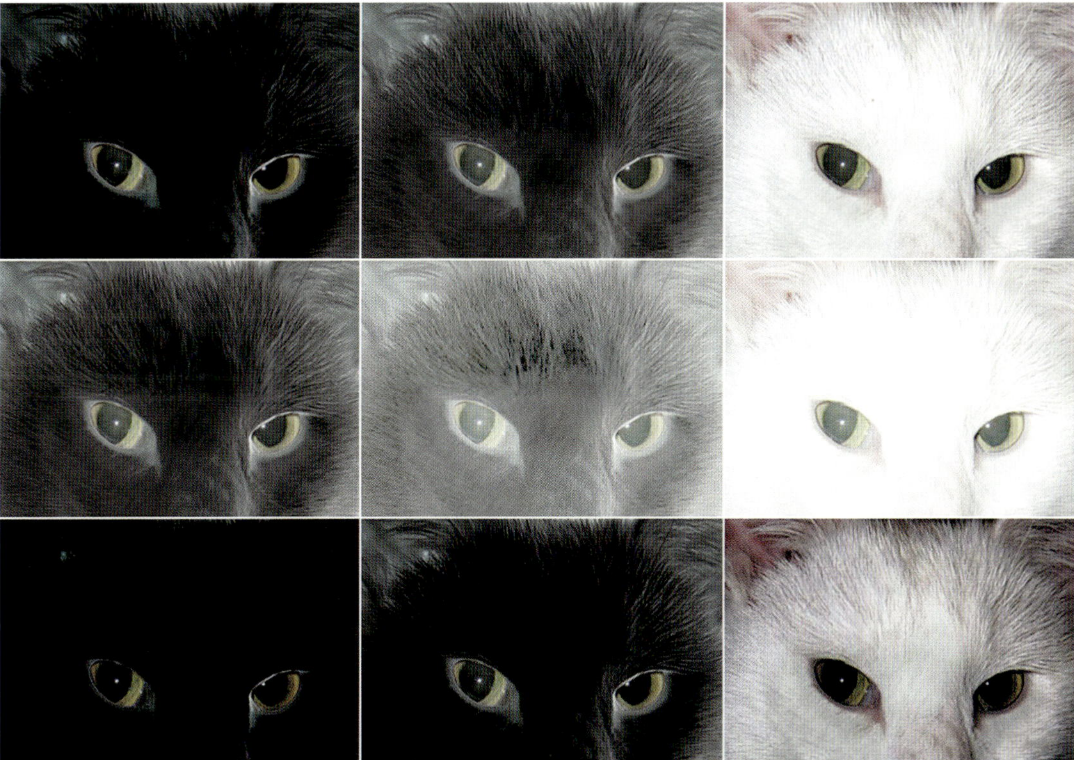

Figure 6.4 Exposure based on the middle-gray cat (top); dark gray cat (center); and white cat (bottom).

As you can see, the ideal way to measure exposure is to meter from a subject that reflects 12 to 18 percent of the light that reaches it. If you want the most precise exposure calculations, if you don't have a gray cat handy, the solution is to use a stand-in, such as the evenly illuminated gray card I mentioned earlier. But, because the standard Kodak gray card reflects 18 percent of the light that reaches it and, as I said, your camera is calibrated for a somewhat darker 12 percent tone, you would need to add about one-half stop *more* exposure than the value metered from the card.

Another substitute for a gray card is the palm of a human hand (the backside of the hand is too variable). But a human palm, regardless of ethnic group, is even brighter than a standard gray card, so instead of one-half stop more exposure, you need to add one additional stop. That is, if your meter reading is 1/500th of a second at f/11, use 1/500th second at f/8 or 1/250th second at f/11 instead. (Both exposures are equivalent.)

If you actually wanted to use a gray card, place it in your frame near your main subject, facing the camera, and with the exact same even illumination falling on it that is falling on your subject. Then, use the Spot metering function (described in the next section) to calculate exposure. Of course, in most situations, it's not necessary to do this. Your camera's light meter will do a good job of calculating the right exposure, especially if you use the exposure tips in the next section. But, I felt that explaining exactly what is going on during exposure calculation would help you understand how your D3500's metering system works.

WHY THE GRAY CARD CONFUSION?

Why are so many photographers under the impression that cameras and meters are calibrated to the 18 percent "standard," rather than the true value, which may be 12 to 14 percent, depending on the vendor? You'll find this misinformation in an alarming number of places. I've seen the 18 percent "myth" taught in camera classes; I've found it in books, and even been given this wrong information from the technical staff of camera vendors. (They should know better—the same vendors' engineers who design and calibrate the cameras have the right figure.)

The most common explanation is that during a revision of Kodak's instructions for its gray cards in the 1970s, the advice to open up an extra half stop was omitted, and a whole generation of shooters grew up thinking that a measurement off a gray card could be used as-is. The proviso returned to the instructions by 1987, it's said, but by then it was too late. Next to me is a (c)2006 version of the instructions for KODAK Gray Cards, Publication R-27Q, and the current directions read (with a bit of paraphrasing from me in italics):

- For subjects of normal reflectance increase the indicated exposure by 1/2 stop.

- For light subjects use the indicated exposure; for very light subjects, decrease the exposure by 1/2 stop. *(That is, you're measuring a cat that's lighter than middle gray.)*

- If the subject is dark to very dark, increase the indicated exposure by 1 to 1-1/2 stops. *(You're shooting a black cat.)*

EXTERNAL METERS CAN BE CALIBRATED

The light meters built into your camera are calibrated at the factory. But if you use a hand-held incident or reflective light meter, you *can* calibrate it, using the instructions supplied with your meter. Because a hand-held meter *can* be calibrated to the 18 percent gray standard (or any other value you choose), my rant about the myth of the 18 percent gray card doesn't apply.

To meter properly you'll want to choose both the *metering method* (how light is evaluated) and *exposure method* (how the appropriate shutter speeds and apertures are chosen). I'll describe both in the following sections.

MODES, MODES, AND MORE MODES

Call them modes or methods, the Nikon D3500 seems to have a lot of different sets of options that are described using similar terms. Here's how to sort them out:

- **Metering method.** These modes determine the *parts of the image* within the 420-segment sensor array that are examined in order to calculate exposure. The D3500 may look at many different points within the image, segregate them by zone (Matrix metering), examine the same number of points, but give greater weight to those located in the middle of the frame (Center-weighted metering), or evaluate only a limited number of points in a limited area (Spot metering).
- **Exposure method.** These modes determine *which* settings are used to expose the image. The D3500 may adjust the shutter speed, the aperture, or both, depending on the method you choose.

Choosing a Metering Method

The D3500 has three different schemes for evaluating the light received by its exposure sensors: Matrix (with several variations, depending on what lens you have attached), Center-weighted, and Spot metering. Select the mode you want to use by pressing the *i* button to access the information edit screen. Here is what you need to know about each metering method.

Matrix Metering

For its various Matrix metering modes, the D3500 slices up the frame into 420 different zones in an RGB (red/green/blue) array that covers most of the sensor area, shown at left in Figure 6.5. When Matrix metering is active, an icon appears at lower center in the shooting information display (inset in the upper-left corner of the figure—it doesn't actually appear in that location on the LCD monitor screen). In all cases, the D3500 evaluates the differences between the zones, and compares them with a built-in database of several hundred thousand images to make an educated guess about what kind of picture you're taking. For example, if the top sections of a picture are much lighter than the bottom portions, the algorithm can assume that the scene is a landscape photo with lots of sky. An image that includes most of the lighter portions in the center area may be a portrait. A typical image suitable for Matrix metering is shown at right in Figure 6.5.

The Nikon D3500 also uses information other than brightness to make its evaluation:

- **3D Color Matrix metering II.** This metering mode is used by default when the D3500 is equipped with a lens that has a type G, E, or D designator in its name, such as the AF-S DX Nikkor 16-85mm f/3.5-5.6G ED VR lens. In this case, the G after the f/5.6 is the giveaway. (More on lens nomenclature in Chapter 10.) The camera calculates exposure based on brightness, colors of the subject matter (that is, blue pixels in the upper part of the image are probably sky; green pixels in the lower half probably foliage), focus point, and distance information. The D3500 is able to use that additional distance data to better calculate what kind of scene you have framed. For example, if you're shooting a portrait with a longer focal-length lens focused to about 5 to 12 feet from the camera, and the upper half of the scene is very bright, the camera assumes you would prefer to meter for the rest of the image, and discount the bright area. However, if the camera has a wide-angle lens attached and is focused at infinity, the D3500 can assume you're taking a landscape photo and take the bright upper area into account to produce better looking sky and clouds.

- **Color Matrix metering II.** If you have a non-G, non-E, or non-D lens equipped with a CPU chip (these are generally older lenses, although chips can sometimes be added to optics that lack them), the distance range is not used. Instead, only focus, brightness, and color information is taken into account to calculate an appropriate exposure.

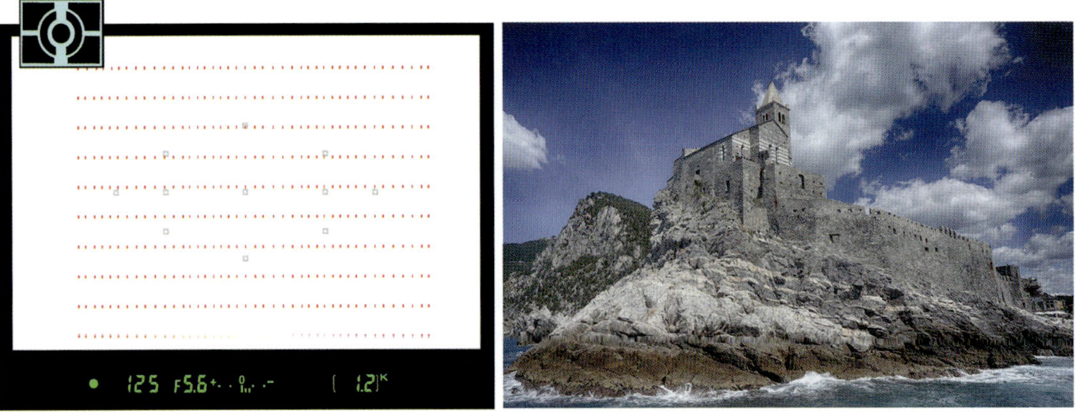

Figure 6.5 Basing exposure on 420 points in the frame, Matrix metering is well-suited for complex scenes.

Matrix metering is best for most general subjects, because it is able to intelligently analyze a scene and make an excellent guess of what kind of subject you're shooting a great deal of the time. The camera can tell the difference between low-contrast and high-contrast subjects by looking at the range of differences in brightness across the scene. Because the D3500 has a fairly good idea about what kind of subject matter you are shooting, it can underexpose slightly when appropriate to preserve highlight detail when image contrast is high. (It's often possible to pull detail out of shadows that are too dark using an image editor, but once highlights are converted to white pixels, they are gone forever.)

> **CAUTION**
>
> If you're using a strong filter, including a polarizing filter, split-color filter, or neutral-density filter (particularly a graduated neutral-density filter), you should switch from Matrix metering to Center-weighted, because the filter can affect the relationships between the different areas of the frame used to calculate a Matrix exposure. For example, a polarizing filter produces a sky that is darker than usual, hindering the Matrix algorithm's recognition of a landscape photo. Extra-dark or colored filters disturb the color relationships used for color Matrix metering, too.

Center-Weighted Metering

In this mode, the exposure meter emphasizes a zone in the center of the frame to calculate exposure, as shown at left in Figure 6.6. About 75 percent of the exposure is based on that central area, and the remaining exposure is based on the rest of the frame. The theory, here, is that, for most pictures, the main subject will be located in the center. So, if the D3500 reads the center portion and determines that the exposure for that region should be f/8 at 1/250th second, while the outer area, which is a bit darker, calls for f/4 at 1/125th second, the camera will give the center portion the most weight and arrive at a final exposure of f/5.6 at 1/250th second.

Center-weighting works best for portraits, architectural photos, backlit subjects with extra-bright backgrounds (such as snow or sand), and other pictures in which the most important subject is located in the middle of the frame, as shown at right in Figure 6.6. As the name suggests, the light reading is *weighted* toward the central portion, but information is also used from the rest of the frame. If your main subject is surrounded by very bright or very dark areas, the exposure might not be exactly right. However, this scheme works well in many situations if you don't want to use one of the other modes. This mode can be useful for close-ups of subjects like flowers, or for portraits.

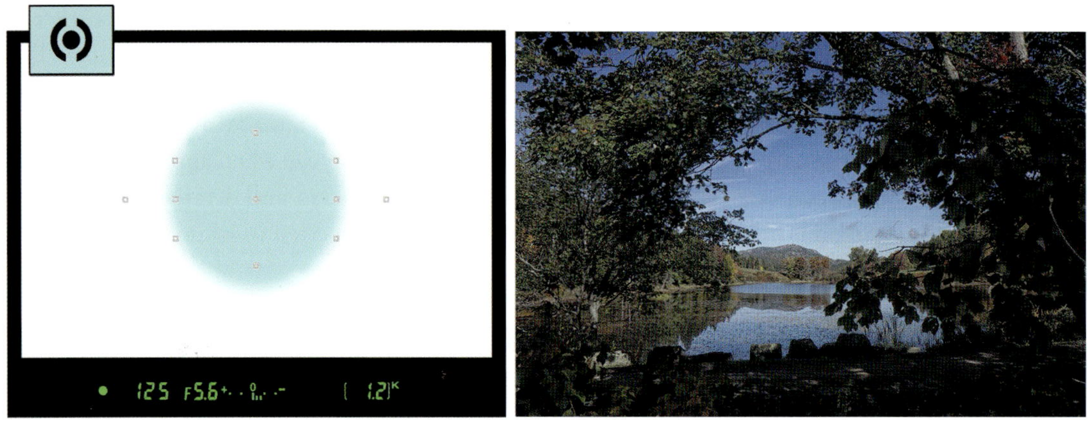

Figure 6.6 Center-weighted metering allots 75 percent of the exposure to the center area (left). Scenes with the main subject in the center, surrounded by areas that are significantly darker or lighter, are perfect (right).

Spot Metering

Spot metering is favored by those of us who used a hand-held light meter to measure exposure at various points (such as metering highlights and shadows separately). However, you can use Spot metering in any situation where you want to individually measure the light reflecting from light, midtone, or dark areas of your subject—or any combination of areas.

This mode confines the reading to a limited 3.5mm area in the viewfinder, making up only 2.5 percent of the image, as shown at left in Figure 6.7. The circle is centered on the *current focus point* (which can be *any* of the focus points, *not* just the center one shown in the figure), *but is larger than the focus point*, so don't fall into the trap of believing that exposure is being measured only within the brackets that represent the active focus point. This is the only metering method you can use to tell the D3500 exactly where to measure exposure when using the optical viewfinder. However, if a non-CPU lens is mounted, or you have selected Auto-area AF, only the center focus point is used to spot meter.

You'll find Spot metering useful when you want to base exposure on a small area in the frame. If that area is in the center of the frame, so much the better. If not, you'll have to make your meter reading for an off-center subject using an appropriate focus point, and then lock exposure by pressing the shutter release halfway, or by pressing the AE-L/AF-L button. This mode is best for subjects where the background is significantly brighter or darker, as in Figure 6.7, right, for which I metered off the area roughly in the center.

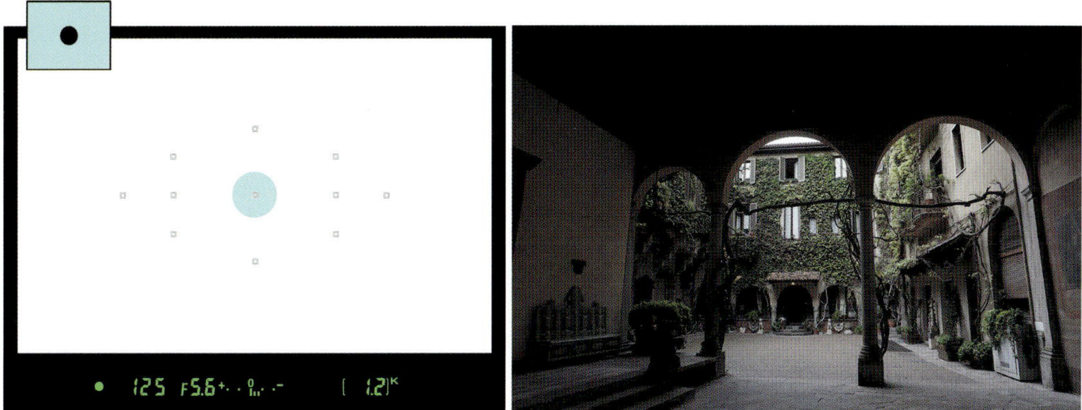

Figure 6.7 Spot metering calculates exposure based on a center spot that's only 2.5 percent of the image area, centered around the current focus point.

Choosing an Exposure Method

You'll find four methods for choosing the appropriate shutter speed and aperture when using the semi-automatic/manual modes. (Scene modes, which use their own exposure biases, are described next.) You can choose among Program, Aperture-priority, Shutter-priority, or Manual options by rotating the mode dial on top of the camera. Your choice of which is best for a given shooting situation will depend on things like your need for lots of (or less) depth-of-field, a desire to freeze action or allow motion blur, or how much noise you find acceptable in an image. Each of the D3500's exposure methods emphasizes one aspect of image capture or another. This section introduces you to all four.

Aperture-Priority

In Aperture-priority mode, you specify the lens opening used, and the D3500 selects the shutter speed. Aperture-priority is especially good when you want to use a particular lens opening to achieve a desired effect. Perhaps you'd like to use the smallest f/stop possible to maximize depth-of-field in a close-up picture. Or, you might want to use a large f/stop to throw everything except your main subject out of focus, such as the bird in Figure 6.8. Maybe you'd just like to "lock in" a particular f/stop because it's the sharpest available aperture with that lens. Or, you might prefer to use, say, f/2.8 on a lens with a maximum aperture of f/1.4, because you want the best compromise between speed and sharpness.

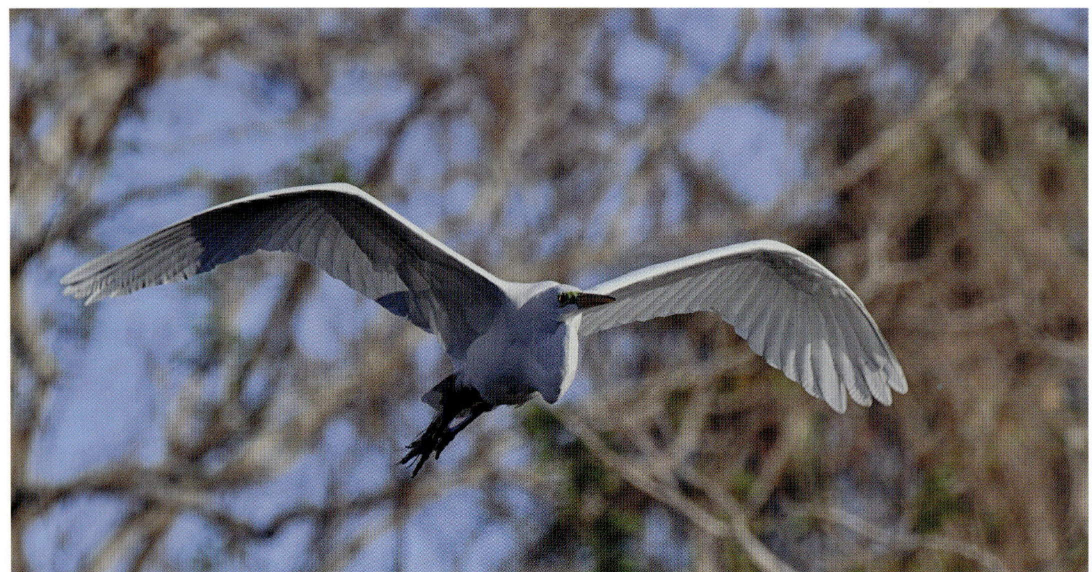

Figure 6.8 Use Aperture-priority to "lock in" a large f/stop when you want to blur the background.

Aperture-priority can even be used to specify a *range* of shutter speeds you want to use under varying lighting conditions, which seems almost contradictory. But think about it. You're shooting a soccer game outdoors with a telephoto lens and want a relatively high shutter speed, but you don't care if the speed changes a little should the sun duck behind a cloud. Set your D3500 to A, and adjust the aperture until a shutter speed of, say, 1/1,000th second is selected at your current ISO setting. (In bright sunlight at ISO 400, that aperture is likely to be around f/11.) Then, go ahead and shoot, knowing that your D3500 will maintain that f/11 aperture (for sufficient depth-of-field as the soccer players move about the field), but will drop down to 1/800th or 1/500th second if necessary should the lighting change a little.

A flashing question mark in the viewfinder, accompanied by a Subject Is Too Dark or Subject Is Too Bright warning and flashing shutter speed or aperture on the LCD monitor indicates that the D3500 is unable to select an appropriate shutter speed at the selected aperture and that over- or underexposure will occur at the current ISO setting. That's the major pitfall of using Aperture-priority: you might select an f/stop that is too small or too large to allow an optimal exposure with the available shutter speeds. For example, if you choose f/2.8 as your aperture and the illumination is quite bright (say, at the beach or in snow), even your camera's fastest shutter speed might not be able to cut down the amount of light reaching the sensor to provide the right exposure. Or, if you select f/8 in a dimly lit room, you might find yourself shooting with a very slow shutter speed that can cause blurring from subject movement or camera shake. Aperture-priority is best used by those with a bit of experience in choosing settings. Many seasoned photographers leave their D3500 set on Aperture-priority all the time.

Shutter-Priority

Shutter-priority (S) is the inverse of Aperture-priority: you choose the shutter speed you'd like to use, and the camera's metering system selects the appropriate f/stop. Perhaps you're shooting action photos and you want to use the absolute fastest shutter speed available with your camera (see Figure 6.9); in other cases, you might want to use a slow shutter speed to add some blur to the tires of a speeding stock car, or hovering helicopter. Shutter-priority mode gives you some control over how much action-freezing capability your digital camera brings to bear in a particular situation.

You'll also encounter the same problem as with Aperture-priority when you select a shutter speed that's too long or too short for correct exposure under some conditions. I've shot outdoor soccer games on sunny fall evenings and used Shutter-priority mode to lock in a 1/1,000th second shutter speed, and was unable to continue when the sun dipped behind some trees and there was no longer enough light to shoot at that speed, even with the lens wide open.

Like Aperture-priority mode, it's possible to choose an inappropriate shutter speed. If that's the case, the displays will flash.

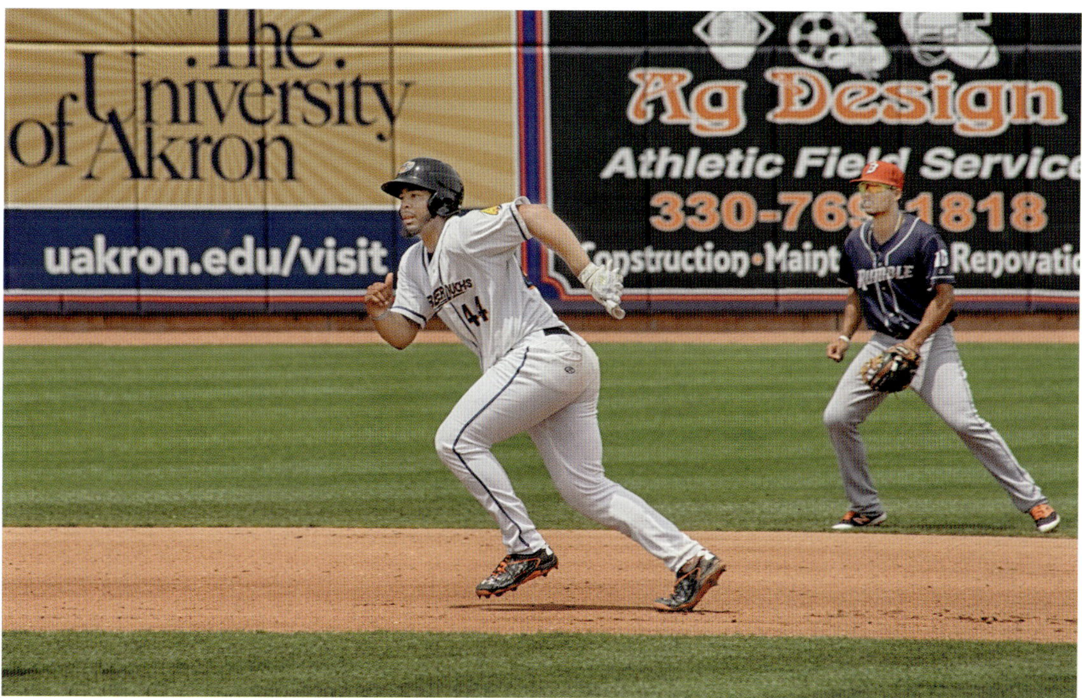

Figure 6.9 Lock the shutter at a specific speed to introduce blur into an action shot.

Program Mode

Program mode (P) uses the D3500's built-in smarts to select the correct f/stop and shutter speed using a database of picture information that tells it which combination of shutter speed and aperture will work best for a particular photo. If the correct exposure cannot be achieved at a current fixed ISO setting, the flashing question mark in the viewfinder and flashing shutter speed/aperture on the LCD monitor will appear. You can then boost or reduce the ISO to increase or decrease sensitivity. Or, switching to ISO Auto allows the camera to make those adjustments for you.

The D3500's recommended exposure can be overridden if you want. Use the EV setting feature (described later, because it also applies to Shutter-priority and Aperture-priority modes) to add or subtract exposure from the metered value. And, as I mentioned earlier in this chapter, in Program mode you can rotate the command dial to change from the recommended setting to an equivalent setting (as shown in Table 6.1) that produces the same exposure, but using a different combination of f/stop and shutter speed.

This is called "Flexible Program" by Nikon. Rotate the command dial left to reduce the size of the aperture (going from, say, f/4 to f/5.6), so that the D3500 will automatically use a slower shutter speed (going from, say, 1/250th second to 1/125th second). Rotate the command dial right to use a larger f/stop, while automatically producing a shorter shutter speed that provides the same equivalent exposure as metered in P mode. An asterisk appears next to the P in the LCD monitor and viewfinder so you'll know you've overridden the D3500's default program setting. Your adjustment remains in force until you rotate the command dial until the asterisk disappears, or you switch to a different exposure mode, or turn the D3500 off.

MAKING EV CHANGES

Sometimes you'll want more or less exposure than indicated by the D3500's metering system. Perhaps you want to underexpose to create a silhouette effect, or overexpose to produce a high-key look. It's easy to use the D3500's exposure compensation system to override the exposure recommendations. Press and hold the EV button on the top of the camera (just southeast of the shutter release). Then rotate the command dial right to add exposure, and left to subtract exposure. The EV change you've made remains for the exposures that follow, until you manually zero out the EV setting. The EV plus/minus icon appears in the viewfinder to warn you that an exposure compensation change has been entered. You can increase or decrease exposure over a range of plus or minus five stops.

Manual Exposure

Part of being an experienced photographer comes from knowing when to rely on your D3500's automation (with Scene modes or P mode), when to go semi-automatic (with Shutter-priority or Aperture-priority), and when to set exposure manually (using M). Some photographers actually prefer to set their exposure manually, as the D3500 will be happy to provide an indication of when its metering system judges your manual settings provide the proper exposure, using the analog exposure scale at the bottom of the viewfinder and on the status LCD monitor.

Manual exposure can come in handy in some situations. You might be taking a silhouette photo and find that none of the exposure modes or EV correction features give you exactly the effect you want. Set the exposure manually to use the exact shutter speed and f/stop you need. Or, you might be working in a studio environment using multiple flash units. The additional flash units are triggered by slave devices (gadgets that set off the flash when they sense the light from another flash, or, perhaps from a radio or infrared remote control). Your camera's exposure meter doesn't compensate for the extra illumination, so you need to set the aperture manually.

Although, depending on your proclivities, you might not need to set exposure manually very often, you should still make sure you understand how it works. Fortunately, the D3500 makes setting exposure manually very easy. Just rotate the mode dial to change to Manual mode, and then turn the command dial to set the shutter speed, and hold down the Aperture/EV button (just southeast of the shutter release button) while rotating the command dial to adjust the aperture. Press the shutter release halfway or press the AE lock button, and the exposure scale in the viewfinder shows you how far your chosen setting diverges from the metered exposure.

Using Scene Modes

As described in Chapter 2, the D3500 retains the "quickie" exposure modes found in Nikon's earlier entry-level cameras, but absent from the company's "pro" and "semi-pro" models. Of course, anyone who uses a D3500 for more than a day will see that it is just as advanced as many cameras (from Nikon or other vendors) that cost hundreds of dollars more. But because the D3500 is a basic model, it includes Scene modes.

As an avid photographer, you probably won't use Scene modes much, except when you're in a hurry to capture a grab shot and don't have time to make any decisions about what advanced exposure mode to use. You want to shoot a macro photo, so you rotate the mode dial to the Close-up position and you're all set. Nothing could be easier and—surprise, surprise—you will probably end up with some nice macro images. You don't have all the creative control you might need for a more studied image, but a grab shot that's not perfect trumps any photo you don't take because you're fiddling with settings.

Scene modes are also useful when you loan your camera to someone and don't want to explain to them how to use the D3500. Scene modes not only make decisions about basic exposure, but they select some focusing options, whether or not to use flash, and what shutter speeds/apertures are best for a particular type of subject. I'll recap the descriptions of these modes that I originally provided in Chapter 2:

- **Auto.** In this mode, the D3500 makes all the exposure decisions for you, and will pop up the internal flash if needed under low-light conditions. The camera automatically focuses on the subject closest to the camera (unless you've set the lens to manual focus), and the autofocus assist illuminator lamp on the front of the camera will light up to help the camera focus in low-light conditions.

- **Auto (Flash Off).** Identical to Auto mode, except that the flash will not pop up under any circumstances. You'd want to use this in a museum, during religious ceremonies, concerts, or any environment where flash is forbidden or distracting.

- **Portrait.** Use this mode when you're taking a portrait of a subject standing relatively close to the camera and want to de-emphasize the background, maximize sharpness, and produce flattering skin tones. The built-in flash will pop up if needed.

- **Sports.** Use this mode to freeze fast-moving subjects. The D3500 selects a fast shutter speed to stop action, and focuses continuously on the center focus point while you have the shutter release button pressed halfway. However, you can select one of the other two focus points to the left or right of the center by pressing the multi selector left/right buttons. The built-in electronic flash and focus assist illuminator lamp are disabled.

- **Close-Up.** This mode is helpful when you are shooting close-up pictures of a subject from about one foot away or less, such as flowers, bugs, and small items. The D3500 focuses on the closest subject in the center of the frame, but you can use the multi selector right and left buttons to focus on a different point. Use a tripod in this mode, as exposures may be long enough to cause blurring from camera movement. The built-in flash will pop up if needed.

- **Night Portrait.** Choose this mode when you want to illuminate a subject in the foreground with flash (it will pop up automatically, if needed), but still allow the background to be exposed properly by the available light. The camera focuses on the closest main subject. Be prepared to use a tripod or a vibration-resistant lens like the 18-55 VR kit lens to reduce the effects of camera shake. (You'll find more about VR and camera shake in Chapter 10.)

Using Special Effects Modes

Although the D3500's Special Effects modes are a type of Scene mode selection, I've elected to describe them here, but they are actually more closely related to retouching effects we explored in Chapter 5. Indeed, three of them are essentially identical to retouching effects, but are simply applied during shooting rather than after the image has already been captured.

To use Special Effects, set the mode dial to the EFFECTS position, and then rotate the command dial to cycle through the 10 effects and select the one you want to use. Then, you can take pictures as always. However, when using Night Vision, Color Sketch, Miniature Effect, or Select Color special effects, only JPEG Fine images will be saved. No RAW image is created. The flash and AF-assist beam are disabled when using all these effects. Your choices include:

- **Night Vision.** This effect gives you a monochrome image recorded at high ISO under very low light conditions. Because the light is so dim, autofocus is available only in live view. You can use manual focus instead. The D3500's flash and AF-assist beam are disabled. You'll probably want to use a tripod, because this mode can use longer shutter speeds that accentuate camera movement. (See Figure 6.10, upper left.)

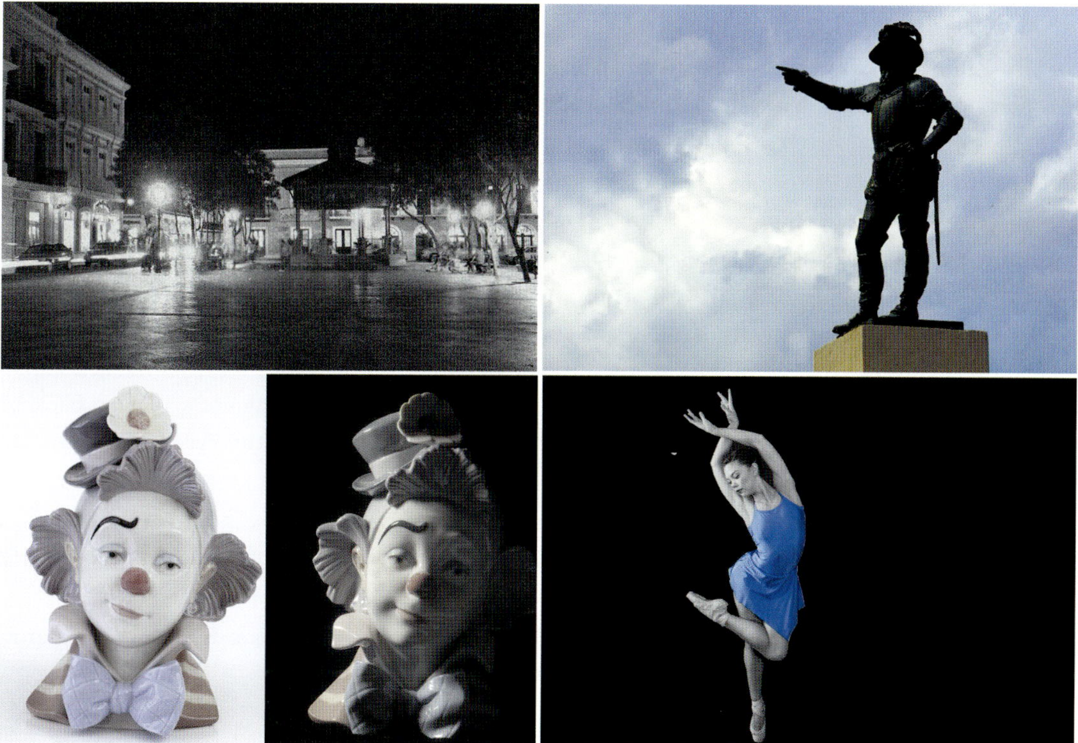

Figure 6.10 Special effects include Night Vision (upper left), Silhouette (upper right), High/Low Key (lower left), and Selective Color (lower right).

- **Super Vivid.** Both color richness (saturation) and contrast are boosted to make the image more vibrant, if a bit unrealistic. You might want to use this on cloudy, overcast days to counter the overall gray mood of an outdoor scene.

- **Pop.** Increases saturation but does not increase contrast, giving a more realistic, if vivid, image.

- **Photo Illustration.** Creates a posterization effect, with blocky colors and outlines around their edges. In live view, you can adjust the thickness of the outlines by pressing the left/right directional buttons. Press OK when done specifying thickness. If you like, you can then exit live view and shoot using the viewfinder with the thickness settings you've specified in effect. You can also shoot movies in this mode; they play back like as a series of still pictures. Note that autofocus is not available in movie mode. Flash is disabled when using Photo Illustration.

- **Toy Camera Effect.** Produces an image that looks like it was taken with a toy camera. In live view you can preview the effect and make adjustments before the shot. Press the OK button, and Vividness and Vignetting options pop up. Choose one with the up/down buttons, and adjust the selected parameter with the left/right buttons.

- **Miniature Effect.** This setting produces the same look as the Miniature Effect retouching option. Shoot from an elevated vantage point to enhance the miniature look. You can adjust the effect when shooting in live view. Use the multi selector buttons to select a point of focus in the image, and press the shutter release halfway to lock in focus on that point. You can press the Zoom In button to cancel miniature effect options and zoom in on your image to select a new point of focus. Press the Zoom Out button to return to miniature effect view.

  You can then use the left/right buttons to adjust the orientation of the area that will be in focus, and the up/down buttons to adjust its width. Press OK when all settings are complete. You can shoot miniature effect images in live view, or press the Lv button to exit and take pictures using those same settings using the viewfinder instead.

  I've seen some great video clips shot with this effect, making, in one example, Disneyland appear to be a miniature amusement park. No sound is recorded, but you can add your own audio later. Note that autofocus is not available in Movie mode. However, the finished clip is played back at high speed, like an old-time movie. A 45-minute sequence will play back in roughly three minutes (a 15x speed-up factor!). The built-in flash and AF-assist beam are disabled.

- **Selective Color.** This setting creates an image with selective color effects. As with most other special effects, the built-in flash is disabled. Directions for using Selective Color are in the sidebar that follows. (See Figure 6.10, lower right.)

- **Silhouette.** Produces silhouettes against bright backgrounds, and flash is disabled. (See Figure 6.10, upper right.)

SELECTIVE COLOR

1. In live view, press OK to view the Selective Color options.

2. Place the white square in the center of an image over a color you want to retain. You can use the Zoom In and Zoom Out buttons to zero in on an area with the desired color more precisely.

3. Press the up button to select the color. You can now press the up/down buttons to choose a "tolerance" for similar hues (say, other shades of red if you've selected a red tone). The range is 1–7.

4. Rotate the control dial to move highlighting to one of the other two boxes in the top row. You can repeat Steps 2 and 3 to add more colors.

5. Press the Trash button to reset and start over, or OK when done specifying colors.

6. As with other Effects, you can exit live view and take images with the viewfinder, using your settings. Your images will look like Figure 6.10, lower right.

- **High Key.** Creates bright scenes. This effects tool, like the Low Key effect described next, can't work miracles. It won't produce a high-key image from a low-key subject. But if you have a scene that is filled with bright light, this effect will accentuate that. Flash is disabled in this mode. High Key effect and Low Key effect (described next) are shown at lower left in Figure 6.10.

- **Low Key.** Gives you dark, foreboding images. You'll need contrasty lighting to achieve this effect, but given the right subject, you can end up with an image like the ones shown in the figure. Flash is disabled in this mode.

Adjusting Exposure with ISO Settings

Another way of adjusting exposures is by changing the ISO sensitivity setting. Sometimes photographers forget about this option, because the common practice is to set the ISO once for a particular shooting session (say, at ISO 200 for bright sunlight outdoors, or ISO 800 when shooting indoors) and then forget about ISO. ISOs higher than ISO 200 or 400 are seen as "bad" or "necessary evils." However, changing the ISO is a valid way of adjusting exposure settings, particularly with the Nikon D3500, which produces good results at ISO settings that create grainy, unusable pictures with some other camera models.

Indeed, I find myself using ISO adjustment as a convenient alternate way of adding or subtracting EV when shooting in Manual mode, and as a quick way of choosing equivalent exposures when in Program or Shutter-priority or Aperture-priority modes. For example, I've selected a Manual exposure with both f/stop and shutter speed suitable for my image using, say, ISO 200. I can change the exposure in 1/3-stop increments by holding down the ISO button located on the left side of the camera next to the LCD monitor, and spinning the command dial one click at a time. The difference in image quality/noise at ISO 200 is negligible if I dial in ISO 160 or ISO 125 to reduce exposure a little, or change to ISO 250 or 320 to increase exposure. I keep my preferred f/stop and shutter speed, but still adjust the exposure.

Or, perhaps, I am using S mode and the metered exposure at ISO 200 is 1/500th second at f/11. If I decide on the spur of the moment I'd rather use 1/500th second at f/8, I can press the Fn button (unless you've redefined its behavior to some other function) and spin the command dial three clicks counterclockwise to switch to ISO 100. You can also use the *i* button to summon the information edit screen. Of course, it's a good idea to monitor your ISO changes, so you don't end up at ISO 6400 accidentally. An ISO indicator appears in the viewfinder to remind you what sensitivity setting has been dialed in.

ISO settings can, of course, also be used to boost or reduce sensitivity in particular shooting situations. The D3500 can use ISO settings from ISO 100 up to ISO 25600. The camera can also adjust the ISO automatically as appropriate for various lighting conditions. When you choose the Auto ISO setting in the Shooting menu, as described in Chapter 4, the D3500 adjusts the sensitivity dynamically to suit the subject matter, based on minimum shutter speed and ISO limits you have prescribed. As I noted in Chapter 4, you should use Auto ISO cautiously if you don't want the D3500 to use an ISO higher than you might otherwise have selected.

Dealing with Noise

Visual image noise is that random grainy effect that some like to use as a special effect, but which, most of the time, is objectionable because it robs your image of detail even as it adds that "interesting" texture. Noise is caused by two different phenomena: high ISO settings and long exposures.

High ISO noise commonly appears when you raise your camera's sensitivity setting above ISO 800. With the Nikon D3500, noise may become visible at ISO 1600, and is often fairly noticeable at ISO 3200. At ISO 6400 and above, noise is usually quite bothersome. You can expect noise and increase in contrast in any pictures taken at these lofty ratings. High ISO noise appears as a result of the amplification needed to increase the sensitivity of the sensor. While higher ISOs do pull details out of dark areas, they also amplify non-signal information randomly, creating noise. You'll find a High ISO NR choice in the Shooting menu, where you can specify Off or On. Because noise reduction tends to soften the grainy look while robbing an image of detail, you may want to disable the feature if you're willing to accept a little noise in exchange for more details.

A similar noisy phenomenon occurs during long time exposures, which allow more photons to reach the sensor, increasing your ability to capture a picture under low-light conditions. However, the longer exposures also increase the likelihood that some pixels will register random phantom photons, often because the longer an imager is "hot," the warmer it gets, and that heat can be mistaken for photons. There's also a special kind of noise that CMOS sensors like the one used in the D3500 are potentially susceptible to. With a CCD, the entire signal is conveyed off the chip and funneled through a single amplifier and analog-to-digital conversion circuit. Any noise introduced there is, at least, consistent. CMOS imagers, on the other hand, contain millions of individual amplifiers and A/D converters, all working in unison. Because these circuits don't necessarily all process in precisely the same way all the time, they can introduce something called fixed-pattern noise into the image data.

You can also apply noise reduction to a lesser extent using Photoshop, and when converting RAW files to some other format, using your favorite RAW converter, or an industrial-strength product like Noise Ninja (www.picturecode.com) to wipe out noise after you've already taken the picture.

Fixing Exposures with Histograms

While you can often recover poorly exposed photos in your image editor, your best bet is to arrive at the correct exposure in the camera, minimizing the tweaks that you have to make in post-processing. However, you can't always judge exposure just by viewing the image on your D3500's LCD monitor after the shot is made. Nor can you get a 100 percent accurately exposed picture by using live view. Ambient light may make the LCD difficult to see, and the brightness level you've set can affect the appearance of the playback image.

Instead, you can use a histogram, which is a chart displayed on the D3500's LCD monitor that shows the number of tones being captured at each brightness level. You can use the information to provide correction for the next shot you take. The D3500 offers four histogram variations in three screens: three histograms that show overall brightness levels for an image and an alternate version that separates the red, green, and blue channels of your image into separate histograms.

DISPLAYING HISTOGRAMS

To view all the available histograms on your screen, you must have the D3500 set up properly. First, you'll need to mark Histograms using the Playback Display Options entry in the Playback menu, as described in Chapter 4. That will make the Histograms screen visible when you cycle among the informational screens while pressing the multi selector up/down buttons while an image is displayed.

The most basic histogram is displayed during playback when you press the multi selector up/down buttons to produce the Overview Data screen, as described briefly in Chapter 4. This screen provides a small histogram at the right side that displays the distribution of luminance or brightness. The most useful histogram screen is the one shown in Figure 6.11, which displays both a luminance chart and separate red, green, and blue charts.

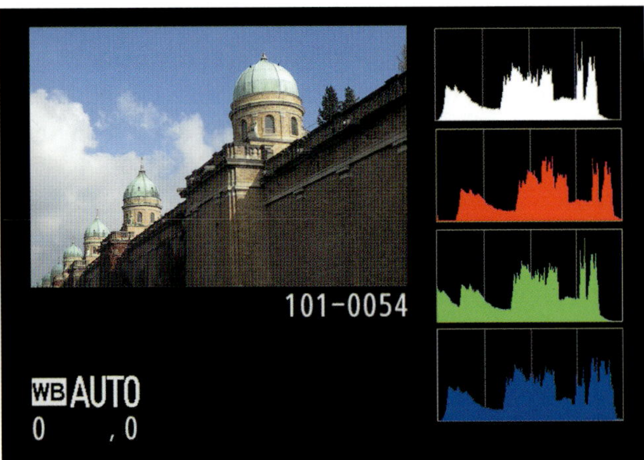

Figure 6.11
The D3500's most complete histogram screen shows both luminance and separate red, green, and blue histograms.

Both luminance and RGB histograms are charts that include a representation of up to 256 vertical lines on a horizontal axis that show the number of pixels in the image at each brightness level, from 0 (black) on the left side to 255 (white) on the right. (The three-inch LCD monitor doesn't have enough pixels to show each and every one of the 256 lines, but, instead provides a representation of the shape of the curve formed.) The more pixels at a given level, the taller the bar at that position. If no bar appears at a particular position on the scale from left to right, there are no pixels at that particular brightness level.

As you can see, a typical histogram produces a mountain-like shape, with most of the pixels bunched in the middle tones, with fewer pixels at the dark and light ends of the scale. Ideally, though, there will be at least some pixels at either extreme, so that your image has both a true black and a true white representing some details. Learn to spot histograms that represent over- and underexposure, and add or subtract exposure using an EV modification to compensate.

For example, Figure 6.12 (top) shows the histogram (in the inset) for an image that is badly underexposed. You can guess from the shape of the histogram that many of the dark tones to the left of the graph have been clipped off. There's plenty of room on the right side for additional pixels to reside without having them become overexposed. Or, a histogram might look like the inset in Figure 6.12 (center), which is overexposed. In either case, you can increase or decrease the exposure (either by changing the f/stop or shutter speed in Manual mode or by adding or subtracting an EV value in A or S modes) to produce the corrected histogram shown inset in Figure 6.12 (bottom), in which the tones are more evenly distributed, reaching both left and right sides of the scale. See "Making EV Changes," above for information on dialing in exposure compensation.

The histogram can also be used to aid in fixing the contrast of an image, although gauging incorrect contrast is more difficult. For example, if the histogram shows all the tones bunched up in one place in the image, the photo will be low in contrast. If the tones are spread out more or less evenly, the image is probably high in contrast. In either case, your best bet may be to switch to RAW (if

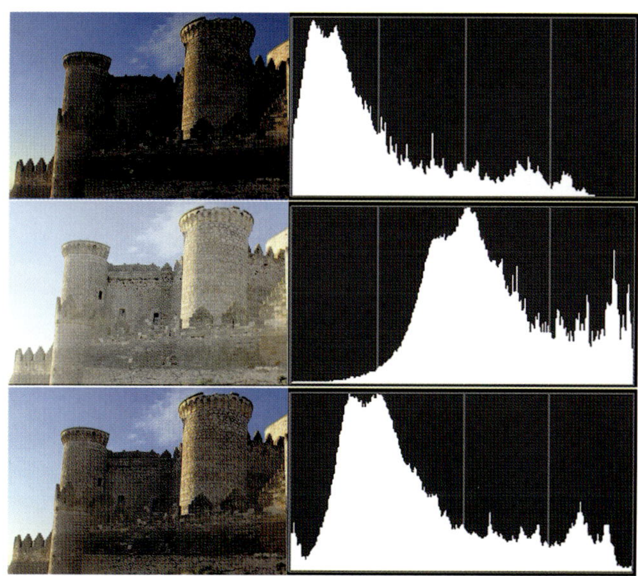

Figure 6.12
This histogram shows an underexposed image (top). This histogram reveals that the image is overexposed (center). A histogram for a properly exposed image should look like this (bottom).

you're not already using that format) so you can adjust contrast in post-processing. However, you can also change to a user-defined Picture Control with contrast set lower (–1 to –3) or higher (+1 to +3) as required. You'll find instructions for creating Picture Controls in Chapter 4.

One useful, but often overlooked tool in evaluating histograms is the Highlights display accessed by cycling though the playback display options with the up/down keys, which shows blown-out highlights with a black blinking border for the selected active channel. Highlights can give you a better picture of what information is being lost to overexposure.

In working with histograms, your goal should be to have all the tones in an image spread out between the edges, with none clipped off at the left and right sides. Underexposing (to preserve highlights) should be done only as a last resort, because retrieving the underexposed shadows in your image editor will frequently increase the noise, even if you're working with RAW files. A better course of action is to expose for the highlights, but, when the subject matter makes it practical, fill in the shadows with additional light, using reflectors, fill flash, or other techniques rather than allowing them to be seriously underexposed.

The more you work with histograms, the more useful they become. One of the first things that histogram veterans notice is that it's possible to overexpose one channel even if the overall exposure appears to be correct. For example, flower photographers soon discover that it's really, really difficult to get a good picture of a rose, like the one shown at top in Figure 6.13. The exposure looks okay—but there's no detail in the rose's petals. Looking at the histogram (at bottom in the figure) shows why: the red channel is blown out. If you look at the red histogram, there's a peak at the right edge that indicates that highlight information has been lost. In fact, the green channel has been blown, too, and so the green parts of the flower also lack detail. Only the blue channel's histogram

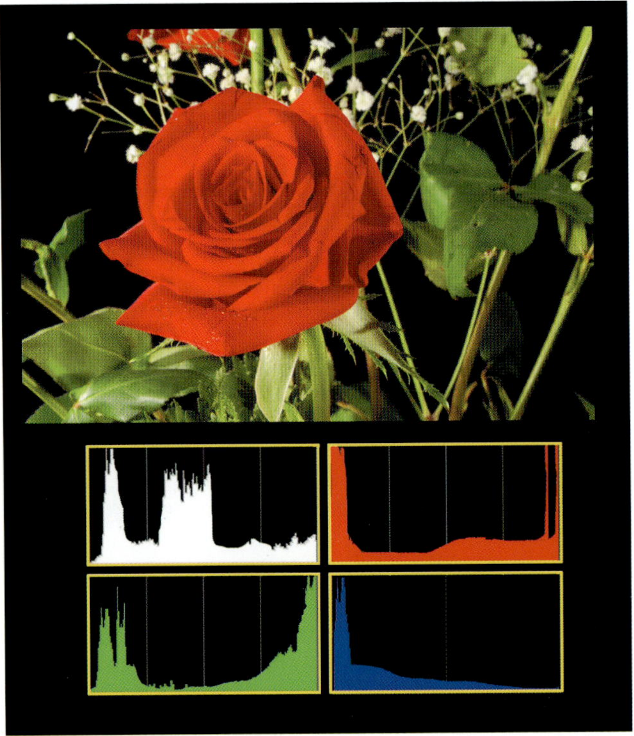

Figure 6.13
The red channel is blown out, leaving little detail in the rose.

is entirely contained within the boundaries of the chart, and, on first glance, the white luminance histogram at top of the column of graphs seems fairly normal.

Any of the primary channels, red, green, or blue, can blow out all by themselves, although bright reds seem to be the most common problem area. More difficult to diagnose are overexposed tones in one of the "in-between" hues on the color wheel. Overexposed yellows (which are very common) will be shown by blowouts in *both* the red and green channels. Too-bright cyans will manifest as excessive blue and green highlights, while overexposure in the red and blue channels reduces detail in magenta colors. As you gain experience, you'll be able to see exactly how anomalies in the RGB channels translate into poor highlights and murky shadows.

The only way to correct for color channel blowouts is to reduce exposure. As I mentioned earlier, you might want to consider filling in the shadows with additional light to keep them from becoming too dark when you decrease exposure. In practice, you'll want to monitor the red channel most closely, followed by the blue channel, and slightly decrease exposure to see if that helps. Because of the way our eyes perceive color, we are more sensitive to variations in green, so green channel blowouts are less of a problem, unless your main subject is heavily colored in that hue. If you plan on photographing a frog hopping around on your front lawn, you'll want to be extra careful to preserve detail in the green channel, using bracketing or other exposure techniques outlined in this chapter.

Bracketing

Bracketing is a method for shooting several consecutive exposures using different settings, as a way of improving the odds that one will be exactly right. Before digital cameras took over the universe, it was common to bracket exposures, shooting, say, a series of three photos at 1/125th second, but varying the f/stop from f/8 to f/11 to f/16. In practice, smaller than whole-stop increments were used for greater precision, and lenses with apertures that were set manually commonly had half-stop detents on their aperture rings, or could easily be set to a mid-way position between whole f/stops. It was just as common to keep the same aperture and vary the shutter speed, although in the days before electronic shutters, film cameras often had only whole-increment shutter speeds available.

Today, cameras like the D3500 can bracket exposures much more precisely, using "in between" settings. Unfortunately, the D3500 doesn't have automatic bracketing, like some of its more advanced siblings, but you can still bracket manually by adding and/or subtracting EV values, as described in the "Making EV Changes," sidebar earlier in the chapter, or by shooting in Manual mode to select the shutter speed and aperture that will be used.

Bracketing and Merge to HDR

One reason you might want to use manual bracketing is to create high dynamic range (HDR) photographs, which have become all the rage as a way to extend the number of tones that a digital camera like the D3500 can capture. While my goal in this book is to show you how to take great photos *in the camera* rather than how to fix your errors in Photoshop, the Merge to HDR Pro (high dynamic range) feature in Adobe's flagship image editor is too cool to ignore. The ability to have a bracketed set of exposures that are identical except for exposure, is key to getting good results with this Photoshop feature, which allows you to produce images with a full, rich dynamic range that includes a level of detail in the highlights and shadows that is almost impossible to achieve with digital cameras. In contrasty lighting situations, even the Nikon D3500 has a tendency to blow out highlights when you expose solely for the shadows or midtones.

Suppose you wanted to photograph a dimly lit room that had a bright window showing an outdoors scene. Proper exposure for the room might be on the order of 1/60th second at f/2.8 at ISO 200, while the outdoors scene probably would require f/11 at 1/400th second. That's almost a 7 EV step difference (approximately 7 f/stops) and well beyond the dynamic range of any digital camera, including the Nikon D3500.

When you're using Merge to HDR Pro, you'd take three pictures, one for the shadows, one for the highlights, and perhaps one for the midtones. Then, you'd use the Merge to HDR Pro command to combine all of the images into one HDR image that integrates the well-exposed sections of each version.

The images should be as identical as possible, except for exposure. So, it's a good idea to mount the D3500 on a tripod, use the self timer, and take all the exposures in one continuous series. Just follow these steps:

1. **Set up the camera.** Mount the D3500 on a tripod.

2. **Set the camera for Manual exposure.** Use the mode dial to select Manual exposure.

3. **Choose an f/stop.** Select an aperture that will provide a correct exposure at your initial manual settings for the series of manually bracketed shots. *And then leave this adjustment alone!* You don't want the aperture to change for your series, as that would change the depth-of-field. You want to adjust exposure *only* with the shutter speed.

4. **Choose a shutter speed for the initial exposure.** For this exercise, we'll be shooting three different bracketed exposures, so set the shutter speed such that the first image will be properly exposed. If necessary, take a test shot to find the "correct" exposure and adjust from there.

5. **Choose manual focus.** You don't want the focus to change between shots, so set the D3500 to manual focus, and carefully focus your shot.

6. **Choose RAW exposures.** Set the camera to take RAW files, which will give you the widest range of tones in your images.

7. **Take the first shot.** Carefully press the shutter release and take the first exposure, which will be correctly exposed, as seen at top left in Figure 6.14.

8. **Adjust shutter speed to give one stop less exposure.** For example, if your first shot was at 1/250th second at f/11, *gently* change to 1/500th second.

9. **Take the second shot.** Press the button on the shutter release and take the second exposure, which will be one stop underexposed, as seen at center left in Figure 6.14.

10. **Repeat steps 8 and 9 once more.** Create an exposure one stop overexposed. You'll end up with a third picture, overexposed so the shadows have detail, but highlights are washed out, as shown at bottom left in Figure 6.14.

11. **Continue with the Merge to HDR Pro steps listed next.** You can also use a different program, such as Photomatix (www.hdrsoft.com), if you know how to use it. Note that these steps could also be carried out using Aperture-priority, and using EV adjustments to achieve the different exposures over the same range. I find manual bracketing to be just as fast.

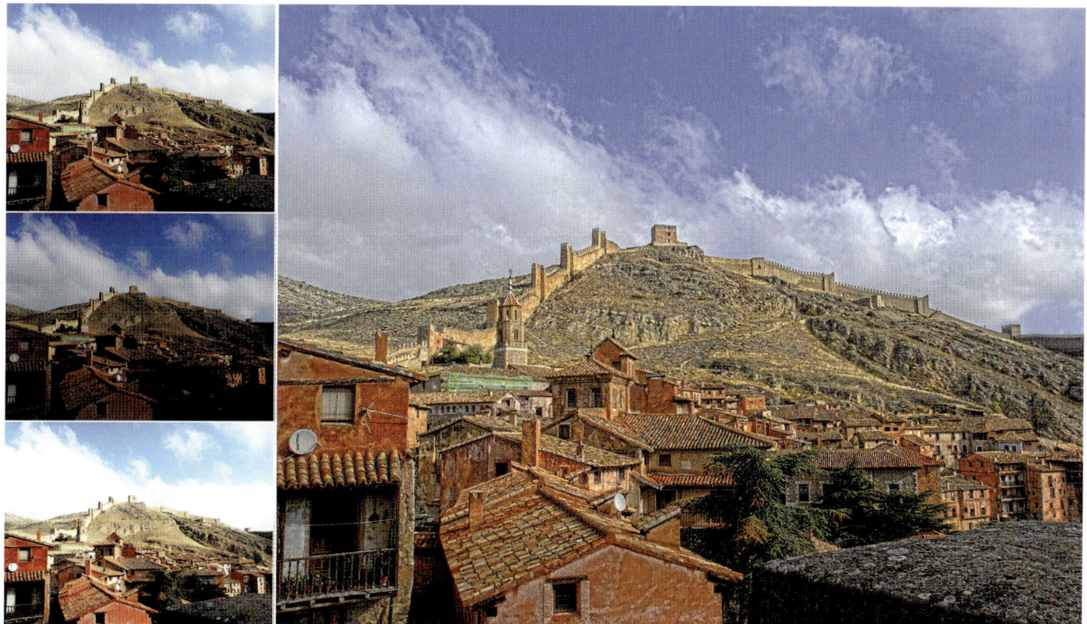

Figure 6.14 With three different exposures (left), you'll end up with an extended dynamic range photo like this one (right).

The next steps show you how to combine the separate exposures into one merged high dynamic range image.

1. **Copy your images to your computer.** If you use an application to transfer the files to your computer, make sure it does not make any adjustments to brightness, contrast, or exposure. You want the real raw information for Merge to HDR Pro to work with.

2. **Activate Merge to HDR Pro.** Choose File > Automate > Merge to HDR Pro.

3. **Select the photos to be merged.** Use the Browse feature to locate and select your photos to be merged. You'll note a checkbox that can be used to automatically align the images if they were not taken with the camera mounted on a rock-steady support. This will adjust for any slight movement of the camera that might have occurred when you changed exposure settings.

4. **Choose parameters (optional).** The first time you use Merge to HDR Pro, you can let the program work with its default parameters. Once you've played with the feature a few times, you can read the Adobe help files and learn more about the options than I can present in this non-software-oriented camera guide.

5. **Click OK.** The merger begins.

6. **Save.** Once HDR merge has done its thing, save the file to your computer.

If you do everything correctly, you'll end up with a photo like the one shown at right in Figure 6.14. Note that, ideally, nothing should move between shots. That means ocean waves and waterfalls aren't your best subjects for HDR, unless you're looking for a special effect.

What if you don't have the opportunity, inclination, or skills to create several images at different exposures, as described? If you shoot in RAW format, you can still use Merge to HDR, working with a *single* original image file. What you do is import the image into Photoshop several times, using Adobe Camera Raw to create multiple copies of the file at different exposure levels.

For example, you'd create one copy that's too dark, so the shadows lose detail, but the highlights are preserved. Create another copy with the shadows intact and allow the highlights to wash out. Then, you can use Merge to HDR to combine the two and end up with a finished image that has the extended dynamic range you're looking for.

7

Mastering the Mysteries of Autofocus

Getting the right exposure is one of the foundations of a great photograph, but a lot more goes into a compelling shot than good tonal values. A sharp image, proper white balance, good color, and other factors all can help elevate your image from good to exceptional. So, now that you've got a good understanding of exposure tucked away, you'll want to learn how to work with some additional exposure options, use the automatic and manual focusing controls available with the Nikon D3500, and master some of the many ways you can fine-tune your images.

One key problem is that the camera doesn't have any way of determining, for certain, what subject you want to be in sharp focus. It may select an object and lock in focus with lightning speed—even though the subject is not the one that's the center of interest of your photograph. Or, the camera may lock focus too soon, or too late. This chapter will help you choose the options available with your Nikon D3500 that will help the camera understand what you want to focus on, when, and maybe even why.

How Focus Works

Although Nikon added autofocus capabilities to its cameras in the 1980s, back in the day of film, prior to that focusing was always done manually. Honest. Even though viewfinders were bigger and brighter than they are today, special focusing screens, magnifiers, and other gadgets were often used to help the photographer achieve correct focus. Imagine what it must have been like to focus manually under demanding, fast-moving conditions such as sports photography.

Focusing was problematic because our eyes and brains have poor memory for correct focus, which is why your eye doctor must shift back and forth between sets of lenses and ask, "Does that look sharper—or was it sharper before?" in determining your correct prescription. Similarly, manual focusing involves jogging the focus ring back and forth as you go from almost in focus, to sharp focus, to almost focused again. The little clockwise and counterclockwise arcs decrease in size until you've zeroed in on the point of correct focus. What you're looking for is the image with the most contrast between the edges of elements in the image.

The camera also looks for these contrast differences among pixels to determine relative sharpness. There are two primary ways that sharp focus is determined: phase detection and contrast detection. As you'll see, these can be applied in several different ways, with options changing dramatically when you switch from composing through the optical viewfinder, and when you're using live view to shoot stills or movies. First, let's get the primary focus methods out of the way. I'll cover the focus variations available in Live View/Movie modes in Chapter 8.

There are two ways that sharp focus is determined: Contrast detection (used when shooting stills and movies with live view), and Phase detection (used when framing your image through the optical viewfinder). I'm going to provide a quick overview of contrast detection first, and then devote the rest of this chapter to ways of working with phase detection.

Contrast Detection

This is a slower, but potentially more accurate, mode, best suited for static subjects, and used by the D3500 in Live View and Movie modes. It's a bit easier to understand, and is illustrated by Figure 7.1, a close-up of some weathered wood. At top in the figure, the transitions between the edges found in the image are soft and blurred because of the low contrast between them. Whether the edges are horizontal, vertical, or diagonal doesn't matter in the least; the focus system looks only for contrast between edges, and those edges can run in any direction.

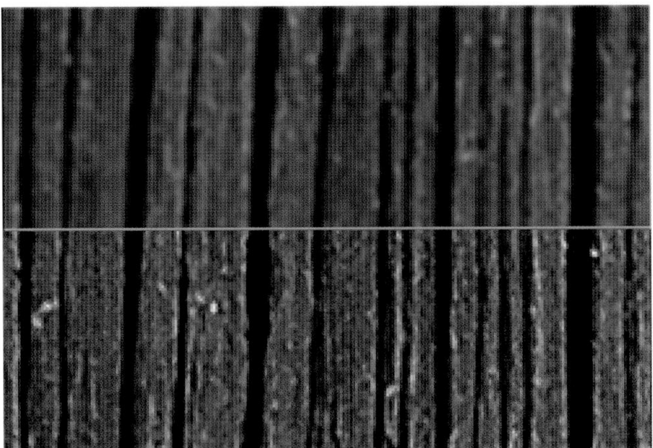

Figure 7.1
Focus in contrast detection mode evaluates the increase in contrast in the edges of subjects, starting with a blurry image (top) and producing a sharp, contrasty image (bottom).

At the bottom of Figure 7.1, the image has been brought into sharp focus, and the edges have much more contrast; the transitions are sharp and clear. Although this example is a bit exaggerated so you can see the results on the printed page, it's easy to understand that when maximum contrast in a subject is achieved, it can be deemed to be in sharp focus. Although achieving focus with contrast detection is generally quite a bit slower, there are several advantages to this method:

- **Works with more image types.** Any subject that has edges will work.

- **Focus on any point.** With contrast detection, any portion of the image can be used to focus. Focus is achieved with the actual sensor image, so focus point selection is simply a matter of choosing which part of the sensor image to use. As you'll learn in Chapter 8, you can move the focus frame around on the screen when working with live view.

- **Potentially more accurate.** Contrast detection is clear-cut. The camera can clearly see when the highest contrast has been achieved, as long as there is sufficient light to allow the camera to examine the image produced by the sensor. Some "hunting" may be necessary as the D3500 seeks the ideal focus plane, but the results are generally very accurate.

You'll find more on contrast detection, and its use during live view and movie making, in Chapter 8.

Phase Detection

This mode is used by the autofocus system when you're looking through the optical viewfinder. The autofocus sampling area is divided into two halves by a lens in the sensor. The two halves are compared, much like (actually, exactly like) a two-window rangefinder used in surveying weaponry—and non-SLR cameras like the venerable Leica M film models. The contrast between the two images changes as focus is moved in or out, until sharp focus is achieved when the images are "in phase," or lined up.

The eleven autofocus sensors of Nikon's Multi-CAM 1000 autofocus module are located in the "floor" of the mirror box, just under the flip-up mirror, which is partially silvered so that most of the light reaching it from the lens is bounced upward to the viewfinder, while some light is directed downward toward the focus sensors. If you lock up the mirror of your camera (using the Lock Mirror Up for Cleaning option in the Setup menu), you can see where these sensors are located.

Conceptually, these AF sensors function as shown in Figure 7.2, a simplified illustration of what's going on. The illumination arrives from opposite sides of the lens surface and is directed through separate microlenses, producing two half-images.

When the image is out of focus—or out of phase—as in Figure 7.2 (top), the two halves, each representing a slightly different view from opposite sides of the lens, don't line up. Sharp focus is achieved when the images are "in phase," and aligned, as in Figure 7.2 (bottom).

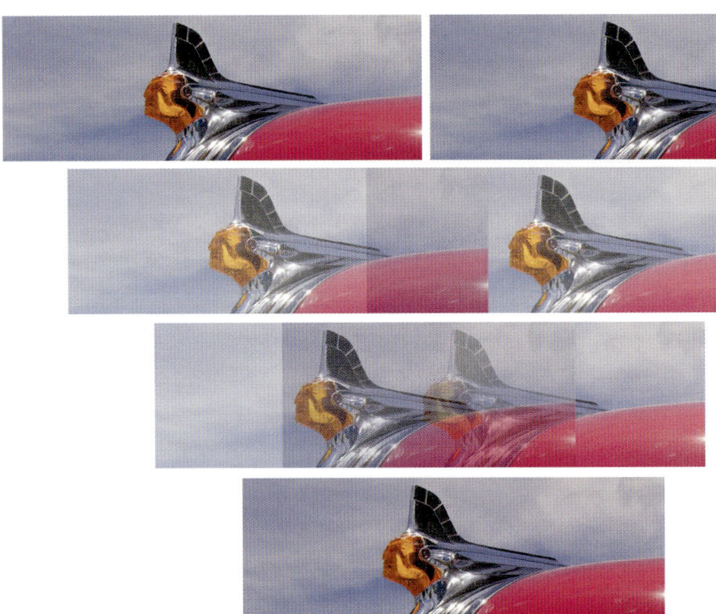

Figure 7.2
Using phase detection, the D3500 is able to align the features of the image and achieve sharp focus quickly.

Fortunately, the "rangefinder" approach of phase detection tells the D3500 exactly how out of focus the image is, and in which direction (focus is too near, or too far) thanks to the amount and direction of the displacement of the split image. The camera can quickly and precisely snap the image into sharp focus and line up the vertical lines, as shown in the figure. Of course, this scenario—vertical lines being interpreted by a horizontally oriented sensor—is ideal. When the same sensor is asked to measure focus for, say, horizontal lines that don't split up quite so conveniently, or, in the worst case, subjects such as the sky (which may have neither vertical nor horizontal lines), focus can slow down drastically, or even become impossible.

Phase detection is the normal mode used by the D3500. As with any rangefinder-like function, accuracy is better when the "base length" between the two images is larger. (Think back to your high school trigonometry; you could calculate a distance more accurately when the separation between the two points where the angles were measured was greater.) For that reason, phase detection autofocus is more accurate with larger (wider) lens openings—especially those with maximum f/stops of f/2.8 or better—than with smaller lens openings, and may not work at all when the f/stop is smaller than f/5.6. As I noted, the D3500 is able to perform these comparisons very quickly.

Cross-Type Focus Point

One feature that new Nikon D3500 owners sometimes overlook is the cross-type focus point at the center position. Why is this important? It helps to take a closer look at the phase detection system when presented with a non-ideal subject.

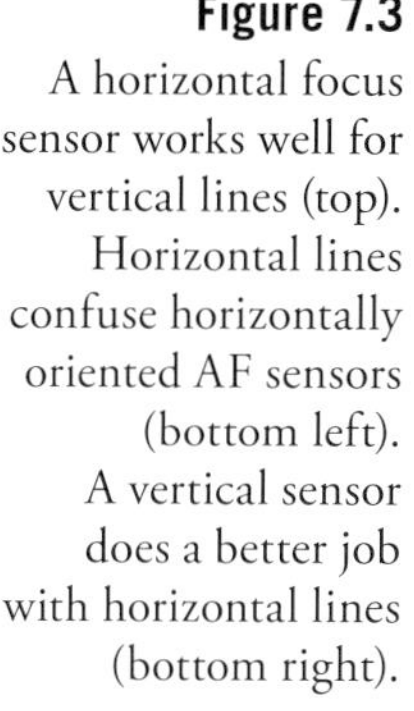

Figure 7.3
A horizontal focus sensor works well for vertical lines (top). Horizontal lines confuse horizontally oriented AF sensors (bottom left). A vertical sensor does a better job with horizontal lines (bottom right).

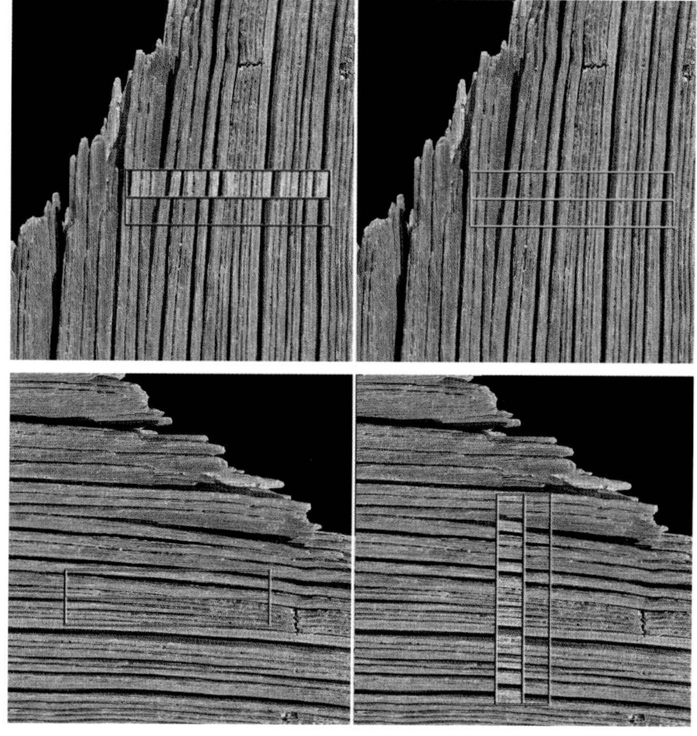

Figure 7.3, top, shows the same weathered wood pictured earlier in Figure 7.1, and illustrates how the AF system is able to align the vertical lines to bring the out-of-focus image (top left) into focus (top right). (This is an overly simplified illustration; your autofocus system looks *nothing* like this.) At bottom left in Figure 7.3, we've chosen to rotate the camera 90 degrees (say, because we want a vertically oriented composition). In the illustration, the image within the focus sensor's area is still split in two and displaced slightly side to side, but the amount and direction of the misalignment is far from obvious. A horizontally oriented focus sensor will be forced to look for less obvious vertical lines to match up. Our best-case subject has been transformed into a worst-case subject for a horizontal focus sensor.

One way to solve the conundrum is to use a vertically oriented AF sensor, as shown in Figure 7.3, bottom right. It has no problem with the horizontal lines. Cross-type sensors combine the best of both worlds, embedding both vertical and horizontal AF sensors with the focus point in the center of the D3500's AF point array. Cross-type sensors can handle horizontal and vertical lines with equal aplomb and, if you think about it, lines at any diagonal angle as well. In lower light levels, with subjects that were moving, or with subjects that have no pattern and less contrast to begin with, the cross-type sensor not only works faster but can focus subjects that a horizontal- or vertical-only sensor can't handle at all. So, you can see that having a center cross-type focus sensor that is extra-sensitive with faster lenses is a definite advantage.

Locking in Focus

The D3500's autofocus mechanism, like all such systems found in SLR cameras, evaluates the degree of focus, but, unlike the human eye, it is able to remember the progression perfectly, so that autofocus can lock in much more quickly and, with an image that has sufficient contrast, more precisely. Unfortunately, while the D3500's focus system finds it easy to measure degrees of apparent focus at each of the focus points in the viewfinder, it doesn't really know with any certainty *which* object should be in sharpest focus. Is it the closest object? The subject in the center? Something lurking *behind* the closest subject? A person standing over at the side of the picture? Many of the techniques for using autofocus effectively involve telling the Nikon D3500 exactly what it should be focusing on, by choosing a focus zone or by allowing the camera to choose a focus zone for you. I'll address that topic shortly.

As the camera collects focus information from the sensors, it then evaluates it to determine whether the desired sharp focus has been achieved. The calculations may include whether the subject is moving, and whether the camera needs to "predict" where the subject will be when the shutter release button is fully depressed and the picture is taken. The speed with which the camera is able to evaluate focus and then move the lens elements into the proper position to achieve the sharpest focus determines how fast the autofocus mechanism is. Although your D3500 will almost always focus more quickly than a human, there are types of shooting situations where that's not fast enough. For example, if you're having problems shooting sports because the D3500's autofocus system manically follows each moving subject, a better choice might be to switch Autofocus modes or shift into Manual and prefocus on a spot where you anticipate the action will be, such as a goal line or soccer net. At night football games, for example, when I am shooting with a telephoto lens almost wide open, I sometimes focus manually on one of the referees who happens to be standing where I expect the action to be taking place (say, a halfback run or a pass reception).

Focus Modes

When you're using the optical viewfinder (and, therefore, phase detection autofocus), the D3500 has three AF modes: AF-S (also known as Single autofocus or Single-servo autofocus), AF-C (Continuous autofocus or Continuous-servo autofocus), and AF-A (which switches between the two as appropriate). I'll explain these in more detail later in this section. But first, some confusion…

MANUAL FOCUS

Manual focus is activated by sliding the switch on the lens (if present) to the M position. There are some advantages and disadvantages to focusing yourself. While your batteries will last longer in manual focus mode, it will take you longer to focus the camera for each photo, a process that can be difficult. Modern digital cameras, even dSLRs, depend so much on autofocus that the viewfinders of models that have less than full-frame-sized sensors are no longer designed for optimum manual focus. Pick up any film camera and you'll see a bigger, brighter viewfinder with a focusing screen that's a joy to focus on manually.

Adding Circles of Confusion

You know that increased depth-of-field brings more of your subject into focus. But more depth-of-field also makes autofocusing (or manual focusing) more difficult because the contrast is lower between objects at different distances. So, autofocus with a 200mm lens (or zoom setting) may be easier than at a 28mm focal length (or zoom setting) because the longer lens has less apparent depth-of-field. By the same token, a lens with a maximum aperture of f/1.8 will be easier to auto-focus (or manually focus) than one of the same focal length with an f/4 maximum aperture, because the f/4 lens has more depth-of-field *and* a dimmer view. That's yet another reason why lenses with a maximum aperture smaller than f/5.6 can give your D3500's autofocus system fits—increased depth-of-field joins forces with a dimmer image, and more difficulty in achieving phase detection.

To make things even more complicated, many subjects aren't polite enough to remain still. They move around in the frame, so that even if the D3500 is sharply focused on your main subject, it may change position and require refocusing. (This is where the Subject-tracking mode available in live view is handy; once you've specified an area of focus, the D3500 is smart enough to follow your subject around the frame as your subject moves or you reframe the picture. I'll explain Subject-tracking in detail later in this chapter.)

In other cases, an intervening subject may pop into the frame and pass between you and the subject you meant to photograph. You (or the D3500) have to decide whether to lock focus on this new subject, or remain focused on the original subject. Finally, there are some kinds of subjects that are difficult to bring into sharp focus because they lack enough contrast to allow the D3500's AF system (or our eyes) to lock in. Blank walls, a clear blue sky, or other subject matter may make focusing difficult.

If you find all these focus factors confusing, you're on the right track. Focus is, in fact, measured using something called a *circle of confusion*. An ideal image consists of zillions of tiny little points, which, like all points, theoretically have no height or width. There is perfect contrast between the point and its surroundings. You can think of each point as a pinpoint of light in a darkened room. When a given point is out of focus, its edges decrease in contrast and it changes from a perfect point to a tiny disc with blurry edges (remember, blur is the lack of contrast between boundaries in an image). (See Figure 7.4.)

Figure 7.4
When a pinpoint of light (left) goes out of focus, its blurry edges form a circle of confusion (center and right).

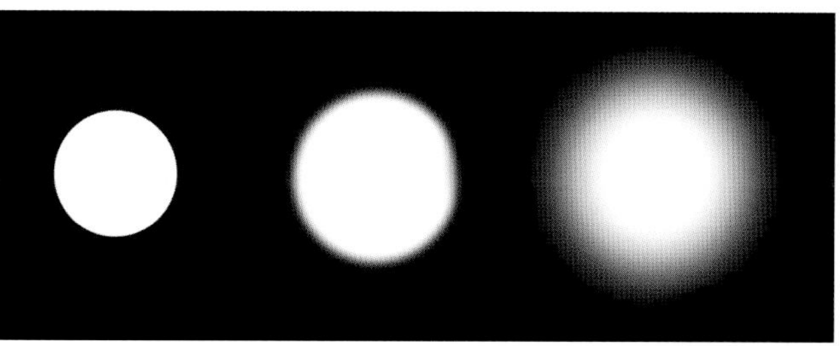

If this blurry disc—the circle of confusion—is small enough, our eye still perceives it as a point. It's only when the disc grows large enough that we can see it as a blur rather than a sharp point that a given point is viewed as out of focus. You can see, then, that enlarging an image, either by displaying it larger on your computer monitor or by making a large print, also enlarges the size of each circle of confusion. Moving closer to the image does the same thing. So, parts of an image that may look perfectly sharp in a 5 × 7–inch print viewed at arm's length, might appear blurry when blown up to 11 × 14 and examined at the same distance. Take a few steps back, however, and it may look sharp again.

To a lesser extent, the viewer also affects the apparent size of these circles of confusion. Some people see details better at a given distance and may perceive smaller circles of confusion than someone standing next to them. For the most part, however, such differences are small. Truly blurry images will look blurry to just about everyone under the same conditions.

Technically, there is just one plane within your picture area, parallel to the back of the camera (or sensor, in the case of a digital camera), that is in sharp focus. That's the plane in which the points of the image are rendered as precise points. At every other plane in front of or behind the focus plane, the points show up as discs that range from slightly blurry to extremely blurry until, as you can see in Figure 7.5, the out-of-focus areas become blurry and less distracting.

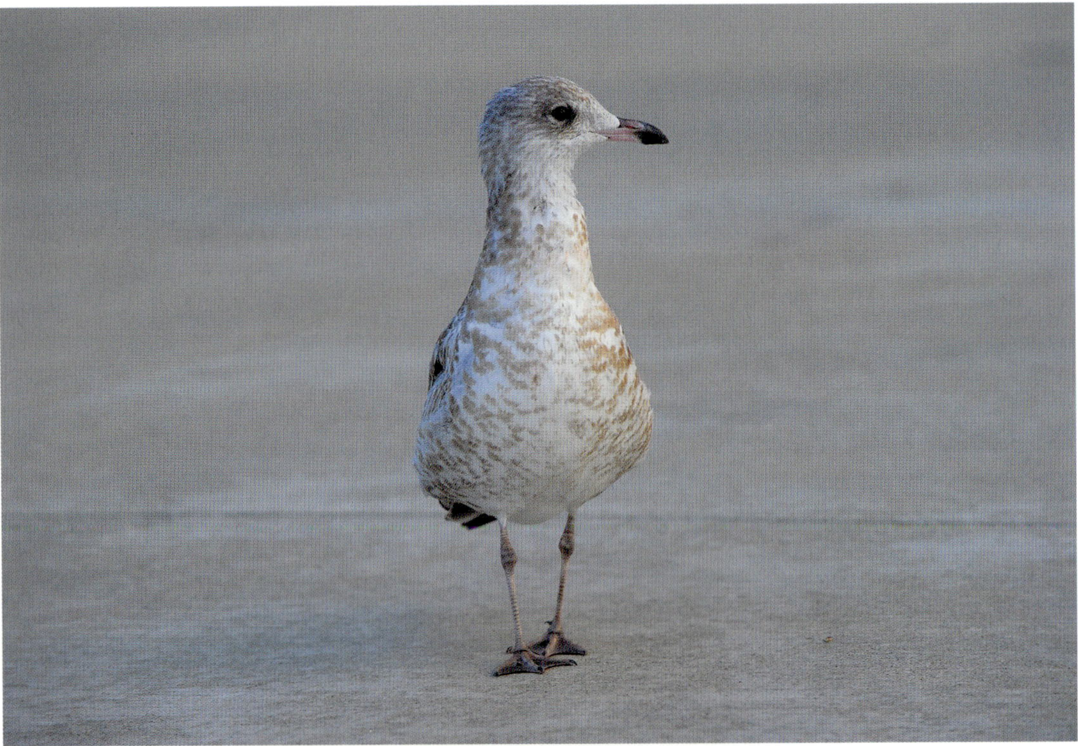

Figure 7.5 With shallow depth-of-field, the background becomes blurry.

In practice, the discs in many of these planes will still be so small that we see them as points, and that's where we get depth-of-field. Depth-of-field is just the range of planes that include discs that we perceive as points rather than blurred splotches. The size of this range increases as the aperture is reduced in size and is allocated roughly one-third in front of the plane of sharpest focus, and two-thirds behind it. The range of sharp focus is always greater behind your subject than in front of it.

Using Autofocus with the Nikon D3500

Autofocus can sometimes be frustrating for the new digital SLR photographer, especially those coming from the point-and-shoot world. That's because correct focus plays a greater role among your creative options with a dSLR, even when photographing the same subjects. Most non-dSLR digital cameras have sensors that are much tinier than the sensor in the D3500. Those smaller sensors require shorter focal lengths, which (as you'll learn in Chapter 10) have, effectively, more depth-of-field.

The bottom line is that with the average point-and-shoot camera, *everything* is in focus from about one foot to infinity and at virtually every f/stop. Unless you're shooting close-up photos a few inches from the camera, the depth-of-field is prodigious, and autofocus is almost a non-factor. The D3500, on the other hand, uses longer focal length lenses to achieve the same field of view with its larger sensor, so there is less depth-of-field. That's a *good* thing, creatively, because you have the choice to use selective focus to isolate subjects. But it does make the correct use of autofocus more critical. To maintain the most creative control, you have to choose three attributes:

- **How much is in focus.** Generally, by choosing the f/stop used, you'll determine the *range* of sharpness/amount of depth-of-field. The larger the DOF, the "easier" it is for the autofocus system's locked-in focus point to be appropriate (even though, strictly speaking, there is only one actual plane of sharp focus). With less depth-of-field, the accuracy of the focus point becomes more critical, because even a small error will result in an out-of-focus shot.

- **What subject is in focus.** The portion of your subject that is zeroed in for autofocus is determined by the autofocus zone that is active, and which is chosen either by you or by the Nikon D3500 (as described next). For example, when shooting portraits, it's actually okay for part of the subject—or even part of the subject's face—to be slightly out of focus as long as the eyes (or even just the *nearest* eye) appear sharp.

- **When focus is applied.** For static shots of objects that aren't moving, *when* focus is applied doesn't matter much. But when you're shooting sports, or birds in flight (see Figure 7.6), or children (traditionally three of the most difficult subjects to capture), the target may move within the viewfinder as you're framing the image. Whether that movement is across the frame or headed right toward you, timing the instant when autofocus is applied can be important.

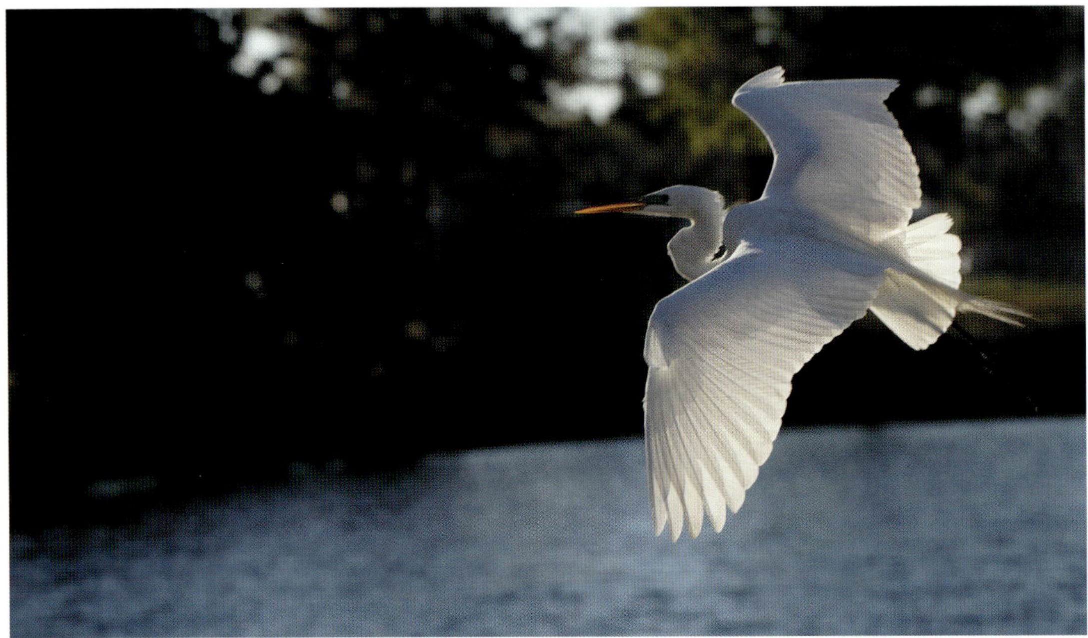

Figure 7.6 When capturing moving subjects, such as birds in flight, timing the instant when autofocus is applied can be important.

Your Autofocus Mode Options

Choosing the right autofocus mode and the way in which focus points are selected is your key to success. Using the wrong mode for a particular type of photography can lead to a series of pictures that are all sharply focused—on the wrong subject. When I first started shooting sports with an autofocus SLR, I covered one game alternating between shots of base runners and outfielders with pictures of a promising young pitcher, all from a position next to the third base dugout. The base runner and outfielder photos were great, because their backgrounds didn't distract the autofocus mechanism. But all my photos of the pitcher had the focus tightly zeroed in on the fans in the stands behind him. A simple change, such as locking in focus or focus zone manually, or even manually focusing, would have done the trick.

There are two main autofocus options you need to master to make sure you get the best possible automatic focus with your Nikon D3500: Autofocus mode and Autofocus Area. I'll explain each of them separately.

Autofocus Mode

This choice determines *when* your D3500 starts to autofocus, and what it does when focus is achieved. Automatic focus is not something that happens all the time when your camera is turned on. To save battery power, your D3500 generally doesn't start to focus the lens until you partially depress the shutter release. (You can also use the AE-L/AF-L button to start autofocus, as described in Chapter 3.) Autofocus isn't some mindless beast out there snapping your pictures in and out of focus with no feedback from you after you press that button. There are several settings you can modify that return at least a modicum of control to you.

Your first decision, if you'll be composing your image through the optical viewfinder, should be whether you set the D3500 to AF-S, AF-C, AF-A, or Manual. (Special issues for focusing in live view are discussed in Chapter 8.) To change to any of the automatic focus modes, use the information edit menu by pressing the *i* button, and select the focus mode (at the left end of the bottom row of options). With the camera set for one of the Scene modes, AF-S will be used automatically, except when using the Sports/Action scene mode. To switch to manual mode, select manual mode in the menu, or slide the AF/M or M-A/M switch on the lens to M.

AF-S

In this mode, also called *Single Autofocus*, focus is set once and remains at that setting until the button is fully depressed, taking the picture, or until you release the shutter button without taking a shot. You can also use the AE-L/AF-L button, as described in Chapter 3, if you've set that button to lock focus when pressed. For non-action photography, this setting is usually your best choice, as it minimizes out-of-focus pictures (at the expense of spontaneity). The drawback here is that you might not be able to take a picture at all while the camera is seeking focus; you're locked out until the autofocus mechanism is happy with the current setting. AF-S/Single Autofocus is sometimes referred to as *focus priority* for that reason. Because of the small delay while the camera zeroes in on correct focus, you might experience slightly more shutter lag. This mode uses less battery power.

When sharp focus is achieved, the focus confirmation light at the lower left will remain green, without flashing. By keeping the shutter button depressed halfway, you'll find you can reframe the image while retaining the focus (and exposure) that's been set.

AF-C

This mode, also known as *Continuous Autofocus*, is the one to use for sports and other fast-moving subjects. In this mode, once the shutter release is partially depressed, the camera sets the focus but continues to monitor the subject, so that if it moves or you move, the lens will be refocused to suit. Focus and exposure aren't really locked until you press the shutter release down all the way to take the picture. You'll often see Continuous Autofocus referred to as *release priority*. If you press the shutter release down all the way while the system is refining focus, the camera will go ahead and take a picture, even if the image is slightly out of focus. You'll find that AF-C produces the least amount of shutter lag of any autofocus mode: press the button and the camera fires. It also uses the most battery power, because the autofocus system operates as long as the shutter release button is partially depressed.

AF-A

This setting is actually a combination of the first two. When selected, the camera focuses using AF-S AF and locks in the focus setting. But, if the subject begins moving, it will switch automatically to AF-C and change the focus to keep the subject sharp. AF-A is a good choice when you're shooting a mixture of action pictures and less dynamic shots and want to use AF-S when possible. The camera will default to that mode, yet switch automatically to AF-C when it would be useful for subjects that might begin moving unexpectedly. However, as with AF-S, the shutter can be released only when the subject at the selected focus point is in focus.

Manual Focus

In this mode, or when you've set the lens autofocus switch to Manual (or when you're using a non-AF-S lens, which lacks an internal autofocus motor), the D3500 always focuses manually using the rotating focus ring on the lens barrel. However, if you are using a lens with a maximum aperture of at least f/5.6, the focus confirmation light in the viewfinder will glow a steady green when the image is correctly manually focused.

In manual focus mode, you can use the rangefinder feature to help you achieve sharp focus when you're shooting in Program, Aperture-priority, or Shutter-priority mode. You'll find an additional description and illustrations for using the rangefinder in Chapter 5. As I noted in Chapter 5, the rangefinder supplements the focus confirmation indicator at the left edge of the viewfinder by using the analog exposure indicator as a focusing "scale."

In Figure 7.7, at top you can see that the focus indicator has illuminated all the bars to the left and right of the "zero" point. That means that the current focus is grossly incorrect. In the middle illustration, the bars are illuminated to the right, indicating that the current focus setting is significantly *behind the true point of focus*. To focus on the piece in front, you'd need to focus more closely. At bottom, correct manual focus has been achieved, and the rangefinder indicator shows just a pair of bars, centered under the zero point.

Figure 7.7
The manual focus scale in the viewfinder shows (top) that the image is very out of focus; (middle) focus is behind the correct point; (bottom) correct focus has been achieved.

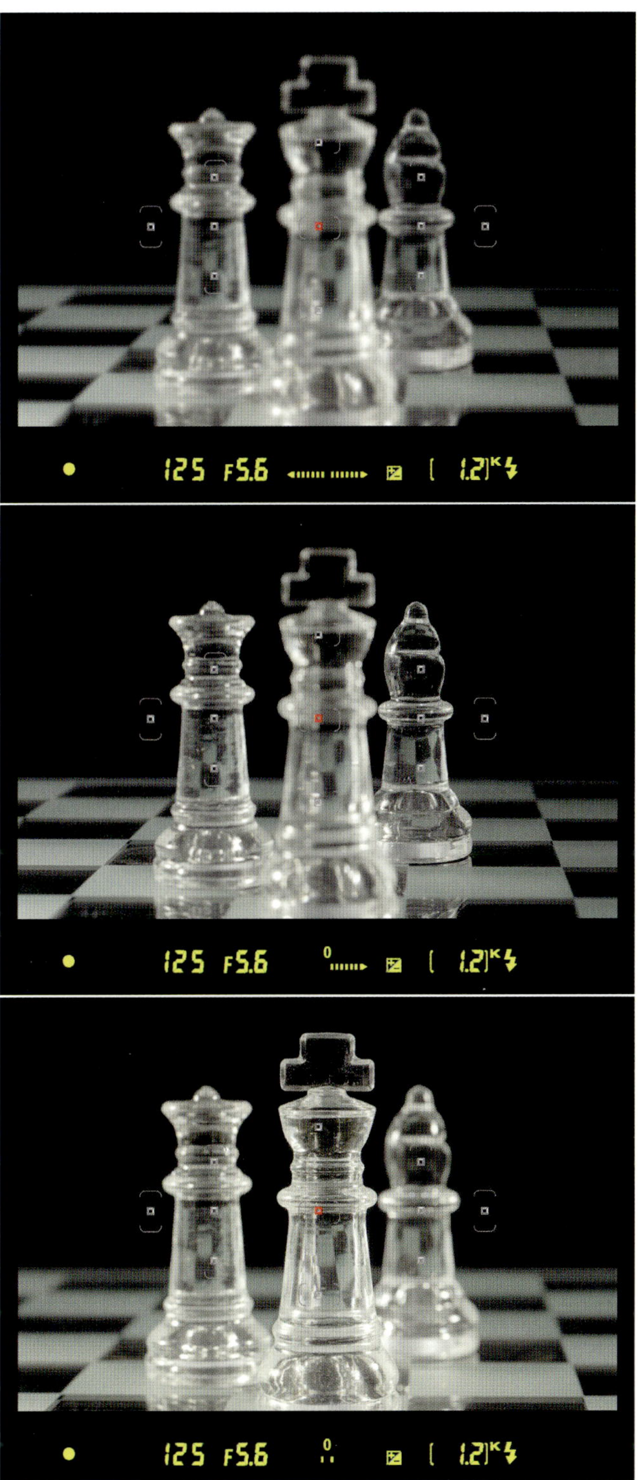

Follow these steps to use the rangefinder:

1. **Activate.** Use the Setup menu's Rangefinder entry to turn on the rangefinder, as described in Chapter 5.

2. **Select a focus point.** Use the multi selector to move the highlighting around in the frame.

3. **Rotate the lens focus ring.** Zoom lenses will have *two* rings; there's no fixed convention as to whether the wider or narrower ring is the focus ring. Choose the one farthest from the zoom scale (on the new collapsible kit lens, the focus ring is a thin band just behind the front of the lens).

4. **Watch the rangefinder.** If the indicator is pointing toward the left, focus farther away. If the scale points toward the right, focus more closely.

5. **Achieve sharp focus.** When the subject you've selected with the focus zone bracket is in sharp focus, only two bars will appear, centered under the 0, and the focus confirmation indicator will stop blinking. If no 0 appears, the camera cannot determine focus.

Autofocus Area

Where autofocus mode chooses *when* to autofocus, the Autofocus Area parameter tells your Nikon D3500 *how to choose which of the 11 focus points* in the viewfinder should be used to evaluate and lock in focus. Ordinarily, your camera would like to be able to choose among the available AF points itself. In fact, that's the default behavior, and when AF-area mode for Viewfinder is set to Auto-area, the D3500 chooses the focus point automatically in Auto, No-Flash, Portrait, Landscape, Night Portrait, and P/A/S (Program, Aperture-priority, and Shutter-priority) exposure modes. Giving the D3500 free rein in selecting a focus point works well much of the time, and you can use this default mode with confidence.

If you want to choose a focus point yourself, you must do two things. When the focus point is unlocked, you can use the multi selector pad to shift the active point to any of the 11 focus points seen in the viewfinder. The available points are shown in Figure 7.8.

The second thing to do is to switch the viewfinder Focus Area mode in the Shooting menu from Auto-area (which *always* chooses the focus point automatically) to Single-point, Dynamic-area, or 3D-tracking (11 Points). (Different focus area options are available for Live View mode, as described later.)

Figure 7.8
There are 11 possible
focus points shown
in the viewfinder.

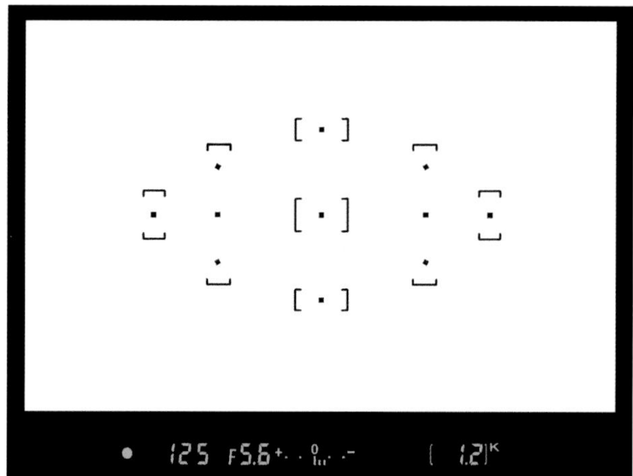

These viewfinder modes change the D3500's behavior as follows:

- **Single-point.** You choose which of the 11 points are used, and the Nikon D3500 sticks with that focus bracket, no matter what. This mode is best for stationary subjects, and is used automatically in Close-up scene mode. In this mode, you always select the focus point manually, using the multi selector button. The D3500 evaluates focus based solely on the point you select, making this a good choice for subjects that don't move much. Once you've moved the focus point, you can return it to the center of the frame by pressing the OK button.

- **Dynamic-area.** You can select the focus point, but the D3500 can use other focus points as well. You'd want to use this mode when photographing subjects that are moving unpredictably, but want the flexibility of being able to choose one of the 11 focus zones yourself. Once you've specified the focus bracket you want using the multi selector's buttons, the D3500 will use that area exclusively in Single-servo autofocus mode (AF-S). If you've chosen Continuous-autofocus mode (AF-C) or Automatic-autofocus mode (AF-A), if the subject begins moving after autofocus is activated, the D3500 will focus based on information from one of the other focus zones. Well suited for sports photography, this mode is applied automatically with the Sports scene setting, and can be used with other types of moving subjects, such as active children.

- **3D-tracking (11 points).** In this mode, you select the focus point using the multi selector, but if you subsequently reframe the picture slightly, the D3500 uses distance information when in AF-C (Continuous Autofocus) or AF-A (Automatic Autofocus) modes to refocus on the original subject if necessary. When using AF-S (Single Autofocus), this mode functions the same as Single-point focus area mode. This mode is useful if you need to reframe a relatively static subject from time to time. If your subject leaves the frame entirely, you'll need to release the shutter button and refocus.

- **Auto-area.** This mode chooses the focus point for you, and can use distance information when working with a G or D lens that supplies that data to the camera. (See Chapter 10 for more on the difference between G/D lenses and other kinds of lenses.)

Focusing in Live View

When you're not using the optical viewfinder, and instead using the D3500's Live View mode on the back-panel color LCD, available modes differ slightly. Instead of using phase detection autofocus (or the human eye's contrast detection system when focusing manually), the D3500 puts contrast detection to work full-time. The camera evaluates the focus of the image as seen by the sensor, and makes adjustments from there.

This section will explain your live view focus options.

Focus Mode

Activate live view by pressing the Lv button on the back of the D3500. Then press the *i* button to view the information edit screen. You can then adjust the focus mode. The available modes differ slightly from those possible when not shooting in live view. The following three choices are possible when your lens is not set to the manual focus position:

- **AF-S.** This single autofocus mode, which Nikon calls single-servo AF, locks focus when the shutter release is pressed halfway. This mode uses *focus priority;* the shutter can be fully released to take a picture only if the D3500 is able to achieve sharp focus.

- **AF-F.** This new mode is roughly the equivalent of AF-C. Nikon calls it full-time servo AF. The D3500 focuses and refocuses continually as you shoot stills in live view or record movies. Unlike AF-C, this mode also uses focus priority. You can't release the shutter unless the camera has achieved sharp focus.

- **MF.** Manual focus. You focus the image by rotating the focus ring on the camera.

Focus Area

Still in information edit mode, choose the D3500's AF-area mode for live view. (You can also choose AF-area mode in the Shooting menu under AF-Area Mode, using the Live View/Movie entry, as described in Chapter 4.) Your choices are Face-Priority AF, Wide-Area AF, Normal-area AF, Subject-tracking AF, and Manual focus.

- **Face-priority AF.** The camera automatically detects faces, and focuses on subjects facing the camera, as when you're shooting a portrait. You can't select the focus zone yourself. Instead, a double yellow border will be displayed on the LCD when the camera detects a face. You don't need to press the shutter release to activate this behavior. (Up to five faces may be detected; the D3500 focuses on the face that is closest to the camera.) When you press down the shutter release halfway, the camera attempts to focus the face. As sharp focus is achieved, the border turns green (see Figure 7.9). If the camera is unable to focus, the border blinks red. Focus may also be lost if the subject turns away from the camera and is no longer detectable by Face-priority.

- **Wide-area AF.** This is the mode to use for non-portrait subjects, such as landscapes, as you can select the focus zone to be used manually. It's good for shooting hand-held, because the subjects may change as you reframe the image with a hand-held camera, and the wide-area zones are forgiving of these changes. The focus zone will be outlined in red. You can move the focus zone around the screen with the multi selector buttons. When sharp focus is achieved, the focus zone box will turn green. (See Figure 7.10.)

- **Normal-area AF.** This mode uses smaller focus zones, and so is best suited for tripod-mounted images where the camera is held fairly steady. As with Wide-area AF, the focus zone will be outlined in red. You can move the focus zone around the screen with the multi selector buttons. When sharp focus is achieved, the focus zone box will turn green. (See Figure 7.11.)

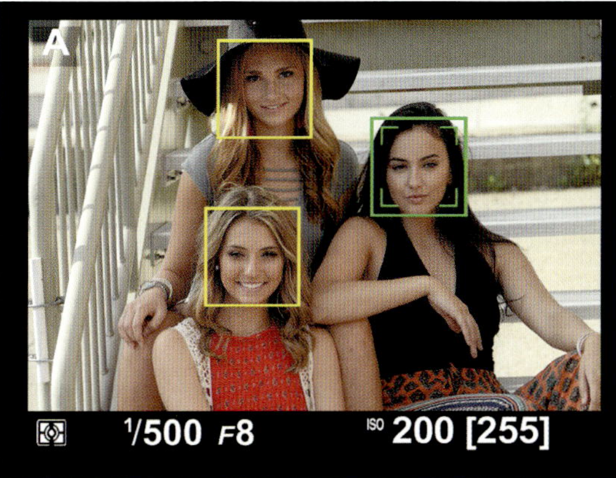

Figure 7.9 Face-priority AF attempts to focus on the face that's closest to the camera.

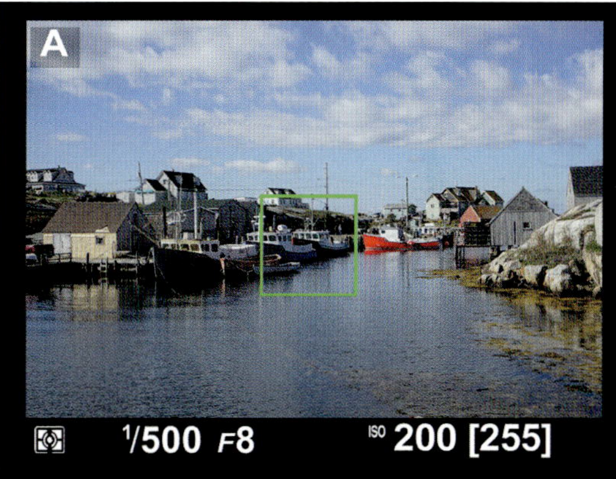

Figure 7.10 Wide-area AF is best for landscapes and other subjects with large elements.

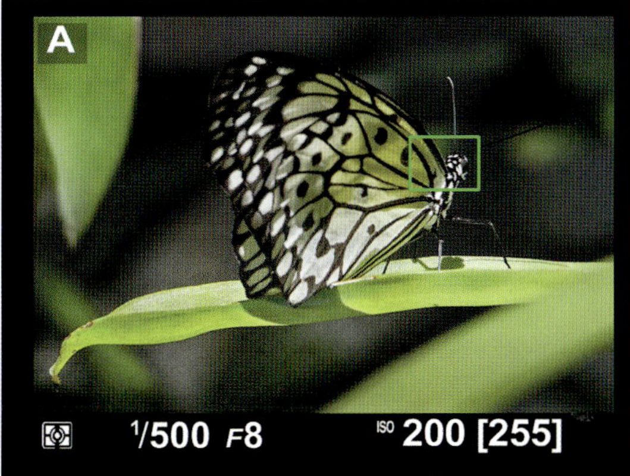

Figure 7.11 Normal-area AF allows you to zero in on a specific point of focus.

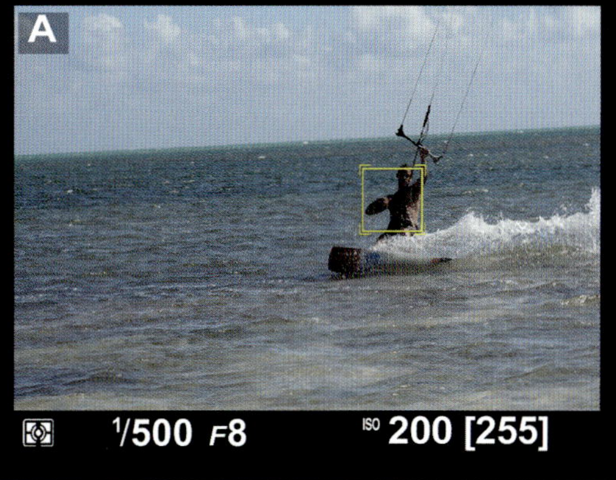

Figure 7.12 Subject-tracking AF can keep focus as it follows your subject around in the frame.

- **Subject-tracking AF.** This mode allows the camera to "grab" a subject, focus, and then follow the subject as it moves within the frame. You can use this mode for subjects that don't remain stationary, such as small children. When using Subject-tracking AF, a border appears in the center of the frame, and changes color when focus is locked in (as described in the section that follows). To activate focus or refocus, press the multi selector up button. I'll explain Subject-tracking in more detail next. (See Figure 7.12.)

- **Manual focus.** In this non-automatic focus mode, you can select the focus zone to use with the multi selector buttons, press the shutter release halfway, and then adjust focus manually by rotating the focus ring on the lens. When sharp focus is achieved, the focus confirmation indicator at the lower left of the viewfinder will turn a steady green.

Introducing Subject-Tracking

The useful Subject-tracking autofocus feature is one of those features that can be confusing at first, but once you get the hang of it, it's remarkably easy to use. Face-priority, in comparison, is almost intuitive to learn. Here's the quick introduction you need to Subject-tracking.

- **Ready, aim…** When you've activated Subject-tracking, a border appears in the center of the frame. Use that border to "aim" the camera until the subject you want to focus on and track is located within the border.

- **…focus.** When you've pinpointed your subject, press the OK button to activate the D3500's contrast detection autofocus feature. The focus frame will change color and the camera will emit a beep (unless you've disabled the beep within the Setup menu) when locked in. To stop subject-tracking press OK again.

- **Reframe as desired.** Once the focus frame has locked in, it seemingly takes on a life of its own, and will "follow" your subject around on the LCD as you reframe your image. (See Figure 7.12.) (In other words, the subject being tracked doesn't have to be in the center of the frame for the actual photo.) Best of all, if your subject moves, the D3500 will follow it and keep focus as required.

- **Tracking continues.** The only glitches that may pop up might occur if your subject is small and difficult to track, or is too close in tonal value to its background, or if the subject approaches the camera or recedes sufficiently to change its relative size on the LCD significantly.

- **Grab a new subject.** If you want to refocus or grab a new subject, press the OK button again.

8

Live View and Movie Making

As we've seen in our exploration of its features so far, the Nikon D3500 is superbly equipped for taking still photographs of very high quality in a wide variety of shooting environments. But this camera's superior level of performance is not limited to stills. The D3500 camera is unusually capable in the movie-making arena as well. So, even though you may have bought your camera primarily for shooting stationary scenes, you acquired a device that is equipped with a cutting-edge set of features for recording high-quality video clips. This camera can record high-definition (HD) video. Whether you're looking to record informal clips of the family on vacation, the latest viral video for YouTube, or a set of scenes that will be painstakingly crafted into a cinematic masterpiece using editing software, the D3500 will perform admirably.

Working with Live View

Live view is one of those features that experienced SLR users (especially those dating from the film era) originally thought they didn't need—until they tried it. While dSLR veterans didn't really miss what we've come to know as live view, it was at least, in part, because, until the feature became universal, they couldn't miss what they never had. After all, why would you eschew a big, bright, magnified through-the-lens optical view that showed depth-of-field fairly well, and which was easily visible under virtually all ambient light conditions? LCD displays, after all, were small, tended to wash out in bright light, and didn't really provide you with an accurate view of what your picture was going to look like.

The Nikon D3500 has a versatile 3-inch LCD monitor that can be viewed under a variety of lighting conditions and from wide-ranging angles, so you don't have to be exactly behind the display to see it clearly in live view. It offers a 100 percent view of the sensor's capture area (the optical viewfinder shows just 95 percent of the sensor's field of view). It's large enough to allow manual focusing—but if you want to use automatic focus with contrast detection, the D3500 can do that, too. You still have to avoid pointing your D3500 at bright light sources (especially the sun) when using live view, but the real-time preview can be used for fairly long periods without frying the sensor. (Image quality can degrade, but the camera issues a warning when the sensor starts to overheat.)

Fun with Live View

You may not have considered everything you can do with live view. But once you've played with it, you'll discover dozens of applications for this capability, as well as a few things that you can't do. Here's a list of live view considerations:

- **Shoot stills and movies.** You can take still pictures or movies using live view, and alternate between the two.
- **Preview your images on a TV.** Connect your Nikon D3500 to a television using a video cable, and you can preview your image on an HDTV screen.
- **Preview remotely.** Extend the cable between the camera and TV screen, and you can preview your images some distance away from the camera.
- **Continuous shooting.** You can shoot bursts of images using live view, but all shots will use the focus and exposure setting established for the first picture in the series.
- **Shoot from tripod or hand-held.** Of course, holding the camera out at arm's length to preview an image is poor technique, and will introduce a lot of camera shake. If you want to use live view for hand-held images, use an image-stabilized lens and/or a high shutter speed. A tripod is a better choice if you have one.
- **Watch your power.** Live view uses a lot of juice and will deplete your battery rapidly. The optional AC adapter is a useful accessory.

Beginning Live View

Activate live view by pressing the Lv lever on the top-right shoulder of the camera until the mirror flips up and the live view preview is shown on the display. You can change the amount and type of information overlaid on the LCD by pressing the Info button (on top of the camera) repeatedly. This is one special case where the Info button does more than simply turn the information display on or off.

Not all of the information appears all the time. For example, the Time Remaining indicator shows only when there are 30 seconds or less remaining for live view shooting. The indicators overlaid on the image can be displayed or suppressed by pressing the Info button, and the LCD cycles among these screen variations:

- Live view screen overlaid with shooting information.

- Live view screen overlaid with only minimal information.

- Live view screen overlaid with basic information, plus a 16-segment alignment grid.

The first thing to do when entering live view is to double-check three settings that affect how your image or movie is taken. These settings include:

Metering Mode

While using live view, you can press the *i* button to view the information edit screen, which is the same screen you've already worked with in still photo mode. There, you can select the metering option (it's the third selection from the left in the bottom row) and press OK. Then, choose Matrix, Center-weighted, or Spot metering.

Focus Mode

While the information edit screen is visible, adjust the focus mode. As mentioned in the last chapter, the available modes differ slightly from those possible when not shooting in live view. You can select AF-S (single autofocus), AF-F (full-time servo AF), or MF (manual focus).

Focus Area

Also as described in the last chapter, you can choose the D3500's AF-area mode for live view, either using the information edit screen or in the Shooting menu. A recap of your choices are as follows:

- **Face-priority AF.** The camera automatically detects faces, and focuses on subjects facing the camera, as when you're shooting a portrait, and you can't select the specific focus zone.

- **Wide-area AF.** You can select the focus zone with the directional buttons.

- **Normal-area AF.** Includes smaller focus zones for you to choose from with the multi selector directional buttons.

- **Subject-tracking AF.** Select a subject and let the D3500 track it to maintain focus.

- **Manual focus.** In this non-automatic focus mode, you can select the focus zone to use with the multi selector buttons, press the shutter release halfway, and then adjust focus manually by rotating the focus ring on the lens.

Shooting in Live View

Shooting stills and movies in live view is easy. Just follow these steps:

1. **Press the Lv lever.** Activate live view by pressing the lever. The D3500 can be hand-held or mounted on a tripod. (Using a tripod mode makes it easier to obtain and keep sharp focus.) You can exit live view at any time by pressing the Lv lever again.

2. **Zoom in/out.** Check your view by pressing the Zoom In button. A navigation box appears in the lower right of the LCD with a yellow box representing the portion of the image zoomed, just as when you're reviewing photos you've already taken using Playback mode. Use the multi selector keys to change the zoomed area within the full frame. Press the Zoom Out button to zoom out again.

3. **Make exposure adjustments.** While using an automatic exposure mode, you can add or subtract exposure using the EV settings, as described in Chapter 6. Hold down the EV button (just southeast of the shutter release) and rotate the command dial to add or subtract exposure when using P, S, and A modes. The back-panel color LCD monitor will brighten or darken to represent the exposure change you make.

4. **Shoot.** Press the shutter release all the way down to take a still picture, or press the red Movie button to start motion picture filming. Stop filming by pressing the Movie button again. Movies up to 4GB in size can be taken (assuming there is sufficient room on your memory card), which limits you to 20 minutes for an HDTV clip.

Shooting Movies with the D3500

As you've probably gathered, movie making is an extension of the live view concept. Once you've directed the output of the sensor to the LCD monitor, capturing it as a video file—with audio—is relatively easy. All the focus modes and AF-area modes described for plain old Live View mode can be applied to movie making, too. Here are some considerations to think about:

- **Stills, too.** You can take a still photograph even while you're shooting a movie clip by pressing the shutter release all the way down. You won't miss a still shot because you're shooting video. However, movie shooting will cease after you take the still, and must be re-activated by pressing the red Movie button again.

- **Exposure compensation.** When shooting movies, exposure compensation is available in plus/minus 3EV steps in 1/3 EV increments.

- **Size matters.** Individual movie files can be up to 4GB in size (this will vary according to the resolution you select), and are limited in length by the frame rate and image quality you choose. The speed and capacity of your memory card may provide additional restrictions on size/length. For example, videos captured using the Miniature Effect are up to three minutes long when played back. Otherwise, the maximum length video clip possible is:

  - **1920 × 1080/60p.** High Quality: 10 minutes; Normal Quality: 20 minutes.
  - **1920 × 1080/30p/24p.** High Quality: 20 minutes; Normal Quality 29 minutes, 59 seconds.
  - **1280 × 720/60p.** High Quality: 20 minutes; Normal Quality 29 minutes, 59 seconds.

WHAT FRAME RATE: 24 fps, 30 fps, or 60 fps?

Even intermediate movie shooters can be confused by the choice between 24 fps and 30 fps or 60 fps, especially since those are only nominal figures (with the D3500, the 24 fps setting actually yields 23.976 frames per second; 30 fps gives you 29.97 actual "frames" per second; 60 fps is 59.24 fps).

The difference lies in the two "worlds" of motion images, film and video. The standard frame rate for motion picture film is 24 fps, while the video rate, at least in the United States, Japan, and other places using the NTSC standard is 30 fps (actually 60 interlaced *fields* per second) and also manifested as 60 fps. In countries using the PAL system, 25 and 50 fps options are available.

Computer-editing software can handle any of these types, and convert between them. The choice between 24 fps and 30 or 60 fps is determined by what you plan to do with your video.

The short explanation is that, for technical reasons I won't go into here, shooting at 24 fps gives your movie a "film" look, excellent for showing fine detail. However, if your clip has moving subjects, or you pan the camera, 24 fps can produce a jerky effect called "judder." A 30 or 60 fps rate produces a home-video look that some feel is less desirable, but which is smoother and less jittery when displayed on an electronic monitor. I suggest you try both and use the frame rate that best suits your tastes and video-editing software.

In the Movie Settings entry of the Shooting menu (see Figure 8.1), you can make the following choices:

- **Frame size/frame rate.** Choose your resolution. Use the Movie Settings entry in the Shooting menu. Or, when live view is activated, and before you start shooting your video clip, you can select the resolution/frame rate of your movie. All use *progressive scan,* in which all the lines are captured one after another in order. (See Figure 8.2.)

Figure 8.1
Movie settings.

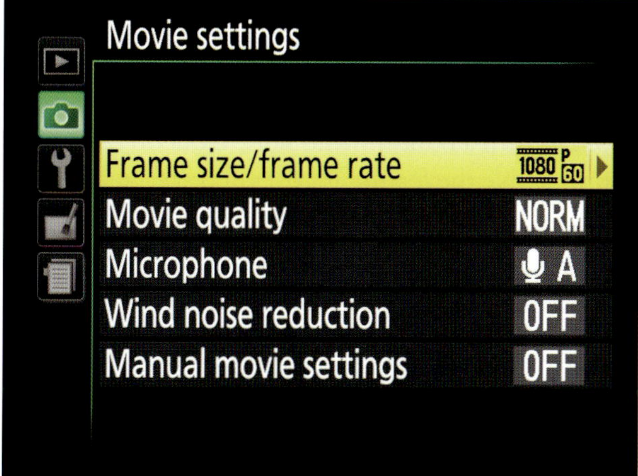

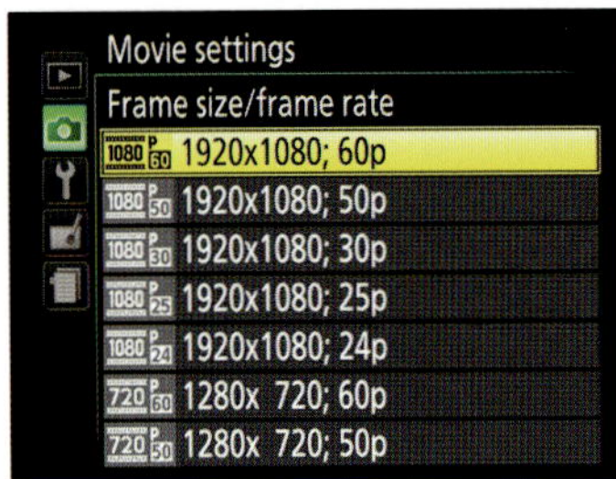
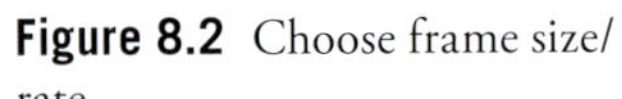

Figure 8.2 Choose frame size/ rate.

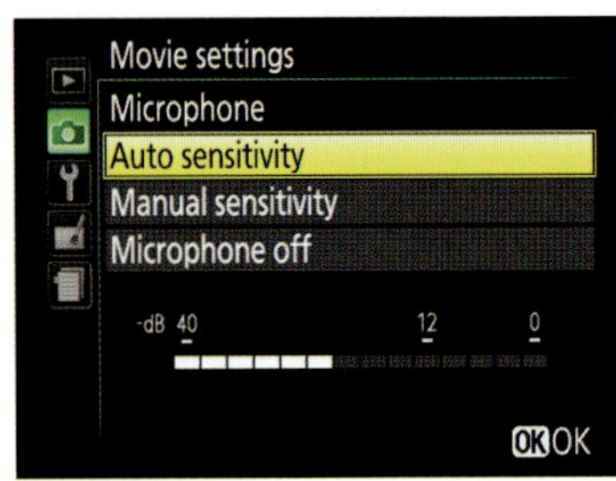

Figure 8.3 Adjust the built-in microphone's sensitivity.

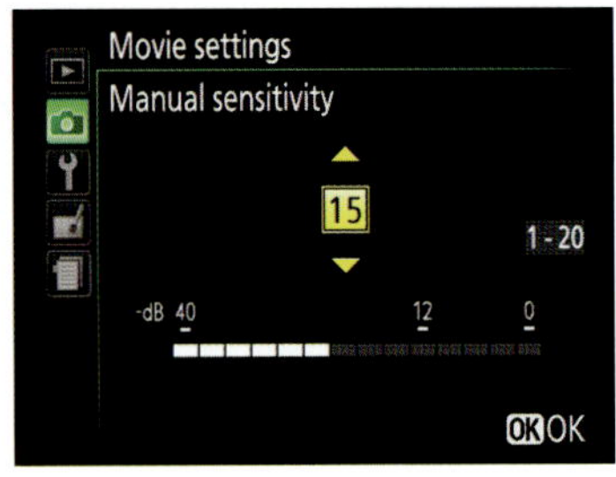

Figure 8.4 You can manually adjust the microphone's sensitivity.

Your options are as follows:

- 1920 × 1080 at 60/50 fps, progressive scan (60p/50p)
- 1920 × 1080 at 30/25 fps, progressive scan (30p/25p)
- 1920 × 1080 at 24 fps, progressive scan (24p)
- 1280 × 720 at 60/50 fps, progressive scan (60p/50p)

■ **Movie Quality.** Choose High quality (to capture up to 10 minutes of action at 60p, or 20 minutes at 30p and 24p) or Normal quality (for up to 20 minutes at 60p or 29 minutes, 59 seconds of video per clip at 30p and 24p). The High setting has a maximum bit rate requirement of 24 Mbps; if your memory card won't handle that, the Normal setting reduces the demand to 12 Mbps, at the cost of some additional compression that reduces the size of the file and cuts resolution/image quality slightly.

■ **Microphone.** Here you can set audio sensitivity for the built-in microphone. (See Figure 8.3.) Choose from Auto Sensitivity, Manual Sensitivity, or Microphone Off. With the Manual Sensitivity setting, a set of volume unit (VU) meter bars appears on the menu screen showing the current sound levels. Press the right directional button to access a screen where you can select a manual sensitivity level from 1 to 20. (See Figure 8.4.)

■ **Wind noise reduction.** Gusts of wind can interfere with clear recording of your desired audio, so this option allows you to turn a built-in wind noise reduction feature on or off. In quiet surroundings you'll want to disable the feature for overall better sound quality.

■ **Manual movie settings.** Select On if you'd like to be able to adjust shutter speed and ISO sensitivity when shooting movies in Manual exposure mode. Select Off if you won't need this capability, which is explained in the next section.

NOT MUCH OF A LIMITATION

Unless you are shooting an entire performance from a fixed position, such as a stage play, the limitations on HDTV movie duration won't put much of a crimp in your style. Good motion picture practice calls for each production to consist of a series of relatively *short* clips, with 10 to 20 seconds a good average. You can assemble and edit your D3500 movies into one long, finished production using one of the many movie-editing software packages available. Andy Warhol might have been successful with his 1963 five-hour epic *Sleep*, but the rest of us will do better with short sequences of the type produced by the Nikon D3500.

To shoot your movies, follow these steps, which are similar to those for using live view:

1. **Start live view.** Activate live view by pressing the Lv lever.

2. **Choose a focus mode.** Select from AF-S, AF-F, or MF, as described earlier.

3. **Choose an AF-area mode.** Choices include Face-priority AF, Wide-area AF, Normal-area AF, or Subject-tracking AF.

4. **Activate and lock in focus.** This was also described under the live view instructions.

5. **Preview framing.** If you want to preview the image area that will be captured when shooting video, you can press the Info button (the one *on top* of the camera) to show movie indicators. During actual capture, the movie frame area will be enlarged to fill the LCD monitor, so what you see is what you get.

6. **Start/Stop recording.** Press the red movie recording button located just southwest of the shutter release. Press again to stop recording.

Movie Exposure

Exposure in Movie mode is much the same as in Live View mode. You can use Manual exposure, any of the semi-automatic modes (Program, Aperture-priority, or Shutter-priority), as well as Auto, Scene, and Effects modes (capturing video in Effects modes can produce some particularly inventive movie "looks").

- **Semi-automatic modes.** As in live view, just rotate the mode dial to the mode you want (P, A, S) prior to capture, whether in live view or non–live view modes. You can change to another mode while capturing video, but the recording will be interrupted and you'll need to press the movie button again.

- **Auto and Scene modes.** Use the mode dial to select Auto, Portrait, Action, Close-up, or Night Portrait modes. If you change Scene modes while capturing video, the recording will be interrupted and you'll need to press the movie button again.

- **Effects modes.** You can select an Effects mode exactly as you do a Scene mode, except that the mode dial needs to be rotated to the EFFECTS position. Just rotate the command dial to choose an Effect from the screen that pops up.

- **Manual exposure.** With the mode dial set to M, and Manual Movie Settings activated in the Movie Settings entry of the Shooting menu, you can select shutter speed and aperture while shooting movies. If your D3500 is set for a "forbidden" shutter speed prior to activating Movie mode, the camera will automatically adjust to an appropriate speed.

The option to increase the shutter speed to a shorter value can be useful when capturing action and you don't want individual frames to have too much blur. Your best bet is to use a shutter speed that is about twice the frame rate, for example, 1/60th second when shooting at 24 fps or 30 fps, and 1/125th second at 60 fps. You can up the speed a notch—say, 1/125th at 24/30 fps or 1/260th at 60 fps. However, using a *much* higher shutter speed, while freezing action, may make your images look jittery and unrealistic. The ability to adjust ISO settings manually allows you to compensate for the higher shutter speeds used, if necessary.

In all cases, however, your shutter speed range is limited to 1/4,000th second at the high end, and no slower than 1/30th second at 30/24 fps rates or no slower than 1/60th second at 60 fps.

Viewing Your Movies

Once you've finished recording your movies, they are available for review. Film clips show up during picture review, the same as still photos, but they are differentiated by a movie camera overlay. Press the OK button to start playback. The screen shown in Figure 8.5 will appear, with the controls overlaid for a few seconds before they blink out of sight until you use one of them.

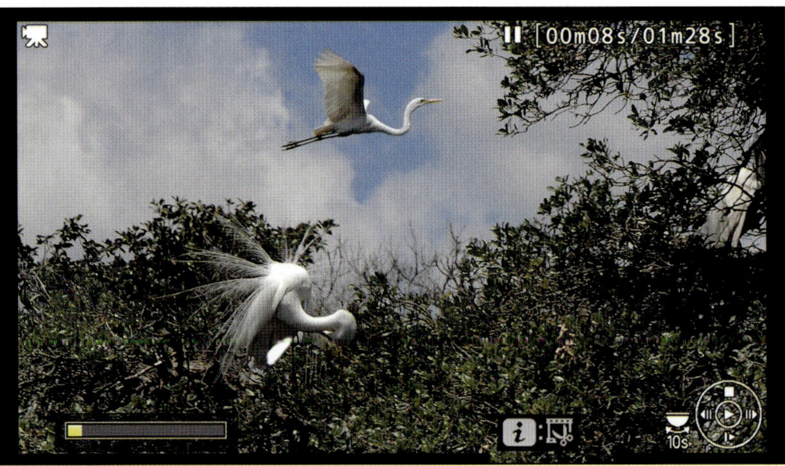

Figure 8.5
Viewing your movie.

During playback, you can perform the following functions:

- **Pause.** Press the multi selector down button to pause the clip during playback. Press the multi selector center button to resume playback.

- **Rewind/Advance.** Press the left/right multi selector buttons to rewind or advance (respectively). Press once for 2X speed, twice for 8X speed, or three times for 16X speed. Hold down the left/right buttons to move to the end or beginning of the clip.

- **Single Frame Rewind/Advance.** Press the multi selector down key to pause the clip, then use the left/right buttons to rewind or advance one frame at a time.

- **Slow-motion.** Press the down button while the movie is paused to begin slow-motion playback.

- **Skip 10 seconds.** Rotate the command dial to skip forward or back 10 seconds.

- **Change volume.** Press the Zoom In and Zoom Out buttons to increase/decrease volume.

- **Trim movie.** Press the AE-L/AF-L button while the movie is paused.

- **Exit Playback.** Press the multi selector up button to exit playback.

- **View menus.** Press the MENU button to interrupt playback to access menus.

Editing Your Movies

In-camera editing is limited to trimming the beginning or end from a clip, and the clip must be at least two seconds long. For more advanced editing, you'll need an application capable of editing AVI movie clips. Google "AVI Editor" to locate any of the hundreds of free video editors available, or use a commercial product like Corel Video Studio, Adobe Premiere Elements, or Pinnacle Studio. These will let you combine several clips into one movie, add titles, special effects, and transitions between scenes.

To do in-camera editing/trimming, follow these steps:

1. **Activate edit.** While viewing a movie clip, press the down button to pause, and then press the *i* button. The Edit Movie prompt will appear. (See Figure 8.6, left.)

2. **Select start/end point.** Select Choose Start/End Point and press OK. Then select Start Point or End Point and press OK again. (See Figure 8.6, right.)

Figure 8.6
Choose a start/end point.

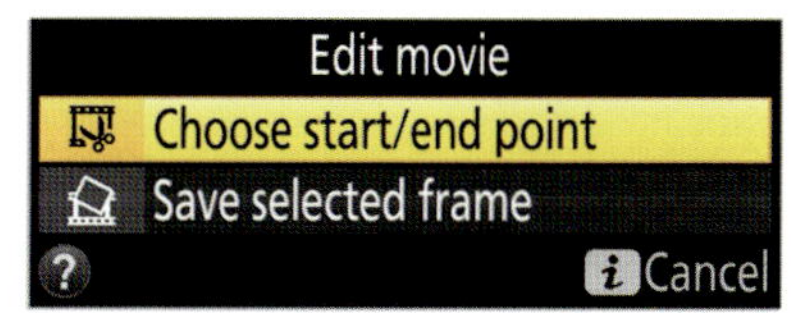

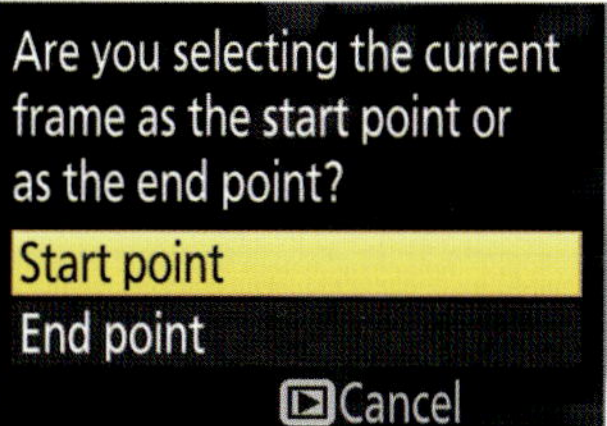

3. **Resume playback.** Press the center button of the multi selector to start or resume playback. You can use the Pause, Rewind, Advance, and Single Frame controls described previously to move around within your clip.

4. **Mark trim point.** When you reach the point where you want to trim, press the Pause button (if the movie is not already paused), and then press the multi selector up button. All frames prior to the pause will be deleted if you're in Choose Start Point mode; all frames *after* the pause will be deleted if you're in Choose End Point mode. Your trimmed movie must be at least two seconds long. (See Figure 8.7.)

5. **Confirm trim.** A Proceed? prompt appears. Choose Yes or No, and press OK.

6. **Save movie.** You'll be asked whether you want to save it as a new movie file or to overwrite an existing file. You can also preview your clipped movie. (See Figure 8.8, top.) When you begin saving the movie you'll see the screen shown in Figure 8.8, bottom, and a green progress bar as the D3500 stores the trimmed clip to your memory card. Storage takes some time, and you don't want to interrupt it to avoid losing your saved clip. So, make sure your camera has a fully charged battery before you start to edit a clip.

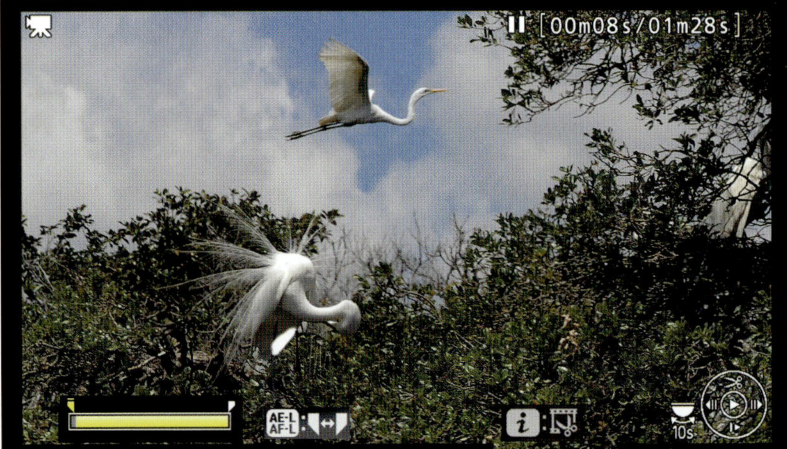

Figure 8.7
Mark the point and continue viewing to the end point.

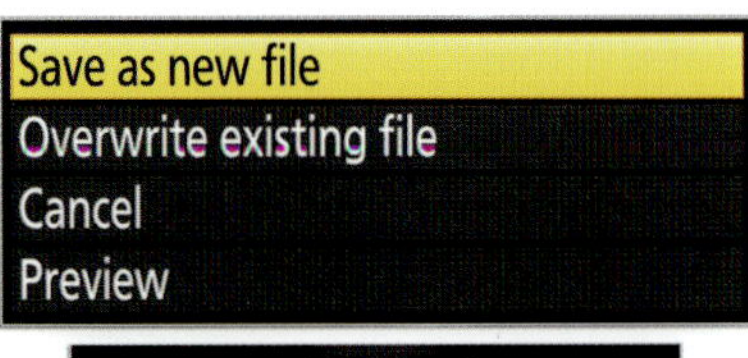

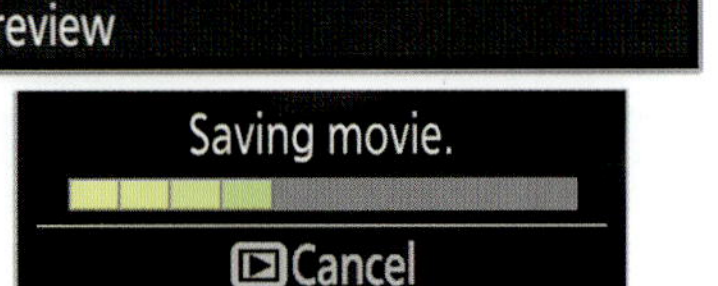

Figure 8.8
Save your edited movie.

Saving a Frame

You can store any frame from one of your movies as a JPEG still, using the resolution of the video format. Just follow these steps:

1. Pause your movie at the frame you want to save. Press the *i* button to access the Edit Movie screen shown in Figure 8.6.

2. Choose Save Selected Frame and press OK.

3. Choose Proceed to confirm.

4. Your frame will be stored on the memory card, and will be marked with a scissors icon.

Some Fundamentals

Recording a video with the Nikon D3500 is extraordinarily easy to accomplish—just press the Lv lever and then press the prominent Movie button (with the red dot) just southwest of the shutter release button, and press it again to stop.

Before you press that button, though, there are some settings to prepare the camera to record the scene the way you want it to. Setting up the camera for recording video can be a bit tricky, because it's not immediately obvious, either from the camera's menus or from Nikon's manuals, which settings apply to video recording and which do not. I will unravel that mystery for you, and throw in a few other tips to help improve your movies.

I'll show you how to optimize your settings before you start shooting video, but here are some considerations to be aware of as you get started. Many of these points will be covered in more detail later in this chapter:

■ **Use the right card.** You'll want to use an SD or SDHC card with Class 6 or higher speed; if you use a slower card, like a Class 4 or especially Class 2, the recording may stop after a minute or two. Chose a memory card with at least 4GB capacity; 8GB or 16GB are even better. If you're going to be recording a lot of HD video, that could be a good reason to take advantage of the ability to use SDXC cards of 64GB capacity. Just make sure your memory card reader is SDXC compatible and your computer can read the files from that type of card. I've standardized on fast Class 6 or Class 10 16GB SDHC cards when I'm shooting movies; one of these cards will hold at least three hours of video. However, the camera cannot shoot a continuous movie scene for more than 20 minutes. You can start shooting the next clip right away, though, missing only about 30 seconds of the action. Of course, that assumes there's enough space on your memory card and adequate battery power.

One aspect that doesn't always occur to new movie shooters is that the capacity of the card matters only with respect to the number and length of video clips you intend to shoot. Larger cards let you capture more and longer sequences. You don't need to upgrade the size of your card because you've upgraded the resolution of your camera. A 36-megapixel D800 and a

24-megapixel D3500 *both* record full HD movies using the exact same 1920 × 1080–pixel resolution. The upscale model may outperform your D3500 in other respects, but when it comes to HD movie making, the playing field is level.

- **Minimize zooming.** While it's great to be able to use the zoom for filling the frame with a distant subject, think twice before zooming during the shot. Because you are not able to use an external mic, the sound of the zoom ring being spun will be picked up by the internal microphone and it will be audible when you play a movie. Any more than the occasional minor zoom will be very distracting to friends who watch your videos.

- **Use a fully charged battery.** A fresh battery will allow about one hour of filming at normal (non-winter) temperatures, but that can be shorter if there are many focus adjustments. Individual clips can be no longer than 20 to 29 minutes (depending on the Quality setting), however.

- **Keep it cool.** Video quality can suffer terribly when the imaging sensor gets hot so keep the camera in a cool place. When shooting on hot days especially, the sensor can get hot more quickly than usual; when there's a risk of overheating, the camera will stop recording and it will shut down about five seconds later. Give it time to cool down before using it again.

- **Press the Movie button.** You don't have to hold it down. Press it again when you're done to stop recording.

Tips for Shooting Better Video

Once upon a time, the ability to shoot video with a digital still camera was one of those "Gee whiz" gimmicks camera makers seemed to include just to have a reason to get you to buy a new camera. That hasn't been true for a couple of years now, as the video quality of many digital still cameras has gotten quite good. The D3500 is a stellar example. It's capable of HD-quality video and is actually capable of outperforming typical modestly priced digital video camcorders, especially when you consider the range of lenses and other helpful accessories available for it.

Producing high-quality videos can be a real challenge for amateur photographers. After all, by comparison we're used to watching the best productions that television, video, and motion pictures can offer. Whether it's fair or not, our efforts are compared to what we're used to seeing produced by experts. While this book can't make you a professional videographer in half a chapter, there is some advice I can give you that will help you improve your results with the camera.

Lens Craft

I'll cover the use of lenses with the D3500 in more detail in Chapter 10, but a discussion of lens selection when shooting movies may be useful at this point. In the video world, not all lenses are created equal. The two most important considerations are depth-of-field, or the beneficial lack thereof, and zooming. I'll address each of these separately.

Depth-of-Field and Video

Have you wondered why professional videographers have gone nuts over still cameras that can also shoot video? The producers of *Saturday Night Live* could afford to have their director of photography use the niftiest, most expensive high-resolution video cameras to shoot the opening sequences of the program. Instead, they opted for a pair of digital SLR cameras. One thing that makes digital still cameras so attractive for video is that they have relatively large sensors, which provides improved low-light performance and results in the oddly attractive reduced depth-of-field, compared with most professional video cameras.

Figure 8.9 provides a comparison of the relative size of sensors. The size of many professional video camera sensors is shown at lower left. The APS-C sensor used in the D3500 is shown just north of it. You can see that it is much larger, especially when compared with the sensor found in the typical point-and-shoot camera shown at right. Compared with the sensors used in many pro video cameras and the even smaller sensors found in the typical computer camcorder, the D3500's image-grabber is much larger. Only the most expensive Super 35 video cameras use a sensor as large as that found in APS-C cameras like the D3500.

As you'll learn in Chapter 10, a larger sensor calls for the use of longer focal lengths to produce the same field of view, so, in effect, a larger sensor has reduced depth-of-field. And *that's* what makes cameras like the D3500 attractive from a creative standpoint. Less depth-of-field means greater control over the range of what's in focus. Your D3500, with its larger sensor, has a distinct advantage over consumer camcorders in this regard, and even does a better job than many professional video cameras.

Figure 8.9
Sensor size comparison.

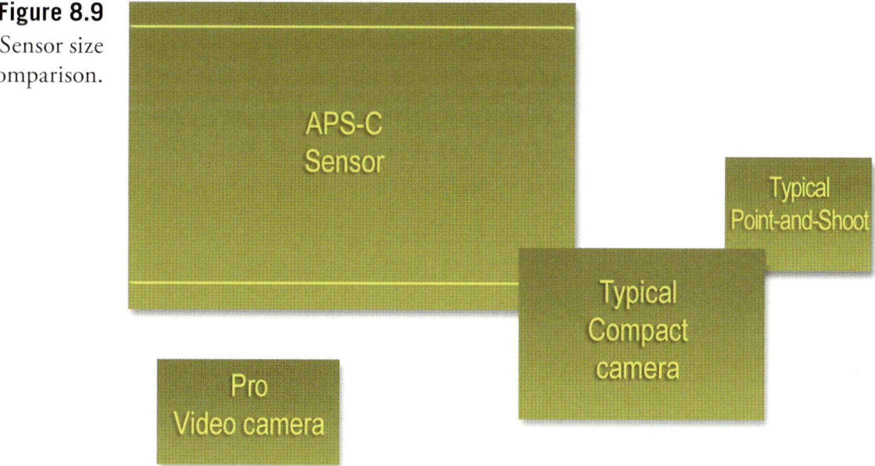

Zooming and Video

We're back to zooming (or not zooming) again! When shooting still photos, a zoom is a zoom is a zoom. The key considerations for a zoom lens used only for still photography are the maximum aperture available at each focal length ("How *fast* is this lens?"), the zoom range ("How far can I zoom in or out?"), and its sharpness at any given f/stop ("Do I lose sharpness when I shoot wide open?").

When shooting video, the priorities may change, and there are two additional parameters to consider. The first two I listed, lens speed and zoom range, have roughly the same importance in both still and video photography. Zoom range gains a bit of importance in videography, because you can always/usually move closer to shoot a still photograph, but when you're zooming during a shot most of us don't have that option (or the funds to buy/rent a dolly to smoothly move the camera during capture). But, oddly enough, overall sharpness may have slightly less importance under certain conditions when shooting video. That's because the image changes in some way many times per second, so any given frame doesn't hang around long enough for our eyes to pick out every single detail. You want a sharp image, of course, but your standards don't need to be quite as high when shooting video.

Here are the remaining considerations:

- **Zoom lens maximum aperture.** The speed of the lens matters in several ways. A zoom with a relatively large maximum aperture lets you shoot in lower light levels, and a big f/stop allows you to minimize depth-of-field for selective focus. Keep in mind that the maximum aperture may change during zooming. A lens that offers an f/3.5 maximum aperture at its widest focal length, may provide only f/5.6 worth of light at the telephoto position.

- **Zoom range.** Use of zoom during actual capture should not be an everyday thing, unless you're shooting a kung-fu movie. However, there are effective uses for a zoom shot, particularly if it's a "long" one from extreme wide angle to extreme close-up (or vice versa). We all can recall those memorable long shots of a building, seen from a distance, followed by a quick zoom in on Steve McGarrett poised outside that building with a steely glint in his eye.

  But, most of the time, you'll use the zoom range to adjust the perspective of the camera *between* shots, and a longer zoom range can mean less trotting back and forth to adjust the field of view. Zoom range also comes into play when you're working with selective focus (longer focal lengths have less depth-of-field), or want to expand or compress the apparent distance between foreground and background subjects. A longer range gives you more flexibility.

- **Linearity.** Interchangeable lenses may have some drawbacks, as many photographers who have been using the video features of their digital SLRs have discovered. That's because, unless a lens is optimized for video shooting, zooming with a particular lens may not necessarily be linear. Rotating the zoom collar manually at a constant speed doesn't always produce a smooth zoom. There may be "jumps" as the elements of the lens shift around during the zoom. Keep that in mind if you plan to zoom during a shot, and are using a lens that has proved from experience to provide a non-linear zoom. (Unfortunately, there's no easy way to tell ahead of time whether you own a lens that is well-suited for zooming during a shot.)

■ **Quiet autofocus motor.** Nikon's latest AF-P lenses have especially quiet autofocus motors, which reduce the possibility of picking up lens noise while shooting video.

Audio

When it comes to making a successful video, audio quality is one of those things that separates the professionals from the amateurs. We're used to watching top-quality productions on television and in the movies, yet the average person has no idea how much effort goes in to producing what seems to be "natural" sound. Much of the sound you hear in such productions is actually recorded on carefully controlled sound stages and "sweetened" with a variety of sound effects and other recordings of "natural" sound.

Tips for Better Audio

Since recording high-quality audio is such a challenge, it's a good idea to do everything possible to maximize recording quality. Although the D3500 does not include a jack for using an external microphone, there are things you can do to improve the quality of the audio your camera records:

■ **Get the camera and its microphone close to the speaker.** The farther the microphone is from the audio source, the less effective it will be in picking up that sound. While having to position the camera and microphone closer to the subject affects your lens choices and lens perspective options, it will make the most of your audio source. Of course, if you're using a very wide-angle lens, getting too close to your subject can have unflattering results, so don't take this advice too far.

■ **Turn off any sound makers you can.** Little things like fans and air handling units aren't obvious to the human ear, but will be picked up by the microphone. Turn off any machinery or devices that you can plus make sure cell phones are set to silent mode. Also, do what you can to minimize sounds such as wind, radio, television, or people talking in the background.

■ **Make sure to record some "natural" sound.** If you're shooting video at an event of some kind, make sure you get some background sound that you can add to your audio as desired in postproduction.

■ **Consider recording audio separately.** Lip-syncing is probably beyond most of the people you're going to be shooting, but there's nothing that says you can't record narration separately and add it later. It's relatively easy if you learn how to use simple software video-editing programs like iMovie (for the Macintosh) or Windows Movie Maker (for Windows PCs). Any time the speaker is off-camera, you can work with separately recorded ■ narration rather than recording the speaker on-camera. This can produce much cleaner sound.

Keep Things Stable and on the Level

Camera shake's enough of a problem with still photography, but it becomes even more of a nuisance when you're shooting video. While the image-stabilization feature provided by some Nikon lenses can help minimize this, it can't work miracles. Placing your camera on a tripod will work much better than trying to hand-hold it while shooting.

Shooting Script

A shooting script is nothing more than a coordinated plan that covers both audio and video and provides order and structure for your video. A detailed script will cover what types of shots you're going after, what dialogue you're going to use, audio effects, transitions, and graphics.

Storyboards

A storyboard is a series of panels providing visuals of what each scene should look like. While the ones produced by Hollywood are generally of very high quality, there's nothing that says drawing skills are important for this step. Stick figures work just fine if that's the best you can do. The storyboard just helps you visualize locations; placement of actors/actresses, props, and furniture; and also helps everyone involved get an idea of what you're trying to show. It also helps show how you want to frame or compose a shot. You can even shoot a series of still photos and transform them into a "storyboard" if you want, such as in Figure 8.10.

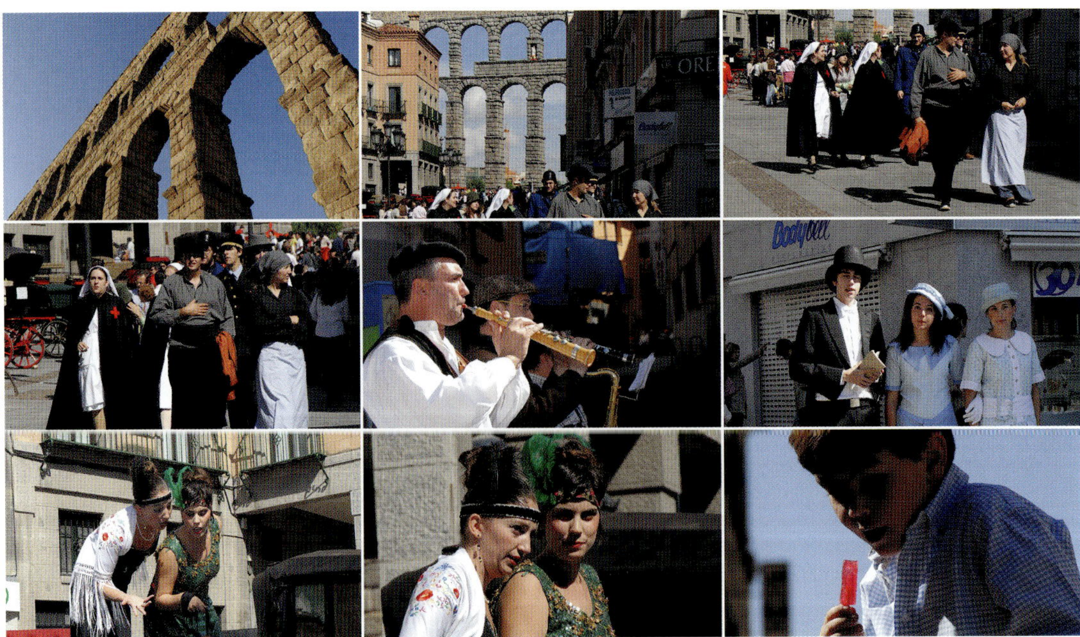

Figure 8.10 A storyboard is a series of simple sketches or photos to help visualize a segment of video.

Storytelling in Video

Today's audience is used to fast-paced, short-scene storytelling. In order to produce interesting video for such viewers, it's important to view video storytelling as a kind of shorthand code for the more leisurely efforts print media offers. Audio and video should always be advancing the story. While it's okay to let the camera linger from time to time, it should only be for a compelling reason and only briefly.

It only takes a second or two for an establishing shot to impart the necessary information. For example, many of the scenes for a video documenting a model being photographed in a Rock and Roll music setting might be close-ups and talking heads, but an establishing shot showing the studio where the video was captured helps set the scene.

Provide variety too. Change camera angles and perspectives often and never leave a static scene on the screen for a long period of time. (You can record a static scene for a reasonably long period and then edit in other shots that cut away and back to the longer scene with close-ups that show each person talking.)

When editing, keep transitions basic! I can't stress this one enough. Watch a television program or movie. The action "jumps" from one scene or person to the next. Fancy transitions that involve exotic "wipes," dissolves, or cross fades take too long for the average viewer and make your video ponderous.

Composition

In movie shooting, several factors restrict your composition and impose requirements you just don't always have in still photography (although other rules of good composition do apply). Here are some of the key differences to keep in mind when composing movie frames:

- **Horizontal compositions only.** Some subjects, such as basketball players and tall buildings, just lend themselves to vertical compositions. But movies are shown in horizontal format only. So, if you're interviewing a local basketball star, you can end up with a worst-case situation like the one shown in Figure 8.11. If you want to show how tall your subject is, it's often impractical to move back far enough to show him full-length. You really can't capture a vertical composition. Tricks like getting down on the floor and shooting up at your subject can exaggerate the perspective, but aren't a perfect solution.

- **Wasted space at the sides.** Moving in to frame the basketball player as outlined by the yellow box in Figure 8.11 means that you're still forced to leave a lot of empty space on either side. (Of course, you can fill that space with other people and/or interesting stuff, but that defeats your intent of concentrating on your main subject.) So, when faced with some types of subjects in a horizontal frame, you can be creative, or move in *really* tight. For example, if I was willing to give up the "height" aspect of my composition, I could have framed the shot as shown by the green box in the figure, and wasted less of the image area at either side.

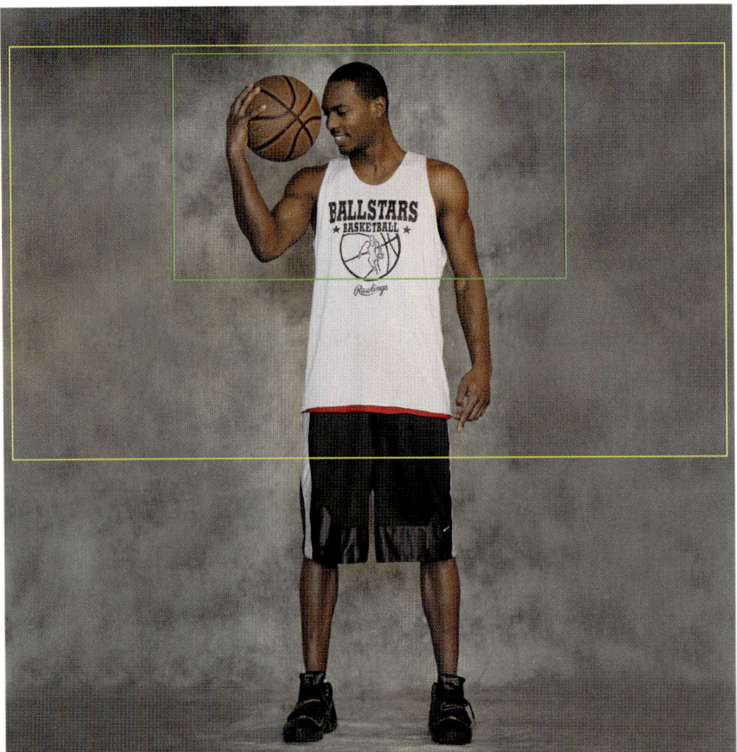

Figure 8.11
Movie shooting
requires you to fit all
your subjects into a
horizontally oriented
frame.

- **Seamless (or seamed) transitions.** Unless you're telling a picture story with a photo essay, still pictures often stand alone. But with movies, each of your compositions must relate to the shot that preceded it, and the one that follows. It can be jarring to jump from a long shot to a tight close-up unless the director—you—is very creative. Another common error is the "jump cut" in which successive shots vary only slightly in camera angle, making it appear that the main subject has "jumped" from one place to another. (Although everyone from French New Wave director Jean-Luc Goddard to Guy Ritchie—Madonna's ex—have used jump cuts effectively in their films.) The rule of thumb is to vary the camera angle by at least 30 degrees between shots to make it appear to be seamless. Unless you prefer that your images flaunt convention and appear to be "seamy."

- **The time dimension.** Unlike still photography, with motion pictures there's a lot more emphasis on using a series of images to build on each other to tell a story. Static shots where the camera is mounted on a tripod and everything is shot from the same distance are a recipe for dull videos. Watch a television program sometime and notice how often camera shots change distances and directions. Viewers are used to this variety and have come to expect it. Professional video productions are often done with multiple cameras shooting from different angles and positions. But many professional productions are shot with just one camera and careful planning, and you can do just fine with your D3500.

Here's a look at the different types of commonly used compositional tools:

■ **Establishing shot.** Much like it sounds, this type of composition, as shown at top left in Figure 8.12, establishes the scene and tells the viewer where the action is taking place. Let's say you're shooting a video of your offspring's move to college; the establishing shot could be a wide shot of the campus with a sign welcoming you to the school in the foreground. Another example would be for a child's birthday party; the establishing shot could be the front of the house decorated with birthday signs and streamers or a shot of the dining room table decked out with party favors and a candle-covered birthday cake. In this case, I wanted to show the studio where the video was shot.

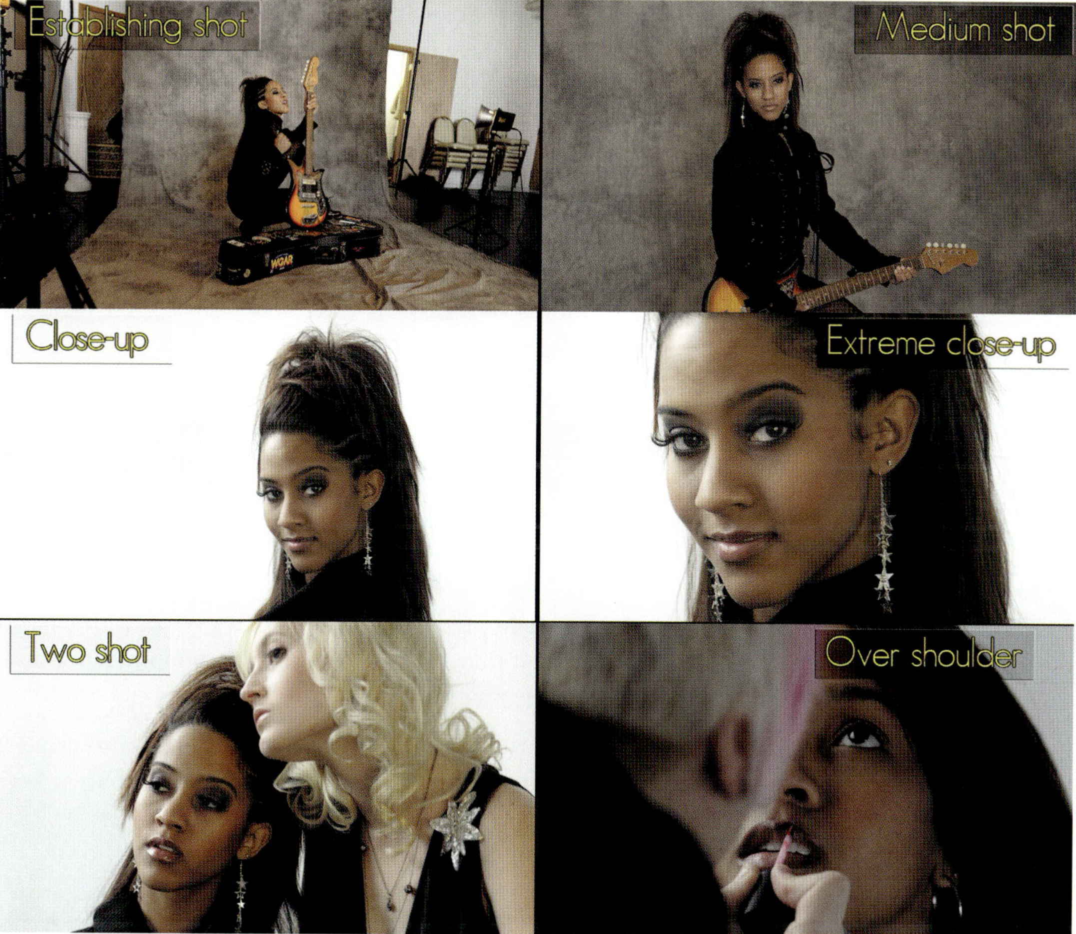

Figure 8.12 Use a full range of shot types.

- **Medium shot.** This shot is composed from about waist to head room (some space above the subject's head). It's useful for providing variety from a series of close-ups and also makes for a useful first look at a speaker. (See Figure 8.12, top right.)

- **Close-up.** The close-up, usually described as "from shirt pocket to head room," provides a good composition for someone talking directly to the camera. Although it's common to have your talking head centered in the shot, that's not a requirement. In the middle left image in Figure 8.12 the subject was offset to the right. This would allow other images, especially graphics or titles, to be superimposed in the frame in a "real" (professional) production. But the compositional technique can be used with videos, too, even if special effects are not going to be added.

- **Extreme close-up.** When I went through broadcast training, this shot was described as the "big talking face" shot and we were actively discouraged from employing it. Styles and tastes change over the years and now the big talking face is much more commonly used (maybe people are better looking these days?) and so this view may be appropriate. Just remember, the D3500 is capable of shooting in high-definition video and you may be playing the video on a high-def TV; be careful that you use this composition on a face that can stand up to high definition. (See middle right, Figure 8.12.)

- **"Two shot."** A two shot shows a pair of subjects in one frame. They can be side by side or one subject in the foreground and one in the background. This does not have to be a head-to-ground composition. Subjects can be standing or seated. A "three shot" is the same principle except that three people are in the frame. (See Figure 8.12, lower left.)

- **Over-the-shoulder shot.** Long a composition of interview programs, the "over-the-shoulder shot" uses the rear of one person's head and shoulder to serve as a frame for the other person. This puts the viewer's perspective as that of the person facing away from the camera. (See Figure 8.12, lower right.)

Lighting for Video

Much like in still photography, how you handle light pretty much can make or break your videography. Lighting for video can be more complicated than lighting for still photography, since both subject and camera movement are often part of the process.

Lighting for video presents several concerns. First off, you want enough illumination to create a useable video. Beyond that, you want to use light to help tell your story or increase drama. Let's take a closer look at both.

Illumination

You can significantly improve the quality of your video by increasing the light falling in the scene. This is true indoors or out, by the way. While it may seem like sunlight is more than enough, it depends on how much contrast you're dealing with. If your subject is in shadow (which can help them from squinting) or wearing a ball cap, a video light can help make them look a lot better.

Lighting choices for amateur videographers are a lot better these days than they were a decade or two ago. An inexpensive incandescent video light, which will easily fit in a camera bag, can be found for $15 or $20. You can even get a good-quality LED video light for less than $100. Work lights sold at many home improvement stores can also serve as video lights since you can set the camera's white balance to correct for any color casts. You'll need to mount these lights on a tripod or other support, or, perhaps, to a bracket that fastens to the tripod socket on the bottom of the camera.

Much of the challenge depends upon whether you're just trying to add some fill light on your subject versus trying to boost the light on an entire scene. A small video light will do just fine for the former. It won't handle the latter. Fortunately, the versatility of the D3500 comes in quite handy here. Since the camera shoots video in Auto ISO mode, it can compensate for lower lighting levels and still produce a decent image. For best results though, better lighting is necessary.

Creative Lighting

While ramping up the light intensity will produce better technical quality in your video, it won't necessarily improve the artistic quality of it. Whether we're outdoors or indoors, we're used to seeing light come from above. Videographers need to consider how they position their lights to provide even illumination while up high enough to angle shadows down low and out of sight of the camera.

When considering lighting for video, there are several factors. One is the quality of the light. It can either be hard (direct) light or soft (diffused). Hard light is good for showing detail, but can also be very harsh and unforgiving. "Softening" the light, but diffusing it somehow, can reduce the intensity of the light but make for a kinder, gentler light as well.

While mixing light sources isn't always a good idea, one approach is to combine window light with supplemental lighting. Position your subject with the window to one side and bring in either a supplemental light or a reflector to the other side for reasonably even lighting.

Lighting Styles

Some lighting styles are more heavily used than others. Some forms are used for special effects, while others are designed to be invisible. At its most basic, lighting just illuminates the scene, but when used properly it can also create drama. Let's look at some types of lighting styles:

- **Three-point lighting.** This is a basic lighting setup for one person. A main light illuminates the strong side of a person's face, while a fill light lights up the other side. A third light is then positioned above and behind the subject to light the back of the head and shoulders. (See Figure 8.13.)

- **Flat lighting.** Use this type of lighting to provide illumination and nothing more. It calls for a variety of lights and diffusers set to raise the light level in a space enough for good video reproduction, but not to create a particular mood or emphasize a particular scene or individual. With flat lighting, you're trying to create even lighting levels throughout the video space and minimize any shadows. Generally, the lights are placed up high and angled downward (or possibly pointed straight up to bounce off of a white ceiling). (See Figure 8.14.)

- **"Ghoul lighting."** This is the style of lighting used for old horror movies. The idea is to position the light down low, pointed upward. It's such an unnatural style of lighting that it makes its targets seem weird and ghoulish.

- **Outdoor lighting.** While shooting outdoors may seem easier because the sun provides more light, it also presents its own problems. As a general rule of thumb, keep the sun behind you when you're shooting video outdoors, except when shooting faces (anything from a medium shot and closer) since the viewer won't want to see a squinting subject. When shooting another human this way, put the sun behind her and use a video light to balance light levels between the foreground and background. If the sun is simply too bright, position the subject in the shade and use the video light for your main illumination. Using reflectors (white board panels or aluminum foil–covered cardboard panels are cheap options) can also help balance light effectively.

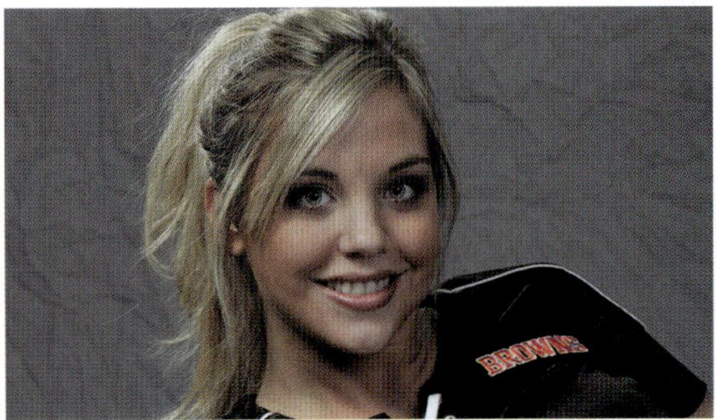

Figure 8.13 With three-point lighting, two lights are placed in front and to the side of the subject (45-degree angles are ideal) and positioned about a foot higher than the subject's head. Another light is directed on the background in order to separate the subject and the background.

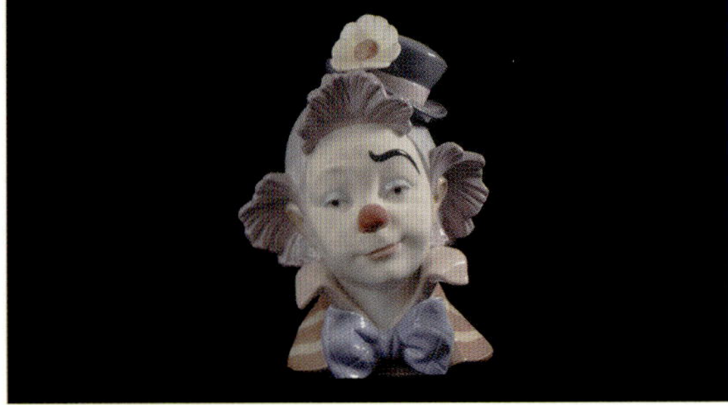

Figure 8.14 Flat lighting is another approach for creating even illumination. Here the lights can be bounced off of a white ceiling and walls to fill in shadows as much as possible. It is a flexible lighting approach since the subject can change positions without needing a change in light direction.

9

Advanced Shooting Tips for Your Nikon D3500

Getting the right exposure is one of the foundations of a great photograph, but a lot more goes into a compelling shot than good tonal values. A sharp image, proper white balance, good color, and other factors all can help elevate your image from good to exceptional. So, now that you've got a good understanding of exposure tucked away, you'll want to learn how to work with some additional exposure options, use the automatic and manual focusing controls available with the Nikon D3500, and master some of the many ways you can fine-tune your images.

In this chapter I'm including some specific advanced shooting techniques you can apply to your Nikon D3500. If you master these concepts, you can be confident that you're well on your way toward mastering your Nikon D3500. In fact, you'll be ready for the discussions of using lenses (Chapter 10) and working with light (Chapter 11).

Continuous Shooting

The Nikon D3500's 5-frames-per-second Continuous shooting release mode reminds me how far digital photography has brought us. The first accessory I purchased when I worked as a newspaper sports photographer some years ago was a motor drive for my film SLR. It enabled me to snap off a series of shots in rapid succession, which came in very handy when a fullback broke through the line and headed for the end zone. Even a seasoned action photographer can miss the decisive instant when a crucial block is made, or a baseball superstar's bat shatters and pieces of cork fly out. Continuous shooting simplifies taking a series of pictures, either to ensure that one has more or less the exact moment you want to capture or to capture a sequence that is interesting as a collection of successive images.

The D3500's "motor drive" capabilities are, in many ways, much superior to what you get with a film camera. For one thing, a motor-driven film camera can eat up film at an incredible pace, which is why many of them were used with cassettes that held hundreds of feet of film stock. At three frames per second (typical of film cameras), a short burst of a few seconds can burn up as much as half of an ordinary 36 exposure roll of film. The Nikon D3500, which fires off bursts at a faster frame rate (up to 5 frames per second), has reusable "film," so if you waste a few dozen shots on non-decisive moments, you can erase them and shoot more. Figure 9.1 shows the kind of results you can expect.

To use the D3500's Continuous shooting mode, press the Release mode button (located just above the Trash button) and use the multi selector to set the camera for continuous shooting. When you partially depress the shutter button, the viewfinder will display at the right side a number representing the maximum number of shots you can take at the current quality settings. As a practical matter, the buffer in the Nikon D3500 will generally allow you to take up to a dozen JPEG shots in a single burst, but only a few RAW photos. It can also not be used when using the built-in flash.

To get the maximum number of shots, reduce the image-quality setting by switching to JPEG only (from RAW+Fine), to a lower JPEG quality setting, or by reducing the D3500's resolution from L to M or S. The reason the size of your bursts is limited is that continuous images are first shuttled into the D3500's internal memory buffer, then doled out to the memory card as quickly as they can be written to the card. Technically, the D3500 takes the RAW data received from the digital image processor and converts it to the output format you've selected—either JPG or NEF (RAW)—and deposits it in the buffer ready to store on the card.

This internal "smart" buffer can suck up photos much more quickly than the memory card and, indeed, some memory cards are significantly faster or slower than others. When the buffer fills, you can't take any more continuous shots until the D3500 has written some of them to the card, making more room in the buffer. (You should keep in mind that faster memory cards write images more quickly, freeing up buffer space faster.)

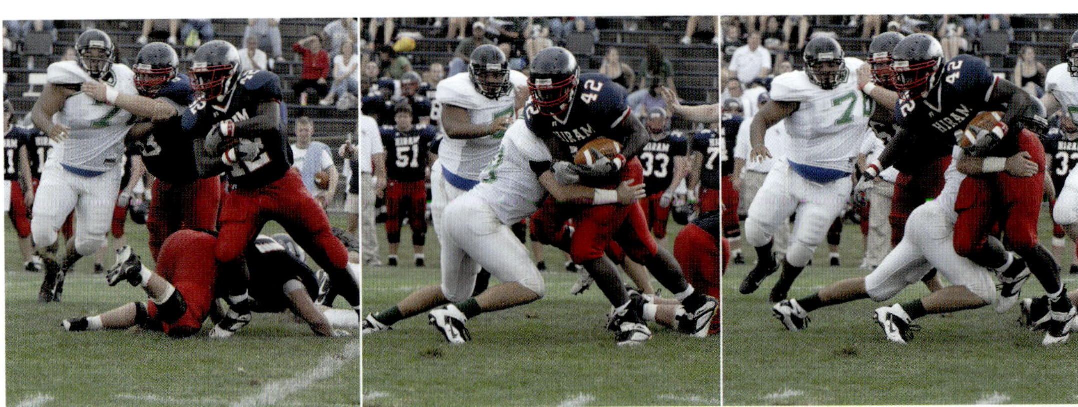

Figure 9.1 Continuous shooting allows you to capture an entire sequence of exciting moments as they unfold.

Exploring Ultra-Fast Exposures

Fast shutter speeds stop action because they capture only a tiny slice of time. Electronic flash also freezes motion by virtue of its extremely short duration—as brief as 1/50,000th second or less. The Nikon D3500 has a top shutter speed of 1/4,000th second and its built-in flash unit fires off brief bursts that can give you more of these ultra-quick glimpses of moving subjects. An external flash, such as one of the Nikon SB-series strobes, offers even more versatility. You can read more about using electronic flash to stop action in Chapter 11.

In this section, I'm going to emphasize the use of short exposures to capture a moment in time. The Nikon D3500 is fully capable of immobilizing all but the fastest movement using only its shutter speeds, which range all the way up to that impressive 1/4,000th second. Some cameras have speeds up to 1/8,000th second, but those ultra-fast shutters are generally overkill when it comes to stopping action, and are rarely needed for achieving the exposure you desire. For example, the image shown in Figure 9.2 required a shutter speed of just 1/2,000th second to freeze the high jumper clearing the bar.

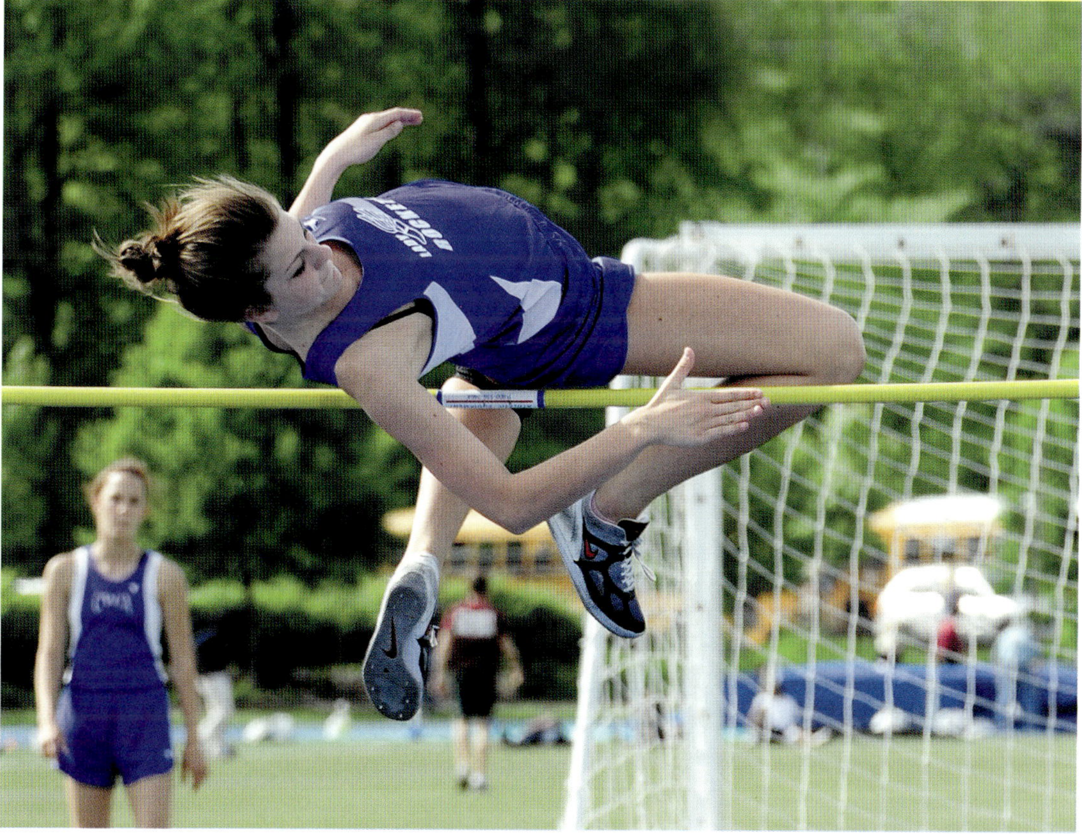

Figure 9.2 A shutter speed of 1/2000th second will stop most action.

When it comes to stopping action, most sports can be frozen at 1/2,000th second or slower, and for many sports a slower shutter speed is actually preferable—for example, to allow the wheels of a racing automobile or motorcycle, or the propeller on a helicopter, to blur realistically.

In practice, shutter speeds faster than 1/4,000th second are rarely required. If you wanted to use an aperture of f/1.8 at ISO 200 outdoors in bright sunlight, say, to throw a background out of focus with a wide aperture's shallow depth-of-field, a shutter speed of 1/4,000th second would more than do the job. You'd need a faster shutter speed only if you moved the ISO setting to a higher sensitivity, and you probably wouldn't do that if your goal were to use the widest f/stop possible. Under *less* than full sunlight, 1/4,000th second is more than fast enough for any conditions you're likely to encounter. That's why electronic flash units work so well for high-speed photography when used as the only source of illumination: they provide both the effect of a very brief shutter speed and the high levels of light needed for an exposure.

Of course, as you'll see, the tiny slices of time extracted by the millisecond duration of an electronic flash exact a penalty. To use flash at its full power setting, you have to use a shutter speed equal to or slower than the *maximum sync speed* of your camera. With the D3500, the top speed usable for flash is 1/200th second (unless you're using the special High-speed sync mode I'll describe in Chapter 11). The sync speed is the fastest speed at which the camera's focal plane shutter is completely open. At shorter speeds, the camera uses a "slit" passed in front of the sensor to make an exposure. The flash will illuminate only the portion of the slit exposed during the duration of the flash.

Indoors, that shutter speed limitation may cause problems: at 1/200th second, there may be enough existing ("ambient") light to cause ghost images. Outdoors, you may find it difficult to achieve a correct exposure. In bright sunlight at the lowest ISO settings available with the cameras, an exposure of 1/200th second at f/13 might be required. So, even if you want to use daylight as your main light source, and work with flash only as a fill for shadows, you can have problems. I'll explain the vagaries of electronic flash in more detail in Chapter 11.

You can have a lot of fun exploring the kinds of pictures you can take using very brief exposure times, whether you decide to take advantage of the action-stopping capabilities of your built-in or external electronic flash or work with the motion-freezing capabilities of the Nikon D3500's faster shutter speeds (between 1/1,000th and 1/4,000th second). Here are a few ideas to get you started:

- **Take revealing images.** Fast shutter speeds can help you reveal the real subject behind the façade, by freezing constant motion to capture an enlightening moment in time. Legendary fashion/portrait photographer Philippe Halsman used leaping photos of famous people, such as the Duke and Duchess of Windsor, Richard Nixon, and Salvador Dali, to illuminate their real selves. Halsman said, *"When you ask a person to jump, his attention is mostly directed toward the act of jumping and the mask falls so that the real person appears."* Try some high-speed portraits of people you know in motion to see how they appear when concentrating on something other than the portrait.

- **Create unreal images.** High-speed photography can also produce photographs that show your subjects in ways that are quite unreal. A helicopter in mid-air with its rotors frozen or a moto-cross cyclist leaping over a ramp, but with all motion stopped so that the rider and machine look as if they were frozen in mid-air, makes for an unusual picture. (See the frozen rotors at top in Figure 9.3.) When we're accustomed to seeing subjects in motion, seeing them stopped in time can verge on the surreal.

- **Capture unseen perspectives.** Some things are *never* seen in real life, except when viewed in a stop-action photograph. MIT professor Dr. Harold Edgerton's famous balloon burst photographs were only a starting point for the inventor of the electronic flash unit. Freeze a hummingbird in flight for a view of wings that never seem to stop. Or, capture the splashes as liquid falls into a bowl, as shown in Figure 9.4. No electronic flash was required for this image (and wouldn't have illuminated the water in the bowl as evenly). Instead, a clutch of high-intensity lamps bounced off a green card and an ISO setting of 1600 allowed the camera to capture this image at 1/2,000th second.

Figure 9.3
Freezing a helicopter's rotors with a fast shutter speed makes for an image that doesn't look natural (top); a little blur helps convey a feeling of motion (bottom).

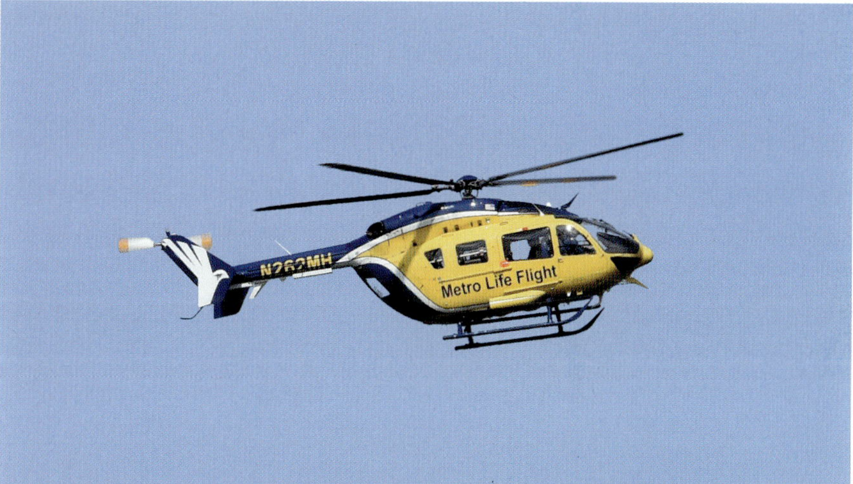

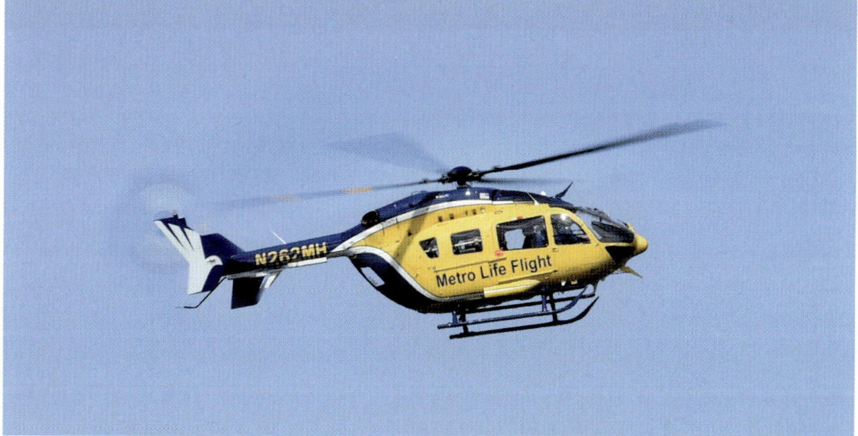

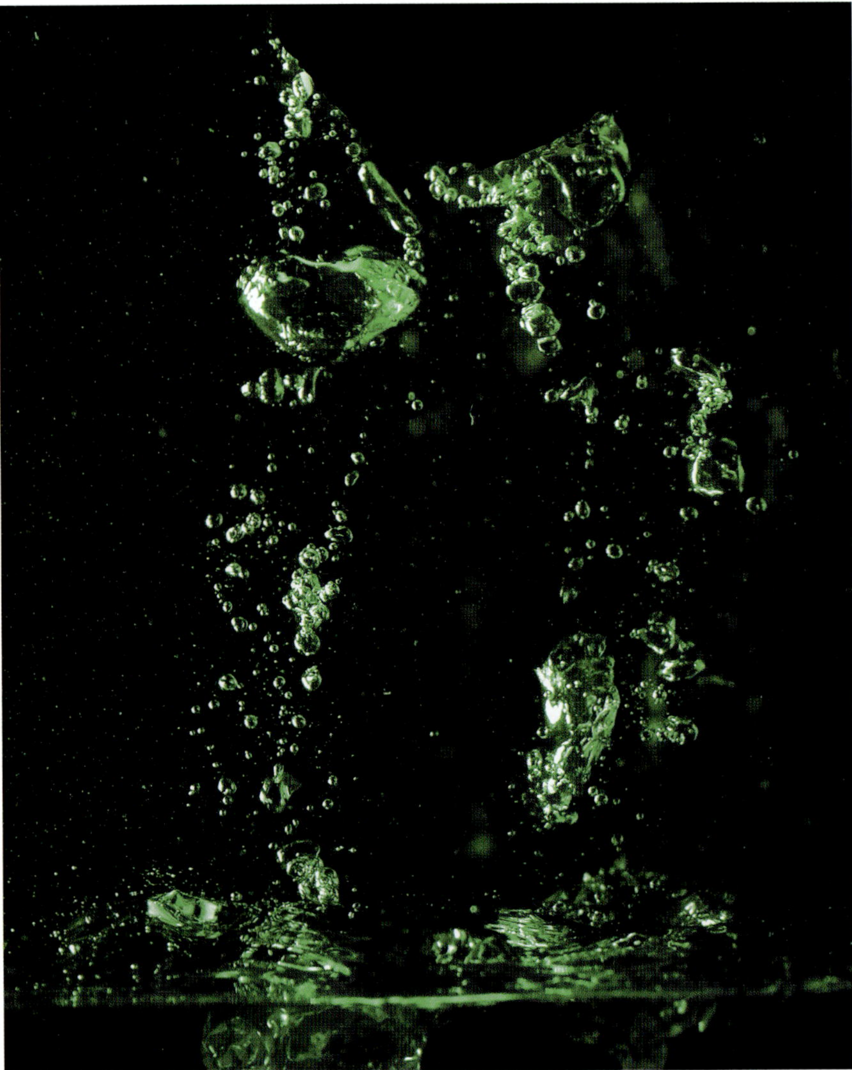

Figure 9.4
A large amount of artificial illumination and an ISO 1600 sensitivity setting allowed capturing this shot at 1/2000th second without use of an electronic flash.

Long Exposures

Longer exposures are a doorway into another world, showing us how even familiar scenes can look much different when photographed over periods measured in seconds. At night, long exposures produce streaks of light from moving, illuminated subjects like automobiles or amusement park rides, such as the Ferris wheel shown in Figure 9.5. Extra-long exposures of seemingly pitch-dark subjects can reveal interesting views using light levels barely bright enough to see by. At any time of day, including daytime (in which case you'll often need the help of neutral-density filters to make the long exposure practical), long exposures can cause moving objects to vanish entirely, because they don't remain stationary long enough to register in a photograph.

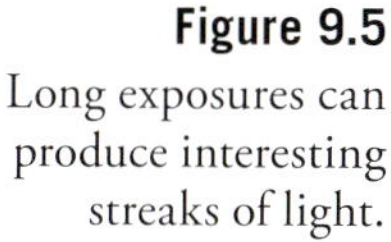

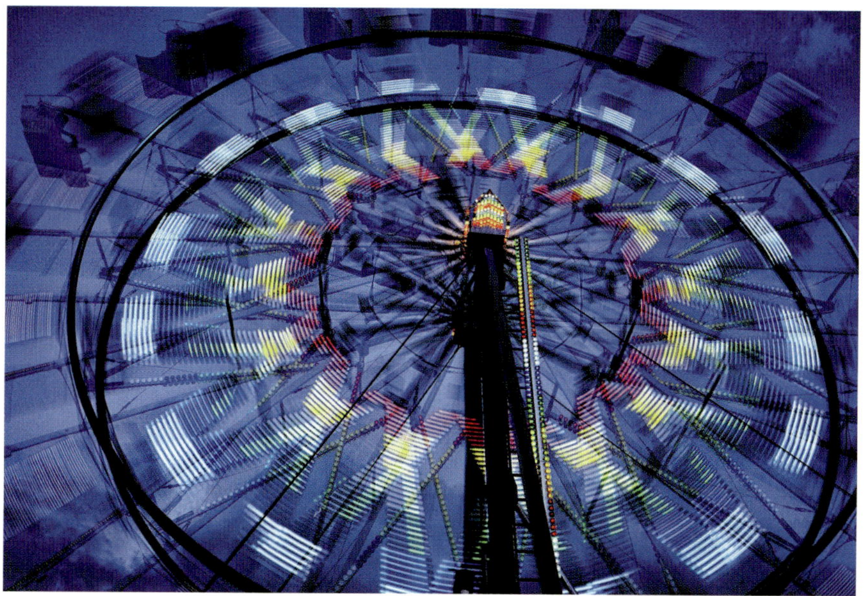

Three Ways to Take Long Exposures

There are actually three common types of lengthy exposures: *timed exposures*, *bulb exposures*, and *time exposures*. The Nikon D3500 offers all three. Because of the length of the exposure, all of the following techniques should be used with a tripod to hold the camera steady.

- **Timed exposures.** These are long exposures from 1 second to 30 seconds, measured by the camera itself. To take a picture in this range, simply use Manual or Shutter-priority mode and use the control dial to set the shutter speed to the length of time you want, choosing from several preset speeds ranging from 1.0 to 30.0 seconds. The advantage of timed exposures is that the camera does all the calculating for you. There's no need for a stopwatch. If you review your image on the EVF or LCD and decide to try again with the exposure doubled or halved, you can dial in the correct exposure with precision. The disadvantage of timed exposures is that you can't take a photo for longer than 30 seconds.

- **Bulb exposures.** This type of exposure is so-called because in the olden days the photographer squeezed and held an air bulb attached to a tube that provided the force necessary to keep the shutter open. Traditionally, a bulb exposure is one that lasts as long as the shutter release button is pressed; when you release the button, the exposure ends. To make a bulb exposure with the Nikon D3500, set the camera on Manual exposure mode and use the control dial to select the shutter speed immediately after 30 seconds, labeled Bulb. Then, press the shutter to start the exposure, and release it to close the shutter.

- **Time exposures.** This is an alternate setting used to produce longer exposures. The shutter opens when you press the shutter release button, and remains open until you press the button again. To use the Time exposure feature, put the D3500 in Manual exposure mode, and select the shutter speed after Bulb, labeled Time. Press the shutter button once to start the exposure, and a second time to stop it. The advantage of this approach is that you can take an exposure of virtually any duration without the need for special equipment, as you can take a time exposure by manually pressing the shutter button. There's no need to remain at the camera holding down the shutter button. You can press the release, go off for a few minutes, and come back to close the shutter (assuming your camera is still there). The disadvantages of this mode are exposures must be timed manually, and with shorter exposures it's possible for the vibration of manually opening and closing the shutter to register in the photo. For longer exposures, the period of vibration is relatively brief and not usually a problem.

Working with Long Exposures

Because the Nikon D3500 produces such good images at longer exposures, and there are so many creative things you can do with long-exposure techniques, you'll want to do some experimenting. Get yourself a tripod or another firm support and take some test shots with long exposure noise reduction both enabled and disabled (to see whether you prefer low noise or high detail) and get started. Here are some things to try:

- **Make people invisible.** One very cool thing about long exposures is that objects that move rapidly enough won't register at all in a photograph, while the subjects that remain stationary are portrayed in the normal way. That makes it easy to produce people-free landscape photos and architectural photos at night or, even, in full daylight if you use a neutral-density filter (or two or three) to allow an exposure of at least a few seconds. At ISO 100, f/22, and a pair of 8X (three-stop) neutral-density filters, you can use exposures of nearly two seconds; overcast days and/or even more neutral-density filtration would work even better if daylight people vanishing is your goal. They'll have to be walking *very* briskly and across the field of view (rather than directly toward the camera) for this to work. At night, it's much easier to achieve this effect with the 20- to 30-second exposures that are possible. (See Figure 9.6.)

- **Create streaks.** If you aren't shooting for total invisibility, long exposures with the camera on a tripod can produce some interesting streaky effects. Even a single 8X ND filter will let you shoot at f/22 and 1/6th second in daylight. Indoors, you can achieve interesting streaks with slow shutter speeds, as shown in Figure 9.7. I shot the dancers using a 1/2-second exposure, triggering the shot at the beginning of a movement.

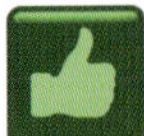

Tip

Neutral-density filters are gray (non-colored) filters that reduce the amount of light passing through the lens, without adding any color or effect of their own.

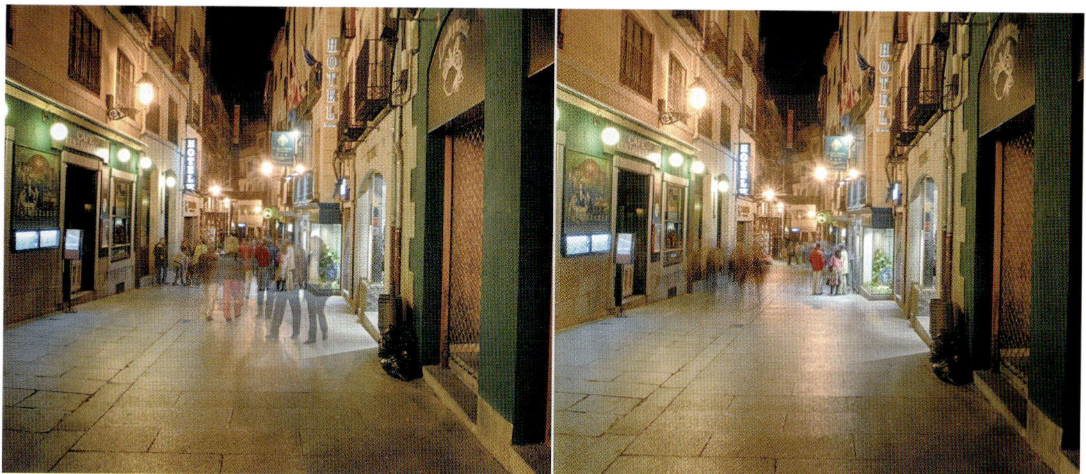

Figure 9.6 This street was packed with tourists (left), but those who were moving were rendered invisible by the 30-second exposure (right).

Figure 9.7
The shutter opened as the dancer began her movement from a standing position, and finished as she rotated.

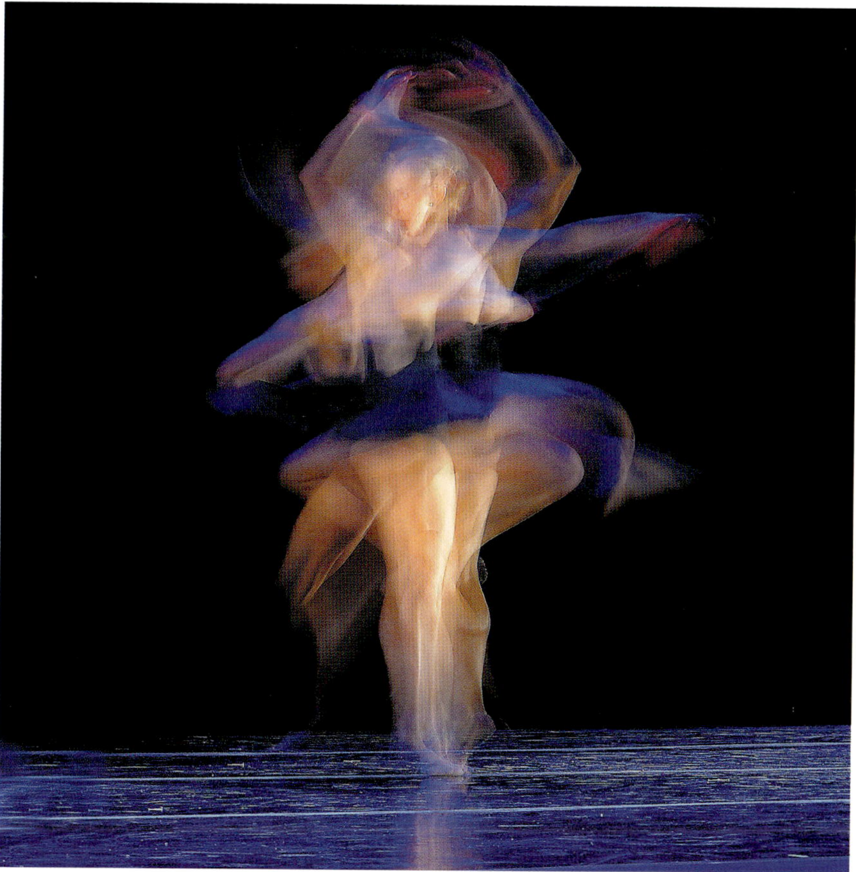

- **Produce light trails.** At night, car headlights, taillights, and other moving sources of illumination can generate interesting light trails. Your camera doesn't even need to be mounted on a tripod; hand-holding the Nikon D3500 for longer exposures adds movement and patterns to your trails. If you're shooting fireworks, a longer exposure—with a tripod—may allow you to capture a burst as it blossoms, as shown in Figure 9.8.

- **Blur waterfalls, etc.** You'll find that waterfalls and other sources of moving liquid produce a special type of long-exposure blur, because the water merges into a fantasy-like veil that looks different at different exposure times, and with different waterfalls. Cascades with turbulent flow produce a rougher look at a given longer exposure than falls that flow smoothly. Although blurred waterfalls have become almost a cliché, there are still plenty of variations for a creative photographer to explore, as you can see in Figure 9.9. For that shot, I incorporated the flowing stream in the background.

- **Show total darkness in new ways.** Even on the darkest, moonless nights, there is enough starlight or glow from distant illumination sources to see by, and, if you use a long exposure, there is enough light to take a picture, too. I was visiting a Great Lakes park hours after sunset, but found that a several-second exposure revealed the skyline scene shown in Figure 9.10, even though in real life, there was barely enough light to make out the boats in the distance. Although the photo appears as if it were taken at twilight or sunset, in fact the shot was made at 10 p.m.

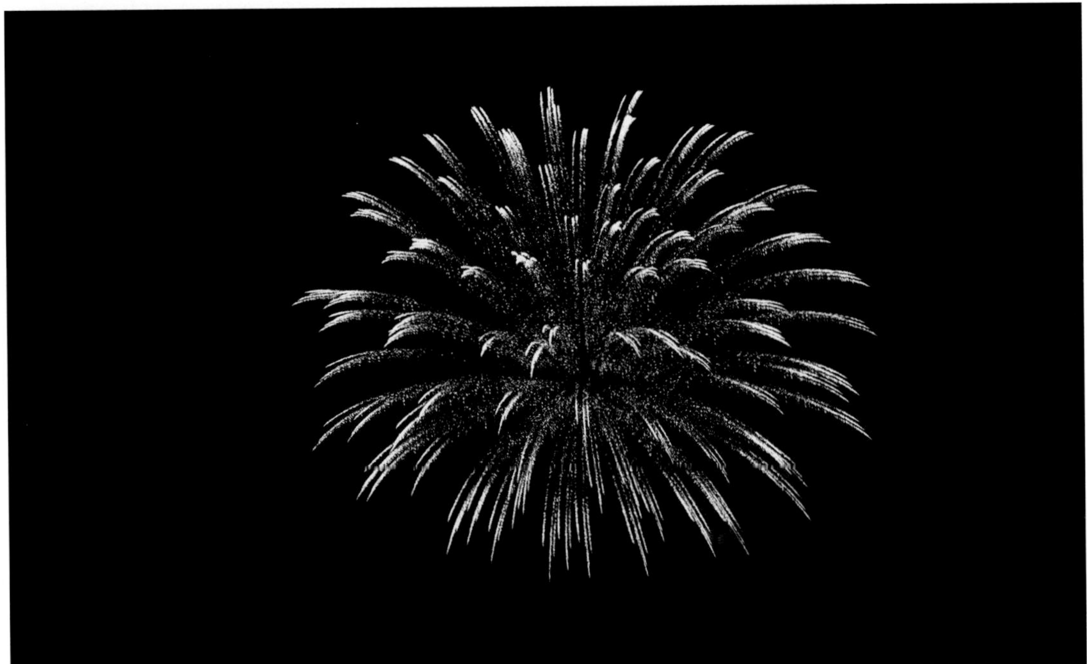

Figure 9.8 I captured these fireworks using a four-second exposure.

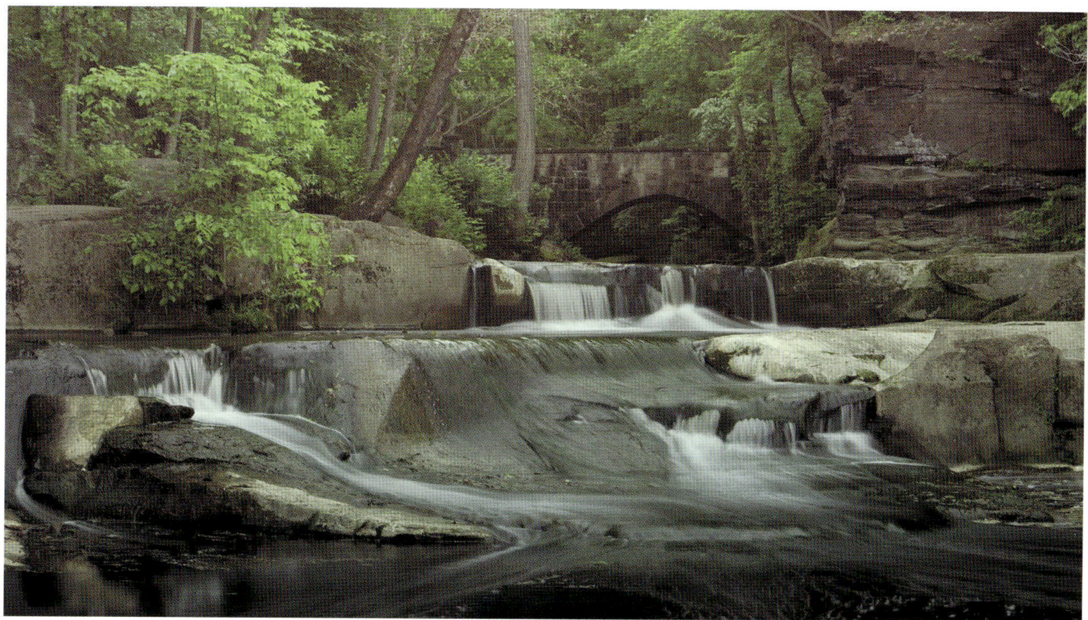

Figure 9.9 Long exposures can transform a waterfall and stream into a display of flowing silk.

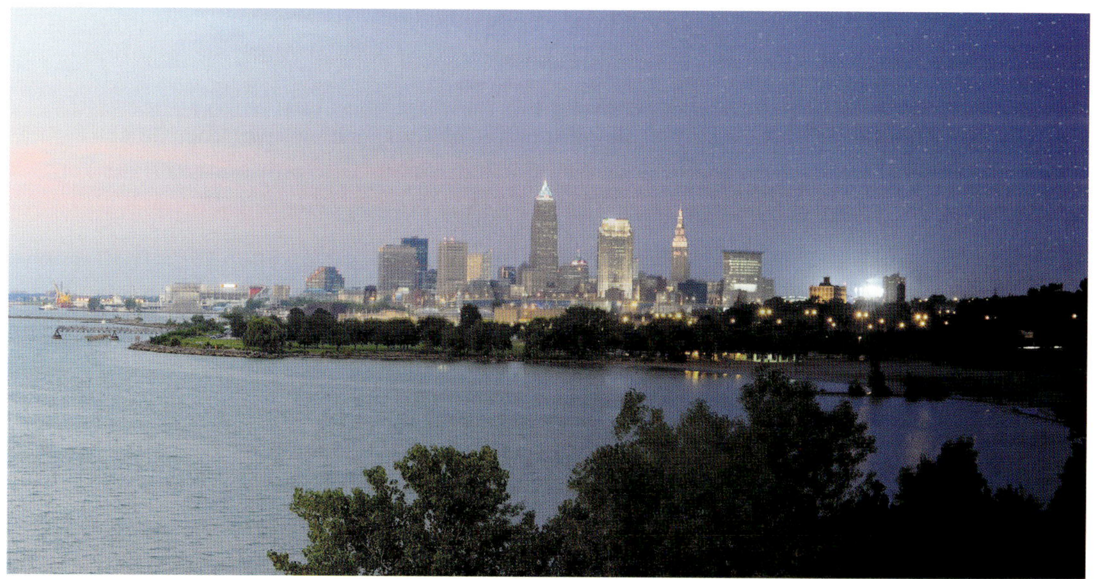

Figure 9.10 A long exposure transformed this night scene into a picture apparently taken at dusk.

Using SnapBridge

Nikon has elected to blaze a trail of its own in implementing wireless connectivity on the D3500, using a new system it calls SnapBridge. SnapBridge provides several useful features in letting you link your camera to a smartphone or tablet. At this time, SnapBridge does *not* allow you to connect your camera to your computer over a Wi-Fi network; communication is strictly between the D3500 and your smart device. Here's what you can do:

- **Bluetooth.** If you own an Android or iOS device that supports Bluetooth 4.1, you can connect your camera and device using the D3500's built-in low-energy Bluetooth connection.

- **Auto uploads.** You can use SnapBridge to automatically upload JPEG images (but not RAW files) from your camera to your smart device.

- **Upload selected photos.** During image review, you can press the *i* button and choose Select to Send to Smart Device/Deselect to choose specific images to transfer to your smart device. You can also use the Select to Send to Smart Device entry in the Playback menu. Up to 1,000 photos can be marked for upload in one session.

- **Resize images.** Obviously uploading full-resolution images to your smart device would be slow and use a lot of storage space on your device. SnapBridge defaults to low-resolution 2-megapixel images (which should be fine for smart device display or sharing on social media), and the app lets you specify an original size.

- **Photo info.** The app also lets you choose to embed comments and copyright information entered in the Setup menu (as described in Chapter 5) or entered using the SnapBridge app itself.

- **Multiple devices.** If you own multiple phones and tablets, you can pair the camera with as many as five different devices. However, the D3500 can connect to only one at a time. You can manually switch between devices using the connection options described shortly.

As I noted earlier, the D3500's SnapBridge app supports only camera-to-smart-device communications. Your first step in using SnapBridge is to download and install the SnapBridge app onto your smart device (Android phone or tablet) from the Google Play store or Nikon's snapbridge.nikon.com web link. You can find the iOS version in the Apple iTunes store. There are several ways to connect your D3500 to your device.

1. Access Connect To Smart Device. You'll find this entry in the Setup menu (see Figure 9.11, upper left). As with all menu entries, and those that follow in this list, proceed by pressing the right directional arrow or pressing OK.

2. When the screen shown at upper right in Figure 9.11 appears, press OK to advance to the screen where you can connect your smart device and the camera.

3. Next, the screen shown at lower left in the figure is displayed on the D3500's LCD monitor. It advises you to install the SnapBridge app (if you haven't already).

4. Open the SnapBridge app on your device and choose Connect. The D3500 should appear on the list of available connections.

5. An authorization screen appears on the D3500 (Figure 9.11, lower right) and on your smart device. The same authorization number should be displayed on each. Press the OK button on the D3500 and Pair on the smart device. When you're successful, the screen shown in Figure 9.12 appears.

6. Press OK again. The Connect screen in the app (shown at left in Figure 9.13) can be used to give permission for the smart device to share location data with the camera. Select Yes and press the right directional button or the OK button to confirm. You can access another version of this screen at any time to enable/disable this feature in the Other > Info/Settings menu of the app on your device.

Figure 9.11

Connecting to a smart device.

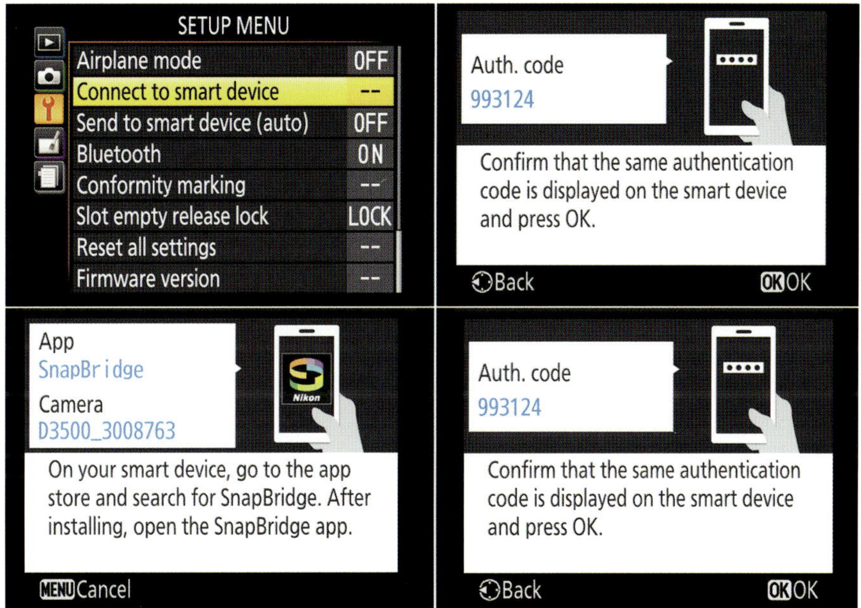

Figure 9.12

Successful connection.

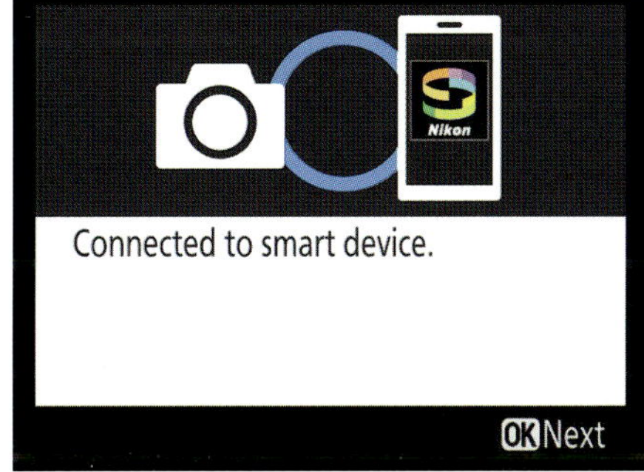

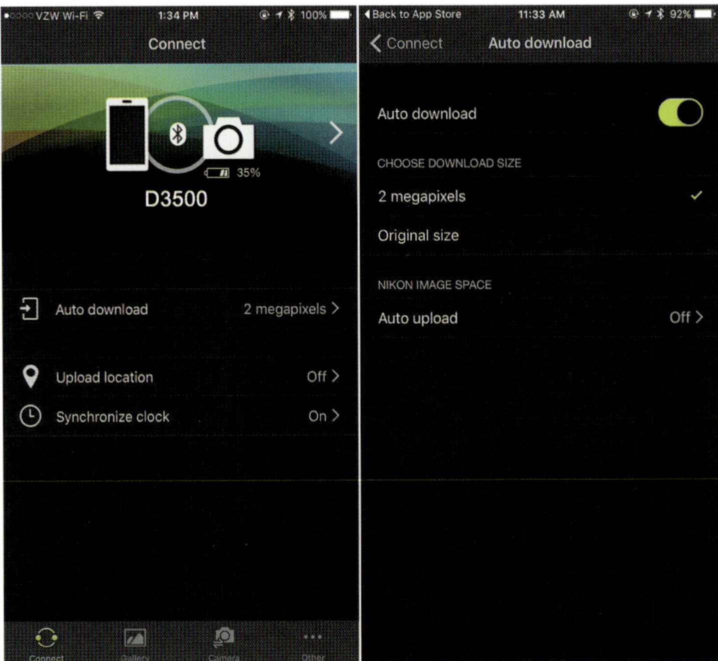

Figure 9.13
Connect screen (left). Choose download size and other parameters (right).

7. The Synchronize Clock screen lets you give permission to allow the smart device to provide the D3500 with time information to synchronize the camera and device. Choose Yes and confirm to finish pairing your device with the camera. The Synchronize Clock feature is also available from the Other > Info/Settings menu any time you are using the app.

8. The Auto Download screen, also available from the Connect screen, lets you tell your smart device that it's OK to automatically download images from your camera. You can choose a compact 2-megapixel size, or original size, as shown at right in Figure 9.13. After you've signed up for a Nikon Image Space account, you can activate the Auto Upload to Nikon Image Space feature.

9. Back in the Setup menu, choose Send to Smart Device (Auto), and in the screen that appears, select and confirm On.

10. Make sure Airplane Mode is turned off, using the entry located just above the two Smart Device entries in the Setup menu. Choose Disable to allow the connectivity features of the D3500 to operate. It's a good idea to Enable Airplane Mode when you don't plan to use SnapBridge in order to save power.

11. Next, find the Bluetooth entry in the Setup menu (see Figure 9.14) and select Send While Off, and confirm it. This allows the camera to maintain a Bluetooth connection with your device and continue to upload images even when the D3500 is powered down. **Note:** this setting will consume even more power if you have many images to upload. Your images will be stored in the Snapshot Gallery in the app.

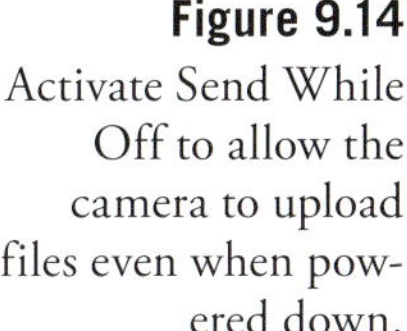

Figure 9.14
Activate Send While Off to allow the camera to upload files even when powered down.

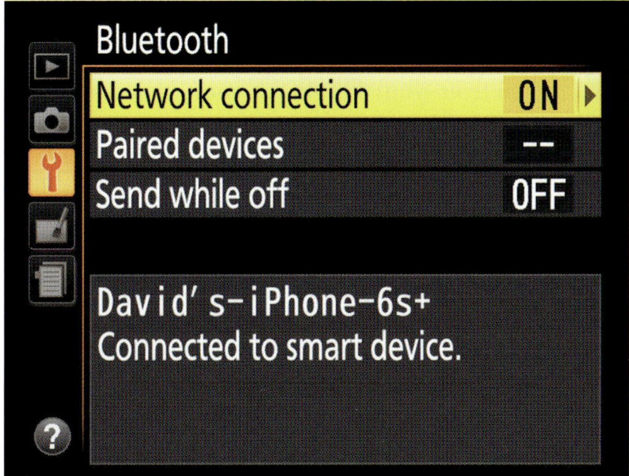

Now that you're all set up and ready to go, you can use the Camera page of the app (see Figure 9.15, left) to select and download only specific photos. If you aren't using automatic upload/download, you can access your photos using the Download Selected Pictures entry on the same menu. First, select the folder containing the camera images you want to access (Figure 9.15, center), and, after the app downloads thumbnails of the images, choose which ones you want to transfer (Figure 9.15,

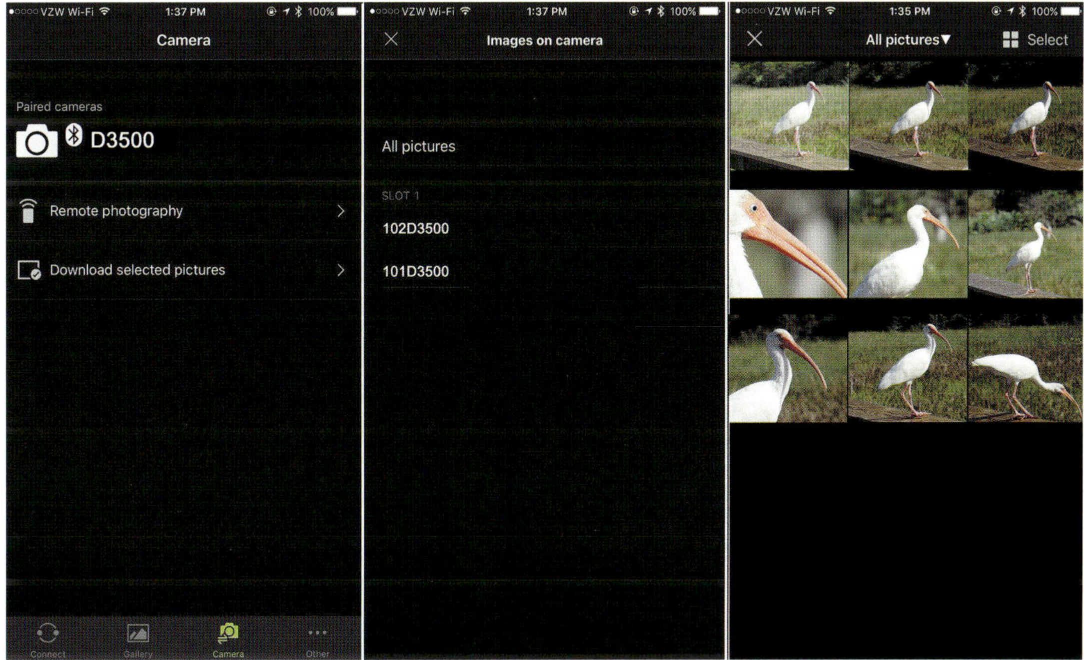

Figure 9.15 Selecting and downloading images.

right). When you tap on a thumbnail, it will appear enlarged in a separate screen. Tap the i icon for information about the photo (such as date shot, resolution, and size). Tap Download at the bottom of that screen to transfer the image from your D3500 to your device.

Don't forget to sign up for Nikon Image Space. It's easy, and can be done using the app. It gives you access to an online image gallery, and you can download many Nikon manuals for easy viewing right on your device. (See Figure 9.16.)

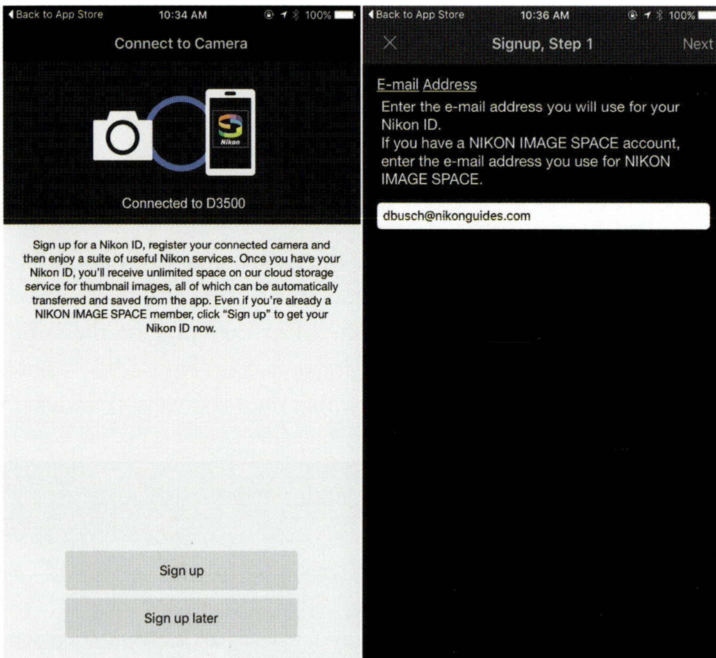

Figure 9.16
Signing up for Nikon Image Space.

10

Working with Lenses

There's no disputing the fact that there is a key reason why many digital SLR buyers choose Nikon cameras: Nikon lenses. Many choose Nikon because of the overall image and build quality of the Nikon lineup. Some favor Nikon cameras because of the broad selection of quality lenses. Others already possess a large collection of Nikon optics (perhaps dating from the owner's photography during the film era), and the ability to use those lenses on the latest digital cameras is a big plus. It's true that there is a mind-bending assortment of high-quality lenses available to enhance the capabilities of Nikon cameras. Nikon has announced the production of its 110 millionth F-mount Nikkor lens. You can use thousands of current and older lenses introduced by Nikon and third-party vendors since 1959, although most manual focus lenses cannot take advantage of the D3500's autoexposure features, and lenses made before 1977 may need an inexpensive $35 modification. That still leaves you with a huge number of autofocus lenses from Nikon and other vendors that work just fine with your camera. This assortment of lenses can give you a wider view, bring distant subjects closer, let you focus closer, shoot under lower light conditions, or provide a more detailed, sharper image for critical work. Other than the sensor itself, the lens you choose for your dSLR is the most important component in determining image quality and perspective of your images.

This chapter explains how to select the best lenses for the kinds of photography you want to do.

Sensor Sensibilities

From time to time, you've heard the term *crop factor*, and you've probably also heard the term *lens multiplier factor*. Both are misleading and inaccurate terms used to describe the same phenomenon: the fact that cameras like the D3500 (and most other affordable digital SLRs) provide a field of view that's smaller and narrower than that produced by certain other (usually much more expensive) cameras, when fitted with exactly the same lens.

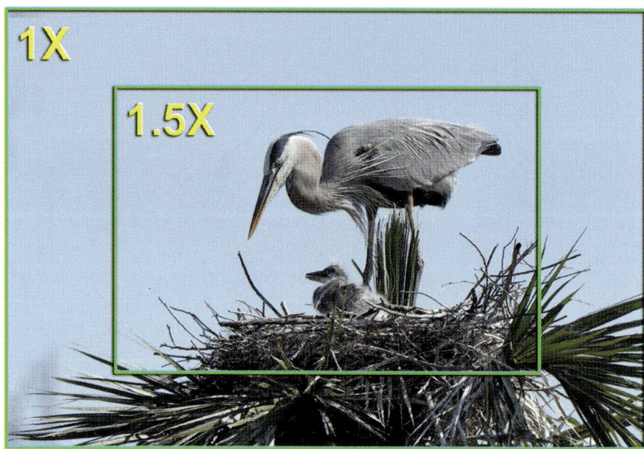

Figure 10.1
The relative fields of
view of full-frame
and DX.

Figure 10.1 quite clearly shows the phenomenon at work. The outer rectangle, marked 1X, shows the field of view you might expect with a 35mm wide-angle lens mounted on one of Nikon's "full-frame" (non-cropped) cameras, like the Nikon D850. The area marked 1.5X shows the field of view you'd get with that 35mm lens installed on a D3500. It's easy to see from the illustration that the outer full-frame rendition provides a wider, more expansive view, while the inner field of view is, in comparison, *cropped* by a factor of 1.5X.

The cropping effect is produced because the sensors of DX cameras like the Nikon D3500 are smaller than the sensors of the Nikon D5, D850, and earlier full-frame cameras. The "full-frame" FX cameras have a sensor that's the size of the standard 35mm film frame, 24mm × 36mm. Your D3500's sensor does *not* measure 24mm × 36mm; instead, it specs out at approximately 23.5mm × 15.6mm.

The cropped sensor effect is most useful when using longer lenses, where extra "reach" is considered a benefit. So, for example, if a 100mm lens is mounted on a D3500, it has the same field of view as a 150mm lens on the Nikon D5.

ARCHAIC NOMENCLATURE?

The common industry term for cameras with this smaller sensor is APS-C, which stands for Advanced Photo System—Classic. It refers to an ill-fated snapshot film format for cameras offered by Kodak and others from 1996 to about 2004. APS-C is one of many film-era terms that live on, including bulb exposure, rangefinder focus, and the designation "full frame" itself. You'll want to remember the APS-C designation when evaluating lenses from third-party vendors, as Nikon is the only company that uses "DX."

This translation is generally useful only if you're accustomed to using full-frame cameras (usually of the film variety) and want to know how a familiar lens will perform on a digital camera. I strongly prefer *crop factor* over *lens multiplier*, because nothing is being multiplied; a 100mm lens doesn't "become" a 150mm lens—the depth-of-field and lens aperture remain the same. (I'll explain more about these later in this chapter.) Only the field of view is cropped. But *crop factor* isn't much better, as it implies that the 24 mm × 36mm frame is "full" and anything else is "less." I get e-mails all the time from photographers who point out that they own full-frame cameras with 33mm × 44mm sensors (such as the Hasselblad X1D-50c and Fujifilm GFX 50S medium-format 50 megapixel digitals). By their reckoning, the "half-size" sensors found in cameras like the Nikon D5 are "cropped."

If you're accustomed to using full-frame film cameras, you might find it helpful to use the crop factor "multiplier" to translate a lens's real focal length into the full-frame equivalent, even though, as I said, nothing is being multiplied. Throughout most of this book, I've been using actual focal lengths and not equivalents, except when referring to specific wide-angle or telephoto focal length ranges and their fields of view.

Crop or Not?

There's a lot of debate over the "advantages" and "disadvantages" of using a camera with a "cropped" sensor, versus one with a "full-frame" sensor. The arguments go like this:

- **"Free" 1.5X teleconverter.** The Nikon D3500 (and other cameras with the 1.5X crop factor) magically transforms any telephoto lens you have into a longer lens, which can be useful for sports, wildlife photography, and other endeavors that benefit from more reach. Yet, your f/stop remains the same. That is, a 300mm f/4 becomes a very fast 450mm f/4 lens. Some discount this advantage, pointing out that the exact same field of view can be had by taking a full-frame image, and trimming it to the cropped equivalent.

- **Dense pixels = more noise.** The other side of the pixel-density coin is that the denser packing of pixels to achieve 24 megapixels in the D3500 sensor means that each pixel must be smaller, and will have less light-gathering capabilities. Larger pixels capture light more efficiently, reducing the need to amplify the signal when boosting ISO sensitivity, and, therefore, producing less noise. In an absolute sense, this is true: the Nikon D750 *also* has 24 megapixels of resolution in a full-frame form factor, so, logically, each of its pixels must be larger. That accounts for its sensational high ISO performance. However, the D3500's sensor—newly developed for this camera—is improved over earlier models, so you'll find it performs very well at higher ISOs.

- **Lack of wide-angle perspective.** Of course, the 1.5X default "crop" factor applies to wide-angle lenses, too, so your 20mm ultra-wide lens becomes a hum-drum 30mm near-wide-angle, and a 35mm focal length is transformed into what photographers call a "normal" lens. Zoom lenses, like the 16-80mm f/2.8-4 lens that is often purchased with the D3500, have less wide-angle perspective at their minimum focal length. The 16-80mm optic, for example, is the equivalent of a 24mm moderate wide angle when zoomed to its widest setting. Nikon has "fixed" this problem by providing several different extra-wide zooms specifically for the DX format, including the (relatively) affordable 12-24mm and 10-24mm DX Nikkors, and a relatively new affordable $309 AF-P DX Nikkor 10-20mm f/4.5-5.6G VR lens. You'll never really lack for wide-angle lenses, but some of us will need to buy wider optics to regain the expansive view we're looking for.

- **Mixed body mix-up.** There is a relatively small number of Nikon D3500 owners who also have a Nikon full-frame camera, say, to use the D3500 as a backup. These enthusiasts can't ignore the focal-length mix-up factor. If you own both FX- and DX-format cameras, it can be vexing to have to adjust to the different fields of view that the cameras provide. If you remove a given lens from one camera and put it on the other, the effective focal length/field of view changes. That 16-35mm zoom works as an ultra-wide to wide angle on a full-frame Nikon, but functions more as a moderate wide-angle to normal lens on a D3500. To get a somewhat similar "look" on both cameras, you'd need to use a 12-24mm zoom on the D3500, and the 16-35mm zoom on the full-frame model. It's possible to become accustomed to this field of view shake-up and, indeed, some photographers put it to work by mounting their longest telephoto lens on the D3500 and their wide-angle lenses on their full-frame camera. Even if you've never owned both an FX and a DX camera, you should be aware of the possible confusion.

First (and Second) Lens Options

Some Nikon dSLRs are almost always purchased with a lens. The entry- and mid-level Nikon dSLRs, including the Nikon D3500, are often bought by those new to digital photography, frequently by first-time SLR or dSLR owners who find the AF-P 18-55mm f/3.5-5.6 kit lens bundled with the AF-P 70-300mm f/4.5-6.3 telephoto to be an irresistable bargain. Indeed, many of you will never purchase or use any lenses other than those.

I bought my D3500 in the two kit lens bundle (18-55mm and 70-300mm included in the box). Nikon has been known to sell only kit packages of its entry- and mid-level cameras initially, and offer bodies only at some later date. As a reader of this book, you've probably been bitten by the enthusiast bug and are at least considering expanding your optical arsenal. You might even consider alternatives, such as the AF-S DX 18-140mm f/3.5-5.6G ED VR, or older AF-S DX 18-105mm f/3.5-5.6G ED VR, or VR version of the 18-55mm kit lens irresistible bargains. All three have shake-canceling vibration reduction built in.

Depending on which category of photographer you fall into, you'll need to make a decision about what first or second lens to buy, or decide what other kind of lenses you need to fill out your complement of Nikon optics. This section will cover "first lens" concerns, while later in the chapter we'll look at "add-on lens" considerations.

When deciding on a first lens, there are several factors you'll want to consider:

- **Cost.** You might have stretched your budget a bit to purchase your Nikon D3500, so the AF-P 18-55mm kit lens helps you keep the cost of your first lens fairly low. In a kit, this lens may tack on just $100 to the price of the body alone. In addition, there are excellent moderately priced lenses available that will add from $100 to $500 to the price of your camera if purchased at the same time.

- **Zoom range.** If you have only one lens, you'll want a fairly long zoom range to provide as much flexibility as possible. Fortunately, several popular basic lenses for the D3500 have 3X to 7.8X zoom ranges (I'll list some of them next), extending from moderate wide-angle/normal out to medium telephoto. These are all fine for everyday shooting, portraits, and some types of sports.

- **Adequate maximum aperture.** You'll want an f/stop of at least f/3.5 to f/4 for shooting under fairly low light conditions. The thing to watch for is the maximum aperture when the lens is zoomed to its telephoto end. You may end up with no better than an f/5.6 maximum aperture. That's not great, but you can often live with it, particularly with a lens having vibration reduction (VR) capabilities, because you can often shoot at lower shutter speeds to compensate for the limited maximum aperture.

- **Image quality.** Your starter lens should have good image quality, because that's one of the primary factors that will be used to judge your photos. Even at a low price, several of the different lenses that can be used with the D3500 kit (such as the 18-140mm zoom) include extra-low dispersion glass and aspherical elements that minimize distortion and chromatic aberration; they are sharp enough for most applications. If you read the user evaluations in the online photography forums, you know that owners of the kit lenses have been very pleased with their image quality.

- **Size matters.** A good walking-around lens is compact in size and light in weight.

- **Fast autofocusing.** Your first lens should have a speedy autofocus system, such as the Silent Wave motor found in Nikon AF-S lenses, and fast, extra-quiet stepping motor included in the new AF-P lenses. As you'll learn later, lenses used on the D3500 *must* have the AF-S or AF-P designation (which means that the lens itself contains an internal autofocusing motor) if you want automatic focus. (Many—but not all—third-party lenses also have internal focus motors.)

- **Close focusing.** The ability to focus down to 12 inches or closer will let you use your basic lens for some types of macro photography.

You can find comparisons of the lenses discussed in the next section. Because "buying guide" books quickly become out of date, I try to stick to describing Nikon lenses only. There are simply too many options available from third-party vendors like Sigma, Tokina, Tamron, Rokinon/Samyang, and other vendors, and their offerings churn frequently as they upgrade and add to their lines. You can even purchase some incredible Zeiss lenses for your D3500. You can find up-to-date discussions of third-party optics in online groups and websites like DP Review (www.dpreview.com).

Buy Now, Expand Later

A capable camera like the D3500 deserves the best lenses you can afford. The following optics are all good, basic lenses; each can serve you well as a "walk-around" lens (one you keep on the camera most of the time, especially when you're out and about without your camera bag). The number of choices is quite amazing, even if your budget is limited to less than $350 for your first lens. Here's a list of Nikon's best-bet "first" (or "second") lenses. Don't worry about sorting out the alphabet soup right now; I provide a complete list of Nikon lens "codes" later in the chapter.

- **AF-S DX Nikkor 18-140mm f/3.5-5.6G ED VR.** This is the DX kit lens Nikon offers as an upgrade for some of its more upscale non-pro DX bodies. It has an extended 7.8X zoom range, a minimum focus distance of roughly 18 inches, and manual focus override that allows you to fine-tune focus after the D3500 has set basic focus automatically. (That feature is especially useful when shooting macro images or working with selective focus techniques when you might want to select a focus point that's slightly different from what the camera selects.) Its roughly $500 list price makes this lens a better buy in a kit (which lowers the effective tariff to around $300). (See Figure 10.2, left.)

- **AF-S DX 16-80mm f/2.8-4E ED VR.** Introduced in 2015, this lens, at roughly $1,100, is a significant upgrade from the 16-85mm lens it replaced. (See Figure 10.2, center.)

- **AF-P DX Nikkor 18-55mm f/3.5-5.6G VR.** If you already own this $250 lens (see Figure 10.2, right), you can continue to use it with your D3500, mostly likely supplemented by other optics. It is also available without VR for about $50 less. Both have fast stepping motors (with the AF-P designation) instead of the older (but still current) AF-S (Silent Wave) motor. These collapsible lenses are compact, but should not be your first choice, even when costs must be kept low. Fortunately, the vibration reduction ("anti-shake") feature of this lens partially offsets the relatively slow maximum aperture at the telephoto position. If you didn't spring for the bundle that included the AF-P 70-300mm zoom, you can mate this lens with Nikon's AF-S

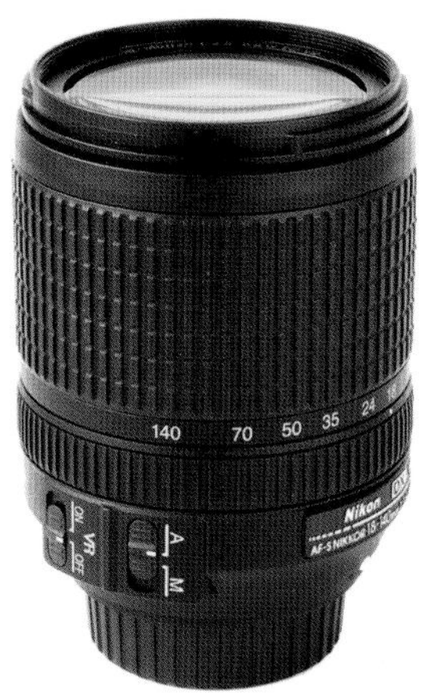
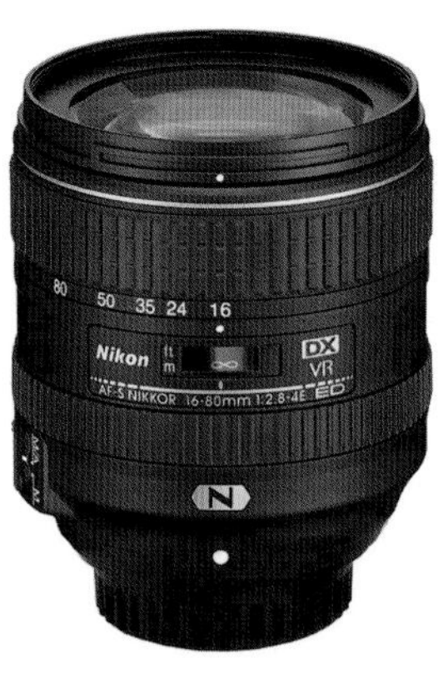
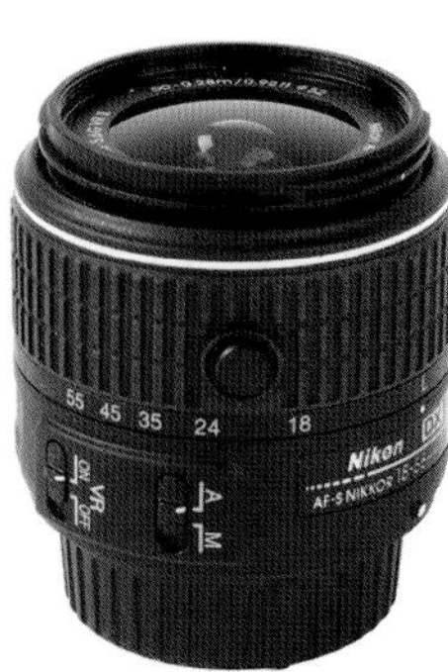

Figure 10.2

The AF-S DX Nikkor 18-140mm f/3.5-5.6G ED VR (left), AF-S DX Nikkor 16-80mm f/2.8-4E ED VR (center), and AF-P DX Nikkor 18-55mm f/3.5-5.6G VR (right), can be purchased as a basic lens for the D3500.

DX VR Zoom-Nikkor 55-200mm f/4-5.6G IF-ED to obtain a two-lens VR pair that will handle everything from 18mm to 200mm, at a relatively low price. (The 55-200mm lens is also available without VR at a lower cost.)

- **AF-S Zoom-Nikkor 24-120mm f/4G ED VR.** If you can live without the focal lengths from 16-23mm (or plan to add a wide-angle zoom that covers that range, such as the Nikon DX 12-24mm or 10-20mm optics), I recommend this one over the 18-140mm kit lens. Theoretically, its $1,100 price is out of the range of a typical D3500 buyer, but if you're planning on upgrading your body or adding a more advanced body in the future, this lens makes an excellent investment. It has a constant f/4 maximum aperture that doesn't change as you zoom, and has a very useful zoom range. As a bonus, it is a full-frame lens, so if you ever decide to upgrade all the way to a full-frame camera, you can take this lens along with you. There are two older versions with f/3.5-f/5.6 variable maximum apertures that you might see available on the used market; they're not as sharp or built as well and should be avoided. (See Figure 10.3.)

- **AF-S DX Nikkor 18-105mm f/3.5-5.6G ED VR II.** This is an older lens but still can be found used (or sometimes new) and is one of my economical choices as a "walking-around" lens for this camera. I much prefer it over the 18-200mm VR (described later), even though it has a more limited zoom range. Its focal length range is quite sufficient for most general photography. You might want this as an everyday lens to use in conjunction with some premium non-zoom primes, like the 85mm f/1.4 or 58mm f/1.4 lenses.

- **AF-S DX Nikkor 16-85mm f/3.5-5.6G ED VR.** The 16-85mm VR lens is the zoom that would make a lot of sense as a kit lens for the D3500 if there weren't better choices available. It's still available new for about $700, but I expect it will probably be discontinued soon, as the 16-80mm lens described above effectively provides a (more expensive) replacement. If you really want to use just a single lens with your camera, this one provides an excellent combination of focal lengths, image quality, and features. Its zoom range extends from a true wide angle (equivalent to a 24mm lens on a full-frame camera) to useful medium telephoto (about 128mm

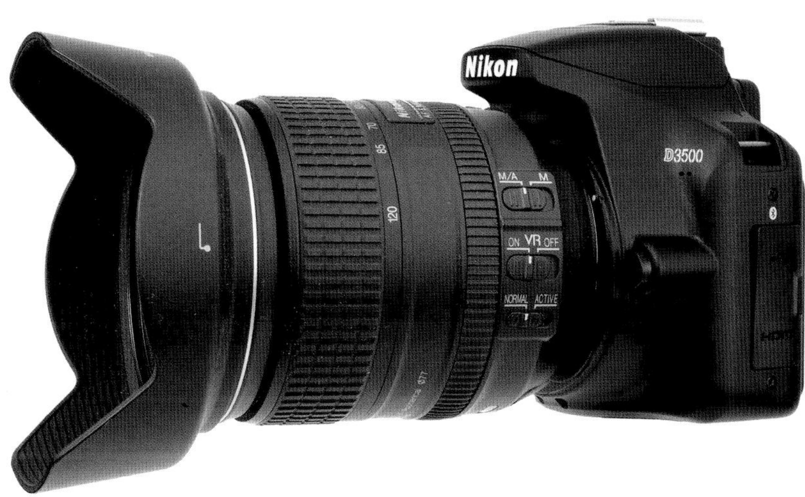

Figure 10.3
The AF-S VR Zoom-Nikkor 24-120mm f/4G ED VR is my recommendation for a first lens for those who plan to cover the super-wide focal length range with an additional lens.

equivalent), and so can be used for everything from architecture to portraiture to sports. If you think vibration reduction is useful only with longer telephoto lenses, you may be surprised at how much it helps you hand-hold your D3500 even at the widest focal lengths. The only disadvantage to this lens is its relatively slow speed (f/5.6) when you crank it out to the telephoto end.

- **AF-S DX Zoom-Nikkor 18-70mm f/3.5-4.5G IF-ED.** If you don't plan on getting a longer zoom-range basic lens and can't afford the 16-80 zoom, I highly recommend this aging, but impressive lens, if you can find one in stock as a used item, as it is long-since discontinued. Originally introduced as the kit lens for the venerable Nikon D70, the 18-70mm zoom quickly gained a reputation as a very sharp lens at a bargain price. It doesn't provide a view that's as long or as wide as the 16-80mm, but it's a half-stop faster at its maximum zoom position. You may have to hunt around to find one of these, but they are available for $200 or even less and well worth it. I own one to this day, and use it regularly, although it spends most of its time installed on my D3200, which has been converted to infrared-only photography.

- **AF-S DX Zoom-Nikkor 18-135mm f/3.5-5.6G IF-ED.** This discontinued lens has been sold as a kit lens for cameras aimed at intermediate amateur-level shooters. While decent, this predecessor of the current 18-140mm VR model is best suited for the crowd who buy one do-everything lens and then never purchase another. Available for less than $300, you won't tie up a lot of money in this lens. There's no VR, so, for most, the 18-105mm VR or 18-140mm VR lens is a better choice.

- **AF-S DX VR II Zoom-Nikkor 18-200mm f/3.5-5.6G IF-ED.** I owned this $650 lens for about three months, and decided it really didn't meet my needs. It was introduced as an ideal "kit" lens for the Nikon D200 many years ago, and, at the time had almost everything you might want. It's a holdover, more upscale kit lens for the D3500. Its stunning 11X zoom range covers everything from the equivalent of 27mm to 300mm when the 1.5X crop factor is figured in, and its VR capabilities plus light weight let you use it without a tripod most of the time. However, I found the image quality to be good, but not outstanding, and the slow maximum aperture at 200mm to be limiting when a fast shutter speed is required to stop action. The "zoom creep" (a tendency for the lens to zoom when the camera is tilted up or down) found in many examples will drive you nuts after a while (see Figure 10.4, left). Fortunately, the newer version with improved VR and with the creep fixed has been available for some time.

- **AF-S VR Zoom-Nikkor 24-85mm f/3.5-4.5G.** Priced at about $500, this lens is reasonably priced, and has the advantage (like the 24-120mm lens) of being a full-frame optic, so if you upgrade in the future to a Nikon FX camera, you can take this one along with you. I happen to own both this lens and Nikon's much more expensive 24-70mm f/2.8 optic (the non-VR version, priced at about $1,800), and tend to use this one (which costs less than one-third as much) much more often. It's not as fast at its maximum zoom setting, but offers a bit more reach, vibration reduction, and is much more compact. This is an excellent walk-around lens for the D3500 if you don't need the extra-wide 18-23mm focal lengths. (See Figure 10.4, center.)

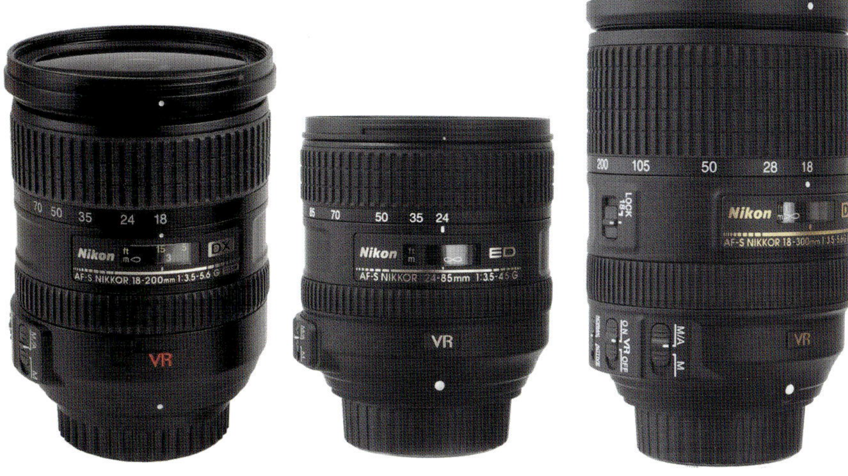

Figure 10.4
The AF-S DX VR Zoom-Nikkor 18-200mm f/3.5-5.6G IF-ED is a lightweight "walk-ing-around" lens (left). The AF-S VR Zoom-Nikkor 24-85mm f/3.5-4.5G lens (center) is affordable, and is compatible with full-frame cameras too. Nikon's 18-300mm offerings (right) cover a full range of focal lengths.

- **AF-S VR Zoom-Nikkor 18-300mm f/3.5-6.3G and f/3.5-5.6G.** Nikon makes *two* 18-300mm super-zoom lenses that cover a full range from moderate wide angle to long telephoto. These ultra-zooms are a special case, and I'll describe them in more detail shortly. One example is shown in Figure 10.4, right.

- **AF-P Zoom-Nikkor 70-300mm f/4.5-6.3G ED.** If you didn't buy this lens with your D3500 in a kit, it's available separately for $350. (See Figure 10.5.) A VR version of the same lens costs $50 more.

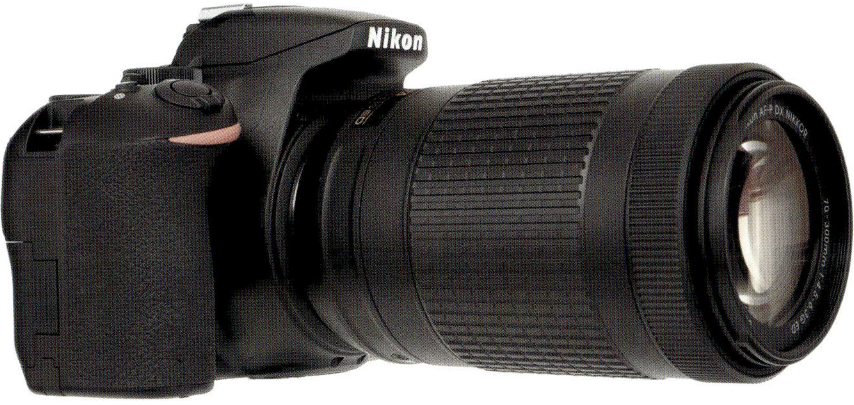

Figure 10.5
The Nikon AF-P 70-300mm f/4.5-6.3G ED "kit" lens is a bargain.

When you're ready to expand your DX lens collection, the following lenses are some of your best-bet options. If an FX camera is in your future, I'll describe some full-frame lenses at the end of this chapter.

- **AF-S DX Nikkor 12-24 f/4G IF-ED.** This $1,150 lens was the original wide zoom for DX cameras, and is great for those who want a fast, constant f/4 maximum aperture and don't need an ultra-wide view. It's still available new, as an extra-cost option with a more rugged build, and a front thread that accepts "professional" 77mm filters.

- **AF-S DX Nikkor 10-24mm f/3.5-4.5G ED.** If you need a wider view and lower price, this newer lens, at $900, is the most popular Nikon ultra-wide lens for the D3500. It focuses nearly three inches closer than its older sibling.

- **AF-P DX Nikkor 10-20mm f/4.5-5.6G VR.** Nikon has blessed bargain-hunters with this new $309 compact, lightweight zoom that features—surprise!—vibration reduction. VR is a feature typically associated with telephoto lenses, because their magnification of the subject also magnifies any camera shake. While VR is less essential for wide-angle lenses like this one, it can be essential for hand-held street photography. It's a reasonable choice for those looking to save money on a wide zoom.

- **AF-S 35mm f/1.8G DX.** If you want a fast, inexpensive "normal" lens for your D3500 for street photography, interiors, photojournalism, or indoor sports, this $200 lens fills the bill.

- **AF-S 40mm f/2.8G DX Micro-Nikkor.** This lens and the 85mm optic described next make up Nikon's reasonably priced macro lens lineup. This one is just $280 and does an excellent job. I describe Nikon's broader range of full-frame macro lenses at the end of this chapter.

- **AF-S 85mm f/3.5G ED DX Micro-Nikkor VR.** A bit more expensive at about $560, this longer Micro-Nikkor gives you a bit more distance from skittish subjects (like insects) and has vibration reduction so you can often shoot nature close-ups hand-held. Keep in mind that VR won't freeze fronds swaying in the breeze; you'll still need to use higher shutter speeds on windy days.

- **AF-S 17-55 f/2.8G DX IF-ED.** This was the first "pro" lens for DX format and remains a popular, if expensive (at around $1,500) option. Personally, if I didn't need a fast f/2.8 constant maximum aperture, I'd prefer to spend those bucks on a similar full-frame lens, like the 24-120mm f/4, which has VR to boot.

- **AF-S 55-300mm f/4.5-5.6G DX VR.** For the price, this lens is an excellent lens in the short telephoto to supertelephoto range. Its $400 price tag won't deplete your pocketbook as much as Nikon's 18-300mm lens if you don't need the wide-angle focal lengths. It's a better performer at the telephoto lens, as well.

- **AF-S 55-200mm f/4-5.6G DX ED VRII / AF-S 55-200mm f4.5-5.6 DX IF-ED VR.** Nikon offers two lenses in the 55-200mm focal length range; a newer version with upgraded VR at $350, and an older model with similar specs, but less advanced vibration reduction. If you can locate one, the latter lens can often be purchased new for around $200. It's not as sharp as its upgraded sibling, but it can make a good addition to your camera bag until you can afford a deluxe version.

Your Best Do-Everything Option?

I mentioned Nikon's pair of 18-300mm zoom offerings earlier. The company has introduced an updated version of this lens, which was originally unveiled in 2012. It might actually be the best do-everything option for a limited number of D3500 shooters, if top-notch image quality at every focal length is not a priority. Both have an incredible 16.7X zoom range, yet are relatively light and compact, focus close, and have image stabilization built in. They've become a standard walk-around lens for many DX format users, because their 27-450mm equivalent focal length range is spectacular for sports and wildlife.

The odd part is that the new version is more compact and weighs less (nine ounces lighter at 1 pound, four ounces), has a *smaller* maximum aperture (f/6.3 versus f/5.6 for the original), and costs less (at $700). The original has the faster maximum aperture, focuses about an inch closer, is marginally sharper, and commands a $300 premium with its $999 MSRP.

The range of these lenses isn't even considered daring anymore since Tamron has introduced an 18-400mm f/3.5-6.3 "all-in-one" lens, and Sigma offers a 60-600mm f/4.5-5.6 zoom. Both are too pricey (the Sigma lists at $2,000) for virtually all D3500 owners. However, Nikon's more affordable (relatively) super-zooms include the following:

- **Ultra-long zoom range.** Used on your D3500, these lenses provide the equivalent field of view as a full-frame 27-450mm lens. That's sort of wide to supertelephoto, without the need to swap optics. That versatility is important when shooting stills, of course, especially with sports and other rapidly changing scenes. But if you're shooting movies, the 18-300mm focal lengths come in especially handy. You can capture a wide establishing shot to set the scene, switch to a medium shot to draw viewer attention to your main subjects, then capture an extreme close-up. Even if you're collecting short clips, the action may be continuing between "takes," so if you had to switch lenses you might miss something. Not so with these lenses. You can change field of view between each shot as quickly as you can rotate the zoom ring. The lens's long range has some possibilities for those mind-boggling quick zooms in or out *during* video capture, too. (Use with restraint!) The only drawback these lenses have is that they are not especially sharp as a telephoto from 200-300mm, nor at the widest-angle settings. If most of your work requires 18-200mm focal lengths and you have an occasional need for the 200-300mm range (and don't want to shoot wide open), these lenses can be very useful.

- **Vibration reduction.** It's so common to have VR in telephoto lenses these days, especially those with equivalent or actual focal lengths of 400mm or more, that you might not stop to think how relatively rare image stabilization has been at the other end of the focal length range. While it's arguable that VR is less essential in a wide-angle lens because camera shake blur is less of a problem, having a lens that starts wide and goes all the way to supertelephoto with optical image stabilization built in is a definite plus.

- **Compact size.** Although it replaces a half-dozen or more lenses, the newer f/6.3 18-300mm zoom measures just 3.3 × 4.7 inches and weighs 1 pound, 4 ounces, which is svelte for a

300mm lens (even if a bit large for an 18mm wide angle). However, it almost doubles in length when cranked out to its full 300mm setting, becoming lanky instead of svelte.

- **Close focusing.** The 18-300mm can focus down to 1.6 feet at 300mm, giving you a 1:3.2X maximum reproduction ratio (about one-third life-size in DX format). The 18-300mm is not a true macro lens, but when you're venturing out with a single lens on your D3500, the ability to focus that closely at 300mm is the next best thing.

- **Good (not great) image quality.** Nikon says that three extra-low dispersion (ED) elements and three aspheric elements deliver the promised minimized chromatic aberration (which can be especially troublesome at wide-angle focal lengths), and the typical aberrations that appear when a lens is used at larger apertures (that's something that will probably happen given the relatively slow f/6.3 maximum aperture at 300mm). As I said earlier, these lenses deliver useful image quality even if they are not the sharpest 300mm lenses you can own.

What Lenses Can You Use?

The previous section helped you sort out what basic lens you need to buy with your Nikon D3500. Now, you're probably wondering what lenses can be added to your growing collection (trust me, it will grow). You need to know which lenses are suitable and, most importantly, which lenses are fully compatible with your Nikon D3500.

With the Nikon D3500, the compatibility issue is a simple one: It can use any modern-era Nikon lens with the AF-S or AF-P designation, with full availability of all autofocus, auto aperture, auto-exposure, and image stabilization features (if present). Older lenses with the AF designation won't autofocus on the D3500, but can still be used for automatic exposure. You can also use any Nikon AI, AI-S, or AI-P lens, which are manual focus lenses that were produced starting in 1977 and continue in production effectively through the present day, because Nikon continues to offer a limited number of manual focus lenses for those who need them. Just remember: AF-S—all features available; non-AF-S (including AF)—no autofocusing possible.

The Nikon D3500, as well as previous entry-level models in the D3xxx, D5xxx, D60, D40, and D40x series don't have an autofocusing motor built into the camera body itself. The motor, present in all other Nikon digital SLRs, allows the camera to adjust the lens focus mechanically. Without that motor in the body, cameras like the D3500 must communicate focus information to the lens, so that the lens's own built-in AF motor can take care of the autofocus process. Because virtually all newer Nikon-brand lenses are of the AF-S or AF-P type, this means your D3500 will have problems only with older Nikon optics.

That's not true with third-party (non-Nikon) lenses. While your D3500 will accept virtually all modern lenses produced by Tokina, Tamron, Sigma, and other vendors, they will autofocus only with those lenses that contain an internal focusing motor, similar to Nikon's AF-S offerings. Vendors have different designators to indicate these lenses, such as HSM (for hypersonic motor). You'll have to check with the manufacturer of non-Nikon lenses to see if they are compatible with the D3500, particularly since some vendors have been gradually introducing revamped versions of their existing lenses with the addition of an internal motor.

There's some good news for those using one of Nikon's focus-motorless entry-level models. These cameras, *unlike* Nikon models that have the camera body focus motor, can safely use lenses offered prior to 1977 (although I expect that, while numerous, most of these aren't used much by those who have modern digital cameras). That's because cameras other than Nikon's entry-level quartet have a pin on the lens mount that can be damaged by an older, unmodified lens. John White at www.aiconversions.com will do the work for about $35 to allow these older lenses to be safely used on any Nikon digital camera. If you own or may someday purchase one of those other cameras, you'll want to consider having the lens conversion done, even though your D3500 doesn't require it to use the lens safely.

Today, in addition to its traditional full-frame lenses, Nikon offers lenses with the DX designation, which is intended for use only on DX-format cameras, like your D3500. While the lens mounting system is the same, DX lenses have a coverage area that fills only the smaller frame, allowing the design of more compact, less-expensive lenses especially for non-full-frame cameras. The AF-S DX Nikkor 35mm f/1.8G, a fixed focal length (non-zoom) lens with a fast f/1.8 maximum aperture, is an example of such a lens.

Ingredients of Nikon's Alphanumeric Soup

Nikon has always been fond of appending cryptic letters and descriptors onto the names of its lenses. Here's an alphabetical list of lens terms you're likely to encounter, either as part of the lens name or in reference to the lens's capabilities. Not all of these are used as parts of a lens's name, but you may come across some of these terms in discussions of particular Nikon optics:

- **AF, AF-D, AF-I, AF-P, AF-S.** In all cases, AF stands for *autofocus* when appended to the name of a Nikon lens. An extra letter is added to provide additional information. A plain old AF lens is an autofocus lens that uses a slot-drive motor in the camera body to provide autofocus functions (and so cannot be used in AF mode on the entry-level models noted earlier). The D means that it's a D-type lens (described later in this listing); the I indicates that focus is through a motor inside the lens; AF-P is used to designate lenses with a very quiet stepper motor that's especially useful for sound video applications. The most common Nikon focus designation is still AF-S, and the S means that a Silent Wave motor in the lens provides focusing. (Don't confuse a Nikon AF-S lens with the AF-S [Single-Servo Autofocus mode].) Nikon has upgraded most of its older AF lenses with AF-S (or AF-P) versions, but it's not safe to assume that *all* newer Nikkors are AF-S/AF-P, or even offer autofocus. For example, the PC-E Nikkor 24mm f/3.5D ED perspective control lens must be focused manually, and Nikon offers a surprising collection of other manual focus lenses to meet specialized needs.

- **AI, AI-S.** All Nikkor lenses produced after 1977 have either automatic aperture indexing (AI) or automatic indexing-shutter (AI-S) features that eliminate the previous requirement to manually align the aperture ring on the camera when mounting a lens. This indexing provides essential information to the camera to allow autoexposure. Unfortunately, the D3500 lacks the required indexing ring, so, while you can use these lenses on your camera, you are limited to both manual focus *and* manual exposure.

- **D.** Appended to the maximum f/stop of the lens (as in f/2.8D), a D-Series lens can send focus distance data to the camera, which uses the information for flash exposure calculation and 3D Color Matrix II metering.

- **DC.** The DC stands for defocus control, which allows managing the out-of-focus parts of an image to produce better-looking portraits and close-ups.

- **DX.** The DX lenses are designed for use with digital cameras using the APS-C-sized sensor having the 1.5X crop factor. The image circle they produce isn't large enough to fill up a full 35mm frame at all focal lengths, but they can be used on Nikon's full-frame models using the automatic/manual DX crop mode.

- **E.** The E designation was used for Nikon's budget-priced E-Series optics, five prime and three zoom manual focus lenses built using aluminum or plastic parts rather than the preferred brass parts of that era, so they were considered less rugged. All are effectively AI-S lenses. They do have good image quality, which makes them a bargain for those who treat their lenses gently and don't need the latest autofocus features. They were available in 28mm f/2.8, 35mm f/2.5, 50mm f/1.8, 100mm f/2.8, and 135mm f/2.8 focal lengths, plus 36-72mm f/3.5, 75-150mm f/3.5, and 70-210mm f/4 zooms. (All these would be considered fairly "fast" today.)

  However, today the E designation is applied to lenses to represent those that stop down the lens to the "taking" aperture electronically. (During framing, focusing, exposure metering, and other pre-photo steps, the lens always remains at its maximum aperture unless you stop it down using a Preview—depth-of-field preview—button.) Non-E lenses use a lever in the camera body that mates with a lever in the lens mount. Lenses with an E in their names, such as the 16-80mm f/2.8-4E ED VR optic, use an electronic mechanism instead. You should be aware that many older film and digital camera bodies (those produced prior to the D3 and D3000, introduced in 2007, plus the Nikon D90 and D3000) are unable to adjust the aperture of this type of E lens, and must be used wide-open.

- **ED (or LD/UD).** The ED (extra-low dispersion) designation indicates that some lens elements are made of a special hard and scratch-resistant glass that minimizes the divergence of the different colors of light as they pass through, thus reducing chromatic aberration (color "fringing") and other image defects. A gold band around the front of the lens indicates an optic with ED elements. You sometimes find LD (low dispersion) or UD (ultra-low dispersion) designations.

- **FX.** When Nikon introduced the Nikon D3 as its first full-frame camera, it coined the term "FX," representing the nominal 24mm × 36mm sensor format as a counterpart to "DX," which was used for its 16mm × 24mm APS-C-sized sensors. Although FX hasn't been officially applied to any Nikon *lenses* so far, expect to see the designation used more often to differentiate between lenses that are compatible with any Nikon digital SLR (FX) and those that operate only on DX-format cameras, or in DX mode when used on an FX camera like the D5.

- **G.** G-type lenses have no aperture ring, and you can use them at other than the maximum aperture only with electronic cameras like the D3500 that set the aperture automatically. Fortunately, this includes all Nikon digital dSLRs.

- **IF.** Nikon's *internal focusing* lenses change focus by shifting only small internal lens groups with no change required in the lens's physical length, unlike conventional double helicoid focusing systems that move all lens groups toward the front or rear during focusing. IF lenses are more compact and lighter in weight, provide better balance, focus more closely, and can be focused more quickly.

- **IX.** These lenses were produced for Nikon's long-discontinued Pronea 6i and S APS film cameras. While the Pronea could use many standard Nikon lenses, IX lenses cannot be mounted on any Nikon digital SLR.

- **Micro.** Nikon uses the term *micro* to designate its close-up lenses. Most other vendors use *macro* instead.

- **N (Nano Crystal Coat).** Nano Crystal lens coating virtually eliminates internal lens element reflections across a wide range of wavelengths, and is particularly effective in reducing ghost and flare peculiar to ultra-wide-angle lenses. Nano Crystal Coat employs multiple layers of Nikon's extra-low refractive index coating, which features ultra-fine crystallized particles of nano size (one nanometer equals one millionth of a mm).

- **NAI.** This is not an official Nikon term, but it is widely used to indicate that a manual focus lens is *Not-AI*, which means that it was manufactured before 1977, and therefore cannot be used safely on modern digital Nikon SLRs (other than the retro Df model) without modification.

- **NOCT** (**Nocturnal).** Used primarily to refer to the prized Nikkor AI-S Noct 58mm f/1.2, a "fast" (wide aperture) prime lens, with aspherical elements, capable of taking photographs in very low light.

- **PC (Perspective Control).** A PC lens can shift the lens from side to side (and up/down) to provide a more realistic perspective when photographing architecture and other subjects that otherwise require tilting the camera so that the sensor plane is not parallel to the subject. Older Nikkor PC lenses offered shifting only, but more modern models, such as the PC-E Nikkor 24mm f/3.5D ED lens introduced early in 2008 allow both shifting and tilting.

- **UV.** This term is applied to special (and expensive) lenses designed to pass ultraviolet light.

- **UW.** Lenses with this designation are designed for underwater photography with Nikonos camera bodies, and cannot be used with Nikon digital SLRs.

- **VR.** Nikon has an expanding line of vibration reduction (VR) lenses, including several very affordable models and the AF-S DX Nikkor 16-85mm f/3.5-5.6G ED VR lens, which shifts lens elements internally to counteract camera shake. The VR feature allows using a shutter speed up to four stops slower than would be possible without vibration reduction, according to Nikon.

Zoom or Prime?

When selecting between zoom and prime lenses, there are several considerations to ponder. Here's a checklist of the most important factors. I already mentioned image quality and maximum aperture earlier, but those aspects take on additional meaning when comparing zooms and primes.

- **Logistics.** As prime lenses offer just a single focal length, you'll need more of them to encompass the full range offered by a single zoom. More lenses mean additional slots in your camera bag, and extra weight to carry. Just within Nikon's line alone you can choose from a good selection of general-purpose (if you can count AF lenses that won't autofocus with the D3500 as "general purpose") prime lenses in 28mm, 35mm, 50mm, 85mm, 100mm, 135mm, and 200mm focal lengths, all of which are overlapped by the 18-200mm zoom I mentioned earlier. Even so, you might be willing to carry an extra prime lens or two to gain the speed or image quality that lens offers.

- **Image quality.** Prime lenses usually produce better image quality at their focal length than even the most sophisticated zoom lenses at the same magnification. Zoom lenses, with their shifting elements and f/stops that can vary from zoom position to zoom position, are in general more complex to design than fixed focal length lenses. That's not to say that the very best prime lenses can't be complicated as well. However, the exotic designs, aspheric elements, and low-dispersion glass can be applied to improving the quality of the lens, rather than wasting a lot of it on compensating for problems caused by the zoom process itself.

- **Maximum aperture.** Because of the same design constraints, zoom lenses usually have smaller maximum apertures than prime lenses, and the most affordable zooms have a lens opening that grows effectively smaller as you zoom in. The difference in lens speed verges on the ridiculous at some focal lengths. For example, the 18-55mm super-bargain kit lens gives you a 55mm f/5.6 lens when zoomed all the way out, while prime lenses in that focal length commonly have f/1.8 or faster maximum apertures. Indeed, the fastest f/2, f/1.8, f/1.4, and f/1.2 lenses are all manual focus primes (at least on the D3500, because they are AF models), and if you require speed, a fixed focal length lens is what you should rely on. Figure 10.6 shows an image taken with a 50mm f/1.8 prime lens.

- **Speed.** Using prime lenses takes time and slows you down. It takes a few seconds to remove your current lens and mount a new one, and the more often you need to do that, the more time is wasted. If you choose not to swap lenses, when using a fixed focal length lens, you'll still have to move closer or farther away from your subject to get the field of view you want. A zoom lens allows you to change magnifications and focal lengths with the twist of a ring and generally saves a great deal of time.

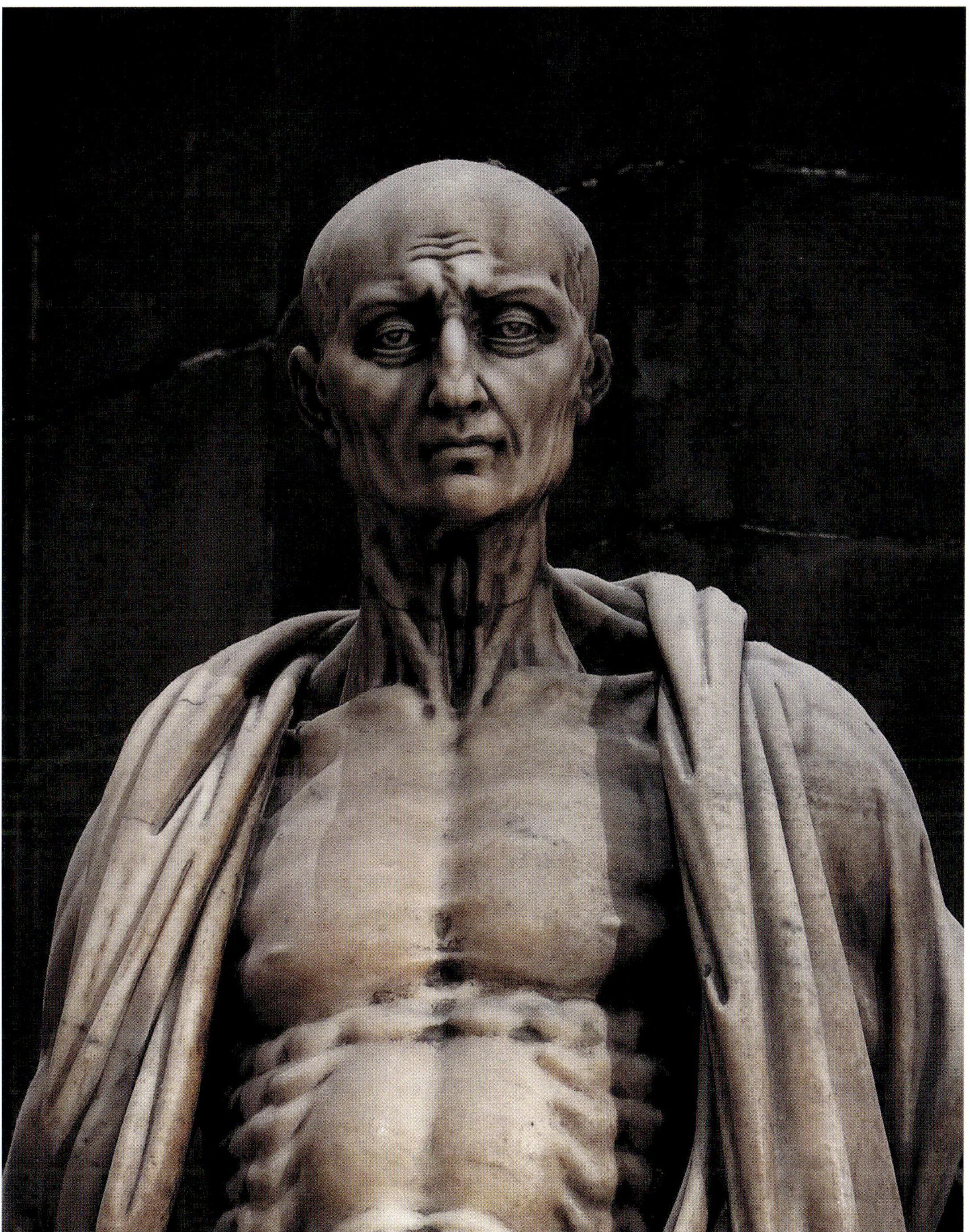

Figure 10.6 A 50mm f/1.8 lens was perfect for this hand-held photo in a dimly lit cathedral in Italy.

Categories of Lenses

Lenses can be categorized by their intended purpose—general photography, macro photography, and so forth—or by their focal length. The range of available focal lengths is usually divided into three main groups: wide angle, normal, and telephoto. Prime lenses fall neatly into one of these classifications. Zooms can overlap designations, with a significant number falling into the catch-all, wide-to-telephoto zoom range. This section provides more information about focal length ranges, and how they are used.

When the 1.5X crop factor (mentioned at the beginning of this chapter) is figured in, any lens with an equivalent focal length of 10mm to 16mm is said to be an *ultra-wide-angle lens*; from about 16mm to 28mm is said to be a *wide-angle lens. Normal lenses* have a focal length roughly equivalent to the diagonal of the film or sensor, in millimeters, and so fall into the range of about 30mm to 40mm on a D3500. *Short telephoto lenses* start at about 40mm to 70mm, with anything from 70mm to 250mm qualifying as a conventional *telephoto.* For the Nikon D3500, anything from about 300mm to 400mm or longer can be considered a *super-telephoto.*

Using Wide-Angle and Wide-Zoom Lenses

To use wide-angle prime lenses and wide zooms, you need to understand how they affect your photography. Here's a quick summary of the things you need to know.

- **More depth-of-field.** Practically speaking, wide-angle lenses offer more depth-of-field at a particular subject distance and aperture. You'll find that helpful when you want to maximize sharpness of a large zone, but not very useful when you'd rather isolate your subject using selective focus (telephoto lenses are better for that).

- **Stepping back.** Wide-angle lenses have the effect of making it seem that you are standing farther from your subject than you really are. They're helpful when you don't want to back up, or can't because there are impediments in your way.

- **Wider field of view.** While making your subject seem farther away, as implied above, a wide-angle lens also provides a larger field of view, including more of the subject in your photos.

- **More foreground.** As background objects retreat, more of the foreground is brought into view by a wide-angle lens. That gives you extra emphasis on the area that's closest to the camera. Photograph your home with a normal lens/normal zoom setting, and the front yard probably looks fairly conventional in your photo (that's why they're called "normal" lenses). Switch to a wider lens and you'll discover that your lawn now makes up much more of the photo. So, wide-angle lenses are great when you want to emphasize that lake in the foreground, but problematic when your intended subject is located farther in the distance.

■ **Super-sized subjects.** The tendency of a wide-angle lens to emphasize objects in the foreground, while de-emphasizing objects in the background can lead to a kind of size distortion that may be more objectionable for some types of subjects than others. Shoot a bed of flowers up close with a wide angle, and you might like the distorted effect of the larger blossoms nearer the lens. Take a photo of a family member with the same lens from the same distance, and you're likely to get some complaints about that gigantic nose in the foreground.

■ **Perspective distortion.** When you tilt the camera so the plane of the sensor is no longer perpendicular to the vertical plane of your subject, some parts of the subject are now closer to the sensor than they were before, while other parts are farther away. So, buildings, flagpoles, or NBA players appear to be falling backward, as you can see in Figure 10.7. While this kind of apparent distortion (it's not caused by a defect in the lens) can happen with any lens, it's most apparent when a wide angle is used.

■ **Steady cam.** Hand-holding a wide-angle lens at slower shutter speeds, without vibration reduction, produces steadier results than with a telephoto lens. The reduced magnification of the wide-lens or wide-zoom setting doesn't emphasize camera shake like a telephoto lens does.

■ **Interesting angles.** Many of the factors already listed combine to produce more interesting angles when shooting with wide-angle lenses. Raising or lowering a telephoto lens a few feet probably will have little effect on the appearance of the distant subjects you're shooting. The same change in elevation can produce a dramatic effect for the much-closer subjects typically captured with a wide-angle lens or wide-zoom setting.

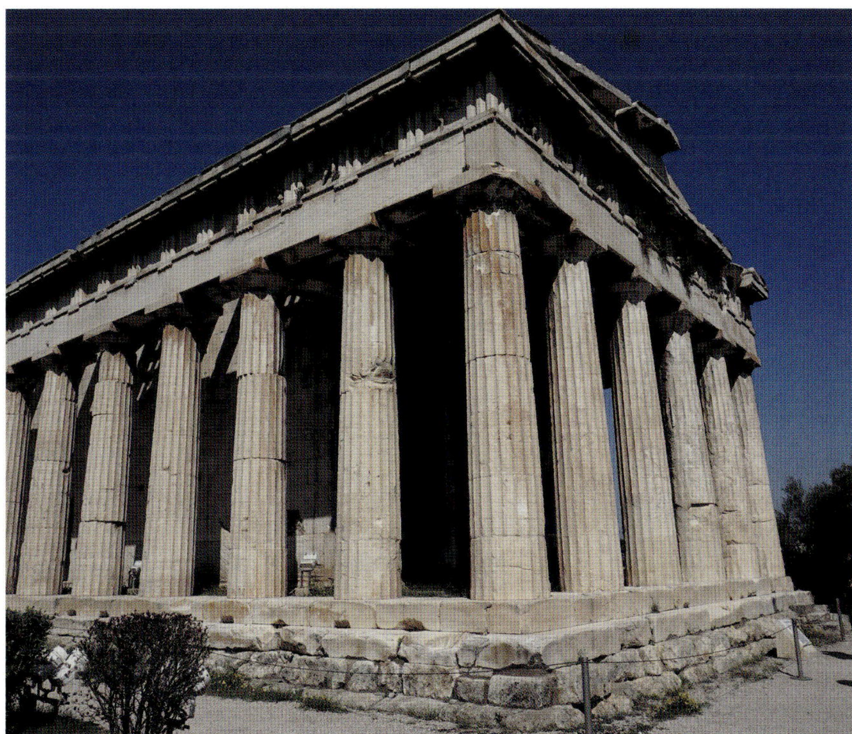

Figure 10.7
Tilting the camera back produces this "falling back" look in architectural photos.

Avoiding Potential Wide-Angle Problems

Wide-angle lenses have a few quirks that you'll want to keep in mind when shooting so you can avoid falling into some common traps. Here's a checklist of tips for avoiding common problems:

- **Symptom: converging lines.** Unless you want to use wildly diverging lines as a creative effect, it's a good idea to keep horizontal and vertical lines in landscapes, architecture, and other subjects carefully aligned with the sides, top, and bottom of the frame. That will help you avoid undesired perspective distortion. Sometimes it helps to shoot from a slightly elevated position so you don't have to tilt the camera up or down.

- **Symptom: color fringes around objects.** Lenses are often plagued with fringes of color around backlit objects, produced by *chromatic aberration*, which is produced when all the colors of light don't focus in the same plane or same lateral position (that is, the colors are offset to one side). This phenomenon is more common in wide-angle lenses and in photos of subjects with contrasty edges. Some kinds of chromatic aberration can be reduced by stopping down the lens, while all sorts can be reduced by using lenses with low diffraction index glass (or ED elements, in Nikon nomenclature) and by incorporating elements that cancel the chromatic aberration of other glass in the lens.

- **Symptom: lines that bow outward.** Some wide-angle lenses cause straight lines to bow outward, with the strongest effect at the edges. In fisheye (or *curvilinear*) lenses, this defect is a feature, as you can see in Figure 10.8, the otherwise difficult-to-capture interior of a cramped barracks at Fort Matanzas, in Florida. When distortion is not desired, you'll need to use a lens

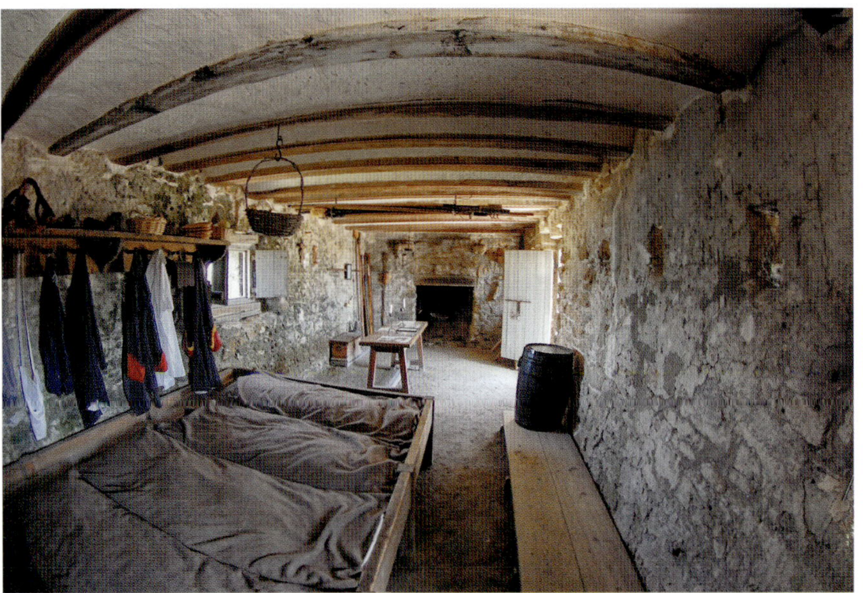

Figure 10.8
Many wide-angle lenses cause lines to bow outward toward the edges of the image; with a fisheye lens, this tendency is considered an interesting feature.

that has corrected barrel distortion. Manufacturers like Nikon do their best to minimize or eliminate it (producing a *rectilinear* lens), often using *aspherical* lens elements (which are not cross-sections of a sphere). You can also minimize barrel distortion simply by framing your photo with some extra space all around, so the edges where the defect is most obvious can be cropped out of the picture. Some image editors, including Photoshop and Photoshop Elements and Nikon Capture NX-D, have a lens distortion correction feature.

- **Symptom: dark corners and shadows in flash photos.** The Nikon D3500's built-in electronic flash is designed to provide even coverage for lenses as wide as 17mm. If you use a wider lens, you can expect darkening, or *vignetting*, in the corners of the frame.

Using Telephoto and Tele-Zoom Lenses

Telephoto lenses also can have a dramatic effect on your photography, and Nikon is especially strong in the long-lens arena, with lots of choices in many focal lengths and zoom ranges. You should be able to find an affordable telephoto or tele-zoom to enhance your photography in several different ways. Here are the most important things you need to know. In the next section, I'll concentrate on telephoto considerations that can be problematic—and how to avoid those problems.

- **Selective focus.** Long lenses have reduced depth-of-field within the frame, allowing you to use selective focus to isolate your subject. You can open the lens up wide to create shallow depth-of-field, or close it down a bit to allow more to be in focus. The flip side of the coin is that when you *want* to make a range of objects sharp, you'll need to use a smaller f/stop to get the depth-of-field you need. Like fire, the depth-of-field of a telephoto lens can be friend or foe. The important thing to remember with selective focus is that it can be used to blur a distracting background (or foreground) beyond recognition, or simply used to place emphasis. For the shot of a military tank and helmet in Figure 10.9, I wanted the hardware in the background to add to the mood of the photo, but wanted the focal point of the image to be the tanker driver's helmet.

- **Getting closer.** Telephoto lenses bring you closer to wildlife, sports action, and candid subjects. No one wants to get a reputation as a surreptitious or "sneaky" photographer (except for paparazzi), but when applied to candids in an open and honest way, a long lens can help you capture memorable moments while retaining enough distance to stay out of the way of events as they transpire.

- **Reduced foreground/increased compression.** Telephoto lenses have the opposite effect of wide angles: they reduce the importance of things in the foreground by squeezing everything together. This compression even makes distant objects appear to be closer to subjects in the foreground and middle ranges. You can use this effect as a creative tool to squeeze subjects together. You'll find the effect used all the time in TV shows, where the hero dashes toward the camera while racing between slow-moving automobiles, seemingly each just a foot or two apart.

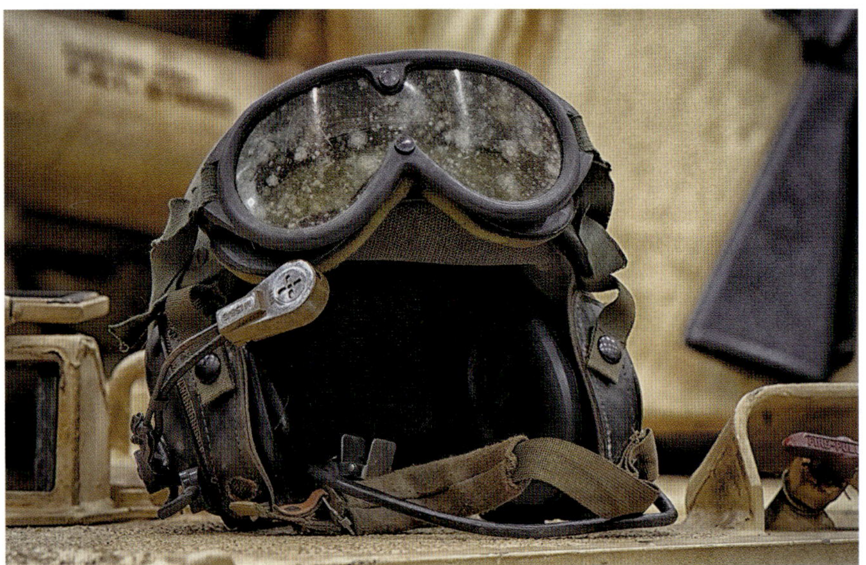

Figure 10.9
A wide f/stop helped isolate the tanker's helmet from the military gear in the background.

- **Accentuates camera shakiness.** Telephoto focal lengths hit you with a double whammy in terms of camera/photographer shake. The lenses themselves are bulkier, more difficult to hold steady, and may even produce a barely perceptible see-saw rocking effect when you support them with one hand halfway down the lens barrel. Telephotos also magnify any camera shake. It's no wonder that vibration reduction is popular in longer lenses.

- **Interesting angles require creativity.** Telephoto lenses require more imagination in selecting interesting angles, because the "angle" you do get on your subjects is so narrow. Moving from side to side or a bit higher or lower can make a dramatic difference in a wide-angle shot, but raising or lowering a telephoto lens a few feet probably will have little effect on the appearance of the distant subjects you're shooting.

Avoiding Telephoto Lens Problems

Many of the "problems" that telephoto lenses pose are really just challenges and are not that difficult to overcome. Here is a list of the seven most common picture maladies and suggested solutions.

- **Symptom: flat faces in portraits.** Head-and-shoulders portraits of humans tend to be more flattering when a focal length of 50mm to 85mm is used. Longer focal lengths compress the distance between features like noses and ears, making the face look wider and flat. A wide angle might make noses look huge and ears tiny when you fill the frame with a face. So, stick with 50mm to 85mm focal lengths, going longer only when you're forced to shoot from a greater distance, and wider only when shooting three-quarters/full-length portraits, or group shots.

- **Symptom: blur due to camera shake.** Use a higher shutter speed (boosting ISO if necessary), consider an image-stabilized lens, or mount your camera on a tripod, monopod, or brace it with some other support. Of those three solutions, only the first will reduce blur caused by *subject* motion; a VR lens or tripod won't help you freeze a race car in mid-lap.

■ **Symptom: color fringes.** Chromatic aberration is the most pernicious optical problem found in telephoto lenses. There are others, including spherical aberration, astigmatism, coma, curvature of field, and similarly scary-sounding phenomena. The best solution for any of these is to use a better lens that offers the proper degree of correction, or stop down the lens to minimize the problem. But that's not always possible. Your second-best choice may be to correct the fringing in your favorite RAW conversion tool or image editor. Photoshop's Lens Correction filter offers sliders that minimize both red/cyan and blue/yellow fringing.

■ **Symptom: lines that curve inward.** Pincushion distortion is found in many telephoto lenses. You might find after a bit of testing that it is worse at certain focal lengths with your particular zoom lens. Like chromatic aberration, it can be partially corrected using tools like the correction tools built into Photoshop and Photoshop Elements. You can see an exaggerated example in Figure 10.10, especially at the edge; pincushion distortion isn't always this obvious.

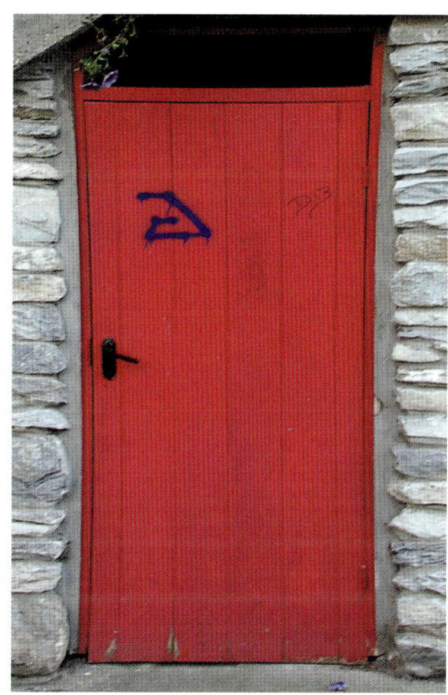

Figure 10.10 Pincushion distortion in telephoto lenses causes lines to bow inward from the edges.

■ **Symptom: low contrast from haze or fog.** When you're photographing distant objects, a long lens shoots through a lot more atmosphere, which generally is muddied up with extra haze and fog. That dirt or moisture in the atmosphere can reduce contrast and mute colors. Some feel that a skylight or UV filter can help, but this practice is mostly a holdover from the film days. Digital sensors are not sensitive enough to UV light for a UV filter to have much effect. So, you should be prepared to boost contrast and color saturation in your Picture Controls menu or image editor if necessary.

■ **Symptom: low contrast from flare.** Lenses are furnished with lens hoods for a good reason: to reduce flare from bright light sources at the periphery of the picture area, or completely outside it. Because telephoto lenses often create images that are lower in contrast in the first place, you'll want to be especially careful to use a lens hood to prevent further effects on your image (or shade the front of the lens with your hand).

■ **Symptom: dark flash photos.** Edge-to-edge flash coverage isn't a problem with telephoto lenses as it is with wide angles. The shooting distance is. A long lens might make a subject that's 50 feet away look as if it's right next to you, but your camera's flash isn't fooled. You'll need extra power for distant flash shots. The pricey Nikon SB-5000 and SB-910 Speedlights, for example, can automatically zoom coverage to illuminate the area captured by a 200mm telephoto lens, with three light distribution patterns (Standard, Center-weighted, and Even).

Telephotos and Bokeh

Bokeh describes the aesthetic qualities of the out-of-focus parts of an image and whether out-of-focus points of light—circles of confusion—are rendered as distracting fuzzy discs or smoothly fade into the background. *Boke* is a Japanese word for "blur," and the h was added to keep English speakers from rendering it monosyllabically to rhyme with *broke*. Although bokeh is visible in blurry portions of any image, it's of particular concern with telephoto lenses, which, thanks to the magic of reduced depth-of-field, produce more obviously out-of-focus areas. (See Figure 10.11, top.)

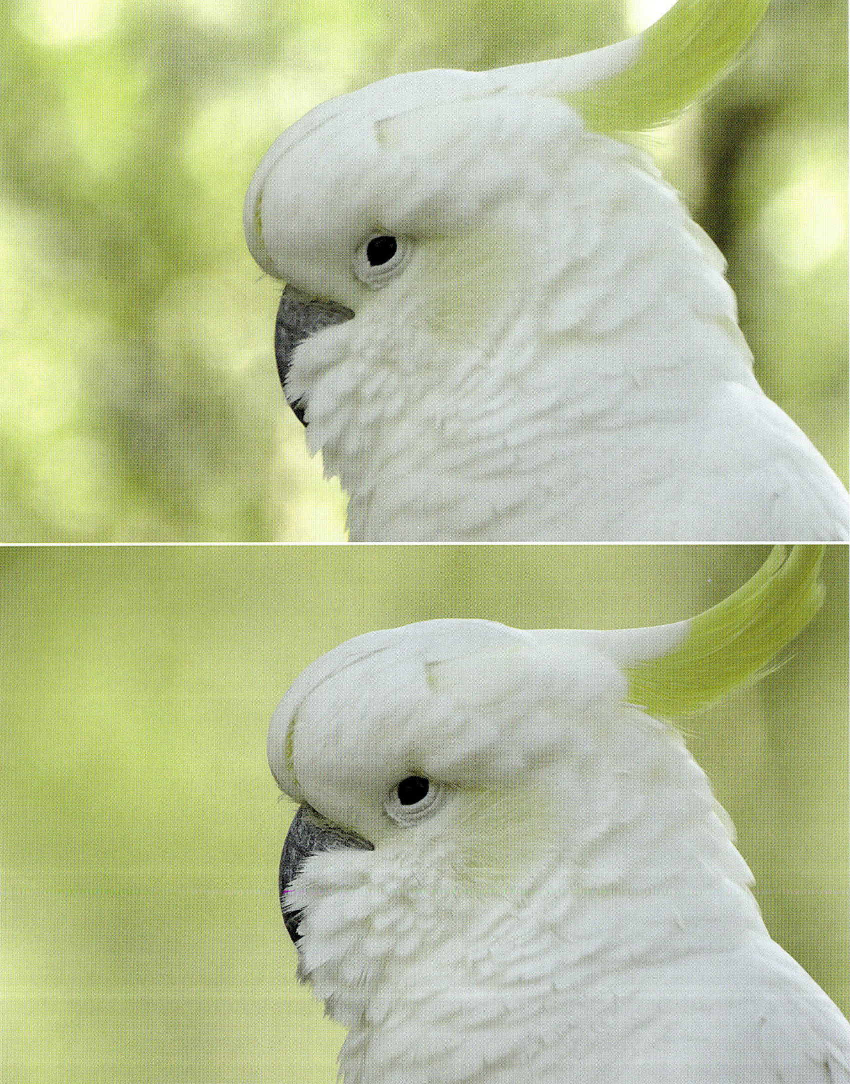

Figure 10.11
Bokeh is less pleasing when the discs are prominent (top), and less obtrusive when they blend into the background (bottom).

Bokeh can vary from lens to lens, or even within a given lens depending on the f/stop in use. Bokeh becomes objectionable when the circles of confusion are evenly illuminated, making them stand out as distinct discs, or, worse, when these circles are darker in the center, producing an ugly "doughnut" effect. A lens defect called spherical aberration may produce out-of-focus discs that are brighter on the edges and darker in the center, because the lens doesn't focus light passing through the edges of the lens exactly as it does light going through the center. (Mirror or *catadioptric* lenses also produce this effect.)

Other kinds of spherical aberration generate circles of confusion that are brightest in the center and fade out at the edges, producing a smooth blending effect, as you can see at bottom in Figure 10.11. Ironically, when no spherical aberration is present at all, the discs are a uniform shade, which, while better than the doughnut effect, is not as pleasing as the bright center/dark edge rendition. The shape of the disc also comes into play, with round smooth circles considered the best, and nonagonal or some other polygon (determined by the shape of the lens diaphragm) considered less desirable.

If you plan to use selective focus a lot, you should investigate the bokeh characteristics of a particular lens before you buy. Nikon user groups and forums will usually be full of comments and questions about bokeh, so the research is fairly easy.

Add-ons and Special Features

Once you've purchased your telephoto lens, you'll want to think about some appropriate accessories for it. There are some handy add-ons available that can be valuable. Here are a couple of them to think about.

Lens Hoods

Lens hoods are an important accessory for all lenses, but they're especially valuable with telephotos. As I mentioned earlier, lens hoods do a good job of preserving image contrast by keeping bright light sources outside the field of view from striking the lens and, potentially, bouncing around inside that long tube to generate flare that, when coupled with atmospheric haze, can rob your image of detail and snap. In addition, lens hoods serve as valuable protection for that large, vulnerable, front lens element. It's easy to forget that you've got that long tube sticking out in front of your camera and accidentally whack the front of your lens into something. It's cheaper to replace a lens hood than it is to have a lens repaired, so you might find that a good hood is valuable protection for your prized optics.

When choosing a lens hood, it's important to have the right hood for the lens, usually the one offered for that lens by Nikon or the third-party manufacturer. You want a hood that blocks precisely the right amount of light: neither too much light nor too little. A hood with a front diameter that is too small can show up in your pictures as vignetting. A hood that has a front diameter that's too large isn't stopping all the light it should. Generic lens hoods may not do the job.

When your telephoto is a zoom lens, it's even more important to get the right hood, because you need one that does what it is supposed to at both the wide-angle and telephoto ends of the zoom range. Lens hoods may be cylindrical, rectangular (shaped like the image frame), or petal shaped (that is, cylindrical, but with cut-out areas at the corners that correspond to the actual image area). Lens hoods should be mounted in the correct orientation (a bayonet mount for the hood usually takes care of this).

Telephoto Converters

Teleconverters (often called telephoto extenders outside the Nikon world) multiply the actual focal length of your lens, giving you a longer telephoto for much less than the price of a lens with that actual focal length. These converters fit between the lens and your camera and contain optical elements that magnify the image produced by the lens. Available in 1.4X, 1.7X, and 2.0X configurations from Nikon, a teleconverter transforms, say, a 200mm lens into a 280mm, 340mm, or 400mm optic, respectively. Given the D3500's crop factor, your 200mm lens now has the same field of view as a 420mm, 510mm, or 600mm lens on a full-frame camera. At around $500 each, converters are quite a bargain, compared with the price of a super-long telephoto lens. (See Figure 10.12.)

The only drawback is that Nikon's own TC II and TC III teleconverters can be used only with a limited number of Nikkor AF-S lenses. The compatible models include the AF-S FX Nikkor 200-500mm f/5.6E EDVR, AF-S FX Nikkor 300mm f/4E PF ED VR, 200mm f/2G ED-IF AF-S VR Nikkor, 300mm f/2.8G ED-IF AF-S VR Nikkor, 400mm f/2.8D ED-IF AF-S II Nikkor, 80-200mm f/2.8D ED-IF AF-S Nikkor, 70-200mm f/2.8G ED-IF AF-S VR Zoom-Nikkor, 200-400mm f/4G ED-IF AF-S VR Zoom-Nikkor, 300mm f/4D ED-IF AF-S Nikkor, 500mm f/4D ED-IF AF-S II Nikkor, and 600mm f/4D ED-IF AF-S II Nikkor. These tend to be pricey (or ultra-pricey lenses). Teleconverters from Sigma, Kenko, Tamron, and others cost less, and may be compatible with a broader range of lenses. (They work especially well with lenses from the same vendor that produces the teleconverter.)

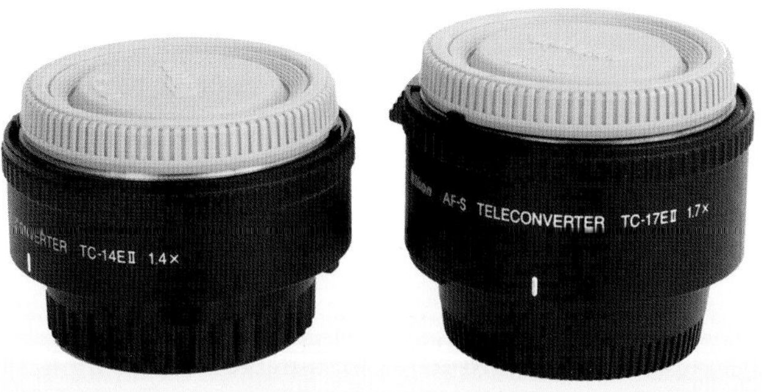

Figure 10.12
Teleconverters multiply the true focal length of your lenses—but at a cost of some sharpness and aperture speed.

There are other downsides. While extenders retain the closest focusing distance of your original lens, autofocus is maintained only if the lens's original maximum aperture is f/4 or larger (for the 1.4X extender) or f/2.8 or larger (for the 2X extender). The components reduce the effective aperture of any lens they are used with, by one f/stop with the 1.4X converter, 1.5 f/stops with the 1.7X converter, and two f/stops with the 2X extender. So, your 200mm f/2.8 lens becomes a 280mm f/4 or 400mm f/5.6 lens. Although Nikon converters are precision optical devices, they do cost you a little sharpness, but that improves when you reduce the aperture by a stop or two. Each of the converters is compatible only with a particular set of lenses greater, so you'll want to check Nikon's compatibility chart to see if the component can be used with the lens you want to attach to it.

If your lenses are compatible and you're shooting under bright lighting conditions, the Nikon extenders make handy accessories. I recommend the 1.4X version because it robs you of very little sharpness and only one f/stop. The 1.7X version also works well, too, but I've found the 2X teleconverter—even the new, improved TC III version—to exact too much of a sharpness and speed penalty to be of much use.

Macro Focusing

Some telephotos and telephoto zooms available for the Nikon D3500 have particularly close focusing capabilities, making them *macro* lenses. Of course, the object is not necessarily to get close (get too close and you'll find it difficult to light your subject). What you're really looking for in a macro lens is to magnify the apparent size of the subject in the final image. Camera-to-subject distance is most important when you want to back up farther from your subject (say, to avoid spooking skittish insects or small animals). In that case, you'll want a macro lens with a longer focal length to allow that distance while retaining the desired magnification.

Nikon makes an assortment of lenses that are officially designated as macro lenses. The most popular include:

- **AF-S Micro-Nikkor 60mm f/2.8G ED.** This type-G lens supposedly replaces the type-D lens listed next, adding an internal Silent Wave autofocus motor that should operate faster, and which is also compatible with cameras lacking a body motor, such as the Nikon D40/D40x and D3500. It also has ED lens elements for improved image quality. However, because it lacks an aperture ring, you can control the f/stop only when the lens is mounted directly on the camera or used with automatic extension tubes. Should you want to reverse a macro lens using a special adapter (the Nikon BR2-A ring) to improve image quality or mount it on a bellows, you're better off with a lens having an aperture ring.

- **AF Micro-Nikkor 60mm f/2.8D.** This non-AF-S lens won't autofocus on the Nikon D3500, but, then, you might be manually focusing most of the time when shooting close-ups, and may appreciate the lower cost of an "obsolete" lens.

■ **AF-S Micro-Nikkor 40mm f/2.8 DX.** The latest macro lens in the lineup, this one is an inexpensive (roughly $250) non-full-frame lens produced especially for DX-format cameras like the D3500. It's sharp and affordable.

■ **AF-S VR Micro-Nikkor 105mm f/2.8G IF-ED.** This G-series lens did replace a similar D-type, non-AF-S version that also lacked VR. I own the older lens, too, and am keeping it because I find VR a rather specialized tool for macro work. Some 99 percent of the time, I shoot close-ups with my D3500 mounted on a tripod or, at the very least, on a monopod, so camera vibration is not much of a concern. Indeed, *subject* movement is a more serious problem, especially when shooting plant life outdoors on days plagued with even slight breezes. Because my outdoor subjects are likely to move while I am composing my photo, I find both VR and autofocus not very useful. I end up focusing manually most of the time, too. This lens provides a little extra camera-to-subject distance, so you'll find it very useful, but consider the older non-G, non-VR version, too, if you're in the market and don't mind losing autofocus features.

■ **AF Micro-Nikkor 200mm f/4D IF-ED.** With a price tag of about $1,800, you'd probably want this lens only if you planned a great deal of close-up shooting at greater distances. It focuses down to 1.6 feet, and is manual focus only with the D3500, but provides enough magnification to allow interesting close-ups of subjects that are farther away—a specialized tool for specialized shooting.

■ **AF-S DX Micro 85mm f/3.5 ED VR.** This lens was designed especially for cropped sensor (DX) models like the D3500. It autofocuses on the D3500, it has vibration reduction, and it's relatively fast at f/3.5, making it an excellent choice for hand-held close-up photography.

■ **PC Micro-Nikkor 85mm f/2.8D.** Priced about the same as the 200mm Micro-Nikkor, this is a manual focus lens (on *any* camera; it doesn't offer autofocus features) that has both tilt and shift capabilities, so you can adjust the perspective of the subject as you shoot. The tilt feature lets you "tilt" the plane of focus, providing the illusion of greater depth-of-field, while the shift capabilities make it possible to shoot down on a subject from an angle and still maintain its correct proportions. If you need one of these for perspective control, you already know it; if you're still wondering how you'd use one, you probably have no need for these specialized capabilities. However, I have recently watched some very creative fashion and wedding photographers use this lens for portraits, applying the tilting features to throw parts of the image wildly out of focus to concentrate interest on faces, and so forth. None of these are likely pursuits of the average Nikon D3500 photographer, but I couldn't resist mentioning this interesting lens.

You'll also find macro lenses, macro zooms, and other close-focusing lenses available from Sigma, Tamron, and Tokina. If you want to focus closer with a macro lens, or any other lens, you can add an accessory called an *extension tube,* or a *bellows extension.* These add-ons move the lens farther from the focal plane, allowing it to focus more closely. Nikon also sells add-on close-up lenses, which look like filters, and allow lenses to focus more closely.

Vibration Reduction

Nikon has a burgeoning line of lenses with built-in vibration reduction (VR) capabilities. The VR feature uses lens elements that are shifted internally in response to vertical or horizontal motion of the lens, which compensates for any camera shake in those directions. Vibration reduction is particularly effective when used with telephoto lenses, which magnify the effects of camera and photographer motion. However, VR can be useful for lenses of shorter focal lengths, such as Nikon's 16-80mm, 18-140mm, and 18-55mm VR lenses. Other Nikon VR lenses provide stabilization with zooms that are as wide as 24mm.

Vibration reduction offers two to three shutter speed increments' worth of shake reduction. (Nikon claims a four-stop gain, which I feel may be optimistic.) This extra margin can be invaluable when you're shooting under dim lighting conditions or hand-holding a lens for, say, wildlife photography. Perhaps that shot of a foraging deer would require a shutter speed of 1/2,000th second at f/5.6 with your telephoto. Relax. You can shoot at 1/250th second at f/11 and get a photo that is just as sharp, as long as the deer doesn't decide to bound off. Or, perhaps you're shooting indoors and would prefer to shoot at 1/15th second at f/4. Your 16-140mm VR lens can grab the shot for you at its wide-angle position. However, consider these facts:

- **VR doesn't freeze subject motion.** Vibration reduction won't freeze moving subjects in their tracks, because it is effective only at compensating for *camera* motion. It's best used in reduced illumination, to steady the up-down swaying of telephoto lenses, and to improve close-up photography. If your subject is in motion, you'll still need a shutter speed that's fast enough to stop the action.

- **VR adds to shutter lag.** The process of adjusting the lens elements, like autofocus, takes time, so vibration reduction may contribute to a slight increase in shutter lag. If you're shooting sports, that delay may be annoying, but I still use my VR lenses for sports all the time!

- **Use when appropriate.** You may find that your results are worse when using VR while panning, although newer Nikon VR lenses work fine when the camera is deliberately moved from side to side during exposure. Older lenses can confuse the panning motion with camera wobble and provide too much compensation. You might want to switch off VR when panning or when your camera is mounted on a tripod.

- **Do you need VR at all?** Remember that an inexpensive monopod might be able to provide the same additional steadiness as a VR lens, at a much lower cost. If you're out in the field shooting wild animals or flowers and think a tripod isn't practical, try a monopod first.

VIBRATION REDUCTION: IN THE CAMERA OR IN THE LENS?

The adoption of image stabilization/anti-shake technology into the camera bodies of models from Sony, Olympus, Pentax, and Samsung has revived an old debate about whether VR belongs in the camera or in the lens. Perhaps it's my Nikon bias showing, but I am quite happy not to have vibration reduction available in the body itself. Here are some reasons:

- Should in-camera VR fail, you have to send the whole camera in for repair, and camera repairs are generally more expensive than lens repairs. I like being able to simply switch to another lens if I have a VR problem.

- VR in the camera doesn't steady your view in the viewfinder, whereas a VR lens shows you a steadied image as you shoot.

- You're stuck with the VR system built in to your camera. If an improved system is incorporated into a lens and the improvements are important to you, just trade in your old lens for the new one.

- When building VR in the camera, a compromise system that works with all lenses must be designed. VR in the lens, however, can be custom-tailored to each specific lens's needs.

11

Making Light Work for You

Successful photographers and artists have an intimate understanding of the importance of light in shaping an image. Rembrandt was a master of using light to create moods and reveal the character of his subjects. Late artist Thomas Kinkade's official tagline was "Painter of Light." Dean Collins, co-founder of Finelight Studios, revolutionized how a whole generation of photographers learned and used lighting. It's impossible to underestimate how the use of light adds to—and how misuse can detract from—your photographs.

All forms of visual art use light to shape the finished product. Sculptors don't have control over the light used to illuminate their finished work, so they must create shapes using planes and curved surfaces so that the form envisioned by the artist comes to life from a variety of viewing and lighting angles. Painters, in contrast, have absolute control over both shape and light in their work, as well as the viewing angle, so they can use both the contours of their two-dimensional subjects and the qualities of the "light" they use to illuminate those subjects to evoke the image they want to produce.

Photography is a third form of art. The photographer may have little or no control over the subject (other than posing human subjects) but can often adjust both viewing angle *and* the nature of the light source to create a particular compelling image. The direction and intensity of the light sources create the shapes and textures that we see. The distribution and proportions determine the contrast and tonal values: whether the image is stark or high key, or muted and low in contrast. The colors of the light (because even "white" light has a color balance that the sensor can detect), and how much of those colors the subject reflects or absorbs, paint the hues visible in the image.

As a Nikon D3500 photographer, you must learn to be a painter and sculptor of light if you want to move from *taking* a picture to *making* a photograph. This chapter provides an introduction to using the two main types of illumination: *continuous* lighting (such as daylight, incandescent, or fluorescent sources) and the brief, but brilliant snippets of light we call *electronic flash*.

Continuous Illumination versus Electronic Flash

Continuous lighting is exactly what you might think: uninterrupted illumination that is available all the time during a shooting session. Daylight, moonlight, and the artificial lighting encountered both indoors and outdoors count as continuous light sources (although all of them can be "interrupted" by passing clouds, solar eclipses, a blown fuse, or simply by switching off a lamp). Indoor continuous illumination includes both the lights that are there already (such as incandescent lamps or overhead fluorescent lights indoors) and fixtures you supply yourself, including photoflood lamps or reflectors used to bounce existing light onto your subject.

Your D3500 has a flip-up electronic flash unit built in. But you can also use an external flash, either mounted on the D3500's accessory shoe or used off-camera and linked with a cable or triggered by a wireless trigger or a slave light (which sets off a flash when it senses the firing of another unit). Studio flash units are electronic flash, too, and aren't limited to "professional" shooters, as there are economical "monolight" (one-piece flash/power supply) units available in the $200 price range. Serious photographers with some spare cash can buy a couple to store in a closet and use to set up a home studio, or use as supplementary lighting when traveling away from home. You'll need a remote trigger mounted on the D3500's accessory/hot shoe, or an accessory/hot shoe–to-PC connector adapter to use studio flash with your camera.

There are advantages and disadvantages to each type of illumination. Here's a quick checklist of pros and cons:

- **Lighting preview—Pro: continuous lighting.** With continuous lighting, you always know exactly what kind of lighting effect you're going to get and, if multiple lights are used, how they will interact with each other, as shown in Figure 11.1. With electronic flash, the general effect you're going to see may be a mystery until you've built some experience, and you may need to review a shot on the LCD monitor, make some adjustments, and then reshoot to get the look you want. (In this sense, a digital camera's review capabilities replace the Polaroid test shots pro photographers relied on in decades past.)

- **Lighting preview—Con: electronic flash.** With flash, the general effect you're going to see may be a mystery until you've built some experience, and you may need to review a shot on the LCD monitor, make some adjustments, and then reshoot to get the look you want. (In this sense, a digital camera's review capabilities replace the Polaroid test shots pro photographers relied on in decades past.)

- **Exposure calculation—Pro: continuous lighting.** Your D3500 has no problem calculating exposure for continuous lighting, because it remains constant and can be measured through the 420-pixel sensor that interprets the light reaching the viewfinder. The amount of light available just before the exposure will, in almost all cases, be the same amount of light present when the shutter is released. The D3500's Spot metering mode can be used to measure and compare the proportions of light in the highlights and shadows, so you can make an adjustment (such as using more or less fill light) if necessary. You can even use a hand-held light meter to measure the light yourself, and then set the shutter speed and aperture to match.

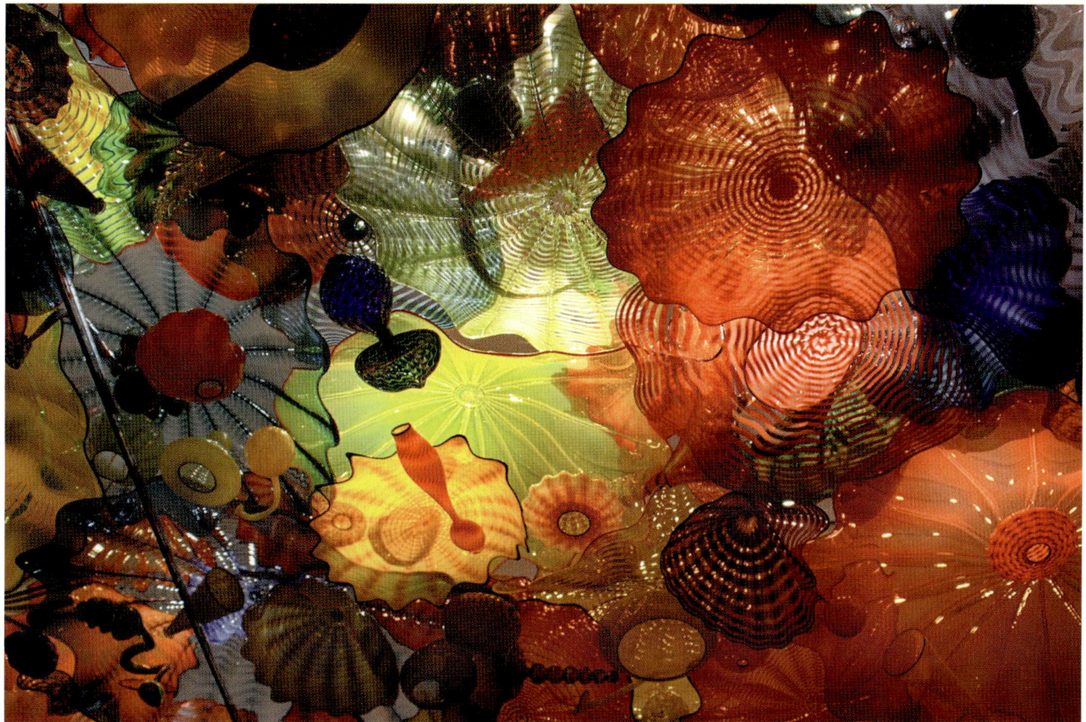

Figure 11.1 You always know how the lighting will look when using continuous illumination.

- **Exposure calculation—Con: electronic flash.** Electronic flash illumination doesn't exist until the flash fires, and so can't be measured by the D3500's exposure sensor when the mirror is flipped up at the moment of exposure. Instead, the light must be measured by metering the intensity of a *pre-flash* triggered an instant before the main flash, as it is reflected back to the camera and through the lens. A less attractive alternative, available with higher-end Nikon flash units like the SB-5000 or SB-910, is to use a sensor built into the external flash itself and measure reflected light that bounces back, but which has not traveled through the lens. If you have a do-it-yourself bent, there are hand-held flash meters, too, including models that measure both flash and continuous light, so you need only one meter for both types of illumination.

- **Evenness of illumination—Pro/con: continuous lighting.** Of the continuous light sources, daylight, in particular, provides illumination that tends to fill an image completely, lighting up the foreground, background, and your subject almost equally. Shadows do come into play, of course, so you might need to use reflectors or fill in additional light sources to even out the illumination further. But, barring objects that block large sections of your image from daylight, the light is spread fairly evenly. Indoors, however, continuous lighting is commonly less evenly distributed. The average living room, for example, has hot spots near the lamps and overhead lights, and dark corners located farther from those light sources. But on the plus side, you can easily *see* this uneven illumination and compensate with additional lamps.

- **Evenness of illumination—Con: electronic flash.** Electronic flash units, like continuous light sources such as lamps that don't have the advantage of being located 93 million miles from the subject, suffer from the effects of their proximity. The *inverse square law*, first applied to both gravity and light by Sir Isaac Newton, dictates that as a light source's distance increases from the subject, the amount of light reaching the subject falls off proportionately to the square of the distance. In plain English, that means that a flash or lamp that's twelve feet away from a subject provides only one-quarter as much illumination as a source that's six feet away (rather than half as much). (See Figure 11.2.) This translates into relatively shallow "depth-of-light."

- **Action stopping—Pro: electronic flash.** When it comes to the ability to freeze moving objects in their tracks, the advantage goes to electronic flash. The brief duration of electronic flash serves as a very high "shutter speed" when the flash is the main or only source of illumination for the photo. Your D3500's shutter speed may be set for 1/2,00th second during a flash exposure, but if the flash illumination predominates, the *effective* exposure time will be the 1/1,000th to 1/50,000th second or less duration of the flash, as you can see in Figure 11.3, in a shot of an olive dropping into a glass. The only fly in the ointment is that, if the ambient light is strong enough, it may produce a secondary, "ghost" exposure, as I'll explain later in this chapter.

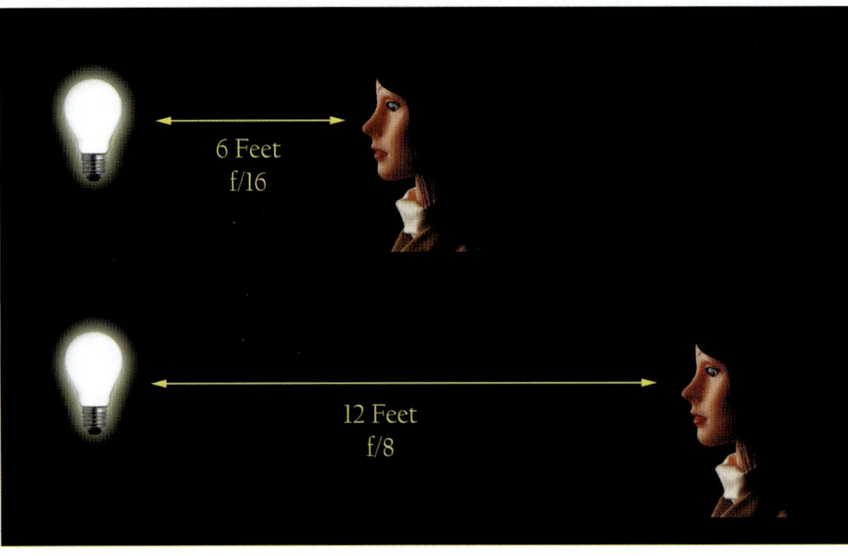

Figure 11.2
A light source that is twice as far away provides only one-quarter as much illumination.

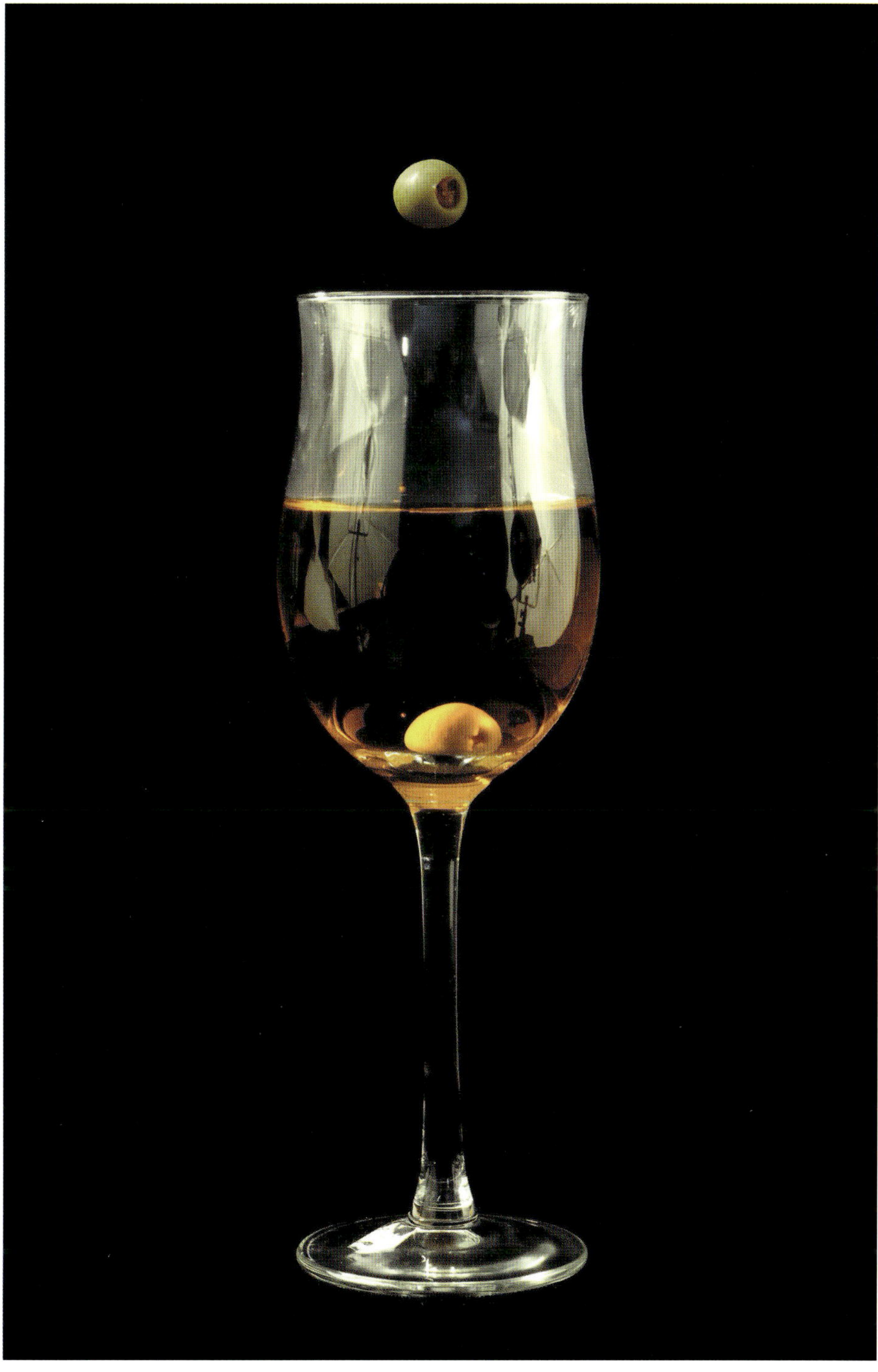

Figure 11.3 Electronic flash can freeze almost any action.

- **Action stopping—Con: continuous lighting.** Action stopping with continuous light sources is completely dependent on the shutter speed you've dialed in on the camera. And the speeds available are dependent on the amount of light available and your ISO sensitivity setting. Outdoors in daylight, there will probably be enough sunlight to let you shoot at 1/2,000th second and f/6.3 with a non-grainy sensitivity setting for your D3500 of ISO 400. That's a fairly useful combination of settings if you're not using a super-telephoto with a small maximum aperture. But inside, the reduced illumination quickly has you pushing your D3500 to its limits. For example, if you're shooting indoor sports, there probably won't be enough available light to allow you to use a 1/2,000th second shutter speed (although I routinely shoot indoor basketball with my D3500 at ISO 1600 and 1/500th second at f/4). In many indoor sports situations, the lack of available light, and the D3500's increased visual noise at settings of ISO 6400 and above, you may find yourself limited to 1/500th second or slower.

- **Cost—Pro: continuous lighting.** Incandescent, LED, or fluorescent lamps are generally much less expensive than electronic flash units, which can easily cost several hundred dollars. I've used everything from desktop high-intensity lamps to reflector flood lights for continuous illumination at very little cost. There are lamps made especially for photographic purposes, too. Maintenance is economical: even LED bulbs suitable for photography now cost only a few dollars.

- **Cost—Con: electronic flash.** Electronic flash units aren't particularly cheap. The lowest-cost dedicated flash designed specifically for the Nikon dSLRs is about $150 (the SB-300). However, such units are limited in features. If you plan to use flash a great deal, plan on spending some money to get the features that a more sophisticated electronic flash offers.

- **Flexibility—Pro: electronic flash.** Electronic flash's action-freezing power allows you to work without a tripod in the studio (and elsewhere), adding flexibility and speed when choosing angles and positions. Flash units can be easily filtered, and, because the filtration is placed over the light source rather than the lens, you don't need to use high-quality filter material. For example, Roscoe or Lee lighting gels, which may be too flimsy to use in front of the lens, can be mounted or taped in front of your flash with ease.

- **Flexibility—Con: continuous lighting.** Because incandescent, LED, and fluorescent lamps are not as bright as electronic flash, the slower shutter speeds required (see "Action stopping," above) mean that you may have to use a tripod more often, especially when shooting portraits. The incandescent variety of continuous lighting gets hot, especially in the studio, and the side effects range from discomfort (for your human models) to disintegration (if you happen to be shooting perishable foods like ice cream). The heat also makes it more difficult to add filtration to incandescent sources. These disadvantages are among the reasons LED illumination is becoming increasingly popular for photography.

Continuous Lighting Basics

While continuous lighting and its effects are generally much easier to visualize and use than electronic flash, there are some factors you need to take into account, particularly the color temperature of the light. (Color temperature concerns aren't exclusive to continuous light sources, of course, but the variations tend to be more extreme and less predictable than those of electronic flash, which output relatively consistent daylight-like illumination.)

Color temperature, in practical terms, is how "bluish" or how "reddish" the light appears to be to the digital camera's sensor. Indoor illumination is quite warm, comparatively, and appears reddish to the sensor. Daylight, in contrast, seems much bluer to the sensor. Our eyes (our brains, actually) are quite adaptable to these variations, so white objects don't appear to have an orange tinge when viewed indoors, nor do they seem excessively blue outdoors in full daylight. Yet, these color temperature variations are real and the sensor is not fooled. To capture the most accurate colors, we need to take the color temperature into account in setting the color balance (or *white balance*) of the D3500—either automatically using the camera's smarts or manually using our own knowledge and experience.

When using the Nikon D3500, you don't need to think in terms of actual color temperature (although you can measure existing color temperature using the Preset feature described later), because the camera won't let you set white balance using color temperature values, which are measured in *degrees Kelvin*. But it is useful to know that warmer (more reddish) color temperatures (measured in degrees Kelvin) are the *lower* numbers, while cooler (bluer) color temperatures are *higher* numbers. It might not make sense to say that 3,400K is warmer than 6,000K, but that's the way it is. If it helps, think of a glowing red ember contrasted with a white-hot welder's torch, rather than fire and ice.

You can set white balance by type of illumination, and then fine-tune it in the D3500 using the Shooting menu's White Balance option. In most cases, however, the Nikon D3500 will do an acceptable job of calculating white balance for you, so Auto can be used as your choice most of the time. Use the preset values or set a custom white balance that matches the current shooting conditions when you need to. The only really problematic light sources are likely to be fluorescents.

Remember that if you shoot RAW, you can specify the white balance of your image when you import it into Photoshop, Photoshop Elements, or another image editor using ViewNX-i, Nikon Capture NX-D, Adobe Camera Raw, or your preferred RAW converter. While color-balancing filters that fit on the front of the lens exist, they are primarily useful for film cameras, because film's color balance can't be tweaked as extensively as that of a sensor.

Daylight

Daylight is produced by the sun, and so is moonlight (which is just reflected sunlight). Daylight is present, of course, even when you can't see the sun. When sunlight is direct, it can be bright and harsh. If daylight is diffused by clouds, softened by bouncing off objects such as walls or your photo reflectors, or filtered by shade, it can be much dimmer and less contrasty.

Daylight's color temperature can vary quite widely. It is highest in temperature (most blue) at noon when the sun is directly overhead, because the light is traveling through a minimum amount of the filtering layer we call the atmosphere. The color temperature at high noon may be 6,000K. At other times of day, the sun is lower in the sky and the particles in the air provide a filtering effect that warms the illumination to about 5,500K for most of the day. Starting an hour before dusk and for an hour after sunrise, the warm appearance of the sunlight is even visible to our eyes when the color temperature may dip to 5,000K–4,500K, as shown in Figure 11.4.

Incandescent/Tungsten Light

The term *incandescent* or *tungsten illumination* is usually applied to the direct descendants of Thomas Edison's original electric lamp. Such lights consist of a glass bulb that contains a vacuum, or is filled with a halogen gas, and contains a tungsten filament that is heated by an electrical current, producing photons and heat. Tungsten-halogen lamps are a variation on the basic lightbulb, using a more rugged (and longer-lasting) filament that can be heated to a higher temperature, housed in a thicker glass or quartz envelope, and filled with iodine or bromine ("halogen") gases. The higher temperature allows tungsten-halogen (or quartz-halogen/quartz-iodine, depending on their construction) lamps to burn "hotter" and whiter. Although popular for automobile headlamps today, they've also been used for photographic illumination.

Although incandescent illumination isn't a perfect black body radiator, it's close enough that the color temperature of such lamps can be precisely calculated and used for photography without concerns about color variation (at least, until the very end of the lamp's life).

The other qualities of this type of lighting, such as contrast, are dependent on the distance of the lamp from the subject, type of reflectors used, and other factors that I'll explain later in this chapter.

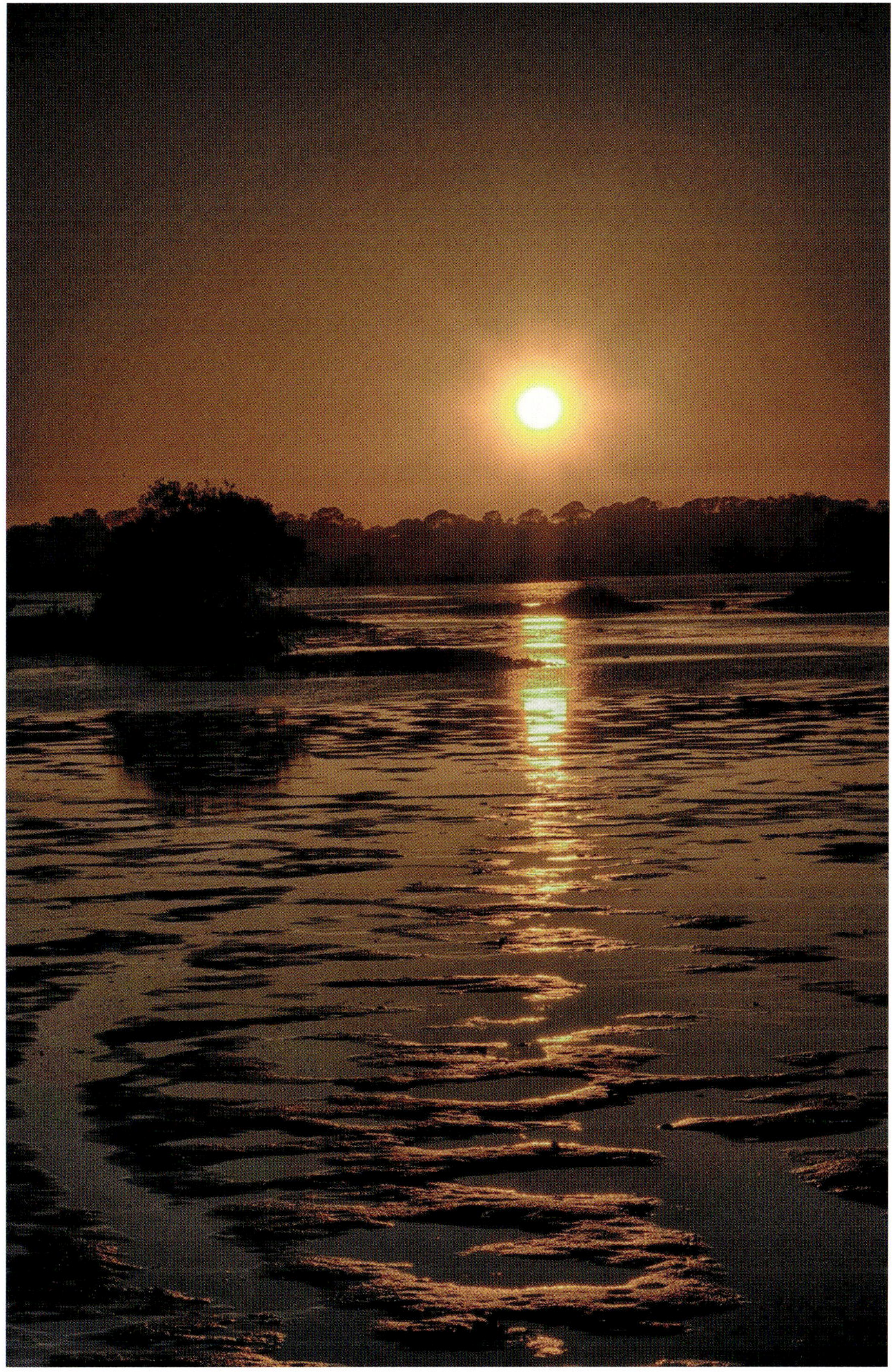

Figure 11.4 At dawn and dusk, the color temperature of daylight may dip as low as 4,500K, and at sunset can go even lower.

Fluorescent and LED Lamps

Fluorescent and LED illumination each have some advantages in terms of illumination, as well as some disadvantages from a photographic standpoint. Fluorescent lights—whether configured as the familiar long tubes or as compact fluorescent lamps (CFLs) all generate light through an electro-chemical reaction that emits most of its energy as visible light, rather than heat, which is why the such bulbs don't get as hot as incandescent lamps. The type of light produced varies depending on the phosphor coatings and type of gas in the tube. So, the illumination fluorescent bulbs produce can vary widely in its characteristics.

That's not great news for photographers. Different types of lamps have different "color tempera-tures" that can't be precisely measured in degrees Kelvin, because the light isn't produced by heat-ing. Worse, fluorescent lamps have a discontinuous spectrum of light that can have some colors missing entirely. A particular type of tube can lack certain shades of red or other colors (see Figure 11.5), which is why fluorescent lamps and other alternative technologies such as sodium-vapor illumination can produce ghastly looking human skin tones if the white balance isn't set correctly. Their spectra can lack the reddish tones we associate with healthy skin and emphasize the blues and greens popular in horror movies.

CFLs don't work in all fixtures and for all applications, such as dimmers (even if you purchase special "dimmable" CFLs), electronic timer or "dusk-to-dawn" light controllers, some illuminated wall switches, or with motion sensors. Only certain types of CFLs (cold cathode models) operate outside in cold weather; they emit IR signals that can confuse the remote control of your TV, air conditioner, etc.

LED illumination, like fluorescents, also produces cooler light (in terms of heat generated by the lamp). Consequently, they have much lower power requirements (a popular 250W LED light from Savage uses only 30W of electricity), making some of them practical for battery operation (a virtual must for video shooting). Units with even lower power needs are available in the form of compact units that clip onto the camera and provide a continuous beam of light to fill in shadows indoors or out, and/or to provide illumination when shooting video inside. Several sources have introduced LED studio lights that are bright enough for general-purpose shooting.

I personally use the Lume Cube (www.lumecube.com), which is a rechargeable LED light with 10 brightness settings, a daylight color temperature, and which can be used as both a constant light source and as a wireless "flash" with variable durations settings (it has a built-in optical slave sensor). This $80 3.5-ounce gadget also includes Bluetooth so you can control it and change settings from an iOS/Android app. It's waterproof, too, down to 100 feet. (I screw it onto my Nikon AW100 underwater point-and-shoot camera.)

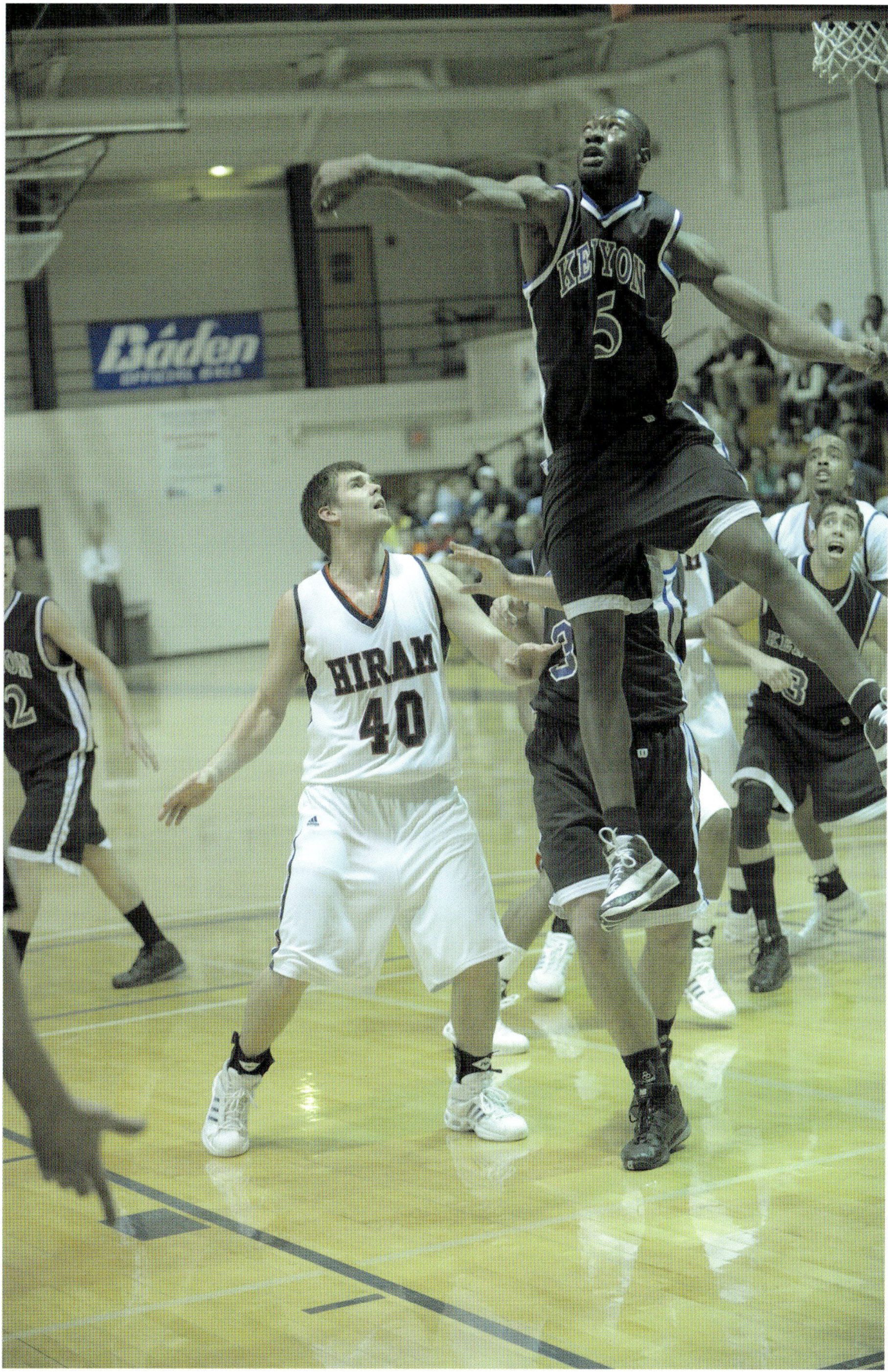

Figure 11.5 The uncorrected fluorescent lighting in the gym added a distinct greenish cast to this image when exposed with a daylight white balance setting.

As I mentioned, different types of lamps have different "color temperatures" that can't be precisely measured in degrees Kelvin, because the light isn't produced by heating. LED lights are generally available only in daylight or warm ("indoor") versions. There are multiple types of fluorescent lights, all of which have a "discontinuous" spectrum of light that can have some colors missing entirely. A particular type of light source can lack certain shades of red or other colors, which is why fluorescent lamps and other alternative technologies such as sodium-vapor illumination can produce ghastly looking human skin tones. Their spectra can lack the reddish tones we associate with healthy skin and emphasize the blues and greens popular in horror movies.

Vendors may provide a figure known as the *color rendering index* (or CRI), which is a measure of how accurately a light source represents standard colors, using a scale of 0 (some sodium-vapor lamps) to 100 (daylight and most incandescent lamps). LED lights generally have a CRI of 80 or above, and the value will be shown on the package.

Adjusting White Balance

I showed you how to adjust white balance in Chapter 4, using the D3500's built-in presets, and white balance shift capabilities.

In most cases, however, the D3500 will do a good job of calculating white balance for you, so Auto can be used as your choice most of the time. Use the preset values or set a custom white balance that matches the current shooting conditions when you need to. The only really problematic light sources are likely to be fluorescents. Daylight fluorescents and deluxe cool white fluorescents might have a CRI of about 79 to 95, which is perfectly acceptable for most photographic applications. Warm white fluorescents might have a CRI of 55. White deluxe mercury-vapor lights are less suitable with a CRI of 45, while low-pressure sodium lamps can vary from CRI 0–18.

Remember that if you shoot RAW, you can specify the white balance of your image when you import it into Photoshop, Photoshop Elements, or another image editor using your preferred RAW converter. While color-balancing filters that fit on the front of the lens exist, they are primarily useful for film cameras, because film's color balance can't be tweaked as extensively as that of a sensor.

Electronic Flash Basics

Until you delve into the situation deeply enough, it might appear that serious photographers have a love/hate relationship with electronic flash. You'll often hear that flash photography is less natural looking, and that the built-in flash in most cameras should never be used as the primary source of illumination because it provides a harsh, garish look. Indeed, most "pro" cameras like the Nikon D5 don't have a built-in flash at all. Available ("continuous") lighting is praised, and built-in flash photography seems to be roundly denounced.

In truth, however, the bias is against *bad* flash photography. Indeed, flash has become the studio light source of choice for pro photographers, because it's more intense (and its intensity can be varied to order by the photographer), freezes action, frees you from using a tripod (unless you want to use one to lock down a composition), and has a snappy, consistent light quality that matches daylight. (While color balance changes as the flash duration shortens, some Nikon flash units can communicate to the camera the exact white balance provided for that shot.) And even pros will cede that the built-in flash of the Nikon D3500 has some important uses as an adjunct to existing light, particularly to illuminate dark shadows using a technique called *fill flash*.

But electronic flash isn't as inherently easy to use as continuous lighting. As I noted earlier, electronic flash units are more expensive, don't show you exactly what the lighting effect will be (unless you use a second source called a *modeling light* for a preview), and the exposure of electronic flash units is more difficult to calculate accurately.

How Electronic Flash Works

The bursts of light we call electronic flash are produced by a flash of photons generated by an electrical charge that is accumulated in a component called a *capacitor* and then directed through a glass tube containing xenon gas, which absorbs the energy and emits the brief flash. For the pop-up flash built into the D3500, the full burst of light lasts about 1/1,000th second and provides enough illumination to shoot a subject 10 feet away at f/4 using the ISO 100 setting. In a more typical situation, you'd use ISO 200, f/5.6 to f/8 and photograph something 8 to 10 feet away. As you can see, the built-in flash is somewhat limited in range; you'll see why external flash units are often a good idea later in this chapter.

An electronic flash (whether built in or connected to the D3500 through a cable plugged into an accessory shoe adapter) is triggered at the instant of exposure, during a period when the sensor is fully exposed by the shutter. The D3500 has a vertically traveling shutter that consists of two curtains. The front curtain opens and moves to the opposite side of the frame, at which point the shutter is completely open. The flash can be triggered at this point (so-called *first-curtain sync*, or *front-curtain sync*), making the flash exposure. Then, after a delay that can vary from 30 seconds to 1/200th second (with the D3500; other cameras may sync at a faster or slower speed), a rear curtain begins moving across the sensor plane, covering up the sensor again. If the flash is triggered just before the rear curtain starts to close, then *rear-curtain sync* (also called *second-curtain sync*) is used. In both cases, though, a shutter speed of 1/200th second is the maximum that can be used to take a photo.

Figure 11.6 illustrates how this works, with a fanciful illustration of a generic shutter (your D3500's shutter does *not* look like this, and some vertically traveling shutters move bottom to top rather than the top-to-bottom motion shown). Both curtains are tightly closed at upper left. At upper right, the front curtain begins to move downward, starting to expose a narrow slit that reveals the sensor behind the shutter. At lower left, the front curtain moves downward farther until, as you can see at lower right in the figure, the sensor is fully exposed.

When front-curtain sync is used, the flash is triggered at the instant that the sensor is completely exposed. The shutter then remains open for an additional length of time (from 30 seconds to 1/200th second), and the rear curtain begins to move downward, covering the sensor once more. When rear-curtain sync is activated, the flash is triggered *after* the main exposure is over, just before the rear curtain begins to move downward.

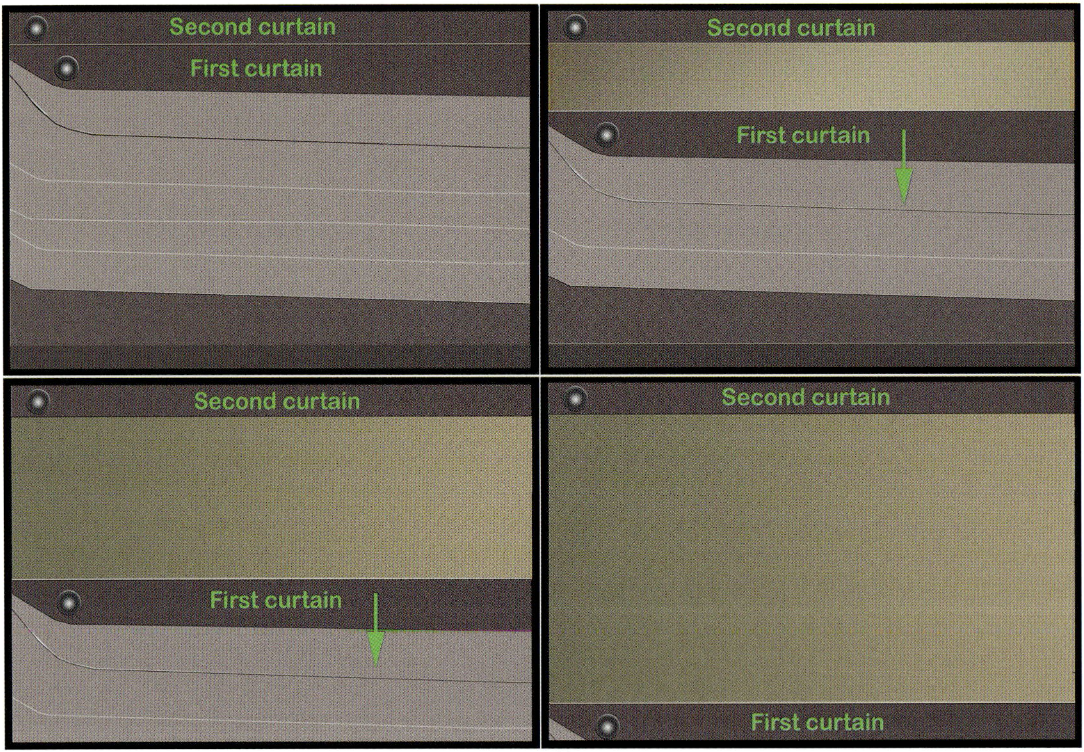

Figure 11.6 A focal plane shutter has two curtains, the first, or front curtain, and a second, rear curtain.

Ghost Images

The difference between triggering the flash when the shutter just opens, or just when it begins to close might not seem like much. But whether you use front-curtain sync (the default setting) or rear-curtain sync (an optional setting) can make a significant difference to your photograph *if the ambient light in your scene also contributes to the image.*

At faster shutter speeds, particularly 1/200th second, there isn't much time for the ambient light to register, unless it is very bright. It's likely that the electronic flash will provide almost all the illumination, so front-curtain sync or rear-curtain sync isn't very important. However, at slower shutter speeds, or with very bright ambient light levels, there is a significant difference, particularly if your subject is moving, or the camera isn't steady.

In any of those situations, the ambient light will register as a second image accompanying the flash exposure, and if there is movement (camera or subject), that additional image will not be in the same place as the flash exposure. It will show as a ghost image and, if the movement is significant enough, as a blurred ghost image trailing in front of or behind your subject in the direction of the movement (see Figure 11.7).

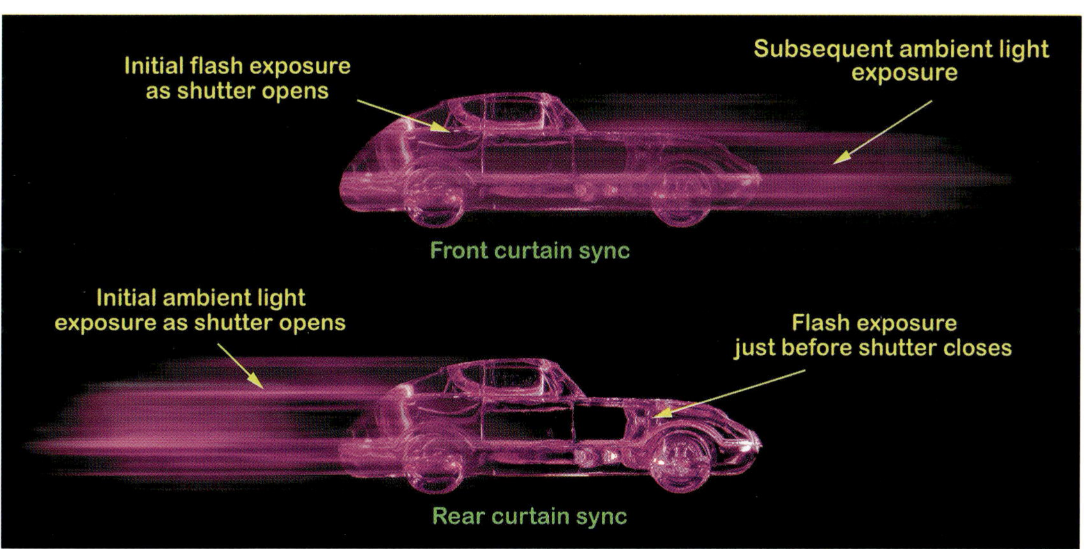

Figure 11.7 Front-curtain sync produces an image that trails in front of the flash exposure (top), while rear-curtain sync creates a more "natural-looking" trail behind the flash image.

As I noted, when you're using front-curtain sync, the flash's main burst goes off the instant the shutter opens fully (a pre-flash used to measure exposure in auto flash modes fires *before* the shutter opens). This produces an image of the subject on the sensor. Then, the shutter remains open for an additional period (30 seconds to 1/200th second, as I said). If your subject is moving, say, toward the right side of the frame, the ghost image produced by the ambient light will produce a blur on the right side of the original subject image, making it look as if your sharp (flash-produced) image is chasing the ghost. For those of us who grew up with lightning-fast superheroes who always left a ghost trail *behind them*, that looks unnatural (see Figure 11.7).

So, Nikon uses rear-curtain sync to remedy the situation. In that mode, the shutter opens, as before. The shutter remains open for its designated duration, and the ghost image forms. If your subject moves from the left side of the frame to the right side, the ghost will move from left to right, too. *Then*, about 1.5 milliseconds before the rear shutter curtain closes, the flash is triggered, producing a nice, sharp flash image *ahead* of the ghost image. Voilà! We have monsieur *Speed Racer* outdriving his own trailing image.

Avoiding Sync Speed Problems

Using a shutter speed faster than 1/200th second can cause problems. Triggering the electronic flash only when the shutter is completely open makes a lot of sense if you think about what's going on. To obtain shutter speeds faster than 1/200th second, the D3500 exposes only part of the sensor at one time, by starting the rear curtain on its journey before the front curtain has completely opened, as shown in Figure 11.8. That effectively provides a briefer exposure as a slit that's narrower than the full height of the sensor passes over the surface of the sensor. If the flash were to fire during the time when the front and rear curtains partially obscured the sensor, only the slit that was actually open would be exposed.

You'd end up with only a narrow band, representing the portion of the sensor that was exposed when the picture is taken. For shutter speeds *faster* than 1/200th second, the rear curtain begins moving *before* the front curtain reaches the bottom of the frame. As a result, a moving slit, the distance between the front and rear curtains, exposes one portion of the sensor at a time as it moves from the bottom to the top. Figure 11.8 shows three views of our typical (but imaginary) focal plane shutter. At left is pictured the closed shutter; in the middle version you can see the front curtain has moved down about 1/4 of the distance from the top; and in the right-hand version, the rear curtain has started to "chase" the front curtain across the frame toward the bottom.

If the flash is triggered while this slit is moving, only the exposed portion of the sensor will receive any illumination. You end up with a photo like the one shown in Figure 11.9. Note that a band across the bottom of the image is black. That's a shadow of the rear shutter curtain, which had started to move when the flash was triggered. Sharp-eyed readers will wonder why the black band is at the *bottom* of the frame rather than at the top, where the rear curtain begins its journey. The answer is simple: your lens flips the image upside down and forms it on the sensor in a reversed position. You never notice that, because the camera is smart enough to show you the pixels that make up your photo in their proper orientation during picture review. But this image flip is why, if your sensor gets dirty and you detect a spot of dust in the upper half of a test photo, if cleaning manually, you need to look for the speck in the *bottom* half of the sensor.

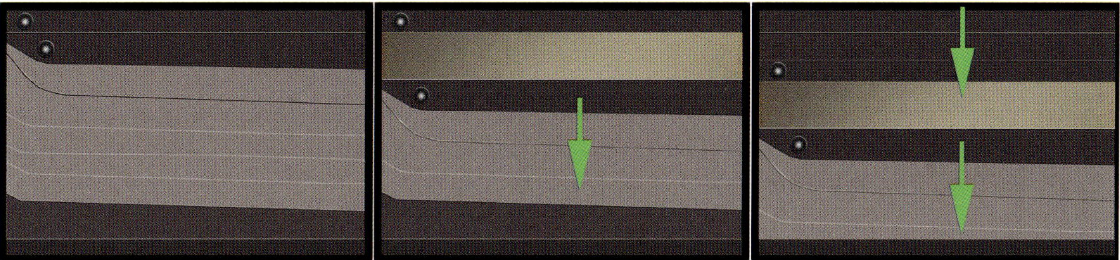

Figure 11.8 A closed shutter (left); partially open shutter as the front curtain begins to move downward (middle); only part of the sensor is exposed as the slit moves (right).

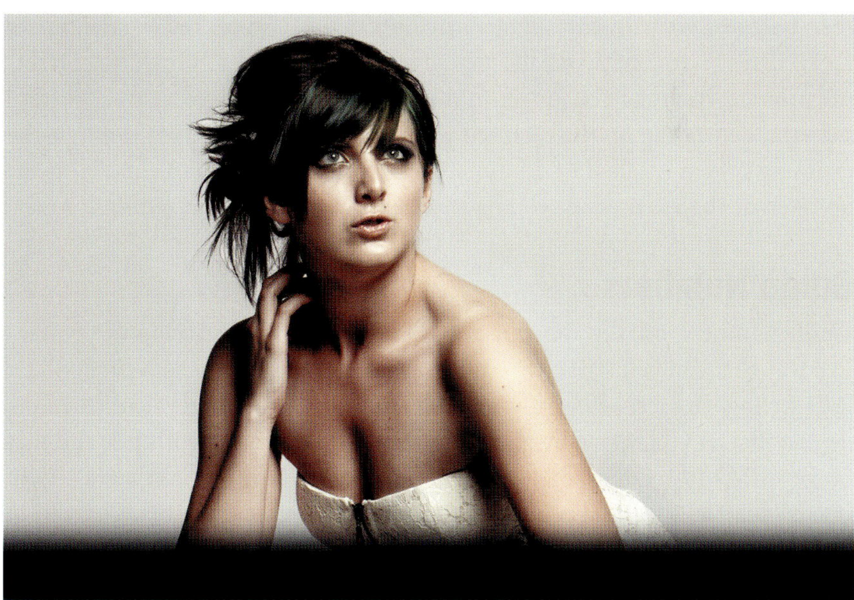

Figure 11.9
If a shutter speed faster than 1/200th second is used, you can end up photographing only a portion of the image.

I generally end up with sync speed problems only when shooting in the studio, using studio flash units rather than my D3500's built-in flash or a Nikon dedicated Speedlight. That's because if you're using either type of "smart" flash, the camera knows that a strobe is attached, and remedies any unintentional goof in shutter speed settings. If you happen to set the D3500's shutter to a faster speed in S or M mode, the camera will automatically adjust the shutter speed down to 1/200th second. In A, P, or any of the Scene modes, where the D3500 selects the shutter speed, it will never choose a shutter speed higher than 1/200th second when using flash. In P mode, shutter speed is automatically set between 1/60th to 1/200th second when using flash. But when using a non-dedicated flash, such as a studio unit plugged into the D3500's accessory shoe adapter, the camera has no way of knowing that a flash is connected, so shutter speeds faster than 1/200th second can be set inadvertently.

Determining Exposure

Calculating the proper exposure for an electronic flash photograph is a bit more complicated than determining the settings for continuous light. The right exposure isn't simply a function of how far away your subject is (which the D3500 can figure out based on the autofocus distance that's locked in just prior to taking the picture). Various objects reflect more or less light at the same distance so, obviously, the camera needs to measure the amount of light reflected back and through the lens. Yet, as the flash itself isn't available for measuring until it's triggered, the D3500 has nothing to measure.

The solution is to fire the flash twice. The initial shot is a *monitor pre-flash* that can be analyzed, then followed virtually instantaneously by a main flash (to the eye the bursts appear to be a single flash) that's given exactly the calculated intensity needed to provide a correct exposure. As a result, the primary flash may be longer in duration for distant objects and shorter in duration for closer subjects, depending on the required intensity for exposure. This through-the-lens evaluative flash exposure system is called i-TTL (intelligent Through-The-Lens), and it operates whenever the pop-up internal flash is used, or you have attached a Nikon dedicated flash unit to the D3500.

Guide Numbers

Guide numbers, usually abbreviated GN, are a way of specifying the power of an electronic flash in a way that can be used to determine the right f/stop to use at a particular shooting distance and ISO setting. In fact, before automatic flash units became prevalent, the GN was actually used to do just that. A GN is usually given as a pair of numbers for both feet and meters that represent the range at ISO 100. For example, the Nikon D3500's built-in flash has a GN in i-TTL mode of 7/22 (meters/feet) at ISO 100. In Manual mode, the true guide number is a fraction higher: 8/26 meters/feet. To calculate the right exposure at that ISO setting, you'd divide the guide number by the distance to arrive at the appropriate f/stop.

Using the D3500's built-in flash as an example, at ISO 100 with its GN of 26 in Manual mode, if you wanted to shoot a subject at a distance of 12 feet, you'd use f/2 (26 divided by 12). At 5 feet, an f/stop of f/5 would be used. Some quick mental calculations with the GN will give you any particular electronic flash's range. You can easily see that the built-in flash would begin to peter out at about 9 feet if you stuck to the lowest ISO of 100, because you'd need an aperture of f/2.8. Of course, in the real world you'd probably bump the sensitivity up to a setting of ISO 800 so you could use a more practical f/5.6 at 9 feet, and the flash would be effective all the way out to 18 feet at f/2.8.

Today, guide numbers are most useful for comparing the power of various flash units, rather than actually calculating what exposure to use. You don't need to be a math genius to see that an electronic flash with a GN in feet of, say, 111.5 at ISO 100 (like the SB-5000) would be *a lot* more powerful than your built-in flash. At ISO 100, you could use f/5.6 to shoot as far as 20 feet.

Flash Control

The Nikon D3500's built-in flash has two modes, TTL (in two variations) and Manual. It does not have a repeating flash option, nor can it be used to trigger other Nikon flashes in Commander mode, unlike most of its siblings. You can choose between TTL and Manual modes using the Flash Control for Built-In Flash entry in the Shooting menu, as first described in Chapter 4. Note that the label on this menu listing changes to Optional Flash when some external flash units, such as the SB-500, are mounted on the D3500 and powered up. You can then make the same flash mode changes for the SB-500 as you can for the built-in flash. Other Nikon external flash units, such as the Nikon SB-5000, have additional exposure modes, which I'll discuss later in this chapter. Your Flash Control options are as follows:

- **TTL.** When the built-in flash is triggered, the D3500 first fires a pre-flash and measures the light reflected back and through the lens to calculate the proper exposure when the full flash is emitted a fraction of a second later. Either i-TTL Balanced Fill-Flash or Standard i-TTL Fill-Flash exposure calculation modes are used. I'll explain these modes next.

- **Manual.** You can set the level of the built-in flash from full power to 1/32 power. A flash icon blinks in the viewfinder and on the shooting information display when you're using Manual mode, and the built-in flash has been flipped up. External flashes can be set in the range from full power to 1/128th power.

Flash Metering Mode

You don't select the way your flash meters the exposure directly; the two modes, i-TTL Balanced Fill-Flash and Standard i-TTL Fill-Flash, are determined by the camera metering mode—Matrix, Center-weighted, or Spot—that you select. Indeed, the built-in flash in the Nikon D3500, as well as external flash units attached to the camera, use the same three metering modes that are available for continuous light sources: Matrix, Center-weighted, and Spot. So, you can choose the flash's metering mode based on the same subject factors as those explained in reference to non-flash exposure techniques in Chapter 4 (for example, use Spot metering to measure exposure from an isolated subject within the frame). Choice of a metering mode determines how the flash reacts to balance the existing light with the light from the electronic unit:

- **i-TTL Balanced Fill-Flash.** This flash mode is used automatically when you choose Matrix or Center-weighted exposure metering. The Nikon D3500 measures the available light and then adjusts the flash output to produce a natural balance between main subject and background. This setting is useful for most photographic situations.

- **Standard i-TTL Fill-Flash.** This mode is activated when you use Spot metering or choose the standard mode with an external flash unit's controls. The flash output is adjusted only for the main subject of your photograph, and the brightness of the background is not factored in. Use this mode when you want to emphasize the main subject at the expense of proper exposure for the background.

Choosing a Flash Sync Mode

The Nikon D3500 has five flash sync modes that determine when and how the flash is fired (as I'll explain shortly). They are selected from the information edit screen, or by holding down the Flash button on the front of the camera lens housing while rotating the command dial. In both cases, the mode chosen appears in the information edit screen as the selection is made.

Not all sync modes are available with all exposure modes. Depending on whether you're using Scene modes, or Program, Aperture-priority, Shutter-priority, or Manual exposure modes, one or more of the following sync modes may not be available. I'm going to list the sync options available for each exposure mode separately, although that produces a little duplication among the options that are available with several exposure modes. However, this approach should reduce the confusion over which sync method is available with which exposure mode.

In Program and Aperture-priority modes you can select these flash modes:

■ **Front-Curtain Sync/Fill Flash.** In this mode, represented by a lightning bolt symbol, the flash fires as soon as the front curtain opens completely. The shutter then remains open for the duration of the exposure, until the rear curtain closes. If the subject is moving and ambient light levels are high enough, the movement will cause a secondary "ghost" exposure that appears to be a stream of light advancing ahead of the flash exposure of the same subject. You'll find more on "ghost" exposures next.

■ **Rear-Curtain Sync.** With this setting, the front curtain opens completely and remains open for the duration of the exposure. Then, the flash is fired and the rear curtain closes. If the subject is moving and ambient light levels are high enough, the movement will cause a secondary "ghost" exposure that appears to stream *behind* the flash exposure. In Program and Aperture-priority modes, the D3500 will combine rear-curtain sync with slow shutter speeds (just like slow sync, discussed below) to balance ambient light with flash illumination. (It's best to use a tripod to avoid blur at these slow shutter speeds.)

■ **Red-Eye Reduction.** In this mode, there is a one-second lag after pressing the shutter release before the picture is actually taken, during which the D3500's red-eye reduction lamp lights, causing the subject's pupils to contract (assuming they are looking at the camera), and thus reducing potential red-eye effects. Don't use with moving subjects or when you can't abide the delay.

■ **Slow Sync.** This setting allows the D3500 in Program and Aperture-priority modes to use shutter speeds as slow as 30 seconds with the flash to help balance a background illuminated with ambient light with your main subject, which will be lit by the electronic flash. You'll want to use a tripod at slower shutter speeds, of course. As shown in Figure 11.10, it's common that the ambient light will be much warmer than the electronic flash's "daylight" balance, so, if you want the two sources to match, you may want to use a warming filter on the flash. That can be done with a gel if you're using an external flash like the SB-910, or by taping an appropriate warm filter over the D3500's built-in flash. (That's not a convenient approach, and many find the warm/cool mismatch not objectionable and don't bother with filtration.)

■ **Red-Eye Reduction with Slow Sync.** This mode combines slow sync with the D3500's red-eye reduction behavior when using Program or Aperture-priority modes.

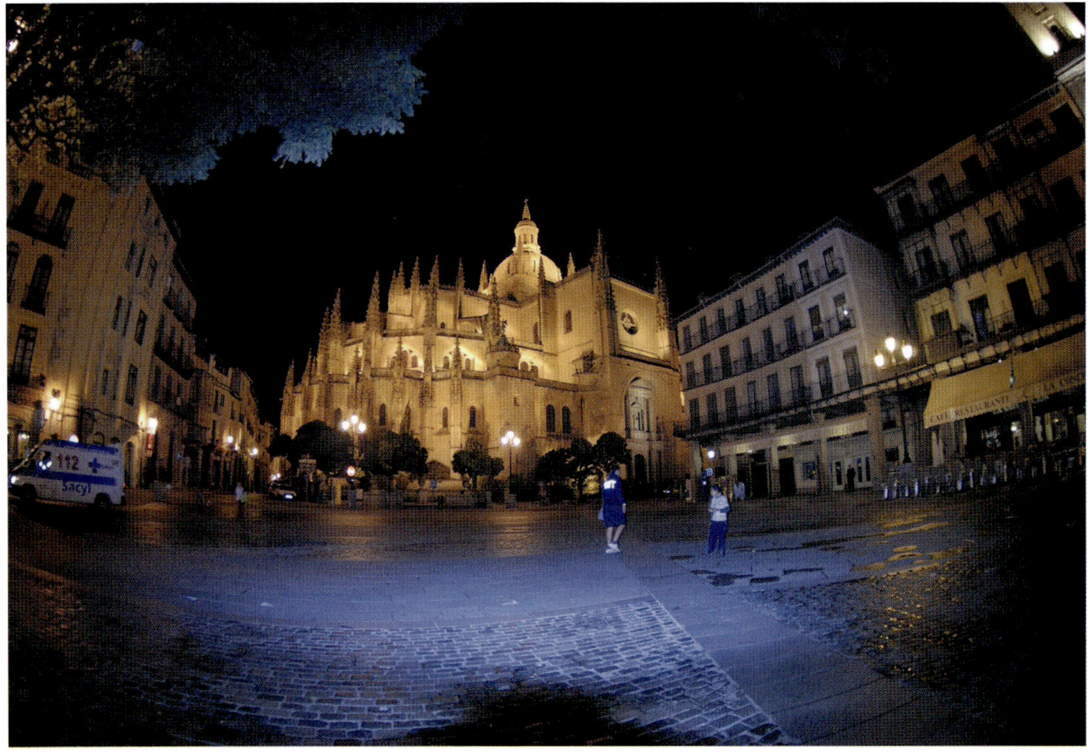

Figure 11.10 I deliberately used flash and slow sync with a scene otherwise illuminated by tungsten light to create this unconventional mixed-lighting image.

In Shutter-priority and Manual exposure modes, you can select the following three flash synchronization settings:

- **Front-Curtain Sync/Fill Flash.** This setting should be your default setting. This mode is also available in Program and Aperture-priority mode, as described above, and, with high ambient light levels, can produce ghost images.
- **Red-Eye Reduction.** This mode, with its one-second lag and red-eye lamp flash, is described above.
- **Rear-Curtain Sync.** As noted previously, in this sync mode, the front curtain opens completely and remains open for the duration of the exposure. Then, the flash is fired and the rear curtain closes. If the subject is moving and ambient light levels are high enough, the movement will cause that "ghost" exposure that appears to be trailing the flash exposure.

In Auto, Portrait, and Close-Up, scene modes, the following flash sync options are available:

- **Auto.** This setting is the same as front-curtain sync, but the flash pops up automatically in dim lighting conditions.

- **Red-Eye Reduction Auto.** In this mode, there is a one-second lag after pressing the shutter release before the picture is actually taken, during which the D3500's red-eye reduction lamp lights, causing the subject's pupils to contract (assuming they are looking at the camera), and thus reducing potential red-eye effects. Don't use with moving subjects or when you can't abide the delay.

- **Flash Off.** This is not really a sync setting, although it is available from the same selection screen. It disables the flash for those situations in which you absolutely do not want it to pop up and fire.

In Night Portrait mode, only slow synchronization flash and flash off modes are available:

- **Auto Slow Sync.** This setting allows the D3500 to select shutter speeds as slow as 30 seconds with the flash to help balance a background illuminated with ambient light with your main subject, which will be lit by the electronic flash. Best for shooting pictures at night when the subjects in the foreground are important, and you want to avoid a pitch-black background. I recommend using a tripod in this mode.

- **Auto Red-Eye Reduction with Slow Sync.** Another mode that calls for a tripod, this sync setting mode combines slow sync with the D3500's red-eye reduction pre-flash. This is the mode to use when your subjects are people who will be facing the camera.

- **Flash Off.** Disables the flash in museums, concerts, religious ceremonies, and other situations in which you absolutely do not want it to pop up and fire.

A Typical Electronic Flash Sequence

Here's what happens when you take a photo using electronic flash, either the unit built into the Nikon D3500 or an external flash like the Nikon SB-500:

1. **Sync mode.** Choose the flash sync mode by holding down the Flash button and rotating the command dial to choose the sync mode, as described above.

2. **Metering method.** When working in P, S, A, or M exposure modes, choose the metering method you want, from Matrix, Center-weighted, or Spot metering, using the information edit screen.

3. **Activate flash.** Press the flash pop-up button to flip up the built-in flash, or mount (or connect with a cable) an external flash and turn it on. A ready light appears in the viewfinder and on the back of the flash when the unit is ready to take a picture.

4. **Check exposure.** Select a shutter speed when using Manual, Program, or Shutter-priority modes; select an aperture when using Aperture-priority and Manual exposure modes. The D3500 will set both shutter speed and aperture if you're using a Scene mode.

5. **Take photo.** Press the shutter release down all the way.

6. **D3500 receives distance data.** An E-, D-, or G-series lens now supplies focus distance to the D3500.

7. **Pre-flash emitted.** The internal flash, if used, or external flash sends out one pre-flash burst used to determine exposure.

8. **Exposure calculated.** The pre-flash bounces back and is measured by the 420-pixel RGB sensor in the viewfinder. It measures brightness and contrast of the image to calculate exposure. If you're using Matrix metering, the D3500 evaluates the scene to determine whether the subject may be backlit (for fill flash), or a subject that requires extra ambient light exposure to balance the scene with the flash exposure, or classifies the scene in some other way. The camera to subject information as well as the degree of sharp focus of the subject matter is used to locate the subject within the frame. If you've selected Spot metering, only standard i-TTL (without balanced fill-flash) is used.

9. **Mirror up.** The mirror flips up. At this point exposure and focus are locked in.

10. **Flash fired.** At the correct triggering moment (depending on whether front or rear sync is used), the camera sends a signal to one or more flashes to start flash discharge. The flash is quenched as soon as the correct exposure has been achieved.

11. **Shutter closes.** The shutter closes and mirror flips down. You're ready to take another picture.

12. **Exposure confirmed.** Ordinarily, the full charge in the flash may not be required. If the flash indicator in the viewfinder blinks for about three seconds after the exposure, that means that the entire flash charge was required, and it *could* mean that the full charge wasn't enough for a proper exposure. Be sure to review your image on the LCD monitor to make sure it's not underexposed, and, if it is, make adjustments (such as increasing the ISO setting of the D3500) to remedy the situation.

Working with Nikon Flash Units

If you want to work with dedicated Nikon flash units, at this time your best choices include the D3500's built-in flash, the Nikon SB-5000, SB-900/910, SB-700, SB-500, SB-400, SB-300 on-camera flash units, and the SB-R200/R1 wireless remote flash systems. These share certain features, which I'll discuss while pointing out differences among them. Nikon may introduce additional flash units during the life of this book, but the current batch and the Nikon Creative Lighting System ushered in with them were significant steps forward.

Nikon D3500 Built-In Flash

In automatic mode, the built-in flash has a guide number of 7/22 (meters/feet) at ISO 100, and must be activated by manually flipping it up when not using one of the Scene modes that feature automatic pop-up. This flash is powerful enough to provide primary direct flash illumination when required, but can't be angled up for diffuse bounce flash off the ceiling. It's useful for balanced fill flash, but cannot operate in Commander mode, which allows the built-in flash to trigger one or more off-camera flash units. You can use Manual flash mode and the Flash Control For Built-in Flash settings in the Shooting menu to dial down the intensity of the built-in flash to 1/32 power to reduce the output.

Changing settings is easy:

- **Elevate the built-in flash.** Press the Flash button on the front left side of the viewfinder housing to pop up the flash.

- **Choose sync mode.** If you want to change the flash sync mode, after the flash is elevated, hold down the Flash button and rotate the command dial. The sync mode you've selected will appear on the shooting information screen.

- **Apply flash exposure compensation.** If your pictures in a session are consistently overexposed or underexposed, you can dial in flash compensation by holding down the compensation button (just southeast of the shutter release) and the Flash button at the same time, and rotating the main dial. The amount of compensation from +1.0 to –3.0EV is displayed on the shooting information screen.

- **Use the information edit screen.** You can also choose sync mode and flash compensation using the information edit screen. Press the Info button, navigate to the function you want to adjust, press OK, and use the up/down buttons to enter the value.

- **Set color temperature.** The D3500's Auto color temperature setting will adjust for the built-in flash nicely. But there might be times when you want to set the color temperature manually. For example, you might be shooting under incandescent illumination and have put an orange gel over your internal or external flash so both light sources match. You'd want to set the color temperature manually to incandescent. Or, you might want to use an oddball setting as a special effect. Use the information edit screen to adjust the color temperature to Flash, Incandescent, or any of the other choices, as described in Chapter 2.

Because the built-in flash draws its power from the D3500's battery, extensive use will reduce the power available to take pictures. For that reason alone, use of an external flash unit can be a good idea when you plan to take a lot of flash pictures.

Nikon Add-On Flash Units

Nikon offers a wide range of external flash units that are compatible with your D3500, ranging from the top-of-the-line SB-5000 to the entry-level SB-300, and will probably introduce more Speedlights during the life of this book. In addition, there are a number of older units that have been officially or unofficially discontinued, such as the SB-600, SB-400, SB-800, and SB-910/ SB-900, which are still available, in both new and used condition. I'm going to concentrate on the most recent in the following sections.

Nikon SB-300

This entry-level Speedlight, at about $150, is the smallest and most basic of the Nikon series of Speedlights. The SB-300 has a limited, easy-to-use feature set suited for point-and-shoot photography and some slightly more advanced techniques. Do note however that it does not support wireless off-camera flash. The SB-300 has a moderate guide number of 18/59 at ISO 100. Its main advantage, then, is to provide some additional elevation of the flash above the camera to provide an improved coverage angle and less chance of red-eye effects. Its flash head tilts up to 120 degrees, with click stops at 120, 90, 75, and 60 degrees when the flash is pointed directly ahead. It has a zoom flash head. The SB-300 is lighter in weight at 3.4 ounces than the SB-400 it replaces, and uses two AAA batteries.

Nikon SB-400

Recently discontinued, but still widely available new from many retailers, this entry-level Speedlight has a limited, easy-to-use feature set suited for point-and-shoot photography and some slightly more advanced techniques. Do note however that, like the SB-300, it does not support wireless off-camera flash. The 4.5-ounce SB-400 has a moderate guide number of 21/69 at ISO 100 when the zooming head (which can be set to either 18mm or 27mm) is at the 18mm position. It tilts up to 90 degrees, allowing you to bounce the light off of a ceiling, but it cannot be rotated to the side.

Nikon SB-500

This Nikon flash unit ($250) has a guide number of 24/79 at ISO 100, a speedy recycle time of about 3.5 seconds, and runs on 2 AA batteries for up to 140 flashes. It includes a built-in LED video light with three output levels, and can also be used for still photography as fill light, especially at the brightest setting. (See Figure 11.11.) It's perfect for wireless mode (discussed in Chapter 10), with four wireless channels and two groups available in Commander mode. The SB-500's head tilts up to 90 degrees, with click-stops at 0, 60, 75, and 90. It rotates horizontally 180 degrees to the left and right, for flexible bounce-flash lighting. If you need a zoom head to adjust flash output to better distribute light at various focal lengths, you're better off with the SB-700 even with its limited zoom range (described next); this unit lacks zooming capabilities.

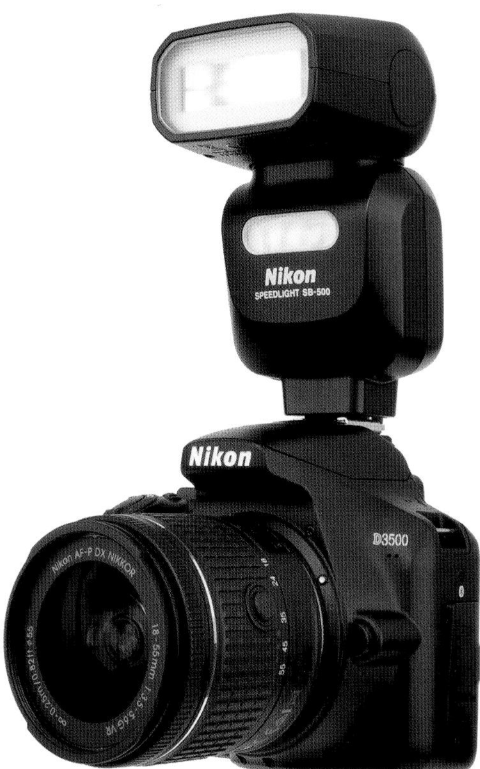

Figure 11.11 The Nikon SB-500 is an entry-level flash ideal for the Nikon D3500.

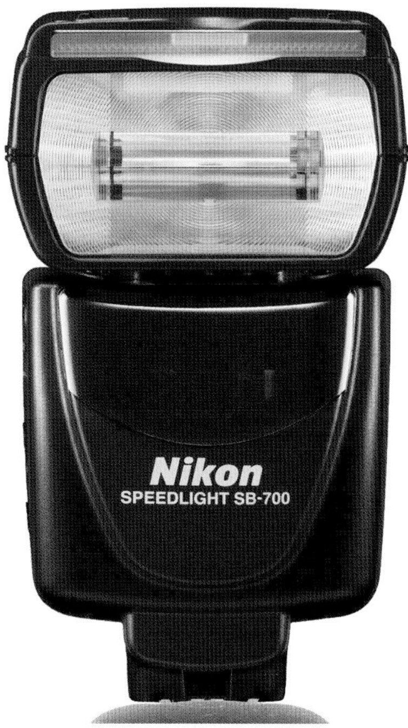

Figure 11.12 The Nikon SB-700 has most features a D3500 owner might want.

Nikon SB-700

This upscale (about $330) unit has a guide number of 28/92 (meters/feet) at ISO 100 when set to the 35mm zoom position. It has many of the top-model SB-910's features, including zoomable flash coverage equal to the field of view of a 16-56mm lens on the D3500 (24-120mm settings with a full-frame camera), and 14mm with a built-in diffuser panel. It has a built-in modeling flash feature, and a wireless Commander mode.

But the SB-700 (see Figure 11.12) lacks some important features found in the SB-910 and SB-5000. Depending on how you use your Speedlight, these differences may or may not be important to you. They include:

- **No repeating flash mode.** You can't shoot interesting stroboscopic effects with the SB-700, as you can with the SB-5000 or older SB-910/900 units.

- **No external PC/X sync socket.** This option, not found on the SB-700, is of limited use for those who want to attach an off-camera flash to the camera, which does not have a PC/X contact.

- **Limited zoom range.** The SB-700's zoom head is limited to 24-120mm, plus 14mm with the diffuser panel. The ability to match the zoom head to the focal length you're using can match the coverage to the field of view, so the flash's output isn't wasted illuminating areas that aren't within the actual frame.

Nikon SB-R200

One oddball flash unit in the Nikon line is the SB-R200. This $165 unit is a specialized wireless-only flash that's especially useful for close-up photography, and is often purchased in pairs for use with the Nikon R1 and R1C1 Wireless Close-Up Speedlight systems. Its output power is low at 10/33 (meters/feet) for ISO 100 as you might expect for a unit used to photograph subjects that are often inches from the camera. It has a fixed coverage angle of 78 degrees horizontal and 60 degrees vertical, but the flash head tilts down to 60 degrees and up to 45 degrees (with detents every 15 degrees in both directions). In this case, "up" and "down" has a different meaning, because the SB-R200 can be mounted on the SX-1 Attachment Ring mounted around the lens, so the pair of flash units are on the sides and titled toward or away from the optical axis. It supports i-TTL, D-TTL, TTL (for film cameras), and Manual modes.

Nikon SB-910

The Nikon SB-910 was the flagship of the Nikon flash lineup until the SB-5000 model was unveiled. However, the SB-910 remains one of the most-used Nikon flash units (along with its predecessor, the SB-900), so I'll continue to include it in my coverage of Speedlights for the foreseeable future. It's still widely available new or used for as little as $350, and has a guide number of 34/111.5 (meters/feet) when the "zooming" flash head (which can be set to adjust the coverage angle of the lens) is set to the 35mm position. It includes Commander mode, repeating flash, modeling light, and selectable power output, along with some extra capabilities.

The SB-910 was basically a slight reboot of the older SB-900, which gained a bad reputation for overheating and then shutting down after a relatively small number of consecutive exposures (as few as a dozen or so shots). The SB-910 also can overheat, but features a different thermal protection system. Instead of disabling the flash as it begins warming up, the SB-910 increases the recycle time between flashes, giving the unit additional time to cool a bit before the next shot. While this "improvement" is not a real fix, it does encourage you to slow your shooting pace a bit to stretch out the number of flashes this Speedlight produces before it must be shut down for additional cooling.

Nikon estimates that you should be able to get 190 flashes from the SB-910 when using AA 2600 mAh rechargeable batteries, if firing the Speedlight at full output once every 30 seconds, with a minimum recycling time of 2.3 seconds (which gradually becomes longer as the flash heats up and the thermal protection kicks in). To get the maximum number of shots from your batteries, Nikon figures that AF-assist illumination, power zoom, and the LCD panel illumination are switched off.

There are some improvements, such as illuminated buttons and a restyled soft case, but, in general, the SB-910 is very similar to the SB-900 that we Nikon photographers have learned to know and fear. For example, you can angle the flash and rotate it to provide bounce flash. It includes additional, non-through-the-lens exposure modes, thanks to its built-in light sensor, and can "zoom" and diffuse its coverage angle to illuminate the field of view of lenses from 8mm to 200mm.

The SB-910/SB-900 also has its own powerful focus assist lamp to aid autofocus in dim lighting, and has reduced red-eye effects simply because the unit, even when attached to the D3500 and not used off-camera, is mounted in a higher position that tends to eliminate reflections from the eye back to the camera lens.

Note that the SB-910, like your camera, contains firmware that can be updated. The custom settings readouts on the flash itself will tell you what firmware version you currently have. If an update is required, you'll need to download the firmware module from the Nikon website. Load it onto a memory card, and then mount the flash on your D3500 and power it up. You'll find a fourth entry in the Firmware section of the Setup menu, marked S (for Speedlight or Strobe). The SB-910's firmware can be updated through the camera/flash connection just like the camera's own firmware.

Nikon SB-5000

This $600 Speedlight, introduced at the same time as the D5 and D500, is the new flagship of the Nikon flash lineup, although it's not really a practical unit for D3500 owners. While it resembles the SB-910 and has a virtually identical guide number (34.5 meters, 113 feet), it more or less solves the overheating problem that plagued its top-line predecessors. A novel internal cooling system purportedly allows up to 90 consecutive shots, or 120 shots at five-second intervals without overheating. (Wedding photographers will love this.) However, the big news—the unit's radio control capabilities—won't excite D3500 owners, as the Nikon radio trigger, the WR-R10 wireless remote adapter, is not compatible with the camera. I'm mentioning the SB-5000 only for completeness.

Working with Wireless Commander Mode

The D3500's built-in flash cannot be set to Commander mode and used to control other compatible flash units. However, if you mount one of several compatible external dedicated flash units, such as the Nikon SB-500, SB-700, or SB-910, any can serve as a flash "Commander" to communicate with and trigger other flash units. Nikon offers a unit called the SU-800, which is a commander unit that has no built-in visible flash, and which controls other units using infrared signals.

Once you have set the external flash as the Master/Commander, you can specify a shooting mode, either Manual with a power output setting you determine from 1/1 to 1/128 or for TTL automatic exposure. When using TTL, you can dial in from −1.0 to +3.0 flash exposure compensation for the master flash. You can also specify a channel (1, 2, 3, or 4) that all flashes will use to communicate among themselves. (If other Nikon photographers are present, choosing a different channel prevents your flash from triggering their remotes, and vice versa.)

Each remote flash unit can also be set to one of three groups (A, B, or C), so you can set the exposure compensation and exposure mode of each group separately. For example, one or more flashes in one group can be reduced in output compared to the flashes in the other group, to produce a particular lighting ratio of effect. You'll find instructions for setting exposure mode, channel, and compensation in the manual that came with your particular flash unit.

Connecting External Flash

You have three basic choices for linking an external flash unit to your Nikon D3500. They are as follows:

- **Mount on the accessory shoe.** Sliding a compatible flash unit into the Nikon D3500's accessory shoe provides a direct connection. With a Nikon dedicated flash, all functions of the flash are supported.

- **Connect to the accessory shoe with a cable or adapter.** The Nikon SC-28 and SC-29 TTL coiled remote cords have an accessory shoe on one end of a nine-foot cable to accept a flash, and a foot that slides into the camera accessory shoe on the other end, providing a link that is the same as when the flash is mounted directly on the camera. The SC-29 version also includes a focus assist lamp, like that on the camera and SB-900/910. You can also use an adapter in the accessory shoe that accepts a standard flash cable. In all cases, you should make sure that the external flash doesn't use a triggering voltage high enough to "fry" your camera's circuitry.

- **Wireless link.** Certain external Nikon electronic flash can be triggered by another master flash such as the Nikon SB-500/700/900/910/5000 in Commander mode or by the SU-800 infrared unit.

More Advanced Lighting Techniques

As you advance in your Nikon D3500 photography, you'll want to learn more sophisticated lighting techniques, using more than just straight-on flash, or using just a single flash unit. Entire books have been written on lighting techniques (check out *David Busch's Quick Snap Guide to Lighting*). I'm going to provide a quick introduction to some of the techniques you should be considering.

Diffusing and Softening the Light

Direct light can be harsh and glaring, especially if you're using the flash built in to your camera, or an auxiliary flash mounted in the accessory shoe and pointed directly at your subject. The first thing you should do is stop using direct light (unless you're looking for a stark, contrasty appearance as a creative effect). There are a number of simple things you can do with both continuous and flash illumination.

- **Use diffusers.** Nikon supplies a diffuser dome with the SB-900/910 and SB-700 flash units. You can purchase a similar diffuser for other flash from Nikon, Sto-Fen, and some other vendors that offer clip-on diffusers. They provide a soft, flattering light and can be used as direct flash, as soft fill flash, or bounced as in Figure 11.13.

- **Use window light.** Light coming in a window can be soft and flattering, and a good choice for human subjects. Move your subject close enough to the window that its light provides the primary source of illumination. You might want to turn off other lights in the room, particularly to avoid mixing daylight and incandescent light (see Figure 11.14).

- **Use fill light.** Your D3500's built-in flash makes a perfect fill-in light for the shadows, brightening inky depths with a kicker of illumination (see Figure 11.15).

- **Bounce the light.** External electronic flash units mounted on the D3500 usually have a swivel that allows them to be pointed up at a ceiling for a bounce light effect. You can also bounce the light off a wall. You'll want the ceiling or wall to be white or have a neutral gray color to avoid a color cast.

- **Use reflectors.** Another way to bounce the light is to use reflectors or umbrellas that you can position yourself to provide a greater degree of control over the quantity and direction of the bounced light. Good reflectors can be pieces of foamboard, Mylar, or a reflective disk held in place by a clamp and stand. Although some expensive umbrellas and reflectors are available, spending a lot isn't necessary. A simple piece of white foamboard does the job beautifully. Umbrellas have the advantage of being compact and foldable, while providing a soft, even kind of light. They're relatively cheap, too, with a good 40-inch umbrella available for as little as $20.

Figure 11.13
Flash diffusers can
soften the light.

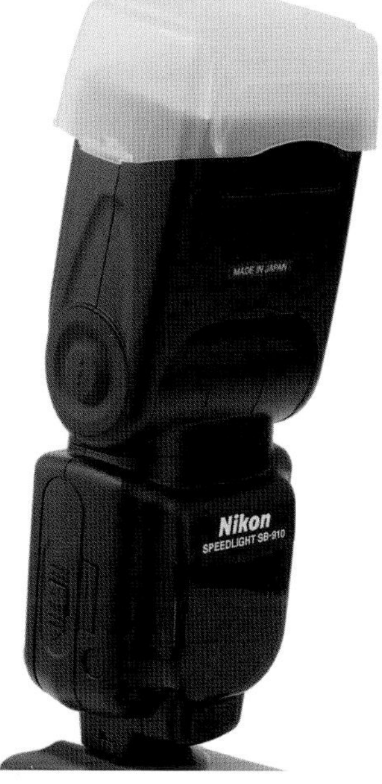

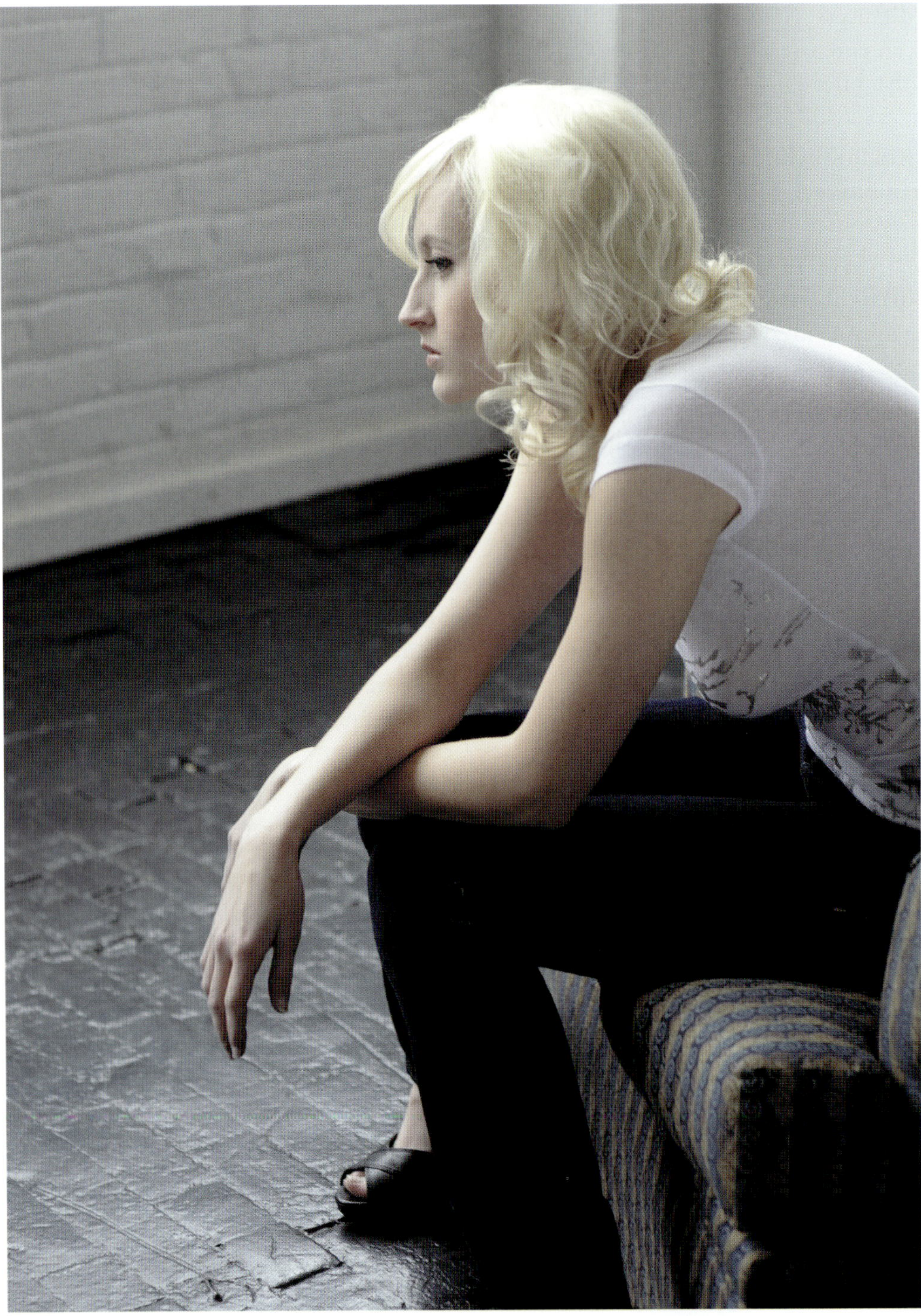

Figure 11.14 Light from the window located off to the upper left makes the perfect diffuse illumination for informal soft-focus portraits like this one.

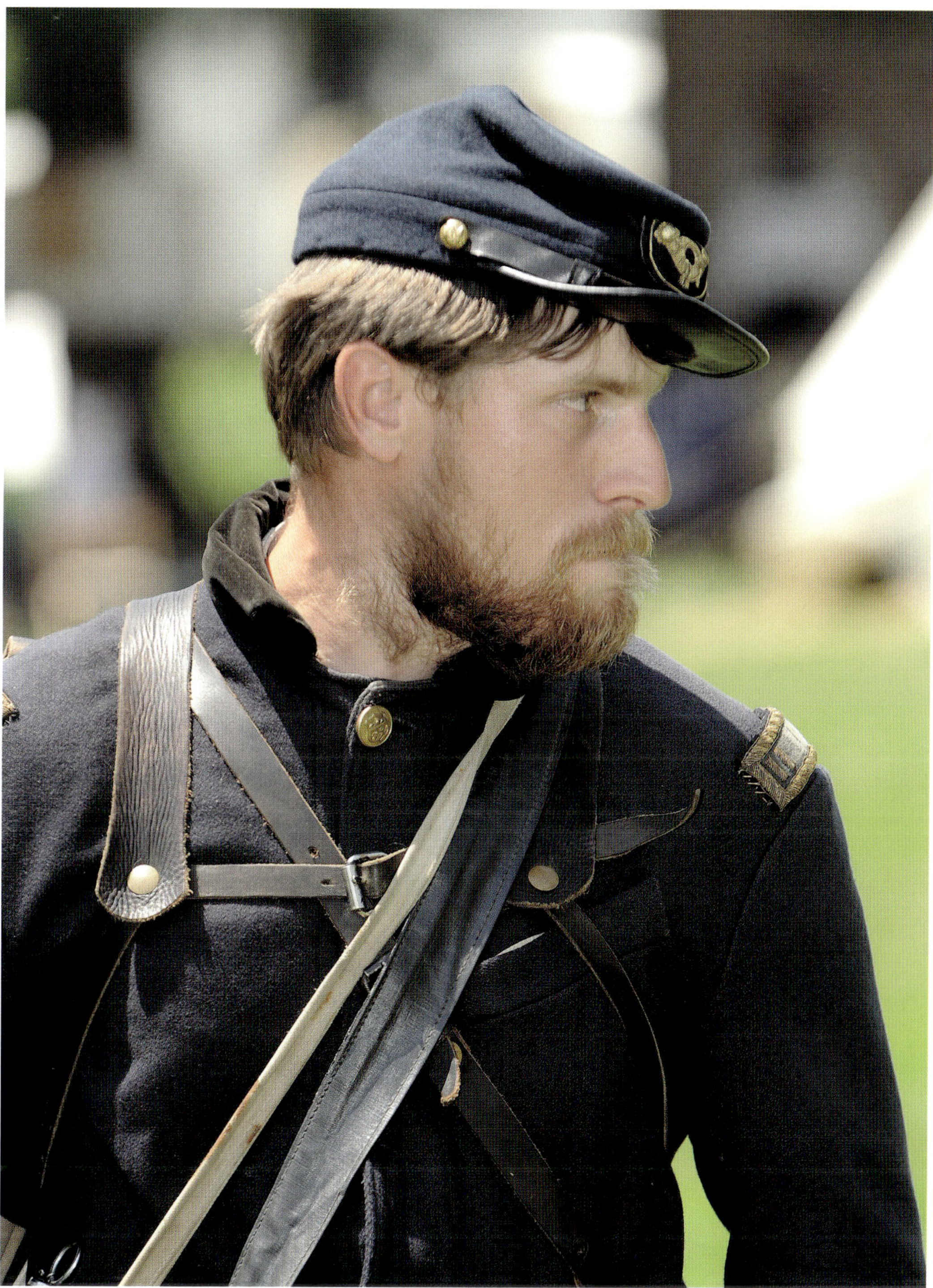

Figure 11.15 Fill flash illuminated the shadows for this candid portrait.

12

Troubleshooting and Prevention

You won't expend a lot of effort keeping your Nikon D3500 humming and operating smoothly. There's not a lot that can go wrong. An electronically controlled camera like the Nikon D3500 has fewer mechanical moving parts to fail, so they are less likely to "wear out." There is no film transport mechanism, no wind lever or motor drive, and, when using lenses with the AF-S or AF-P designation (as described in Chapter 10), no complicated mechanical linkages from camera to lens to adjust the automatic focus. Instead, tiny, reliable motors are built into each lens (and you lose the use of only that lens should something fail), and one of the few major moving parts in the camera itself is a lightweight mirror (its small size is one of the advantages of the D3500's 1.5X crop factor) that flips up and down with each shot.

Of course, the camera also has a moving shutter that can fail, but the shutter is built rugged enough that, even though Nikon doesn't provide an official toughness "rating," many users of previous Nikon entry-level cameras have reported 100,000 trouble-free shutter cycles or more. Unless you're shooting sports in Continuous mode day in and day out, the shutter on your D3500 is likely to last as long as you expect to use the camera.

The only other things on the camera that move are switches, dials, buttons, the flip-up electronic flash, and the door that slides open to allow you to remove and insert the Secure Digital card. Unless you're extraordinarily clumsy or unlucky and manage to give your built-in flash a good whack while it is in use, there's not a lot that can go wrong mechanically with your Nikon D3500.

There are numerous electrical and electronic connections in the camera (many connected to those mechanical switches and dials), and components like the color LCD that can potentially fail or suffer damage. You must contend with dust lodging itself on your sensor, and, from time to time, perhaps the need to periodically update your camera's internal software, called *firmware*. This chapter will show you how to diagnose problems, fix some common ills, and, importantly, learn how to avoid many of them in the future.

Battery Powered

One of the chief liabilities of modern electronic cameras is that they are modern *electronic* cameras. Your D3500 is fully dependent on two different batteries. Without them, the camera can't be used. Photographers from both the film and digital eras have grown used to this limitation, and I've grown to live with the need for batteries even though I shot for years using all-mechanical Nikon cameras that had no batteries (or even a built-in light meter!). The need for electrical power is the price we pay for modern conveniences like autofocus, autoexposure, LCD image display, backlit menus, and, of course, digital images.

KEEPING TRACK OF YOUR BATTERIES AND MEMORY CARDS

Here's a trick I use to keep track of which batteries are fresh/discharged, and which memory cards are blank/exposed. I cut up some small slips of paper and fold them in half, forming a tiny "booklet." Then I write EXPOSED in red on the "inside" pages of the booklet and UNEXPOSED in green on the outside pages. Folded one way, the slips read EXPOSED on both sides; folded the other way, the slips read UNEXPOSED. I slip them inside the plastic battery cover, which you should *always* use when the batteries are not in the camera (to avoid shorting out the contacts), folded so the appropriate "state" of the batteries is visible. The same slips are used in the translucent plastic cases I use for my memory cards (see Figure 12.1). For my purposes, EXPOSED means the same as DISCHARGED, and UNEXPOSED is the equivalent of CHARGED. The color-coding is an additional clue as to which batteries/memory cards are good to go, or not ready for use.

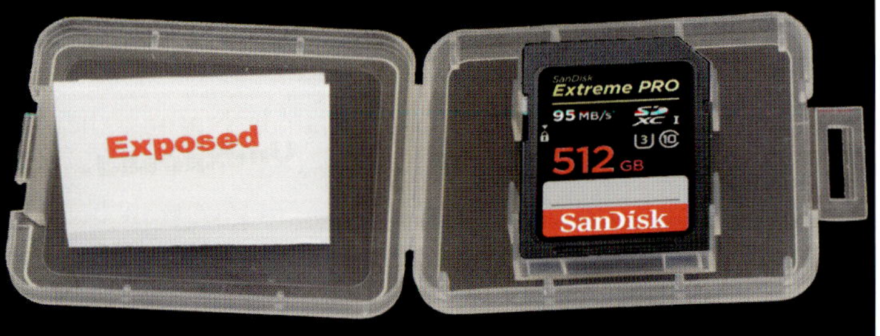

Figure 12.1
Mark your memory cards—or batteries—so you'll know which are ready for use.

One of the batteries you rely on is the EN-EL14a battery installed in the grip. It's rechargeable, can last for as long as 1,550 shots or more, and is user-replaceable if you have a spare. The second power cell in your camera is a so-called *clock battery,* which is also rechargeable, but is tucked away within the innards of the camera and can't be replaced by the user. The clock battery retains the settings of the camera when it's powered down, and, even, when the main battery is removed for charging. If you remove the EN-EL14a for long periods, the clock battery may discharge, but it will be quickly rejuvenated when you replace the main battery. (It's recharged by juice supplied by the EN-EL14a.) Although you can't replace this battery yourself, you can expect it to last for the useful life of the camera.

So, your main concern will be to provide a continuous, reliable source of power for your D3500. As I noted in Chapter 1, you should always have a spare battery or two so you won't need to stop shooting when your internal battery dies. I recommend buying Nikon-brand batteries: saving $20 or so for an after-market battery may seem like a good deal, but it can cost you much more than that if the battery malfunctions and damages your camera.

Updating Your Firmware

The camera relies on its "operating system," or *firmware,* which should be updated in a reasonable fashion as new releases become available. The firmware in your Nikon D3500 handles everything from menu display (including fonts, colors, and the actual entries themselves), what languages are available, and even support for specific devices and features. Upgrading the firmware to a new version makes it possible to add or fine-tune features while fixing some of the bugs that sneak in.

Firmware upgrades are used most frequently to fix bugs in the software, and much less frequently to add or enhance features. The exact changes made to the firmware are generally spelled out in the firmware release announcement. You can examine the remedies provided and decide if a given firmware patch is important to you. If not, you can usually safely wait a while before going through the bother of upgrading your firmware—at least long enough for the early adopters (such as those who haunt the Digital Photography Review forums at www.dpreview.com) to report whether the bug fixes have introduced new bugs of their own. Each new firmware release incorporates the changes from previous releases, so if you skip a minor upgrade you should have no problems.

WHEN TO UPGRADE YOUR FIRMWARE

I *always* recommend waiting at least two weeks after a firmware upgrade is announced before changing the software in your camera. This is often in direct contradiction to the online Nikon "gurus" who breathlessly announce each new firmware release on their web pages, usually with links to where you can download the latest software. *Don't do it!* Yet. Nikon has, in the past, introduced firmware upgrades that were buggy and added problems of their own. If you own a camera affected by a new round of firmware upgrades, I urge you to wait and let a few million over-eager fellow users "beta test" this upgrade for you. Within a few weeks, any problems (although I don't expect there will be any) will surface and you'll know whether the update is safe. Your camera is working fine right now, so why take the chance?

How It Works

If you're computer savvy, you might wonder how your Nikon D3500 is able to overwrite its own operating system—that is, how can the existing firmware be used to load the new version on top of itself? It's a little like lifting yourself by reaching down and pulling up on your bootstraps. Not ironically, that's almost exactly what happens: At your command (when you start the upgrade process), the D3500 shifts into a special mode in which it is no longer operating from its firmware but, rather, from a small piece of software called a *bootstrap loader,* a separate, protected software program that functions only at startup or when upgrading firmware. The loader's function is to look for firmware to launch or, when directed, to copy new firmware from a Secure Digital card to the internal memory space where the old firmware is located.

The loader software isn't set up to go hunting through your Secure Digital card for the firmware file. It looks only in the top or root directory of your card, so that's where you must copy the firmware you download. Once you've determined that a new firmware update is available for your camera and that you want to install it, just follow these steps. (If you chicken out, any Nikon Service Center can install the firmware upgrade for you.)

Why Four Firmware Modules?

Your Nikon D3500's firmware is divided into four parts: Firmware C (for Camera), Firmware LD (for Lens Distortion), Firmware LF (Lens Firmware), and Firmware S (Speedlight). These four modules can be updated separately, and account for bug fixes and feature additions/adjustments that Nikon makes for your camera, lenses, and electronic flash after the camera was released for production. The current firmware numbers can be found in the Firmware Version entry in the Setup menu. The S firmware appears only when a Nikon Speedlight is attached and powered up.

> **WARNING**
>
> Use a fully charged EN-EL14a battery or a Nikon AC adapter to ensure that you'll have enough power to operate the camera for the entire upgrade. Moreover, you should not turn off the camera while your old firmware is being overwritten. Don't open the Secure Digital card door or do anything else that might disrupt operation of the D3500 while the firmware is being installed.

Getting Ready

The first thing to do is determine whether you need the current firmware update. First, confirm the version number of your Nikon D3500's current firmware:

1. Turn on the D3500.
2. Press the MENU button and select Firmware Version from the Setup menu. The camera's firmware version will be displayed, as in Figure 12.2.
3. Write down the version number for each Part.
4. Turn off the D3500.

Next, go to the Nikon support site, locate, and download the firmware update. In the USA, the place to go is http://support.nikontech.com/, and search for firmware from there. Click that link, then click the DSLR link on the page displayed next. Scroll down to the D3500 row in the table, and review the version number for the current update.

Figure 12.2
View your current firmware versions before upgrading.

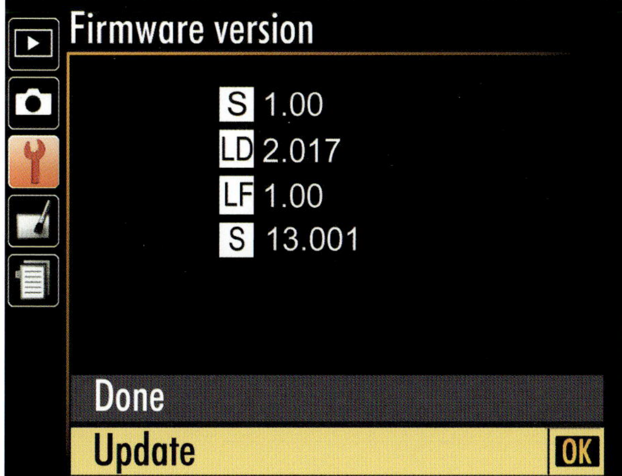

If the version is later than the one you noted in your camera, click the firmware link in either the Windows or Macintosh columns (depending on your computer) to download the file to a new folder on your hard disk. It will have a name like F-D3500-V110W.exe (or .dng for Macs). Then, follow these steps:

1. Run the .exe or .dng application to extract the camera firmware file (which will have a .bin extension) to a folder named "D3500Update" (or something similar).

2. Copy the .bin file to the top level of a memory card that has been formatted in the camera. Be sure to copy the firmware to the root (top-most) directory of the card, as the D3500 will not be able to find it if you use a different folder.

3. Insert the memory card into the D3500's memory card slot.

4. Navigate to the Setup menu and choose Firmware version. Highlight Update and follow the on-screen directions. (See Figure 12.3.)

5. When the camera tells you the update is complete, turn the D3500 off and remove the memory card. (See Figure 12.4.)

6. Power up again and navigate to Firmware Version once more to confirm you've successfully updated to the new version.

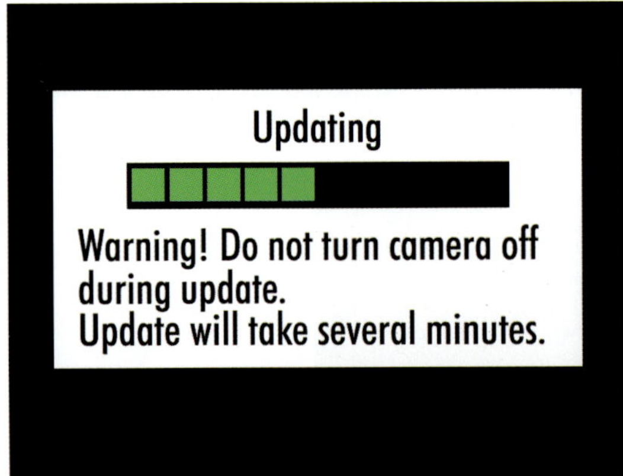

Figure 12.3 Follow the on-screen instructions.

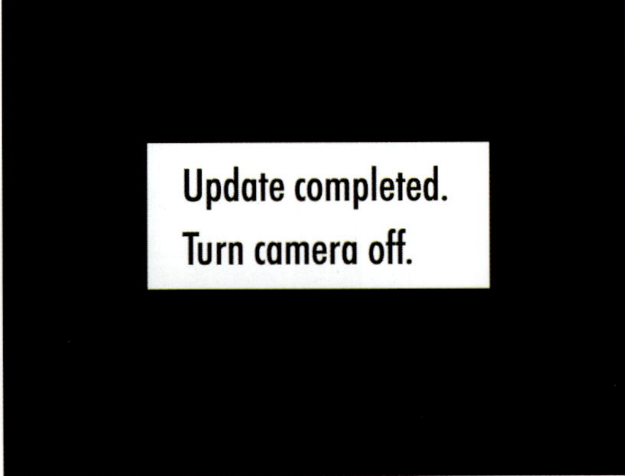

Figure 12.4 Turn off camera when update is complete.

Protecting Your LCD

The large 3-inch color LCD on the back of your Nikon D3500 almost seems like a target for banging, scratching, and other abuse. The LCD itself is quite rugged, and a few errant knocks are unlikely to shatter the protective cover over the LCD, and scratches won't easily mar its surface. However, if you want to be on the safe side, there are a number of protective products you can purchase to keep your LCD safe.

- **Plastic overlays.** The simplest solution (although not always the cheapest) is to apply a plastic overlay sheet or "skin" cut to fit your LCD. These adhere either by static electricity or through a light adhesive coating that's even less clingy than stick-it notes. You can cut down overlays made for smartphones (although these can be pricey at up to $19.95 for a set of several sheets), or purchase overlays sold specifically for digital cameras. I personally prefer the Fellowes 9000206 WriteRight Universal Screen Protectors, available in a 10 pack for about $10. When I receive a new camera I immediately trim one of these and apply it to the LCD on a temporary basis. Then, I purchase a tough tempered glass shield (described next) when they become available for that camera.

- **Acrylic/glass shields.** These scratch-resistant acrylic or tempered glass panels, laser cut to fit your camera perfectly, are my choice as the best protection solution, and what I use on my own D3500. I like the GGS/LaArmour brand, available widely for around $12 to $20 each. They attach using strips of sticky adhesive that hold the panel flush and tight, but which allow the protector to be pried off and the adhesive removed easily if you want to remove or replace the shield. They don't attenuate your view of the LCD and are non-reflective enough for use under a variety of lighting conditions. (See Figure 12.5.)

Figure 12.5
A tough glass shield can protect your LCD from scratches.

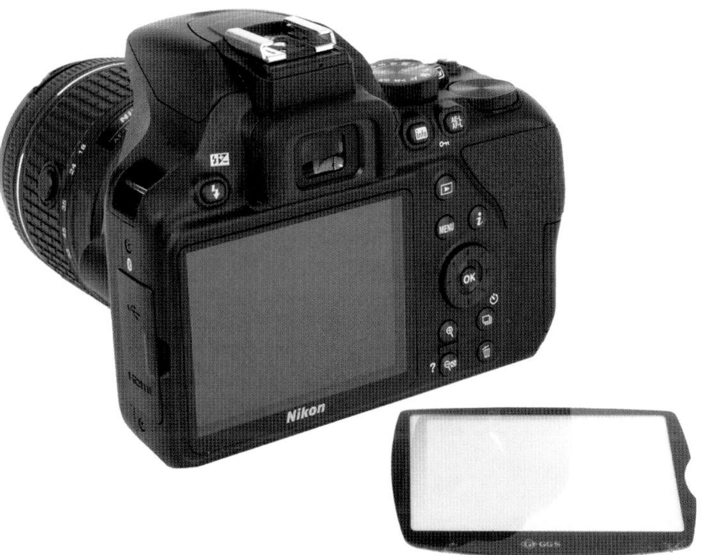

Troubleshooting Memory Cards

Sometimes good memory cards go bad. Sometimes good photographers can treat their memory cards badly. It's possible that a memory card that works fine in one camera won't be recognized when inserted into another. In the worst case, you can have a card full of important photos and find that the card seems to be corrupted and you can't access any of them. Don't panic! If these scenarios sound horrific to you, there are lots of things you can do to prevent them from happening, and a variety of remedies available if they do occur. You'll want to take some time—before disaster strikes—to consider your options.

All Your Eggs in One Basket?

The debate about whether it's better to use one large memory card or several smaller ones has been going on since even before there were memory cards. I can remember when computer users wondered whether it was smarter to install a pair of 200MB (not *gigabyte*) hard drives in their computer, or if they should go for one of those new-fangled 500MB models. By the same token, a few years ago the user groups were full of proponents who insisted that you ought to use 128MB memory cards rather than the huge 512MB versions. Today, most of the arguments involve 8GB cards versus 16GB or 32GB cards, and I expect that as prices for 64GB SD cards continue to drop, they'll find their way into the debate as well, because images from 24MP cameras like the D3500 can quickly fill up smaller cards.

Why all the fuss? Are 32GB memory cards more likely to fail than 16GB cards? Are you risking all your photos if you trust your images to a larger card? Isn't it better to use several smaller cards, so that if one fails you lose only half as many photos? Or, isn't it wiser to put all your photos onto one larger card, because the more cards you use, the better your odds of misplacing or damaging one and losing at least some pictures?

In the end, the "eggs in one basket" argument boils down to statistics, and how you happen to use your D3500. The rationales can go both ways. If you have multiple smaller cards, you do increase your chances of something happening to one of them, so, arguably, you might be boosting the odds of losing some pictures. If all your images are important, the fact that you've lost 100 rather than 200 pictures isn't very comforting.

Also, consider that the eggs/basket scenario assumes that the cards that are lost or damaged are always full. It's actually likely that your 32GB card might suffer a mishap when it's less than half full (indeed, it's more likely that a large card won't be completely filled before it's offloaded to a computer), so you really might not lose any more shots with a single 32GB card than with multiple 16GB cards.

If you shoot photojournalist-type pictures, you probably change memory cards when they're less than completely full in order to avoid the need to do so at a crucial moment. (When I shoot sports, my cards rarely reach 80 to 90 percent of capacity before I change them.) Using multiple smaller cards means you have to change them that more often, which can be a real pain when you're taking a lot of photos. As an example, if you use 1GB memory cards with a Nikon D3500 and shoot RAW+JPEG Fine, you may get only a few dozen pictures on the card. That's not even twice the capacity of a 36-exposure roll of film (remember those?). In my book, I prefer keeping all my eggs in one basket, and then making very sure that nothing happens to that basket.

The other reason comes into play when every single picture is precious to you and the loss of any of them would be a disaster. If you were a wedding photographer, for example, and unlikely to be able to restage the nuptials if a memory card goes bad, you'll probably want to shoot no more pictures than you can afford to lose on a single card, and have an assistant ready to copy each card removed from the camera onto a backup hard drive or DVD onsite.

What Can Go Wrong?

There are lots of things that can go wrong with your memory card, but the ones that aren't caused by human stupidity are statistically very rare. Yes, a Secure Digital card's internal bit bin or controller can suddenly fail due to a manufacturing error or some inexplicable event caused by old age. However, if your SD card works for the first week or two that you own it, it should work forever. There's really not a lot that can wear out.

The typical Secure Digital card is rated for a Mean Time Between Failures of 1,000,000 hours of use. That's constant use 24/7 for more than 100 years! According to the manufacturers, they are good for 10,000 insertions in your camera, and should be able to retain their data (and that's without an external power source) for something on the order of 11 years. Of course, with the millions of SD cards in use, there are bound to be a few lemons here or there.

Given the reliability of solid-state memory compared to magnetic memory, though, it's more likely that your Secure Digital problems will stem from something that you do. SD cards are small and easy to misplace if you're not careful. For that reason, it's a good idea to keep them in their original cases or a "card safe" offered by Gepe (www.gepecardsafe.com), Pelican (www.pelican.com), and others. Always placing your memory card in a case can provide protection from the second-most common mishap that befalls Secure Digital cards: the common household laundry. If you slip a memory card in a pocket, rather than a case or your camera bag often enough, sooner or later it's going to end up in the washing machine and probably the clothes dryer, too. There are plenty of reports of relieved digital camera owners who've laundered their memory cards and found they still worked fine, but it's not uncommon for such mistreatment to do some damage.

Memory cards can also be stomped on, accidentally bent, dropped into the ocean, chewed by pets, and otherwise rendered unusable in myriad ways. Or, if the card is formatted in your computer with a memory card reader, your D3500 may fail to recognize it. Occasionally, I've found that a memory card used in one camera failed if used in a different camera (until I reformatted it in Windows, and then again in the camera). Every once in awhile, a card goes completely bad and—seemingly—can't be salvaged.

Another way to lose images is to do commonplace things with your SD card at an inopportune time. If you remove the card from the D3500 while the camera is writing images to the card, you'll lose any photos in the buffer and may damage the file structure of the card, making it difficult or impossible to retrieve the other pictures you've taken. The same thing can happen if you remove the SD card from your computer's card reader while the computer is writing to the card (say, to erase files you've already moved to your computer). You can avoid this by *not* using your computer to erase files on a Secure Digital card but, instead, always reformatting the card in your D3500 before you use it again.

What Can You Do?

Pay attention: If you're having problems, the *first* thing you should do is *stop* using that memory card. Don't take any more pictures. Don't do anything with the card until you've figured out what's wrong. Your second line of defense (your first line is to be sufficiently careful with your cards that you avoid problems in the first place) is to *do no harm* that hasn't already been done. Read the rest of this section and then, if necessary, decide on a course of action (such as using a data recovery service or software, described later) before you risk damaging the data on your card further.

Now that you've calmed down, the first thing to check is whether you've actually inserted a card in the camera. If you've set the camera so that the No Memory Card? option has been set to allow taking pictures without a card, it's entirely possible (although not particularly plausible) that you've been snapping away with no memory card to store the pictures to, which can lead to massive disappointment later on. You can avoid all this by setting the Slot Empty Release Lock in the Setup menu to Release Locked, and leaving it there.

Things get more exciting when the card itself is put in jeopardy. If you lose a card, there's not a lot you can do other than take a picture of a similar card and print up some "Have You Seen This Lost Flash Memory?" flyers to post on utility poles all around town.

If all you care about is reusing the card, and have resigned yourself to losing the pictures, try reformatting the card in your camera. You may find that reformatting removes the corrupted data and restores your card to health. Sometimes I've had success reformatting a card in my computer using a memory card reader (this is normally a no-no because your operating system doesn't understand the needs of your D3500), and *then* reformatting again in the camera.

If your Secure Digital card is not behaving properly, and you *do* want to recover your images, things get a little more complicated. If your pictures are very valuable, either to you or to others (for example, a wedding), you can always turn to professional data recovery firms. Be prepared to pay hundreds of dollars to get your pictures back, but these pros often do an amazing job. You wouldn't want them working on your memory card on behalf of the police if you'd tried to erase some incriminating pictures. There are many firms of this type, and I've never used them myself, so I can't offer a recommendation. Use a Google search to turn up a ton of them.

A more reasonable approach is to try special data recovery software you can install on your computer and use to attempt to resurrect your "lost" images yourself. They may not actually be gone completely. Perhaps your SD card's "table of contents" is jumbled, or only a few pictures are damaged in such a way that your camera and computer can't read some or any of the pictures on the card. Some of the available software was written specifically to reconstruct lost pictures, while other utilities are more general-purpose applications that can be used with any media, including floppy disks and hard disk drives. They have names like OnTrack, Photo Rescue 2, Digital Image Recovery, MediaRecover, Image Recall, and the aptly named Recover My Photos. You'll find a comprehensive list and links, as well as some picture-recovery tips at www.ultimateslr.com/memory-card-recovery.php. I like the RescuePRO software that SanDisk supplies.

DIMINISHING RETURNS

Usually, once you've recovered any images on a Secure Digital card, reformatted it, and returned it to service, it will function reliably for the rest of its useful life. However, if you find a particular card going bad more than once, you'll almost certainly want to stop using it forever. See if you can get it replaced by the manufacturer if you can, but, in the case of SD card failures, the third time is never the charm.

Preventive Measures

Here are some options for preventing loss of valuable images:

■ **Interleaving.** One option is to *interleave* your shots. Say you don't shoot weddings, but you do go on vacation from time to time. Take 50 or so pictures on one card, or whatever number of images might fill about 25 percent of its capacity. Then, replace it with a different card and shoot about 25 percent of that card's available space. Repeat these steps with diligence (you'd have to be determined to go through this inconvenience), and, if you use four or more memory cards you'll find your pictures from each location scattered among the different memory cards. If you lose or damage one, you'll still have *some* pictures from all the various stops on your trip on the other cards. That's more work than I like to do (I usually tote around a portable hard disk and copy the files to the drive as I go), but it's an option.

- **Transmit your images.** Another option is to transmit your images, as they are shot, to your smartphone or tablet using SnapBridge. You can also upload your images from your phone directly to websites such as Facebook, or Nikon's own My Picturetown.

- **External backup.** You can purchase external hard disk OTG (on-the-go) gadgets which can copy files from your memory cards automatically. More expensive models have color LCD screens so you can review your images. I tend to prefer using a netbook or ultrabook, like the one shown in Figure 12.6. I can store images on the ultrabook's internal hard disk, and make an extra backup copy to an external drive as well. Plus, I can access the Internet from Wi-Fi hotspots, all using a very compact device. Lately, I've been backing up many images on my iPad, which has 64GB of storage—enough for short trips.

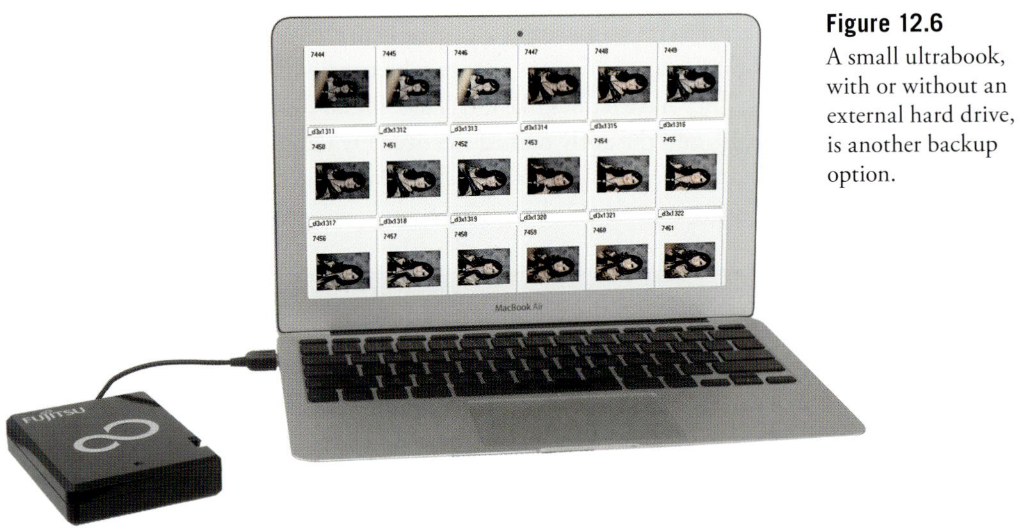

Figure 12.6
A small ultrabook, with or without an external hard drive, is another backup option.

Cleaning Your Sensor

There's no avoiding dust. No matter how careful you are, some of it is going to settle on your camera and on the mounts of your lenses, eventually making its way inside your camera to settle in the mirror chamber. As you take photos, the mirror flipping up and down causes the dust to become airborne and eventually make its way past the shutter curtain to come to rest atop your sensor. There, dust and particles can show up in every single picture you take at a small enough aperture to bring the foreign matter into sharp focus. No matter how careful you are and how cleanly you work, eventually you will get some of this dust on your camera's sensor.

If some dust does collect on your sensor, you can often map it out of your images (making it invisible) using software techniques with the Image Dust Off Ref feature in the Setup menu. Operation of this feature is described in Chapter 5. You may still be required to manually clean your sensor from time to time. This section explains the phenomenon and provides some tips on minimizing dust and eliminating it when it begins to affect your shots.

Dust the FAQs, Ma'am

Here are some of the most frequently asked questions about sensor dust issues.

Q. I see tiny specks in my viewfinder. Do I have dust on my sensor?

A. If you see sharp, well-defined specks, they are clinging to the underside of your focus screen and not on your sensor. They have absolutely no effect on your photographs, and are merely annoying or distracting.

Q. I can see dust on my mirror. How can I remove it?

A. Like focus-screen dust, any artifacts that have settled on your mirror won't affect your photos. You can often remove dust on the mirror or focus screen with a bulb air blower, which will loosen it and whisk it away. Stubborn dust on the focus screen can sometimes be gently flicked away with a soft brush designed for cleaning lenses. I don't recommend brushing the mirror or touching it in any way. The mirror is a special front-surface-silvered optical device (unlike conventional mirrors, which are silvered on the back side of a piece of glass or plastic) and can be easily scratched. If you can't blow mirror dust off, it's best to just forget about it. You can't see it in the viewfinder, anyway.

Q. I see a bright spot in the same place in all of my photos. Is that sensor dust?

A. You've probably got either a "hot" pixel or one that is permanently "stuck" due to a defect in the sensor. A hot pixel is one that shows up as a bright spot only during long exposures as the sensor warms. A pixel stuck in the "on" position always appears in the image. Both show up as bright red, green, or blue pixels, usually surrounded by a small cluster of other improperly illuminated pixels, caused by the camera's interpolating the hot or stuck pixel into its surroundings, as shown in Figure 12.7. A stuck pixel can also be permanently dark. Either kind is likely to show up when they contrast with plain, evenly colored areas of your image.

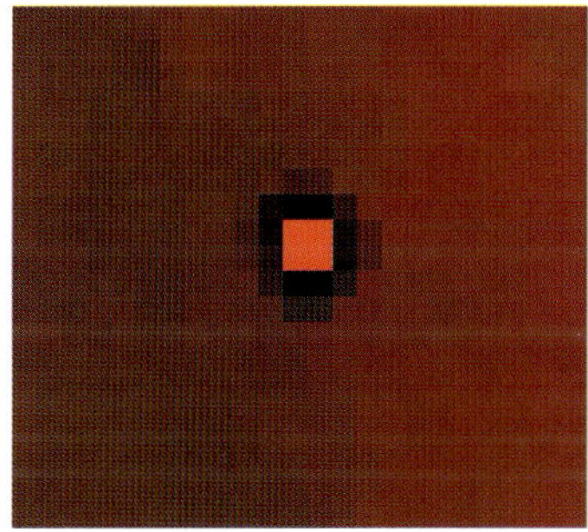

Figure 12.7 A stuck pixel is surrounded by improperly interpolated pixels created by the D3500's demosaicing algorithm.

Finding one or two hot or stuck pixels in your sensor is unfortunately fairly common. They can be "removed" by telling the D3500 to ignore them through a simple process called *pixel mapping*. If the bad pixels become bothersome, Nikon can remap your sensor's pixels with a quick trip to a service center.

Bad pixels can also show up on your camera's color LCD panel, but, unless they are abundant, the wisest course is to just ignore them.

Q. I see an irregular out-of-focus blob in the same place in my photos. Is that sensor dust?

A. Yes. Sensor contaminants can take the form of tiny spots, larger blobs, or even curvy lines if they are caused by minuscule fibers that have settled on the sensor. They'll appear out of focus because they aren't actually on the sensor surface but, rather, a fraction of a millimeter above it on the filter that covers the sensor. The smaller the f/stop used, the more in-focus the dust becomes. At large apertures, it may not be visible at all.

Q. I never see any dust on my sensor. What's all the fuss about?

A. Those who never have dust problems with their Nikon D3500 fall into one of four categories: those for whom the camera's automatic dust removal features are working well; those who seldom change their lenses and have clean working habits that minimize the amount of dust that invades their cameras in the first place; those who simply don't notice the dust (often because they don't shoot many macro photos or other pictures using the small f/stops that makes dust evident in their images); and those who are very, very lucky.

Identifying and Dealing with Dust

Sensor dust is less of a problem than it might be because it shows up only under certain circumstances. Indeed, you might have dust on your sensor right now and not be aware of it. The dust doesn't actually settle on the sensor itself, but, rather, on a protective filter a very tiny distance above the sensor, subjecting it to the phenomenon of *depth-of-focus.* Depth-of-focus is the distance the focal plane can be moved and still render an object in sharp focus. At f/2.8 to f/5.6 or even smaller, sensor dust, particularly if small, is likely to be outside the range of depth-of-focus and blur into an unnoticeable dot.

However, if you're shooting at f/16 to f/22 or smaller, those dust motes suddenly pop into focus. Forget about trying to spot them by peering directly at your sensor with the shutter open and the lens removed. The period at the end of this sentence, about .33mm in diameter, could block a group of pixels measuring 40 × 40 pixels (160 pixels in all!). Dust spots that are even smaller than that can easily show up in your images if you're shooting large, empty areas that are light colored. Dust motes are most likely to show up in the sky, as in Figure 12.8, or in white backgrounds of your seamless product shots and are less likely to be a problem in images that contain lots of dark areas and detail.

To see if you have dust on your sensor, take a few test shots of a plain, blank surface (such as a piece of paper or a cloudless sky) at small f/stops, such as f/22, and a few wide open. Open Photoshop or another image editor, copy several shots into a single document in separate layers, then flip back and forth between layers to see if any spots you see are present in all layers. You may have to boost contrast and sharpness to make the dust easier to spot.

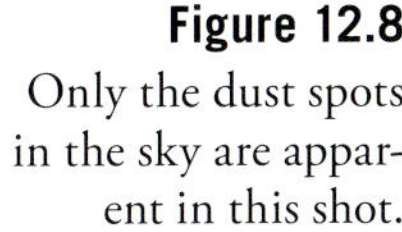

Figure 12.8
Only the dust spots
in the sky are appar-
ent in this shot.

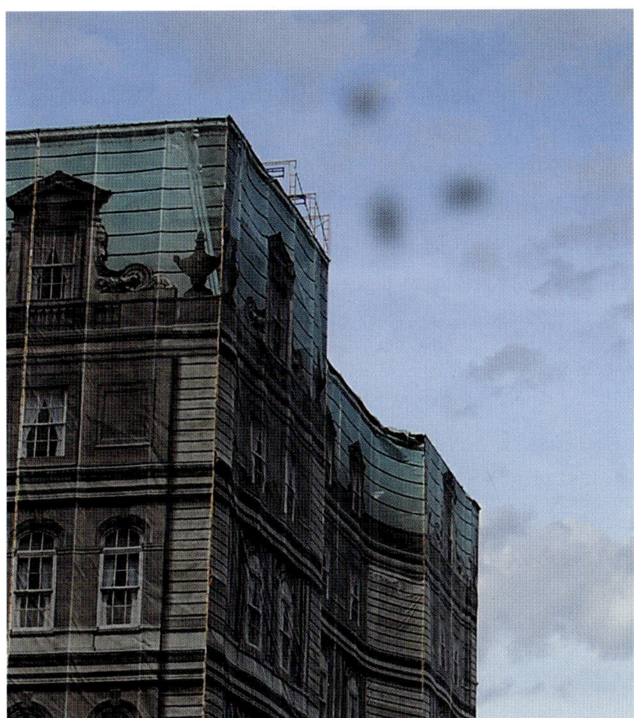

Avoiding Dust

Of course, the easiest way to protect your sensor from dust is to prevent it from settling on the sensor in the first place. Here are my stock tips for eliminating the problem before it begins.

- **Clean environment.** Avoid working in dusty areas if you can do so. Hah! Serious photographers will take this one with a grain of salt, because it usually makes sense to go where the pictures are. Only a few of us are so paranoid about sensor dust (considering that it is so easily removed) that we'll avoid moderately grimy locations just to protect something that is, when you get down to it, just a tool. If you find a great picture opportunity at a raging fire, during a sandstorm, or while surrounded by dust clouds, you might hesitate to take the picture, but, with a little caution (don't remove your lens in these situations, and clean the camera afterward!) you can still shoot. However, it still makes sense to store your camera in a clean environment. One place cameras and lenses pick up a lot of dust is inside a camera bag. Clean your bag from time to time, and you can avoid problems.

- **Clean lenses.** There are a few paranoid types that avoid swapping lenses in order to minimize the chance of dust getting inside their cameras. It makes more sense just to use a blower or brush to dust off the rear lens mount of the replacement lens first, so you won't be introducing dust into your camera simply by attaching a new, dusty lens. Do this before you remove the current lens from your camera, and then avoid stirring up dust before making the exchange.

- **Work fast.** Minimize the time your camera is lensless and exposed to dust. That means having your replacement lens ready and dusted off, and a place to set down the old lens as soon as it is removed, so you can quickly attach the new lens.

- **Let gravity help you.** Face the camera downward when the lens is detached so any dust in the mirror box will tend to fall away from the sensor. Turn your back to any breezes, indoor forced air vents, fans, or other sources of dust to minimize infiltration.

- **Protect the lens you just removed.** Once you've attached the new lens, quickly put the end cap on the one you just removed to reduce the dust that might fall on it.

- **Clean out the vestibule.** From time to time, remove the lens while in a relatively dust-free environment and use a blower bulb like the one shown in Figure 12.9 (*not* compressed air or a vacuum hose) to clean out the mirror box area. A blower bulb is generally safer than a can of compressed air, or a strong positive/negative airflow, which can tend to drive dust further into nooks and crannies.

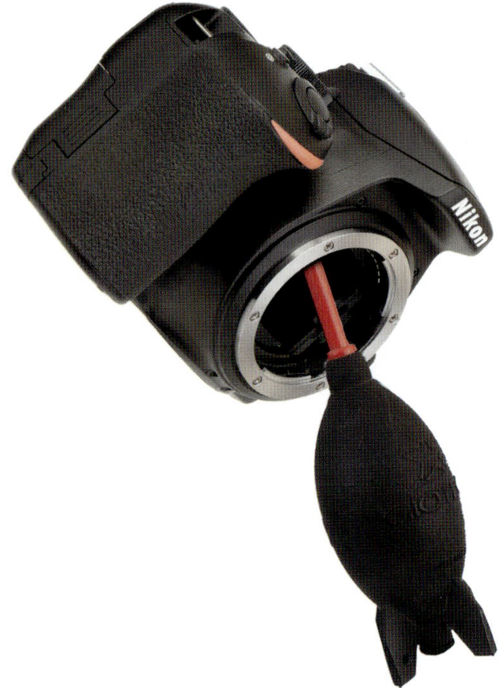

Figure 12.9
Use a robust air bulb for cleaning your sensor.

- **Be prepared.** If you're embarking on an important shooting session, it's a good idea to clean your sensor *now*, rather than come home with hundreds or thousands of images with dust spots caused by flecks that were sitting on your sensor before you even started. Before I left on my most recent trip to Spain, I put both cameras I was taking through a rigid cleaning regimen, figuring they could remain dust-free for a measly 10 days. I even left my bulky blower bulb at home, and took along a new, smaller version for emergencies.

- **Clone out existing spots in your image editor.** Photoshop and other editors have a clone tool or healing brush you can use to copy pixels from surrounding areas over the dust spot or dead pixel. This process can be tedious, especially if you have lots of dust spots and/or lots of images to be corrected. The advantage is that this sort of manual fix-it probably will do the least damage to the rest of your photo. Only the damaged pixels will be affected.

- **Use filtration in your image editor.** A semi-smart filter like Photoshop's Dust & Scratches filter can remove dust and other artifacts by selectively blurring areas that the plug-in decides represent dust spots. This method can work well if you have many dust spots, because you won't need to patch them manually. However, any automated method like this has the possibility of blurring areas of your image that you didn't intend to soften.

Sensor Cleaning

Those new to the concept of sensor dust actually hesitate before deciding to clean their camera themselves. Isn't it a better idea to pack up your D3500 and send it to a Nikon service center so their crack technical staff can do the job for you? Or, at the very least, shouldn't you let the friendly folks at your local camera store do it?

Of course, if you choose to let someone else clean your sensor, they will be using methods that are more or less identical to the techniques you would use yourself. None of these techniques are difficult, and the only difference between their cleaning and your cleaning is that they might have done it dozens or hundreds of times. If you're careful, you can do just as good a job.

Of course vendors like Nikon won't tell you this, but it's not because they don't trust you. It's not that difficult for a real goofball to mess up their camera by hurrying or taking a shortcut. Perhaps the person uses the "Bulb" method of holding the shutter open and a finger slips, allowing the shutter curtain to close on top of a sensor cleaning brush. Or, someone tries to clean the sensor using masking tape, and ends up with goo all over its surface. If Nikon recommended *any* method that's mildly risky, someone would do it wrong, and then the company would face lawsuits from those who'd contend they did it exactly in the way the vendor suggested, so the ruined camera is not their fault.

You can see that vendors like Nikon tend to be conservative in their recommendations, and, in doing so, make it seem as if sensor cleaning is more daunting and dangerous than it really is. Some vendors recommend only dust-off cleaning, through the use of reasonably gentle blasts of air, while condemning more serious scrubbing with swabs and cleaning fluids. However, these cleaning kits for the exact types of cleaning they recommended against are for sale in Japan only, where, apparently, your average photographer is more dexterous than those of us in the rest of the world. These kits are similar to those used by official repair staff to clean your sensor if you decide to send your camera in for a dust-up.

As I noted, sensors can be affected by dust particles that are much smaller than you might be able to spot visually on the surface of your lens. The filters that cover sensors tend to be fairly hard compared to optical glass. Cleaning the 23.5mm × 15.6mm sensor in your Nikon D3500 within the tight confines of the mirror box can call for a steady hand and careful touch. If your sensor's filter becomes scratched through inept cleaning, you can't simply remove it yourself and replace it with a new one.

There are three basic kinds of cleaning processes that can be used to remove dusty and sticky stuff that settles on your dSLR's sensor. All of these must be performed with the shutter locked open. I'll describe these methods and provide instructions for locking the shutter later in this section.

- **Air cleaning.** This process involves squirting blasts of air inside your camera with the shutter locked open. This works well for dust that's not clinging stubbornly to your sensor.
- **Brushing.** A soft, very fine brush is passed across the surface of the sensor's filter, dislodging mildly persistent dust particles and sweeping them off the imager.
- **Liquid cleaning.** A soft swab dipped in a cleaning solution such as ethanol is used to wipe the sensor filter, removing more obstinate particles.

Placing the Mirror/Shutter in the Locked and Fully Upright Position for Landing

Make sure you're using a fully charged battery or an AC adapter. Fortunately, the Nikon D3500 is smart enough that it won't let you try to clean the sensor manually unless the battery has a sufficient charge.

1. Remove the lens from the camera and then turn on the camera.
2. You'll find the Lock Mirror Up for Cleaning menu choice in the Setup menu. Select it.
3. Choose Start. The mirror will flip up and the shutter will open.
4. Use one of the methods described below to remove dust and grime from your sensor. Be careful not to accidentally switch the power off or open the Secure Digital card or battery compartment doors as you work. If that happens, the shutter may be damaged if it closes onto your cleaning tool.
5. When you're finished, turn off the power, replace your lens, and switch your camera back on.

Air Cleaning

Your first attempts at cleaning your sensor should always involve gentle blasts of air. Many times, you'll be able to dislodge dust spots, which will fall off the sensor and, with luck, out of the mirror box. Attempt one of the other methods only when you've already tried air cleaning and it didn't remove all the dust.

Here are some tips for doing air cleaning:

- **Use a clean, powerful air bulb.** Your best bet is bulb cleaners designed for the job, like the Giottos Rocket. Smaller bulbs, like those air bulbs with a brush attached sometimes sold for lens cleaning or weak nasal aspirators may not provide sufficient air or a strong enough blast to do much good.

- **Hold the camera upside down.** Then look up into the mirror box as you squirt your air blasts, increasing the odds that gravity will help pull the expelled dust downward, away from the sensor. You may have to use some imagination in positioning yourself. (See Figure 12.9, earlier, which illustrates how I clean my Nikon D3500.)

- **Never use air canisters.** The propellant inside these cans can permanently coat your sensor if you tilt the can while spraying. It's not worth taking a chance.

- **Avoid air compressors.** Super-strong blasts of air are likely to force dust under the sensor filter.

Brush Cleaning

If your dust is a little more stubborn and can't be dislodged by air alone, you may want to try a brush, charged with static electricity, which can pick off dust spots by electrical attraction. One good, but expensive, option is the Arctic Butterfly sold at www.visibledust.com. A motor built into the brush is used to "flutter" the tip for a few seconds prior to cleaning (see Figure 12.10, left), charging the brush's anti-static properties. Then, the motor is turned off (Figure 12.10, right) and the brush tip is passed above the surface of the sensor. (It's not necessary to touch the sensor.)

Figure 12.10
A proper brush like this Arctic Butterfly is required for dusting off your sensor.

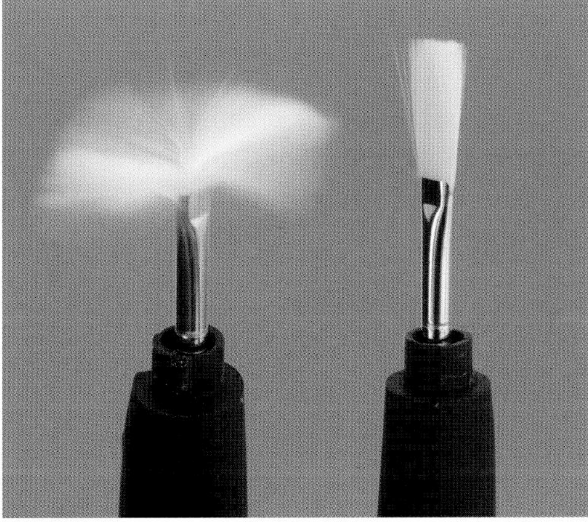

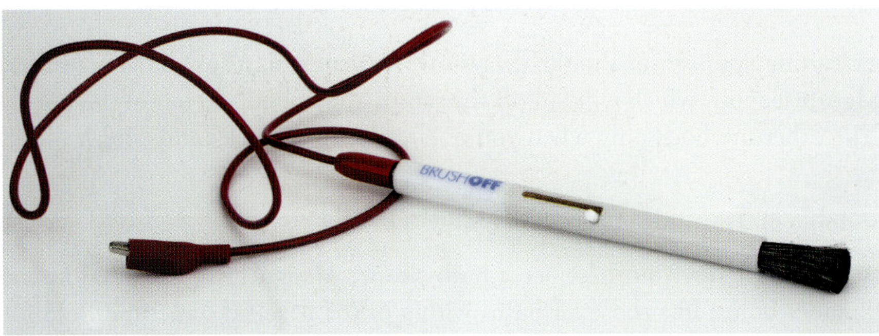

Figure 12.11
This brush includes a grounding lead to siphon off static electricity.

The dust is attracted to the brush and removed by another quick flutter once you've removed the brush from the mirror chamber. Cheaper, inanimate, sensor cleaning brushes can be found on Amazon or other retailers. (See Figure 12.11.) You need a 16mm version. It can be stroked across the short dimension of your D3500's sensor.

Ordinary artist's brushes are much too coarse and stiff and have fibers that are tangled or can come loose and settle on your sensor. A good sensor brush's fibers are resilient and described as "thinner than a human hair." Brush cleaning is done with a dry brush by gently swiping across the surface of the sensor filter with the tip. The dust particles are attracted to the brush particles and cling to them. You should clean the brush with compressed air before and after each use, and store it in an appropriate air-tight container between applications to keep it clean and dust-free. Although these special brushes are expensive, one should last you a long time.

Liquid Cleaning

Unfortunately, you'll often encounter really stubborn dust spots that can't be removed with a blast of air or flick of a brush. These spots may be combined with some grease or a liquid that causes them to stick to the sensor filter's surface. In such cases, liquid cleaning with a swab may be necessary. During my first clumsy attempts to clean my own sensor, I accidentally got my blower bulb tip too close to the sensor, and some sort of deposit from the tip of the bulb ended up on the sensor. I panicked until I discovered that liquid cleaning did a good job of removing whatever it was that took up residence on my sensor.

You want a sturdy swab that won't bend or break so you can apply gentle pressure to the swab as you wipe the sensor surface. Use the swab with methanol (as pure as you can get it, particularly medical grade; other ingredients can leave a residue), or the Eclipse solution also sold by Photographic Solutions. Eclipse is actually quite a bit purer than even medical-grade methanol. A couple drops of solution should be enough, unless you have a spot that's extremely difficult to remove. In that case, you may need to use extra solution on the swab to help "soak" the dirt off.

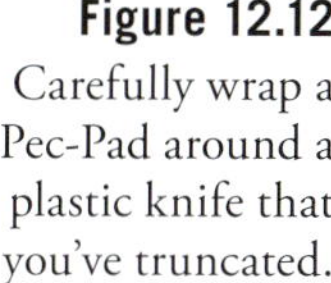

Figure 12.12
Carefully wrap a
Pec-Pad around a
plastic knife that
you've truncated.

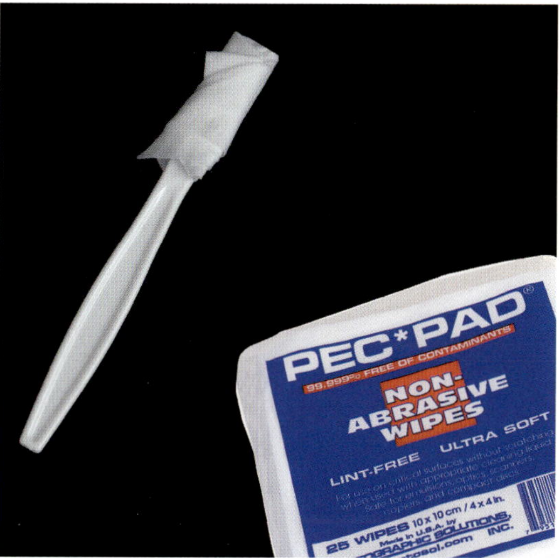

You can make your own swabs out of pieces of plastic (some use fast-food restaurant knives, with the tip cut at an angle to the proper size) covered with a soft cloth or Pec-Pad, as shown in Figure 12.12. However, if you've got the bucks to spend, you can't go wrong with good-quality commercial sensor cleaning swabs, such as those sold by Photographic Solutions, Inc. (www.photosol.com/products.htm).

Once you overcome your nervousness at touching your D3500's sensor, the process is easy. You'll wipe continuously with the swab in one direction, then flip it over and wipe in the other direction. You need to completely wipe the entire surface; otherwise, you may end up depositing the dust you collect at the far end of your stroke. Wipe; don't rub.

Magnifier-Assisted Cleaning

Using a magnifier to view your sensor as you clean it is a good idea. I rely on two types. I have four Carson MiniBrite PO-55 magnifiers (see Figure 12.13), and keep one in each camera bag. So, no matter where I am shooting, I have one of these $8.95 gadgets with me. You can read more about this great tool at my blog (http://dslrguides.com/carson/). When I'm not traveling, I use a SensorKlear loupe (about $100). It's a magnifier with a built-in LED illuminator. There's an opening on one side that allows you to insert a SensorKlear cleaning wand, a lens pen-like stylus with a surface treated to capture dust particles. (See Figure 12.14.) Both the SensorKlear loupe and the SensorKlear wand are available from www.lenspen.com/products.

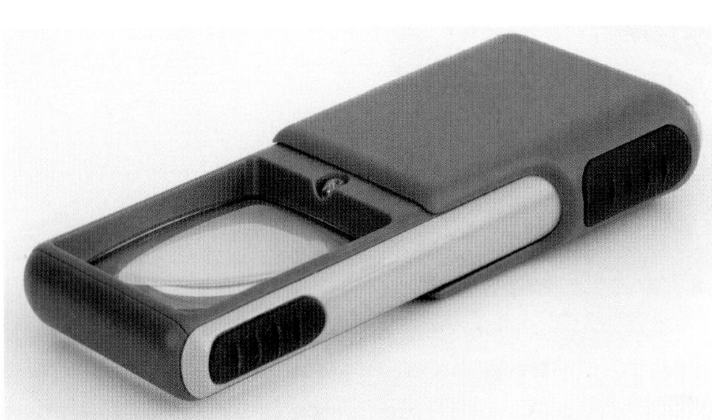

Figure 12.13 The Carson MiniBrite is a good value sensor magnifier.

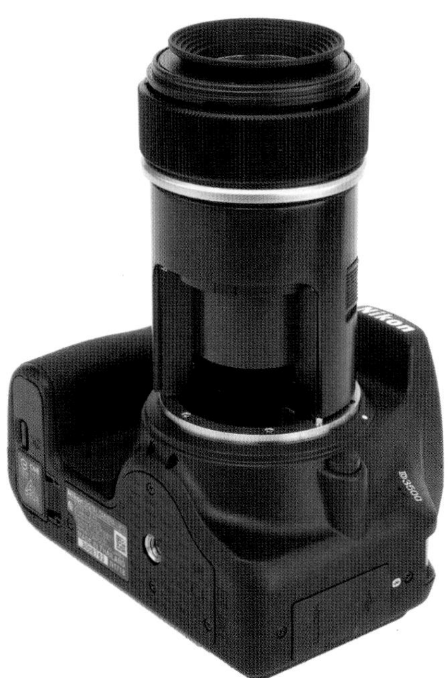

Figure 12.14 The SensorKlear loupe and its accompanying wand (not shown) allow quickly removing multiple dust particles.

When I'm using the MiniBrite, I locate the dust on the sensor with the magnifier, remembering that the position of the dust will be *reversed* from what I might have seen on an image on the camera's LCD (because the camera lens flips the image when making the exposure). Then, I use the SensorKlear's supplied wand or the blower/brush to remove the artifact.

The SensorKlear loupe actually allows you to keep your eye on the prize as you do the cleaning. You can peer through the viewer, rotate the opening to the side opposite the position of the dust, then insert the hinged wand to tap the dust while you're watching. This method allows removing a bunch of dust particles quickly, so it's my preferred procedure when I have the loupe with me.

Index

A

A (Aperture-priority) mode
built-in flash, 27
equivalent exposures, 135
flash sync, 267
using, 21–22

AC adapter EH-5b/Power Connector EF-5a, 7
accessory shoe, 51
action, freezing, 251–252
Active D-Lighting, 48, 50, 82–83
Adobe RGB option, 81–82
advanced modes, choosing, 21–22
Advanced Operation, Guide mode, 31–32
AE-L/AF-L/Protect button, 38–39, 104
AF (autofocus), 105, 222–226, 229, 243–244.
See also focus; macro focusing
AF area mode, 48, 87, 175
AF-A (Auto-servo) mode, 25
AF-area mode, choosing, 24, 87–88
AF-Assist Illuminator, 34–35, 88, 172
AF-C (Continuous-servo AF), 25, 171–172
AF-F mode, 176
AF/MF switch, lenses, 23, 107
AF-S (Single-servo AF), 25, 171, 176
AI (aperture indexing), lenses, 229–230
air cleaning sensors, 299
Airplane Mode, 93, 111
A/M-M switch, lenses, 106-107

aperture
defined, 133
displaying, 48, 55–56
exposure triangle, 130–131
aperture lever, 34–35
aperture ring, 54
aperture/additional functions, 50
Aperture-priority mode, 143–146
APS-C (Advanced Photo System—Classic, 218
audio tips, 193
Auto, Scene mode, 20
Auto (Flash Off), Scene mode, 20
Auto Distortion Control, Shooting menu, 87
Auto Image Rotation, Playback menu, 63
Auto Info Display, 93, 98
Auto modes, 148, 269
Auto Off Timers, 93, 98–100
Auto-area focus, 87, 175
autoexposure lock indicator, 55–56
autofocus
area, 174–175
modes, 48, 170–174
using, 23, 169–170
autofocus-area indicator, 50
Autofocus/Manual focus switch, 53
automatic ISO indicator, 55–56

U

V

W

Z

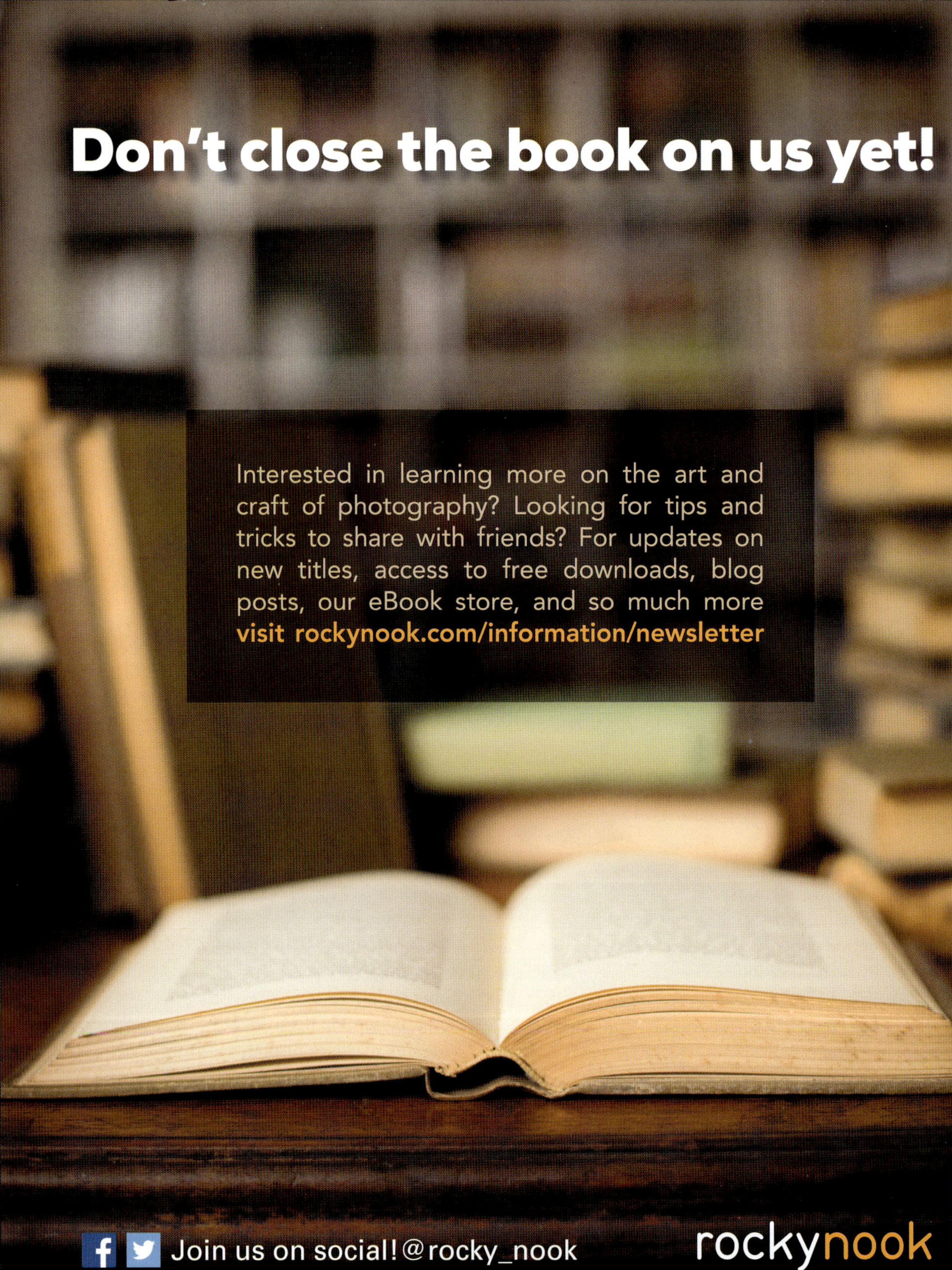